Y0-CCE-114

Table of Contents

Executive Summary

Executive Summary

Effective rule of law reduces corruption, combats poverty and disease, and protects people from injustices large and small. It is the foundation for communities of peace, opportunity, and equity — underpinning development, accountable government, and respect for fundamental rights

The World Justice Project (WJP) joins efforts to produce reliable data on rule of law through the *WJP Rule of Law Index® 2015*, the fifth report in an annual series, which measures rule of law based on the experiences and perceptions of the general public and in-country experts worldwide. We hope this annual publication, anchored in actual experiences, will help identify strengths and weaknesses in each country under review and encourage policy choices that strengthen the rule of law.

The *WJP Rule of Law Index 2015* presents a portrait of the rule of law in each country by providing scores and rankings organized around eight factors: constraints on government powers, absence of corruption, open government, fundamental rights, order and security, regulatory enforcement, civil justice, and criminal justice (a ninth factor, informal justice, is measured but not included in aggregated scores and rankings). These factors are intended to reflect how people experience rule of law in everyday life.

The country scores and rankings for the *WJP Rule of Law Index 2015* are derived from more than 100,000 household and expert surveys in 102 countries and jurisdictions. The Index is the world's most comprehensive data set of its kind and the only to rely solely on primary data, measuring a nation's adherence to the rule of law from the perspective of how ordinary people experience it. These features make the Index a powerful tool that can help identify strengths and weaknesses in each country, and help to inform policy debates, both within and across countries, that advance the rule of law.

Rule of Law Around the World: Scores and Rankings

The table below presents the scores and rankings of the *WJP Rule of Law Index 2015*. Scores range from 0 to 1 (with 1 indicating strongest adherence to the rule of law). Scoring is based on answers drawn from a representative sample of 1,000 respondents in the three largest cities per country and a set of in-country legal practitioners and academics. Tables organized by region and income group, along with disaggregated data for each factor, can be found in the "Scores and Rankings" section of this report. The methodology used to compute the scores and determine the mapping of survey questions to the conceptual framework is available in the methodology section of the WJP Rule of Law Index website (worldjusticeproject.org/methodology).

COUNTRY	SCORE	GLOBAL RANKING	COUNTRY	SCORE	GLOBAL RANKING	COUNTRY	SCORE	GLOBAL RANKING
Denmark	0.87	1	Croatia	0.60	35	Moldova	0.48	69
Norway	0.87	2	South Africa	0.58	36	Ukraine	0.48	70
Sweden	0.85	3	Hungary	0.58	37	China	0.48	71
Finland	0.85	4	Senegal	0.57	38	Tanzania	0.47	72
Netherlands	0.83	5	Malaysia	0.57	39	Zambia	0.47	73
New Zealand	0.83	6	Bosnia and Herzegovina	0.57	40	Kyrgyzstan	0.47	74
Austria	0.82	7	Jordan	0.56	41	Russia	0.47	75
Germany	0.81	8	Jamaica	0.56	42	Cote d'Ivoire	0.47	76
Singapore	0.81	9	Tunisia	0.56	43	Ecuador	0.47	77
Australia	0.80	10	Macedonia, FYR	0.55	44	Burkina Faso	0.47	78
Republic of Korea	0.79	11	Bulgaria	0.55	45	Mexico	0.47	79
United Kingdom	0.78	12	Brazil	0.54	46	Turkey	0.46	80
Japan	0.78	13	Mongolia	0.53	47	Uzbekistan	0.46	81
Canada	0.78	14	Nepal	0.53	48	Madagascar	0.45	82
Estonia	0.77	15	Panama	0.53	49	Liberia	0.45	83
Belgium	0.77	16	Belarus	0.53	50	Kenya	0.45	84
Hong Kong SAR, China	0.76	17	Philippines	0.53	51	Guatemala	0.44	85
France	0.74	18	Indonesia	0.52	52	Egypt	0.44	86
United States	0.73	19	Albania	0.52	53	Sierra Leone	0.44	87
Czech Republic	0.72	20	Argentina	0.52	54	Iran	0.43	88
Poland	0.71	21	Morocco	0.52	55	Nicaragua	0.43	89
Uruguay	0.71	22	Thailand	0.52	56	Honduras	0.42	90
Portugal	0.70	23	El Salvador	0.51	57	Ethiopia	0.42	91
Spain	0.68	24	Sri Lanka	0.51	58	Myanmar	0.42	92
Costa Rica	0.68	25	India	0.51	59	Bangladesh	0.42	93
Chile	0.68	26	Serbia	0.50	60	Bolivia	0.41	94
United Arab Emirates	0.67	27	Malawi	0.50	61	Uganda	0.41	95
Slovenia	0.66	28	Colombia	0.50	62	Nigeria	0.41	96
Georgia	0.65	29	Peru	0.50	63	Cameroon	0.40	97
Italy	0.64	30	Vietnam	0.50	64	Pakistan	0.38	98
Botswana	0.64	31	Kazakhstan	0.50	65	Cambodia	0.37	99
Romania	0.62	32	Belize	0.49	66	Zimbabwe	0.37	100
Greece	0.60	33	Dominican Republic	0.48	67	Afghanistan	0.35	101
Ghana	0.60	34	Lebanon	0.48	68	Venezuela	0.32	102

Country Specific Data and Online Tools

In addition to this written report, an interactive online platform for country-specific WJP Rule of Law Index data is available at data.worldjusticeproject.org. The interactive data site invites viewers to browse each of the 102 country profiles and explore country scores for the eight outcomes of the rule of law. The site features the Index's entire dataset, as well as global, regional, and income group rankings.

Discover each country's overall rule of law scores, as well as individual scores for each of the eight factors: constraints on government powers, absence of corruption, open government, fundamental rights, order and security, regulatory enforcement, civil justice, and criminal justice.

The WJP Rule of Law Index®

The WJP Rule of Law Index

The World Justice Project (WJP) is an independent, multi-disciplinary organization working to advance the rule of law around the world. The rule of law provides the foundation for communities of peace, opportunity, and equity – underpinning development, accountable government, and respect for fundamental rights.

Where the rule of law is weak, medicines fail to reach health facilities, criminal violence goes unchecked, laws are applied unequally across societies, and foreign investments are held back. Effective rule of law helps reduce corruption, improve public health, enhance education, alleviate poverty, and protect people from injustices and dangers large and small.

Strengthening the rule of law is a major goal of governments, donors, businesses, and civil society organizations around the world. To be effective, however, rule of law development requires clarity about the fundamental features of the rule of law, as well as an adequate basis for its evaluation and measurement. In response to this need, the World Justice Project has developed the WJP Rule of Law Index, a quantitative measurement tool that offers a comprehensive picture of the rule of law in practice.

The WJP Rule of Law Index presents a portrait of the rule of law in each country by providing scores and rankings organized around nine themes: constraints on government powers, absence of corruption, open government, fundamental rights, order and security, regulatory enforcement, civil justice, criminal justice, and informal justice. These country scores and rankings are based on answers drawn from more than 100,000 household and expert surveys in 102 countries and jurisdictions.

The WJP Rule of Law Index 2015 is the fifth report in an annual series, and is the product of years of development, intensive consultation, and vetting with academics, practitioners, and community leaders from over 100 countries and 17 professional disciplines. The Index is intended for a broad audience of policy makers, civil society practitioners, academics, and others. The rule of law is not the rule of lawyers and judges: all elements of society are stakeholders. It is our hope that, over time, this diagnostic tool will help identify strengths and weaknesses in each country under review and encourage policy choices that strengthen the rule of law.

Defining the Rule of Law

The rule of law is notoriously difficult to define and measure. A simple way of approaching it is in terms of some of the outcomes that the rule of law brings to societies – such as accountability, respect for fundamental rights, or access to justice – each of which reflects one aspect of the complex concept of the rule of law. The WJP Rule of Law Index seeks to embody these outcomes within a simple and coherent framework to measure the extent to which countries attain these outcomes *in practice* by means of performance indicators.

The WJP Rule of Law Index captures adherence to the rule of law (as defined by the WJP's universal principles, see Box 1) through a comprehensive and multi-dimensional set of outcome indicators, each of which reflects a particular aspect of this complex concept. The theoretical framework linking these outcome indicators draws on two main ideas pertaining to the relationship between the state and the governed: first, that the law imposes limits on the exercise of power by the state and its agents, as well as individuals and private entities. This is measured in factors 1, 2, 3 and 4 of the Index. Second, that the state limits the actions of members of society and fulfills its basic duties towards its population, so that the public interest is served, people are protected from violence and members of society have access to mechanisms to settle disputes and redress grievances This is measured in factors 5,6,7, and 8 of the Index. Although broad in scope, this framework assumes very little about the functions of the state, and when it does, it incorporates functions that are recognized by practically all societies, such as the provisions of justice or the guarantee of order and security.

The resulting set of indicators is also an effort to strike a balance between what scholars call a "thin" or minimalist conception of the rule of law that focuses on formal, procedural rules, and a "thick" conception that includes substantive characteristics, such as self-government and various fundamental rights and freedoms. Striking this balance between "thin" and "thick" conceptions of the rule of law enables the Index to apply to different types of social and political systems, including those which lack many of the features that characterize democratic nations, while including sufficient substantive characteristics to render the rule of law as more than merely a system of rules. Indeed, the Index recognizes that a system of positive law that fails to respect core human rights guaranteed under international law is at best "rule by law" and does not deserve to be called a rule of law system.

Box 1: Four Universal Principles of the Rule of Law

The WJP uses a working definition of the rule of law based on four universal principles, derived from internationally accepted standards. The rule of law is a system where the following four universal principles are upheld:

1. The government and its officials and agents as well as individuals and private entities are accountable under the law.

2. The laws are clear, publicized, stable, and just; are applied evenly; and protect fundamental rights, including the security of persons and property.

3. The process by which the laws are enacted, administered, and enforced is accessible, fair, and efficient.

4. Justice is delivered timely by competent, ethical, and independent representatives and neutrals who are of sufficient number, have adequate resources, and reflect the makeup of the communities they serve.

Box 2: The Rule of Law in Everyday Life

The rule of law affects all of us in our everyday lives. Although we may not be aware of it, the rule of law is profoundly important – and not just to lawyers or judges. It is the foundation for a system of rules to keep us safe, resolve disputes, and enable us to prosper. In fact, every sector of society is a stakeholder in the rule of law. Below are a few examples:

- **Business environment.** Imagine an investor seeking to commit resources abroad. She would probably think twice before investing in a country where corruption is rampant, property rights are ill-defined, and contracts are difficult to enforce. Uneven enforcement of regulations, corruption, insecure property rights, and ineffective means to settle disputes undermine legitimate business and drive away both domestic and foreign investment.

- **Public works.** Consider the bridges, roads, or runways we traverse daily – or the offices and buildings in which we live, work, and play. What if building codes governing their design and safety were not enforced, or if government officials and contractors employed low-quality materials in order to pocket the surplus? Weak regulatory enforcement and corruption decrease the security of physical infrastructures and waste scarce resources, which are essential to a thriving economy.

- **Public health and environment.** Consider the implications of pollution, wildlife poaching, and deforestation for public health, the economy, and the environment. What if a company was pouring harmful chemicals into a river in a highly populated area and the environmental inspector turned a blind eye in exchange for a bribe? While countries around the world have laws to protect the public's health and the environment, these laws are not always enforced. Adherence to the rule of law is essential to effective enforcement of public health and environmental regulations and to hold government, businesses, civil society organizations, and communities accountable for protecting the environment without unduly constraining economic opportunities.

- **Public participation.** What if residents of a neighborhood were not informed of an upcoming construction project commissioned by the government that would cause disruptions to their community? Or what if they did not have the opportunity to present their objections to the relevant government authorities prior to the start of the construction project? Being able to voice opinions about government decisions that directly impact the lives of ordinary people is a key aspect of the rule of law. Public participation ensures that all stakeholders have the chance to be heard and provide valuable input in the decision-making process.

- **Civil Justice**. Imagine an individual having a dispute with another party. What if the system to settle the dispute and obtain a remedy was largely inaccessible, unreliable, or corrupt? Without a well-functioning justice system – a core element of the rule of law – individuals faced with a dispute have few options other than giving up or resorting to violence to settle the conflict.

The WJP Rule of Law Index is comprised of nine factors further disaggregated into 47 specific sub-factors. These sub-factors are presented in Table 1 and are described in detail in the section below.

Constraints on Government Powers. Factor 1 measures the extent to which those who govern are bound by law. It comprises the means, both constitutional and institutional, by which the powers of the government and its officials and agents are limited and held accountable under the law. It also includes non-governmental checks on the government's power, such as a free and independent press.

Governmental checks take many forms; they do not operate solely in systems marked by a formal separation of powers, nor are they necessarily codified in law. What is essential, however, is that authority is distributed, whether by formal rules or by convention, in a manner that ensures that no single organ of government has the practical ability to exercise unchecked power[1]. This factor addresses the effectiveness of the institutional checks on government power by the legislature (1.1), the judiciary (1.2), and independent auditing and review agencies (1.3)[2], as well as the effectiveness of non-governmental oversight by the media and civil society (1.5), which serve an important role in monitoring government actions and holding officials accountable. The extent to which transitions of power occur in accordance with the law is also examined (1.6)[3]. In addition to these checks, this factor also measures the extent to which government officials are held accountable for official misconduct (1.4).

Absence of Corruption. Factor 2 measures the absence of corruption in a number of government agencies. The factor considers three forms of corruption: bribery, improper influence by public or private interests, and misappropriation of public funds or other resources. These three forms of corruption are examined with respect to government officers in the executive branch (2.1), the judiciary (2.2), the military and police (2.3), and the legislature (2.4), and encompass a wide range of possible situations in which corruption – from petty bribery to major kinds of fraud – can occur.

Open Government. Factor 3 measures open government defined as a government that shares information, empowers people with tools to hold the government accountable, and fosters citizen participation in public policy deliberations.

The factor measures whether basic laws and information on legal rights are publicized, and evaluates the quality of information published by the government (3.1). It also measures whether requests for information held by a government agency are properly granted (3.2). Finally, it assesses the effectiveness of civic participation mechanisms –including the protection of freedoms of opinion and expression, assembly and association, and the right to petition (3.3), and whether people can bring specific complaints to the government (3.4).

Fundamental Rights. Factor 4 measures the protection of fundamental human rights. It recognizes that a system of positive law that fails to respect core human rights established under international law is at best "rule by law", and does not deserve to be called a rule of law system. Since there are many other indices that address human rights, and as it would be impossible for the Index to assess adherence to the full range of rights, this factor focuses on a relatively modest menu of rights that are firmly established under the Universal Declaration and are most closely related to rule of law concerns. Accordingly, Factor 4 encompasses adherence to the following fundamental rights: effective enforcement of laws that ensure equal protection (4.1)[4], the right to life and security of the person (4.2)[5], due process of

---

[1] The Index does not address the further question of whether the laws are enacted by democratically elected representatives.

[2] This includes a wide range of institutions, from financial comptrollers and auditing agencies to the diverse array of entities that monitor human rights compliance (e.g. "Human Rights Defender", "Ombudsman", "People's Advocate", "Defensor del Pueblo", "Ouvidoria", "Human Rights Commissioner", "Oiguskantsler", "Mediateur de la Republique", "Citizen's Advocate", "Avocatul Poporului"). In some countries these functions are performed by judges or other state officials; in others, they are carried out by independent agencies.

[3] This sub-factor does not address the issue of whether transitions of political power take place through democratic elections. Rather, it examines whether the rules for the orderly transfer of power are actually observed. This sub-factor looks at the prevalence of electoral fraud and intimidation (for those countries in which elections are held), the frequency of coups d'etat, and the extent to which transition processes are open to public scrutiny.

[4] The laws can be fair only if they do not make arbitrary or irrational distinctions based on economic or social status – the latter defined to include race, color, ethnic or social origin, caste, nationality, alienage, religion, language, political opinion or affiliation, gender, marital status, sexual orientation or gender identity, age, and disability. It must be acknowledged that for some societies, including some traditional societies, certain of these categories may be problematic. In addition, there may be differences both within and among such societies as to whether a given distinction is arbitrary or irrational. Despite these difficulties, it was determined that only an inclusive list would accord full respect to the principles of equality and non-discrimination embodied in the Universal Declaration and emerging norms of international law.

[5] Sub-factor 4.2 concerns police brutality and other abuses – including arbitrary detention, torture and extrajudicial execution – perpetrated by agents of the state against criminal suspects, political dissidents, members of the media, and ordinary people.

law and the rights of the accused (4.3)[6], freedom of opinion and expression (4.4), freedom of belief and religion (4.5), the right to privacy (4.6), freedom of assembly and association (4.7), and fundamental labor rights, including the right to collective bargaining, the prohibition of forced and child labor, and the elimination of discrimination (4.8)[7].

Order and Security. Factor 5 measures how well the society assures the security of persons and property. Security is one of the defining aspects of any rule of law society and a fundamental function of the state. It is also a precondition for the realization of the rights and freedoms that the rule of law seeks to advance. This factor includes three dimensions that cover various threats to order and security: crime (5.1 particularly conventional crime[8]), political violence (5.2 including terrorism, armed conflict, and political unrest), and violence as a socially acceptable means to redress personal grievances (5.3 vigilante justice).

Regulatory Enforcement. Factor 6 measures the extent to which regulations are fairly and effectively implemented and enforced. Regulations, both legal and administrative, structure behaviors within and outside of the government. Strong rule of law requires that these regulations and administrative provisions are enforced effectively (6.1) and are applied and enforced without improper influence by public officials or private interests (6.2). Additionally, strong rule of law requires that administrative proceedings are conducted timely, without unreasonable delays (6.4), that due process is respected in administrative proceedings (6.3), and that there is no expropriation of private property without adequate compensation (6.5).

This factor does not assess which activities a government chooses to regulate, nor does it consider how much regulation of a particular activity is appropriate. Rather, it examines how regulations are implemented and enforced. To facilitate comparisons, this factor considers areas that all countries regulate to one degree or another, such as public health, workplace safety, environmental protection, and commercial activity.

Civil Justice. Factor 7 measures whether ordinary people can resolve their grievances peacefully and effectively through the civil justice system. The delivery of effective civil justice requires that the system be accessible and affordable (7.1), free of discrimination (7.2), free of corruption (7.3), and without improper influence by public officials (7.4). The delivery of effective civil justice also necessitates that court proceedings are conducted in a timely manner and not subject to unreasonable delays (7.5). Finally, recognizing the value of Alternative Dispute Resolution mechanisms (ADRs), this factor also measures the accessibility, impartiality, and efficiency of mediation and arbitration systems that enable parties to resolve civil disputes (7.7).

Criminal Justice. Factor 8 evaluates the criminal justice system. An effective criminal justice system is a key aspect of the rule of law, as it constitutes the conventional mechanism to redress grievances and bring action against individuals for offenses against society. Effective criminal justice systems are capable of investigating and adjudicating criminal offenses successfully and in a timely manner (8.1 and 8.2), through a system that is impartial and non-discriminatory (8.4), and is free of corruption and improper government influence (8.5 and 8.6), all while ensuring that the rights of both victims and the accused are effectively protected (8.7)[9]. The delivery of effective criminal justice also necessitates correctional systems that effectively reduce criminal behavior (8.3). Accordingly, an assessment of the delivery of criminal justice should take into consideration the entire system, including the police, the lawyers, prosecutors, judges, and prison officers.

Informal Justice. Finally, Factor 9 concerns the role played in many countries by customary and 'informal' systems of justice – including traditional, tribal, and religious courts, and community-based systems – in resolving disputes. These systems often play a large role in cultures in which formal legal institutions fail to provide effective remedies for large segments of the population, or when formal institutions are perceived as remote, corrupt, or ineffective. This factor covers three concepts: whether these dispute resolution systems are timely and effective (9.1), whether they are impartial and free of improper influence (9.2), and the extent to which these systems respect and protect fundamental rights (9.3)[10].

---

[6] This includes the presumption of innocence and the opportunity to submit and challenge evidence before public proceedings; freedom from arbitrary arrest, detention, torture and abusive treatment, and access to legal counsel and translators.

[7] Sub-factor 4.8 includes the four fundamental principles recognized by the ILO Declaration of Fundamental Principles and Rights at Work of 1998: (1) the freedom of association and the effective recognition of the right to collective bargaining, (2) the elimination of all forms of forced or compulsory labor, (3) the effective abolition of child labor, and (4) the elimination of discrimination in respect of employment and occupation.

[8] In this category, we include measures of criminal victimization, such as homicide, kidnapping, burglary, armed robbery, extortion, and fraud.

[9] Sub-factor 8.7 includes the presumption of innocence and the opportunity to submit and challenge evidence before public proceedings, freedom from arbitrary arrest, detention, torture and abusive treatment, and access to legal counsel and translators.

[10] WJP has devoted significant effort to collecting data on informal justice in a dozen countries. Nonetheless, the complexities of these systems and the difficulties of measuring their fairness and effectiveness in a manner that is both systematic and comparable across countries, make assessments extraordinarily challenging. Although the WJP has collected data on this dimension, it is not included in the aggregated scores and rankings.

Table 1: The World Justice Project Rule of Law Index

The four universal principles which comprise the WJP's notion of the rule of law are further developed in the nine factors of the WJP Rule of Law Index.

 Factor 1: Constraints on Government Powers

1.1 Government powers are effectively limited by the legislature
1.2 Government powers are effectively limited by the judiciary
1.3 Government powers are effectively limited by independent auditing and review
1.4 Government officials are sanctioned for misconduct
1.5 Government powers are subject to non-governmental checks
1.6 Transition of power is subject to the law

 Factor 2: Absence of Corruption

2.1 Government officials in the executive branch do not use public office for private gain
2.2 Government officials in the judicial branch do not use public office for private gain
2.3 Government officials in the police and the military do not use public office for private gain
2.4 Government officials in the legislative branch do not use public office for private gain

 Factor 3: Open Government

3.1 Publicized laws and government data
3.2 Right to information
3.3 Civic participation
3.4 Complaint mechanisms

 Factor 4: Fundamental Rights

4.1 Equal treatment and absence of discrimination
4.2 The right to life and security of the person is effectively guaranteed
4.3 Due process of law and rights of the accused
4.4 Freedom of opinion and expression is effectively guaranteed
4.5 Freedom of belief and religion is effectively guaranteed
4.6 Freedom from arbitrary interference with privacy is effectively guaranteed
4.7 Freedom of assembly and association is effectively guaranteed
4.8 Fundamental labor rights are effectively guaranteed

 Factor 5: Order and Security

5.1 Crime is effectively controlled
5.2 Civil conflict is effectively limited
5.3 People do not resort to violence to redress personal grievances

 Factor 6: Regulatory Enforcement

6.1 Government regulations are effectively enforced
6.2 Government regulations are applied and enforced without improper influence
6.3 Administrative proceedings are conducted without unreasonable delay
6.4 Due process is respected in administrative proceedings
6.5 The government does not expropriate without lawful process and adequate compensation

 Factor 7: Civil Justice

7.1 People can access and afford civil justice
7.2 Civil justice is free of discrimination
7.3 Civil justice is free of corruption
7.4 Civil justice is free of improper government influence
7.5 Civil justice is not subject to unreasonable delay
7.6 Civil justice is effectively enforced
7.7 ADR is accessible, impartial, and effective

 Factor 8: Criminal Justice

8.1 Criminal investigation system is effective
8.2 Criminal adjudication system is timely and effective
8.3 Correctional system is effective in reducing criminal behavior
8.4 Criminal system is impartial
8.5 Criminal system is free of corruption
8.6 Criminal system is free of improper government influence
8.7 Due process of law and rights of the accused

Factor 9: Informal Justice

9.1 Informal justice is timely and effective
9.2 Informal justice is impartial and free of improper influence
9.3 Informal justice respects and protects fundamental rights

Measuring the Rule of Law

This conceptual framework provides the basis for measuring the rule of law.

The scores and rankings of the 44 sub-factors (factors 1 through 8[1]) draw from two data sources collected by the World Justice Project in each country: (1) a general population poll (GPP) conducted by leading local polling companies using a representative sample of 1,000 respondents in the three largest cities, and (2) qualified respondents' questionnaires (QRQs) consisting of closed-ended questions completed by in-country practitioners and academics with expertise in civil and commercial law, criminal justice, labor law, and public health. Taken together, these two data sources provide up-to-date firsthand information from a large number of people on their experiences and perceptions concerning their dealings with the government, the police, and the courts, as well as the openness and accountability of the state, the extent of corruption, and the magnitude of common crimes to which the general public is exposed.

These data are processed, normalized on a 0 to 1 scale, and aggregated from the variable level all the way up to the dimension level for each country, and then to an overall score and ranking using the data map and weights reported in reported in the methodology section of the WJP Rule of Law Index website. Finally, these scores are validated and cross-checked against qualitative and quantitative third-party sources to identify possible mistakes or inconsistencies within the data.

The WJP has produced the Rule of Law Index for each of the last five years. During this time, the number of countries covered has increased, and the surveys and indicators have evolved to better reflect the rule of law landscape of countries around the world. This year's surveys and indicators are closely aligned with those used in the previous edition. The *WJP Rule of Law Index 2015* report also includes three new countries (Belize, Costa Rica, and Honduras), and covers a total of 102 countries and jurisdictions that account for more than 90 percent of the world's population.

The country scores and rankings presented in this report are based on data collected and analyzed during the fourth quarter of 2014, with the exception of general population data for countries indexed in 2012 and 2013, which were gathered during the fall of 2012 and the fall of 2013.

The scores and rankings have been organized into 102 country profiles, which are available at http://data.worldjusticeproject.org/. Each of these profiles displays 1) the country's overall rule of law score and ranking, 2) the score of each of the eight dimensions of the rule of law as well as the global, regional, and income group rankings, 3) the score of each of the 44 sub-factors together with the average score of the country's region and the country's income group. A detailed description of the process by which data is collected and the rule of law is measured is available online at www.worldjusticeproject.org.

---

[1] Significant effort has been devoted during the last four years to collecting data on informal justice in a dozen countries. Nonetheless, the complexities of these systems and the difficulties of measuring their fairness and effectiveness in a manner that is both systematic and comparable across countries, make assessments extraordinarily challenging. Although the WJP has collected data on this dimension, it is not included in the aggregated scores and rankings.

Box 3: The WJP Rule of Law Index Methodology in a Nutshell

The production of the WJP Rule of Law Index may be summarized in eleven steps:

1

The WJP developed the conceptual framework summarized in the Index's **9 FACTORS** and **47 SUB-FACTORS**, in consultation with academics, practitioners, and community leaders from around the world.

2

The Index team developed a set of **FIVE QUESTIONNAIRES** based on the Index's conceptual framework, to be administered to experts and the general public.

Questionnaires were translated into several languages and adapted to reflect commonly used terms and expressions.

3

The team identified, on average, more than **300 POTENTIAL LOCAL EXPERTS** per country to respond to the experts' questionnaires, and engaged the services of leading local polling companies to implement the house-hold surveys.

4

Polling companies conducted pre-test **PILOT SURVEYS** of the general public in consultation with the Index team, and launched the final survey

5

The team sent the questionnaires to **LOCAL EXPERTS** and engaged in continual interaction with them.

6

The Index team collected and mapped the data onto the **44 SUB-FACTORS** with global comparability.

7

The Index team constructed the final scores using a **FIVE-STEP PROCESS:**

a. Codified the questionnaire items as numeric values.
b. Produced raw country scores by aggregating the responses from several individuals (**EXPERTS OR GENERAL PUBLIC**).
c. Normalized the raw scores.
d. Aggregated the normalized scores into sub-factors and factors using simple averages.
e. Produced the final rankings using the normalized scores.

8

The data were subject to a series of tests to identify possible biases and errors. For example, the Index team cross-checked all sub-factors against more than **60 THIRD-PARTY SOURCES,** including quantitative data and qualitative assessments drawn from local and international organizations.

9

A sensitivity analysis was conducted by the **ECONOMETRICS AND APPLIED STATISTICS UNIT OF THE EUROPEAN COMMISSION'S JOINT RESEARCH CENTRE**, in collaboration with the Index team, to assess the statistical reliability of the results.

10

To illustrate whether the rule of law in a country significantly changed over the course of the past year, a measure of change over time was produced based on the annual difference in the country-level factor scores, the standard errors of these scores (estimated from a set of **100 BOOTSTRAP SAMPLES**), and the results of the corresponding t-tests.

11

The data were organized into **COUNTRY REPORTS, TABLES, AND FIGURES** to facilitate their presentation and interpretation.

✱ *Further information about the methods employed to produce the Index scores and rankings can be found in the "Methodology" section of this report.*

Features of the Rule of Law Index

The WJP Rule of Law Index includes several features that set it apart from other indices and make it useful for a large number of countries:

- **Rule of law in practice:** The Index measures adherence to the rule of law by looking at policy outcomes (such as whether people have access to courts or whether crime is effectively controlled). This stands in contrast to efforts that focus on the laws on the books, or the institutional means by which a society may seek to achieve these policy outcomes.

- **Comprehensive/multi-dimensional:** While other indices cover particular aspects of the rule of law, such as absence of corruption or human rights, they do not yield a full picture of rule of law compliance. The WJP Rule of Law Index is the only global instrument that looks at the rule of law comprehensively.

- **Perspective of the ordinary people:** The WJP Rule of Law Index puts people at its core by looking at a nation's adherence to the rule of law from the perspective of ordinary individuals who are directly affected by the degree of adherence to the rule of law in their societies. The WJP Index examines practical, everyday situations, such as whether people can access public services and whether a dispute among neighbors can be resolved peacefully and cost-effectively by an independent adjudicator.

- **New data anchored in actual experiences:** The Index is the only comprehensive set of indicators on the rule of law that is based on primary data. The Index's scores are built from the assessments of local residents (1,000 respondents per country) and local legal experts, which ensure that the findings reflect the conditions experienced by the population, including marginalized sectors of society.

- **Culturally competent:** The Index has been designed to be applied in countries with vastly different social, cultural, economic, and political systems. No society has ever attained — let alone sustained — a perfect realization of the rule of law. Every nation faces the perpetual challenge of building and renewing the structures, institutions, and norms that can support and sustain a rule of law culture.

Using the WJP Rule of Law Index

The WJP Rule of Law Index has been designed to offer a reliable and independent data source for policy makers, businesses, non-governmental organizations, and other constituencies to assess a nation's adherence to the rule of law as perceived and experienced by the average person, identify a nation's strengths and weaknesses in comparison to similarly situated countries, and track changes over time. The Index has been designed to include several features that set it apart from other indices and make it valuable for a large number of countries, thus providing a powerful resource that can inform policy debates both within and across countries. However, the Index's findings must be interpreted in light of certain inherent limitations.

1. The WJP Rule of Law Index does not identify priorities for reform and is not intended to establish causation or to ascertain the complex relationship among different rule of law dimensions in various countries.

2. The Index's rankings and scores are the product of a rigorous data collection and aggregation methodology. Nonetheless, as with all measures, they are subject to measurement error.

3. Given the uncertainty associated with picking a particular sample of respondents, standard errors have been calculated using bootstrapping methods to test whether the annual changes in the factor scores are statistically significant.

4. Indices and indicators are subject to potential abuse and misinterpretation. Once released to the public, they can take on a life of their own and be used for purposes unanticipated by their creators. If data is taken out of context, it can lead to unintended or erroneous policy decisions.

5. Rule of law concepts measured by the Index may have different meanings across countries. Users are encouraged to consult the specific definitions of the variables employed in the construction of the Index, which are discussed in greater detail in the methodology section of the WJP Rule of Law Index website.

6. The Index is generally intended to be used in combination with other instruments, both quantitative and qualitative. Just as in the areas of health or economics, no single index conveys a full picture of a country's situation. Policymaking in the area of rule of law requires careful consideration of all relevant dimensions – which may vary from country to country – and a combination of sources, instruments, and methods.

7. Pursuant to the sensitivity analysis of the Index data conducted in collaboration with the Econometrics and Applied Statistics Unit of the European Commission's Joint Research Centre, confidence intervals have been calculated for all figures included in the WJP Rule of Law Index. These confidence intervals and other relevant considerations regarding measurement error are reported in Saisana and Saltelli (2015) and Botero and Ponce (2011).

Scores & Rankings

Rule of Law Around the World

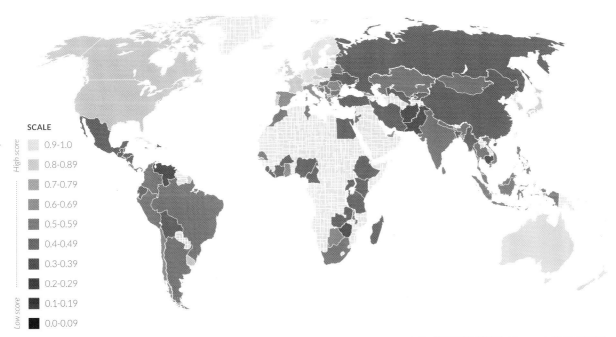

SCALE

High score
- 0.9-1.0
- 0.8-0.89
- 0.7-0.79
- 0.6-0.69
- 0.5-0.59
- 0.4-0.49
- 0.3-0.39
- 0.2-0.29
- 0.1-0.19
- 0.0-0.09
Low score

COUNTRY	SCORE	GLOBAL RANKING	COUNTRY	SCORE	GLOBAL RANKING	COUNTRY	SCORE	GLOBAL RANKING
Denmark	0.87	1	Croatia	0.60	35	Moldova	0.48	69
Norway	0.87	2	South Africa	0.58	36	Ukraine	0.48	70
Sweden	0.85	3	Hungary	0.58	37	China	0.48	71
Finland	0.85	4	Senegal	0.57	38	Tanzania	0.47	72
Netherlands	0.83	5	Malaysia	0.57	39	Zambia	0.47	73
New Zealand	0.83	6	Bosnia and Herzegovina	0.57	40	Kyrgyzstan	0.47	74
Austria	0.82	7	Jordan	0.56	41	Russia	0.47	75
Germany	0.81	8	Jamaica	0.56	42	Cote d'Ivoire	0.47	76
Singapore	0.81	9	Tunisia	0.56	43	Ecuador	0.47	77
Australia	0.80	10	Macedonia, FYR	0.55	44	Burkina Faso	0.47	78
Republic of Korea	0.79	11	Bulgaria	0.55	45	Mexico	0.47	79
United Kingdom	0.78	12	Brazil	0.54	46	Turkey	0.46	80
Japan	0.78	13	Mongolia	0.53	47	Uzbekistan	0.46	81
Canada	0.78	14	Nepal	0.53	48	Madagascar	0.45	82
Estonia	0.77	15	Panama	0.53	49	Liberia	0.45	83
Belgium	0.77	16	Belarus	0.53	50	Kenya	0.45	84
Hong Kong SAR, China	0.76	17	Philippines	0.53	51	Guatemala	0.44	85
France	0.74	18	Indonesia	0.52	52	Egypt	0.44	86
United States	0.73	19	Albania	0.52	53	Sierra Leone	0.44	87
Czech Republic	0.72	20	Argentina	0.52	54	Iran	0.43	88
Poland	0.71	21	Morocco	0.52	55	Nicaragua	0.43	89
Uruguay	0.71	22	Thailand	0.52	56	Honduras	0.42	90
Portugal	0.70	23	El Salvador	0.51	57	Ethiopia	0.42	91
Spain	0.68	24	Sri Lanka	0.51	58	Myanmar	0.42	92
Costa Rica	0.68	25	India	0.51	59	Bangladesh	0.42	93
Chile	0.68	26	Serbia	0.50	60	Bolivia	0.41	94
United Arab Emirates	0.67	27	Malawi	0.50	61	Uganda	0.41	95
Slovenia	0.66	28	Colombia	0.50	62	Nigeria	0.41	96
Georgia	0.65	29	Peru	0.50	63	Cameroon	0.40	97
Italy	0.64	30	Vietnam	0.50	64	Pakistan	0.38	98
Botswana	0.64	31	Kazakhstan	0.50	65	Cambodia	0.37	99
Romania	0.62	32	Belize	0.49	66	Zimbabwe	0.37	100
Greece	0.60	33	Dominican Republic	0.48	67	Afghanistan	0.35	101
Ghana	0.60	34	Lebanon	0.48	68	Venezuela	0.32	102

Rule of Law Around the World by Region

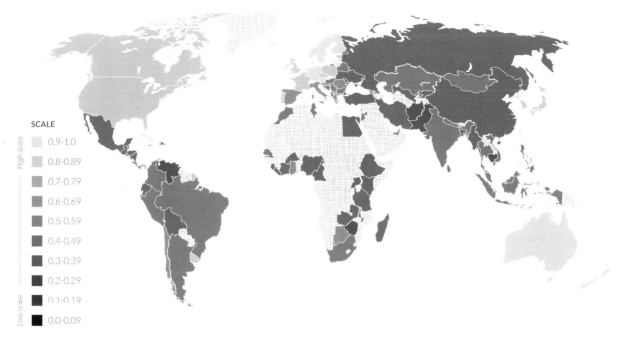

SCALE

	0.9-1.0
	0.8-0.89
	0.7-0.79
	0.6-0.69
	0.5-0.59
	0.4-0.49
	0.3-0.39
	0.2-0.29
	0.1-0.19
	0.0-0.09

High score ... *Low score*

SUB-SAHARAN AFRICA

COUNTRY	SCORE	GLOBAL RANKING
Botswana	0.64	31
Ghana	0.60	34
South Africa	0.58	36
Senegal	0.57	38
Malawi	0.50	61
Tanzania	0.47	72
Zambia	0.47	73
Cote d'Ivoire	0.47	76
Burkina Faso	0.47	78
Madagascar	0.45	82
Liberia	0.45	83
Kenya	0.45	84
Sierra Leone	0.44	87
Ethiopia	0.42	91
Uganda	0.41	95
Nigeria	0.41	96
Cameroon	0.40	97
Zimbabwe	0.37	100

EAST ASIA & PACIFIC

COUNTRY	SCORE	GLOBAL RANKING
New Zealand	0.83	6
Singapore	0.81	9
Australia	0.80	10
Republic of Korea	0.79	11
Japan	0.78	13
Hong Kong SAR, China	0.76	17
Malaysia	0.57	39
Mongolia	0.53	47
Philippines	0.53	51
Indonesia	0.52	52
Thailand	0.52	56
Vietnam	0.50	64
China	0.48	71
Myanmar	0.42	92
Cambodia	0.37	99

EASTERN EUROPE & CENTRAL ASIA

COUNTRY	SCORE	GLOBAL RANKING
Georgia	0.65	29
Bosnia and Herzegovina	0.57	40
Macedonia, FYR	0.55	44
Belarus	0.53	50
Albania	0.52	53
Serbia	0.50	60
Kazakhstan	0.50	65
Moldova	0.48	69
Ukraine	0.48	70
Kyrgyzstan	0.47	74
Russia	0.47	75
Turkey	0.46	80
Uzbekistan	0.46	81

EUROPEAN UNION, EUROPEAN FREE TRADE ASSOCIATION & NORTH AMERICA

COUNTRY	SCORE	GLOBAL RANKING
Denmark	0.87	1
Norway	0.87	2
Sweden	0.85	3
Finland	0.85	4
Netherlands	0.83	5
Austria	0.82	7
Germany	0.81	8
United Kingdom	0.78	12
Canada	0.78	14
Estonia	0.77	15
Belgium	0.77	16
France	0.74	18
United States	0.73	19
Czech Republic	0.72	20
Poland	0.71	21
Portugal	0.70	23
Spain	0.68	24
Slovenia	0.66	28
Italy	0.64	30
Romania	0.62	32
Greece	0.60	33
Croatia	0.60	35
Hungary	0.58	37
Bulgaria	0.55	45

LATIN AMERICAN & CARIBBEAN

COUNTRY	SCORE	GLOBAL RANKING
Uruguay	0.71	22
Costa Rica	0.68	25
Chile	0.68	26
Jamaica	0.56	42
Brazil	0.54	46
Panama	0.53	49
Argentina	0.52	54
El Salvador	0.51	57
Colombia	0.50	62
Peru	0.50	63
Belize	0.49	66
Dominican Republic	0.48	67
Ecuador	0.47	77
Mexico	0.47	79
Guatemala	0.44	85
Nicaragua	0.43	89
Honduras	0.42	90
Bolivia	0.41	94
Venezuela	0.32	102

MIDDLE EAST & NORTH AFRICA

COUNTRY	SCORE	GLOBAL RANKING
United Arab Emirates	0.67	27
Jordan	0.56	41
Tunisia	0.56	43
Morocco	0.52	55
Lebanon	0.48	68
Egypt	0.44	86
Iran	0.43	88

SOUTH ASIA

COUNTRY	SCORE	GLOBAL RANKING
Nepal	0.53	48
Sri Lanka	0.51	58
India	0.51	59
Bangladesh	0.42	93
Pakistan	0.38	98
Afghanistan	0.35	101

Rule of Law Around the World by Income Group

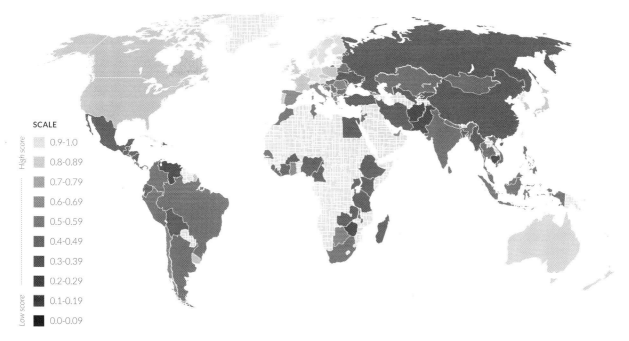

SCALE

	0.9–1.0
	0.8–0.89
	0.7–0.79
	0.6–0.69
	0.5–0.59
	0.4–0.49
	0.3–0.39
	0.2–0.29
	0.1–0.19
	0.0–0.09

High score ... Low score

HIGH INCOME

COUNTRY	SCORE	GLOBAL RANKING
Denmark	0.87	1
Norway	0.87	2
Sweden	0.85	3
Finland	0.85	4
Netherlands	0.83	5
New Zealand	0.83	6
Austria	0.82	7
Germany	0.81	8
Singapore	0.81	9
Australia	0.80	10
Republic of Korea	0.79	11
United Kingdom	0.78	12
Japan	0.78	13
Canada	0.78	14
Estonia	0.77	15
Belgium	0.77	16
Hong Kong SAR, China	0.76	17
France	0.74	18
United States	0.73	19
Czech Republic	0.72	20
Poland	0.71	21
Uruguay	0.71	22
Portugal	0.70	23
Spain	0.68	24
Chile	0.68	26
United Arab Emirates	0.67	27
Slovenia	0.66	28
Italy	0.64	30
Greece	0.60	33
Croatia	0.60	35
Russia	0.47	75

UPPER MIDDLE INCOME

COUNTRY	SCORE	GLOBAL RANKING
Costa Rica	0.68	25
Botswana	0.64	31
Romania	0.62	32
South Africa	0.58	36
Hungary	0.58	37
Malaysia	0.57	39
Bosnia and Herzegovina	0.57	40
Jordan	0.56	41
Jamaica	0.56	42
Tunisia	0.56	43
Macedonia, FYR	0.55	44
Bulgaria	0.55	45
Brazil	0.54	46
Panama	0.53	49
Belarus	0.53	50
Albania	0.52	53
Argentina	0.52	54
Thailand	0.52	56
Serbia	0.50	60
Colombia	0.50	62
Peru	0.50	63
Kazakhstan	0.50	65
Belize	0.49	66
Dominican Republic	0.48	67
Lebanon	0.48	68
China	0.48	71
Ecuador	0.47	77
Mexico	0.47	79
Turkey	0.46	80
Iran	0.43	88
Venezuela	0.32	102

LOWER MIDDLE INCOME

COUNTRY	SCORE	GLOBAL RANKING
Georgia	0.65	29
Ghana	0.60	34
Senegal	0.57	38
Mongolia	0.53	47
Philippines	0.53	51
Indonesia	0.52	52
Morocco	0.52	55
El Salvador	0.51	57
Sri Lanka	0.51	58
India	0.51	59
Vietnam	0.50	64
Moldova	0.48	69
Ukraine	0.48	70
Zambia	0.47	73
Kyrgyzstan	0.47	74
Cote d'Ivoire	0.47	76
Uzbekistan	0.46	81
Guatemala	0.44	85
Egypt	0.44	86
Nicaragua	0.43	89
Honduras	0.42	90
Bolivia	0.41	94
Nigeria	0.41	96
Cameroon	0.40	97
Pakistan	0.38	98

LOW INCOME

COUNTRY	SCORE	GLOBAL RANKING
Nepal	0.53	48
Malawi	0.50	61
Tanzania	0.47	72
Burkina Faso	0.47	78
Madagascar	0.45	82
Liberia	0.45	83
Kenya	0.45	84
Sierra Leone	0.44	87
Ethiopia	0.42	91
Myanmar	0.42	92
Bangladesh	0.42	93
Uganda	0.41	95
Cambodia	0.37	99
Zimbabwe	0.37	100
Afghanistan	0.35	101

The Eight Factors of the WJP Rule of Law Index

The following chart presents country performance on the eight factors of the WJP Rule of Law Index

Factor 1: Constraints on Government Powers

Factor 1 measures the effectiveness of the institutional checks on government power by the legislature, the judiciary, and independent auditing and review agencies, as well as the effectiveness of non-governmental oversight by the media and civil society, which serve an important role in monitoring government actions and holding officials accountable. This factor also measures the extent to which transitions of power occur in accordance with the law and whether government officials are held accountable for official misconduct.

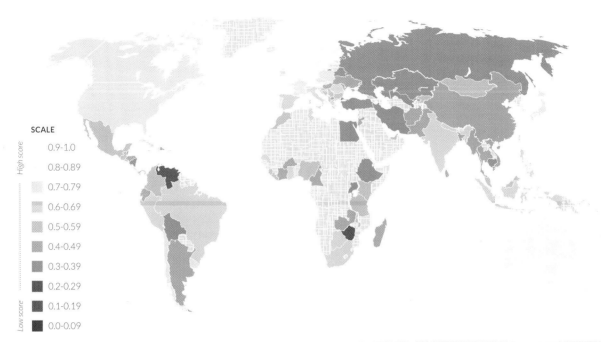

SCALE

High score
- 0.9-1.0
- 0.8-0.89
- 0.7-0.79
- 0.6-0.69
- 0.5-0.59
- 0.4-0.49
- 0.3-0.39
- 0.2-0.29
- 0.1-0.19
- 0.0-0.09

Low score

COUNTRY	SCORE	GLOBAL RANKING	COUNTRY	SCORE	GLOBAL RANKING	COUNTRY	SCORE	GLOBAL RANKING
Denmark	0.92	1	Nepal	0.62	35	Jordan	0.49	69
Finland	0.88	2	Georgia	0.62	36	Dominican Republic	0.49	70
Norway	0.88	3	Slovenia	0.62	37	Argentina	0.49	71
Sweden	0.88	4	India	0.62	38	Cote d'Ivoire	0.47	72
Netherlands	0.87	5	Philippines	0.61	39	Belize	0.47	73
Germany	0.85	6	South Africa	0.61	40	Macedonia, FYR	0.47	74
Austria	0.85	7	Jamaica	0.61	41	Sri Lanka	0.47	75
New Zealand	0.85	8	Brazil	0.61	42	Thailand	0.46	76
Australia	0.83	9	Peru	0.60	43	Ukraine	0.45	77
Belgium	0.81	10	Croatia	0.59	44	Myanmar	0.45	78
United Kingdom	0.80	11	United Arab Emirates	0.58	45	Moldova	0.45	79
Portugal	0.79	12	Bosnia and Herzegovina	0.57	46	Honduras	0.45	80
Estonia	0.79	13	Malawi	0.57	47	Madagascar	0.44	81
Republic of Korea	0.79	14	Morocco	0.57	48	Afghanistan	0.44	82
Costa Rica	0.78	15	Lebanon	0.56	49	Cameroon	0.44	83
France	0.78	16	Kenya	0.56	50	Bangladesh	0.44	84
Canada	0.78	17	Colombia	0.55	51	Vietnam	0.42	85
Poland	0.77	18	Albania	0.55	52	Burkina Faso	0.41	86
Japan	0.76	19	Mongolia	0.54	53	China	0.41	87
Uruguay	0.76	20	Liberia	0.54	54	Ecuador	0.40	88
United States	0.76	21	Tanzania	0.53	55	Uganda	0.39	89
Singapore	0.76	22	Bulgaria	0.53	56	Russia	0.39	90
Chile	0.74	23	Panama	0.53	57	Egypt	0.39	91
Czech Republic	0.74	24	Malaysia	0.52	58	Bolivia	0.38	92
Hong Kong SAR, China	0.71	25	Sierra Leone	0.52	59	Kazakhstan	0.37	93
Spain	0.69	26	El Salvador	0.52	60	Iran	0.37	94
Italy	0.69	27	Mexico	0.51	61	Turkey	0.37	95
Ghana	0.69	28	Kyrgyzstan	0.51	62	Ethiopia	0.36	96
Senegal	0.66	29	Nigeria	0.51	63	Belarus	0.35	97
Greece	0.65	30	Guatemala	0.51	64	Nicaragua	0.35	98
Indonesia	0.64	31	Serbia	0.50	65	Cambodia	0.33	99
Botswana	0.63	32	Hungary	0.49	66	Uzbekistan	0.31	100
Romania	0.63	33	Pakistan	0.49	67	Zimbabwe	0.26	101
Tunisia	0.62	34	Zambia	0.49	68	Venezuela	0.19	102

Factor 2: Absence of Corruption

Factor 2 measures the absence of corruption in government. The factor considers three forms of corruption: bribery, improper influence by public or private interests, and misappropriation of public funds or other resources. These three forms of corruption are examined with respect to government officers in the executive branch, the judiciary, the military, police, and the legislature.

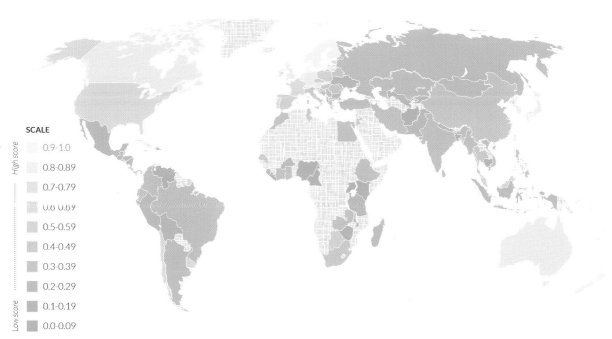

SCALE

High score

- 0.9-1.0
- 0.8-0.89
- 0.7-0.79
- 0.6-0.69
- 0.5-0.59
- 0.4-0.49
- 0.3-0.39
- 0.2-0.29
- 0.1-0.19
- 0.0-0.09

Low score

COUNTRY	SCORE	GLOBAL RANKING	COUNTRY	SCORE	GLOBAL RANKING	COUNTRY	SCORE	GLOBAL RANKING
Denmark	0.96	1	Croatia	0.54	35	Cote d'Ivoire	0.40	69
Norway	0.93	2	Senegal	0.53	36	Zambia	0.40	70
Singapore	0.93	3	Jamaica	0.53	37	Bulgaria	0.39	71
Sweden	0.91	4	Macedonia, FYR	0.52	38	Nepal	0.39	72
Finland	0.90	5	Thailand	0.52	39	Burkina Faso	0.38	73
New Zealand	0.90	6	Romania	0.52	40	Indonesia	0.37	74
Netherlands	0.89	7	China	0.51	41	Nicaragua	0.37	75
Japan	0.86	8	South Africa	0.51	42	Lebanon	0.37	76
Australia	0.84	9	Belarus	0.50	43	Tanzania	0.37	77
Hong Kong SAR, China	0.84	10	Tunisia	0.50	44	Albania	0.36	78
Austria	0.83	11	Hungary	0.50	45	Dominican Republic	0.36	79
Germany	0.83	12	Panama	0.49	46	Malawi	0.36	80
United Arab Emirates	0.82	13	Philippines	0.49	47	Uzbekistan	0.35	81
Republic of Korea	0.82	14	Morocco	0.49	48	Madagascar	0.35	82
United Kingdom	0.82	15	Turkey	0.49	49	Pakistan	0.35	83
Canada	0.81	16	Belize	0.48	50	Ukraine	0.34	84
Belgium	0.81	17	Argentina	0.48	51	Honduras	0.34	85
Uruguay	0.78	18	Egypt	0.47	52	Peru	0.34	86
Estonia	0.78	19	Ethiopia	0.47	53	Bolivia	0.34	87
United States	0.75	20	Sri Lanka	0.46	54	Mexico	0.33	88
France	0.75	21	Brazil	0.46	55	Guatemala	0.33	89
Georgia	0.73	22	Vietnam	0.46	56	Kyrgyzstan	0.30	90
Chile	0.72	23	Ecuador	0.45	57	Sierra Leone	0.30	91
Portugal	0.71	24	Kazakhstan	0.45	58	Zimbabwe	0.28	92
Spain	0.69	25	Ghana	0.44	59	Moldova	0.28	93
Costa Rica	0.68	26	Russia	0.44	60	Liberia	0.28	94
Czech Republic	0.66	27	Bosnia and Herzegovina	0.43	61	Venezuela	0.27	95
Poland	0.65	28	El Salvador	0.43	62	Kenya	0.27	96
Botswana	0.65	29	Colombia	0.43	63	Nigeria	0.27	97
Malaysia	0.63	30	Iran	0.42	64	Bangladesh	0.27	98
Slovenia	0.60	31	Myanmar	0.42	65	Cambodia	0.27	99
Jordan	0.59	32	Mongolia	0.42	66	Uganda	0.27	100
Italy	0.59	33	Serbia	0.41	67	Cameroon	0.25	101
Greece	0.54	34	India	0.40	68	Afghanistan	0.23	102

Factor 3: Open Government

Factor 3 measures whether basic laws and information in legal rights are publicized, and assesses the quality of information published by the government. It also measures whether requests for information held by a government agency are properly granted. Finally, it evaluates the effectiveness of civic participation mechanisms and whether people can bring specific complaints to the government.

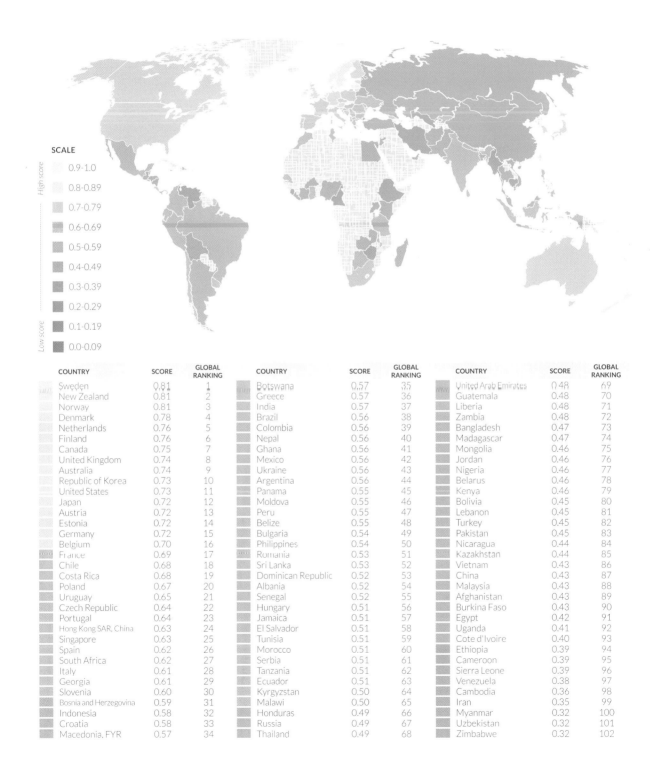

SCALE

High score

	0.9-1.0
	0.8-0.89
	0.7-0.79
	0.6-0.69
	0.5-0.59
	0.4-0.49
	0.3-0.39
	0.2-0.29
	0.1-0.19
	0.0-0.09

Low score

COUNTRY	SCORE	GLOBAL RANKING	COUNTRY	SCORE	GLOBAL RANKING	COUNTRY	SCORE	GLOBAL RANKING
Sweden	0.81	1	Botswana	0.57	35	United Arab Emirates	0.48	69
New Zealand	0.81	2	Greece	0.57	36	Guatemala	0.48	70
Norway	0.81	3	India	0.57	37	Liberia	0.48	71
Denmark	0.78	4	Brazil	0.56	38	Zambia	0.48	72
Netherlands	0.76	5	Colombia	0.56	39	Bangladesh	0.47	73
Finland	0.76	6	Nepal	0.56	40	Madagascar	0.47	74
Canada	0.75	7	Ghana	0.56	41	Mongolia	0.46	75
United Kingdom	0.74	8	Mexico	0.56	42	Jordan	0.46	76
Australia	0.74	9	Ukraine	0.56	43	Nigeria	0.46	77
Republic of Korea	0.73	10	Argentina	0.56	44	Belarus	0.46	78
United States	0.73	11	Panama	0.55	45	Kenya	0.46	79
Japan	0.72	12	Moldova	0.55	46	Bolivia	0.45	80
Austria	0.72	13	Peru	0.55	47	Lebanon	0.45	81
Estonia	0.72	14	Belize	0.55	48	Turkey	0.45	82
Germany	0.72	15	Bulgaria	0.54	49	Pakistan	0.45	83
Belgium	0.70	16	Philippines	0.54	50	Nicaragua	0.44	84
France	0.69	17	Romania	0.53	51	Kazakhstan	0.44	85
Chile	0.68	18	Sri Lanka	0.53	52	Vietnam	0.43	86
Costa Rica	0.68	19	Dominican Republic	0.52	53	China	0.43	87
Poland	0.67	20	Albania	0.52	54	Malaysia	0.43	88
Uruguay	0.65	21	Senegal	0.52	55	Afghanistan	0.43	89
Czech Republic	0.64	22	Hungary	0.51	56	Burkina Faso	0.43	90
Portugal	0.64	23	Jamaica	0.51	57	Egypt	0.42	91
Hong Kong SAR, China	0.63	24	El Salvador	0.51	58	Uganda	0.41	92
Singapore	0.63	25	Tunisia	0.51	59	Cote d'Ivoire	0.40	93
Spain	0.62	26	Morocco	0.51	60	Ethiopia	0.39	94
South Africa	0.62	27	Serbia	0.51	61	Cameroon	0.39	95
Italy	0.61	28	Tanzania	0.51	62	Sierra Leone	0.39	96
Georgia	0.61	29	Ecuador	0.51	63	Venezuela	0.38	97
Slovenia	0.60	30	Kyrgyzstan	0.50	64	Cambodia	0.36	98
Bosnia and Herzegovina	0.59	31	Malawi	0.50	65	Iran	0.35	99
Indonesia	0.58	32	Honduras	0.49	66	Myanmar	0.32	100
Croatia	0.58	33	Russia	0.49	67	Uzbekistan	0.32	101
Macedonia, FYR	0.57	34	Thailand	0.49	68	Zimbabwe	0.32	102

Factor 4: Fundamental Rights

Factor 4 measures the protection of fundamental human rights, including effective enforcement of laws that ensure equal protection, the right to life and security of the person, due process of law and the rights of the accused, freedom of opinion and expression, freedom of belief and religion, the right to privacy, freedom of assembly and association, and fundamental labor rights, including the right to collective bargaining, the prohibition of forced and child labor, and the elimination of discrimination.

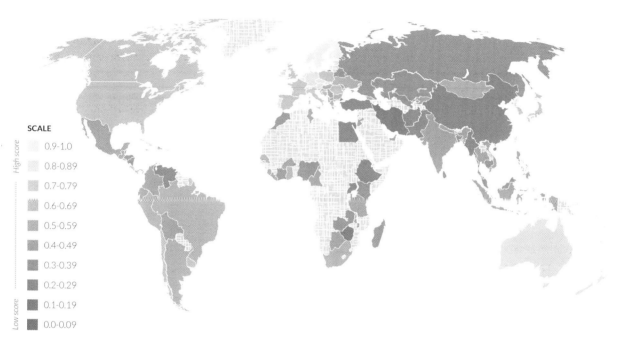

SCALE

High score

- 0.9-1.0
- 0.8-0.89
- 0.7-0.79
- 0.6-0.69
- 0.5-0.59
- 0.4-0.49
- 0.3-0.39
- 0.2-0.29
- 0.1-0.19
- 0.0-0.09

Low score

COUNTRY	SCORE	GLOBAL RANKING	COUNTRY	SCORE	GLOBAL RANKING	COUNTRY	SCORE	GLOBAL RANKING
Finland	0.91	1	Bosnia and Herzegovina	0.66	35	Vietnam	0.52	69
Denmark	0.91	2	Greece	0.65	36	Kyrgyzstan	0.51	70
Norway	0.90	3	Hungary	0.65	37	Tanzania	0.51	71
Sweden	0.90	4	Georgia	0.64	38	Thailand	0.50	72
Austria	0.87	5	South Africa	0.63	39	Belize	0.50	73
Germany	0.87	6	Senegal	0.63	40	Cameroon	0.50	74
Netherlands	0.85	7	El Salvador	0.62	41	United Arab Emirates	0.50	75
Belgium	0.84	8	Panama	0.62	42	Kenya	0.49	76
New Zealand	0.83	9	Dominican Republic	0.61	43	Sri Lanka	0.49	77
Australia	0.82	10	Ukraine	0.61	44	Malaysia	0.48	78
Estonia	0.81	11	Mongolia	0.61	45	Cote d'Ivoire	0.47	79
Portugal	0.80	12	Brazil	0.61	46	Russia	0.47	80
Czech Republic	0.80	13	Peru	0.60	47	Madagascar	0.47	81
United Kingdom	0.79	14	Albania	0.60	48	Belarus	0.46	82
Canada	0.79	15	Malawi	0.59	49	Nicaragua	0.46	83
Uruguay	0.79	16	Liberia	0.58	50	Kazakhstan	0.46	84
Costa Rica	0.78	17	Serbia	0.58	51	Honduras	0.45	85
France	0.78	18	Macedonia, FYR	0.57	52	Morocco	0.45	86
Spain	0.78	19	Nepal	0.56	53	Nigeria	0.44	87
Slovenia	0.77	20	Guatemala	0.56	54	Bangladesh	0.42	88
Poland	0.77	21	Botswana	0.56	55	Zambia	0.42	89
Japan	0.76	22	Mexico	0.56	56	Cambodia	0.42	90
Italy	0.74	23	Lebanon	0.55	57	Uzbekistan	0.41	91
Chile	0.74	24	Burkina Faso	0.55	58	Pakistan	0.39	92
Republic of Korea	0.73	25	Moldova	0.55	59	Venezuela	0.39	93
United States	0.73	26	Colombia	0.55	60	Uganda	0.39	94
Romania	0.73	27	India	0.54	61	Afghanistan	0.38	95
Singapore	0.72	28	Tunisia	0.54	62	Turkey	0.36	96
Hong Kong SAR, China	0.70	29	Sierra Leone	0.53	63	Ethiopia	0.32	97
Ghana	0.69	30	Ecuador	0.53	64	Egypt	0.32	98
Croatia	0.67	31	Bolivia	0.53	65	China	0.32	99
Bulgaria	0.67	32	Indonesia	0.52	66	Myanmar	0.31	100
Argentina	0.66	33	Philippines	0.52	67	Zimbabwe	0.29	101
Jamaica	0.66	34	Jordan	0.52	68	Iran	0.22	102

Factor 5: Order and Security

Factor 5 measures various threats to order and security including conventional crime, political violence, and violence as a means to redress personal grievances.

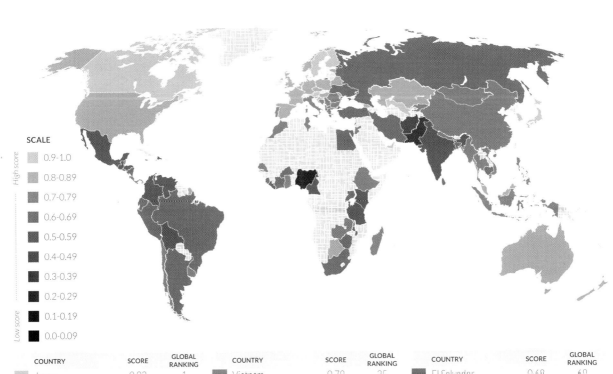

SCALE

High score
- 0.9-1.0
- 0.8-0.89
- 0.7-0.79
- 0.6-0.69
- 0.5-0.59
- 0.4-0.49
- 0.3-0.39
- 0.2-0.29
- 0.1-0.19
- 0.0-0.09
Low score

COUNTRY	SCORE	GLOBAL RANKING	COUNTRY	SCORE	GLOBAL RANKING	COUNTRY	SCORE	GLOBAL RANKING
Japan	0.93	1	Vietnam	0.79	35	El Salvador	0.68	69
Denmark	0.92	2	Bulgaria	0.79	36	Nicaragua	0.68	70
Finland	0.92	3	Mongolia	0.79	37	Belize	0.68	71
Singapore	0.91	4	China	0.78	38	Cambodia	0.68	72
Uzbekistan	0.91	5	Romania	0.78	39	Lebanon	0.68	73
United Arab Emirates	0.91	6	Nepal	0.77	40	Russia	0.67	74
Hong Kong SAR, China	0.91	7	Myanmar	0.77	41	Brazil	0.66	75
Sweden	0.90	8	Indonesia	0.77	42	Bangladesh	0.65	76
Canada	0.90	9	Macedonia, FYR	0.76	43	Cote d'Ivoire	0.63	77
Republic of Korea	0.90	10	Morocco	0.76	44	Zimbabwe	0.63	78
Austria	0.90	11	Portugal	0.76	45	Peru	0.63	79
Czech Republic	0.89	12	Greece	0.76	46	Iran	0.62	80
Australia	0.89	13	Albania	0.76	47	South Africa	0.62	81
Germany	0.88	14	Serbia	0.75	48	Ecuador	0.62	82
New Zealand	0.88	15	Kyrgyzstan	0.75	49	Malawi	0.61	83
Estonia	0.88	16	Tunisia	0.75	50	Argentina	0.61	84
Norway	0.87	17	Thailand	0.75	51	Uganda	0.61	85
Malaysia	0.86	18	Ghana	0.75	52	Sierra Leone	0.60	86
United Kingdom	0.86	19	Italy	0.74	53	Ukraine	0.60	87
Hungary	0.86	20	Madagascar	0.73	54	Dominican Republic	0.59	88
Belgium	0.86	21	Bosnia and Herzegovina	0.72	55	Bolivia	0.59	89
Netherlands	0.85	22	Ethiopia	0.72	56	India	0.58	90
Poland	0.85	23	Uruguay	0.72	57	Tanzania	0.58	91
Georgia	0.83	24	Philippines	0.71	58	Honduras	0.58	92
Moldova	0.82	25	Senegal	0.71	59	Colombia	0.57	93
United States	0.82	26	Chile	0.70	60	Liberia	0.57	94
Slovenia	0.82	27	Panama	0.70	61	Guatemala	0.56	95
Botswana	0.81	28	Zambia	0.70	62	Kenya	0.55	96
Belarus	0.81	29	Costa Rica	0.70	63	Venezuela	0.54	97
France	0.81	30	Jamaica	0.69	64	Cameroon	0.54	98
Croatia	0.81	31	Sri Lanka	0.69	65	Mexico	0.52	99
Kazakhstan	0.81	32	Egypt	0.69	66	Afghanistan	0.42	100
Spain	0.80	33	Burkina Faso	0.69	67	Pakistan	0.30	101
Jordan	0.79	34	Turkey	0.69	68	Nigeria	0.27	102

Factor 6: Regulatory Enforcement

Factor 6 measures the extent to which regulations are effectively implemented and enforced without improper influence by public officials or private interests. It also includes whether administrative proceedings are conducted in a timely manner without unreasonable delays and whether due process is respected in administrative proceedings. This factor also addresses whether the government respects the property rights of people and corporations.

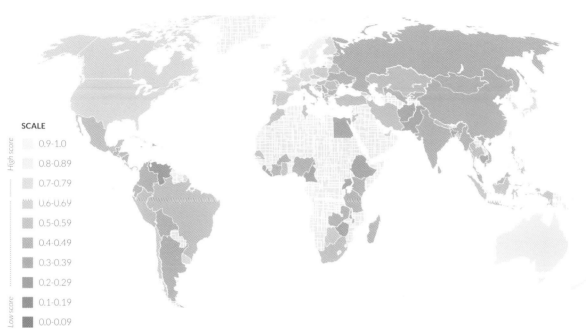

SCALE

High score

- 0.9-1.0
- 0.8-0.89
- 0.7-0.79
- 0.6-0.69
- 0.5-0.59
- 0.4-0.49
- 0.3-0.39
- 0.2-0.29
- 0.1-0.19
- 0.0-0.09

Low score

COUNTRY	SCORE	GLOBAL RANKING	COUNTRY	SCORE	GLOBAL RANKING	COUNTRY	SCORE	GLOBAL RANKING
Singapore	0.86	1	Iran	0.54	35	India	0.45	69
Norway	0.86	2	Greece	0.54	36	Kenya	0.45	70
Sweden	0.82	3	Romania	0.54	37	Albania	0.45	71
Netherlands	0.82	4	Panama	0.54	38	Belize	0.44	72
New Zealand	0.82	5	Morocco	0.53	39	Malawi	0.44	73
Denmark	0.81	6	Jamaica	0.53	40	Nigeria	0.44	74
Austria	0.81	7	Bosnia and Herzegovina	0.53	41	Argentina	0.43	75
Australia	0.81	8	Senegal	0.52	42	Serbia	0.43	76
Finland	0.79	9	Tunisia	0.52	43	Tanzania	0.43	77
Republic of Korea	0.78	10	Kazakhstan	0.51	44	Uzbekistan	0.42	78
Germany	0.77	11	Indonesia	0.51	45	Moldova	0.42	79
United Kingdom	0.77	12	Turkey	0.51	46	Ukraine	0.42	80
Canada	0.77	13	Thailand	0.51	47	Kyrgyzstan	0.42	81
Japan	0.76	14	Hungary	0.51	48	Dominican Republic	0.42	82
Hong Kong SAR, China	0.75	15	Jordan	0.51	49	Lebanon	0.41	83
Estonia	0.75	16	Brazil	0.51	50	Nicaragua	0.41	84
France	0.74	17	Nepal	0.50	51	Vietnam	0.41	85
Belgium	0.73	18	Philippines	0.50	52	Bolivia	0.40	86
Uruguay	0.73	19	Mexico	0.50	53	Madagascar	0.40	87
United States	0.73	20	Macedonia, FYR	0.50	54	Honduras	0.40	88
United Arab Emirates	0.68	21	Peru	0.50	55	Myanmar	0.40	89
Botswana	0.66	22	Bulgaria	0.49	56	Guatemala	0.40	90
Chile	0.65	23	Colombia	0.49	57	Sierra Leone	0.39	91
Czech Republic	0.63	24	Sri Lanka	0.49	58	Cameroon	0.39	92
Georgia	0.62	25	Ecuador	0.49	59	Egypt	0.39	93
Spain	0.62	26	Croatia	0.48	60	Uganda	0.39	94
Costa Rica	0.62	27	Mongolia	0.48	61	Liberia	0.37	95
Slovenia	0.60	28	El Salvador	0.48	62	Bangladesh	0.37	96
Poland	0.60	29	Malaysia	0.47	63	Afghanistan	0.36	97
Portugal	0.57	30	Russia	0.46	64	Ethiopia	0.36	98
Ghana	0.57	31	Cote d'Ivoire	0.46	65	Pakistan	0.36	99
Italy	0.56	32	China	0.46	66	Zimbabwe	0.35	100
South Africa	0.55	33	Burkina Faso	0.46	67	Cambodia	0.33	101
Belarus	0.55	34	Zambia	0.45	68	Venezuela	0.26	102

Factor 7: Civil Justice

Factor 7 measures whether civil justice systems are accessible and affordable, free of discrimination, corruption, and improper influence by public officials. It examines whether court proceedings are conducted without unreasonable delays, and if decisions are enforced effectively. It also measures the accessibility, impartiality, and effectiveness of alternative dispute resolution mechanisms.

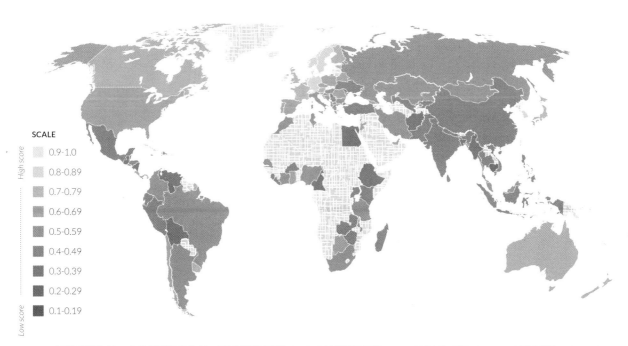

SCALE

High score
- 0.9-1.0
- 0.8-0.89
- 0.7-0.79
- 0.6-0.69
- 0.5-0.59
- 0.4-0.49
- 0.3-0.39
- 0.2-0.29
- 0.1-0.19
Low score

COUNTRY	SCORE	GLOBAL RANKING	COUNTRY	SCORE	GLOBAL RANKING	COUNTRY	SCORE	GLOBAL RANKING
Netherlands	0.86	1	Greece	0.59	35	Sri Lanka	0.47	69
Norway	0.86	2	Italy	0.58	36	Burkina Faso	0.47	70
Singapore	0.84	3	Malaysia	0.57	37	Zambia	0.47	71
Denmark	0.83	4	Macedonia, FYR	0.57	38	Serbia	0.47	72
Germany	0.82	5	South Africa	0.56	39	Kenya	0.47	73
Sweden	0.81	6	Iran	0.56	40	Thailand	0.46	74
Republic of Korea	0.80	7	Mongolia	0.55	41	Philippines	0.46	75
Austria	0.79	8	Argentina	0.55	42	Vietnam	0.46	76
New Zealand	0.78	9	Cote d'Ivoire	0.54	43	Kyrgyzstan	0.46	77
Finland	0.78	10	Bulgaria	0.54	44	Lebanon	0.45	78
Hong Kong SAR, China	0.76	11	Croatia	0.54	45	Zimbabwe	0.45	79
Estonia	0.75	12	Senegal	0.53	46	Honduras	0.45	80
United Kingdom	0.74	13	Hungary	0.53	47	Liberia	0.44	81
Japan	0.74	14	Brazil	0.53	48	Mexico	0.44	82
Australia	0.74	15	Tunisia	0.52	49	Indonesia	0.43	83
Belgium	0.72	16	Malawi	0.52	50	Moldova	0.43	84
Uruguay	0.71	17	Bosnia and Herzegovina	0.52	51	Sierra Leone	0.43	85
Canada	0.70	18	Jamaica	0.52	52	Peru	0.43	86
France	0.70	19	Kazakhstan	0.51	53	Nepal	0.42	87
Czech Republic	0.69	20	Morocco	0.51	54	India	0.42	88
United States	0.67	21	Colombia	0.51	55	Ecuador	0.41	89
Poland	0.65	22	Dominican Republic	0.51	56	Madagascar	0.41	90
Portugal	0.65	23	Tanzania	0.51	57	Pakistan	0.40	91
Spain	0.64	24	El Salvador	0.51	58	Egypt	0.39	92
Slovenia	0.64	25	Albania	0.50	59	Bangladesh	0.39	93
Georgia	0.63	26	Russia	0.50	60	Myanmar	0.37	94
Costa Rica	0.63	27	Panama	0.50	61	Bolivia	0.37	95
Romania	0.63	28	Nigeria	0.50	62	Cameroon	0.37	96
United Arab Emirates	0.63	29	Turkey	0.49	63	Guatemala	0.36	97
Belarus	0.62	30	Belize	0.49	64	Ethiopia	0.36	98
Jordan	0.62	31	Ukraine	0.49	65	Nicaragua	0.36	99
Chile	0.61	32	Uzbekistan	0.49	66	Venezuela	0.35	100
Botswana	0.61	33	China	0.48	67	Afghanistan	0.32	101
Ghana	0.61	34	Uganda	0.48	68	Cambodia	0.29	102

Factor 8: Criminal Justice

Factor 8 measures whether the criminal investigation, adjudication, and correctional systems are effective, and whether the criminal justice system is impartial, free of corruption, free of improper influence, and protective of due process and the rights of the accused.

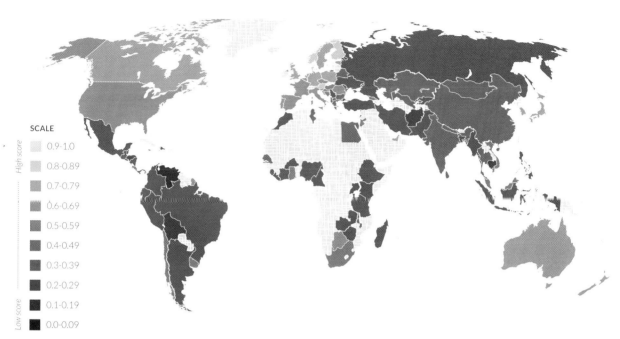

SCALE

High score

- 0.9-1.0
- 0.8-0.89
- 0.7-0.79
- 0.6-0.69
- 0.5-0.59
- 0.4-0.49
- 0.3-0.39
- 0.2-0.29
- 0.1-0.19
- 0.0-0.09

Low score

COUNTRY	SCORE	GLOBAL RANKING	COUNTRY	SCORE	GLOBAL RANKING	COUNTRY	SCORE	GLOBAL RANKING
Finland	0.85	1	Georgia	0.54	35	Dominican Republic	0.37	69
Denmark	0.84	2	Uruguay	0.54	36	Burkina Faso	0.36	70
Singapore	0.82	3	Bosnia and Herzegovina	0.51	37	Ukraine	0.36	71
Norway	0.82	4	South Africa	0.50	38	Zimbabwe	0.36	72
Austria	0.82	5	Vietnam	0.50	39	Nigeria	0.36	73
Hong Kong SAR, China	0.79	6	Ghana	0.50	40	Russia	0.36	74
Sweden	0.78	7	Tunisia	0.49	41	Indonesia	0.35	75
New Zealand	0.77	8	Greece	0.49	42	Turkey	0.35	76
United Arab Emirates	0.77	9	Belarus	0.48	43	Ecuador	0.35	77
Australia	0.77	10	India	0.47	44	Madagascar	0.35	78
United Kingdom	0.76	11	Jamaica	0.46	45	Peru	0.34	79
Germany	0.76	12	Sri Lanka	0.45	46	Uganda	0.34	80
Republic of Korea	0.76	13	China	0.45	47	El Salvador	0.34	81
Netherlands	0.75	14	Malawi	0.45	48	Moldova	0.34	82
Poland	0.74	15	Uzbekistan	0.44	49	Colombia	0.34	83
Japan	0.74	16	Bulgaria	0.44	50	Kyrgyzstan	0.34	84
Canada	0.72	17	Macedonia, FYR	0.44	51	Sierra Leone	0.33	85
Estonia	0.71	18	Senegal	0.44	52	Morocco	0.33	86
Czech Republic	0.69	19	Thailand	0.43	53	Nicaragua	0.33	87
Belgium	0.67	20	Albania	0.43	54	Bangladesh	0.33	88
Portugal	0.67	21	Egypt	0.43	55	Kenya	0.32	89
France	0.66	22	Nepal	0.42	56	Panama	0.32	90
United States	0.64	23	Mongolia	0.42	57	Cameroon	0.32	91
Slovenia	0.63	24	Kazakhstan	0.42	58	Liberia	0.32	92
Italy	0.63	25	Argentina	0.39	59	Mexico	0.31	93
Spain	0.62	26	Iran	0.39	60	Pakistan	0.31	94
Botswana	0.61	27	Ethiopia	0.39	61	Guatemala	0.30	95
Romania	0.60	28	Lebanon	0.39	62	Myanmar	0.30	96
Croatia	0.58	29	Serbia	0.38	63	Belize	0.29	97
Malaysia	0.58	30	Cote d'Ivoire	0.38	64	Cambodia	0.28	98
Costa Rica	0.57	31	Zambia	0.38	65	Bolivia	0.25	99
Chile	0.56	32	Philippines	0.38	66	Afghanistan	0.24	100
Hungary	0.55	33	Tanzania	0.37	67	Honduras	0.21	101
Jordan	0.55	34	Brazil	0.37	68	Venezuela	0.16	102

Global Insights

The *WJP Rule of Law Index 2015* introduces a new feature to the report: global insights on the rule of law. This section presents findings from the Rule of Law Index's main sources of data and presents: 1) individual questions taken from the General Population Poll, and 2) individual questions taken from the expert surveys. This section is intended to complement the Index scores and help users further engage with the data that is used to construct the Index. Visit the WJP Rule of Law Index webpage, http://data.worldjusticeproject.org/, for more information.

Perceptions of Corruption

Corruption is when officials abuse their power for their own interest, making the absence of corruption one of the hallmarks of a society governed by the rule of law. The World Justice Project asked 1,000 citizens in each country how many people they thought were involved in corrupt practices in the five institutions listed below. Forty-seven countries identify parliament/congress as the institution with the most corrupt members. Regionally, people from Sub-Saharan Africa hold the most negative perceptions of corruption in their institutions.

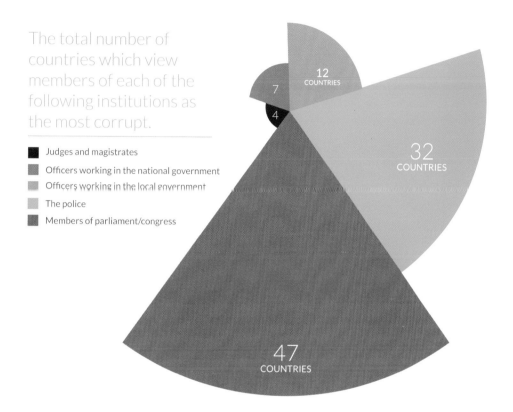

The total number of countries which view members of each of the following institutions as the most corrupt.

- Judges and magistrates
- Officers working in the national government
- Officers working in the local government
- The police
- Members of parliament/congress

12 COUNTRIES
7
4
32 COUNTRIES
47 COUNTRIES

How many of the following people in your country do you think are involved in corrupt practices?

- Officers working in the national government
- Officers working in the local government
- Members of parliament/congress
- Judges and magistrates
- The police

% saying "All of them" or "Most of them"

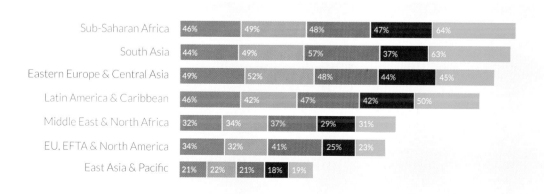

Sub-Saharan Africa	46%	49%	48%	47%	64%
South Asia	44%	49%	57%	37%	63%
Eastern Europe & Central Asia	49%	52%	48%	44%	45%
Latin America & Caribbean	46%	42%	47%	42%	50%
Middle East & North Africa	32%	34%	37%	29%	31%
EU, EFTA & North America	34%	32%	41%	25%	23%
East Asia & Pacific	21%	22%	21%	18%	19%

Regional Experiences with Petty Bribery

Corruption can take many forms – including bribery, nepotism, extortion, fraud, embezzlement, and involvement with organized crime – and may involve a variety of public servants. The chart below presents regional averages for people who had to pay a bribe in their dealings with the police, in order to receive medical treatment, or to obtain a government permit.

During the past three years, did you or someone in your household have to pay a bribe when...

- Receiving medical attention at a public hospital or clinic
- Stopped or detained by the police
- Requesting a government permit or processing a document

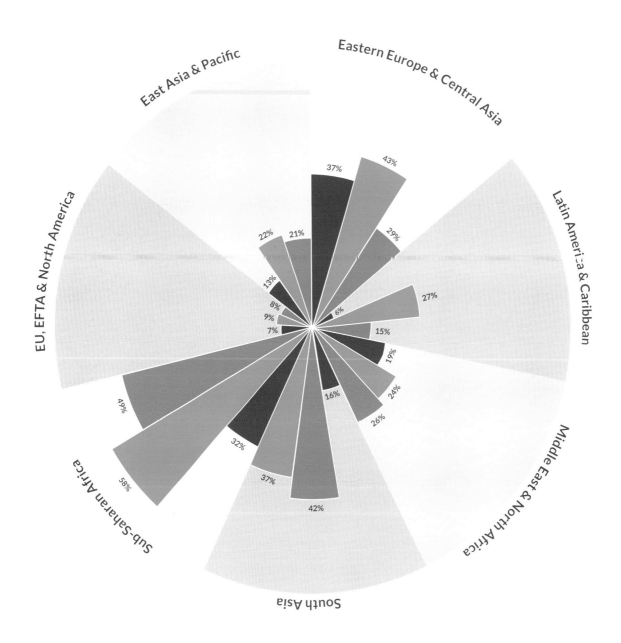

The Global Status of Requesting Government Information

Governments are the custodians of public information on behalf of the people. In an open government citizens have the right to access and use public records freely. The following chart reflects worldwide experiences of those who requested information from the government. Data for each of the 102 countries surveyed can also be found at data.worldjusticeproject.org/opengov

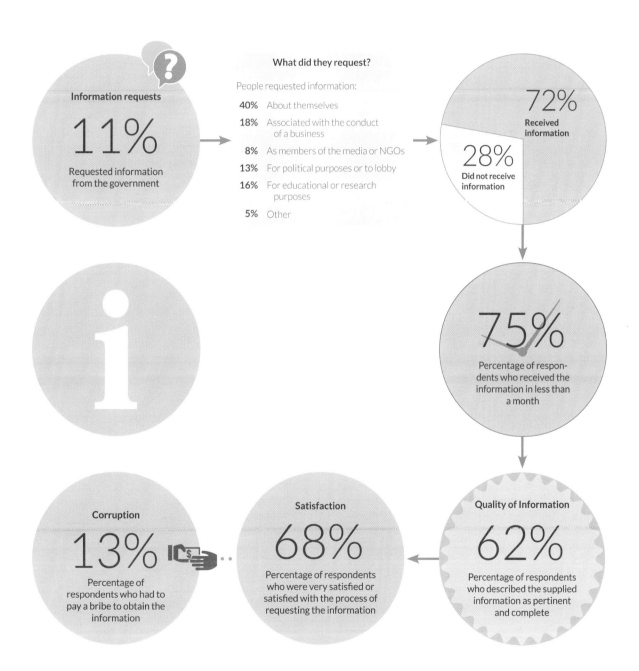

Information requests

11%

Requested information from the government

What did they request?

People requested information:

- **40%** About themselves
- **18%** Associated with the conduct of a business
- **8%** As members of the media or NGOs
- **13%** For political purposes or to lobby
- **16%** For educational or research purposes
- **5%** Other

72%
Received information

28%
Did not receive information

75%
Percentage of respondents who received the information in less than a month

Quality of Information

62%
Percentage of respondents who described the supplied information as pertinent and complete

Satisfaction

68%
Percentage of respondents who were very satisfied or satisfied with the process of requesting the information

Corruption

13%
Percentage of respondents who had to pay a bribe to obtain the information

Freedom of Opinion and Expression

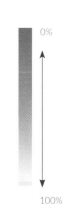

FACTOR 4: Fundamental Rights

As a basic human right, freedom of speech enables people to freely comment on government policies, to peacefully disagree with each other and their government, and ultimately to engage in policymaking and ensure government responsiveness. The following chart presents the percentage of respondents who answered "Strongly agree" or "Agree" to the following statements: a) people, b) civil society organizations, c) political parties, d) the media can express opinions against government policies and actions without fear of retaliation.

	The people	Civil society organizations	Political parties	The media
	% Agree + % Strongly agree			
Afghanistan	70%	66%	67%	70%
Albania	73%	40%	58%	50%
Argentina	79%	68%	74%	68%
Australia	91%	84%	87%	82%
Austria	88%	76%	83%	78%
Bangladesh	40%	31%	31%	28%
Belarus	31%	18%	40%	31%
Belgium	82%	76%	79%	78%
Belize	72%	72%	73%	60%
Bolivia	67%	55%	54%	48%
Bosnia and Herzegovina	65%	52%	70%	31%
Botswana	87%	88%	92%	83%
Brazil	71%	61%	66%	53%
Bulgaria	89%	73%	81%	46%
Burkina Faso	56%	46%	50%	38%
Cambodia	51%	50%	53%	26%
Cameroon	60%	53%	69%	53%
Canada	90%	81%	84%	82%
Chile	78%	70%	79%	68%
China	0%	0%	0%	8%
Colombia	68%	49%	57%	48%
Costa Rica	83%	78%	84%	74%
Cote d'Ivoire	56%	46%	50%	43%
Croatia	68%	49%	73%	45%
Czech Republic	87%	68%	77%	61%
Denmark	93%	89%	89%	88%
Dominican Republic	83%	79%	83%	80%
Ecuador	63%	60%	63%	60%
El Salvador	69%	67%	70%	68%
Estonia	76%	67%	71%	74%
Ethiopia	44%	35%	44%	34%
Finland	88%	82%	84%	83%
France	82%	68%	80%	67%
Georgia	92%	89%	93%	89%
Germany	89%	84%	86%	86%
Ghana	87%	79%	88%	81%
Greece	75%	51%	60%	38%
Guatemala	66%	58%	68%	65%
Honduras	64%	57%	69%	58%
Hong Kong SAR, China	32%	34%	35%	21%
Hungary	54%	31%	48%	25%
India	72%	61%	63%	74%
Indonesia	84%	81%	87%	89%
Iran		20%	22%	23%
Italy	77%	61%	72%	51%
Jamaica	76%	69%	76%	60%
Japan	91%	91%	91%	89%
Jordan	47%	46%	48%	66%
Kazakhstan	34%	36%	47%	47%
Kenya	66%	71%	76%	61%

	The people	Civil society organizations	Political parties	The media
	% Agree + % Strongly agree			
Kyrgyzstan	68%	60%	64%	58%
Lebanon	73%	70%	72%	69%
Liberia	92%	90%	87%	85%
Macedonia, FYR	54%	34%	49%	33%
Madagascar	66%	70%	71%	58%
Malawi	80%	75%	79%	68%
Malaysia	44%	41%	45%	48%
Mexico	58%	48%	51%	36%
Moldova	66%	49%	53%	23%
Mongolia	67%	59%	62%	55%
Morocco	63%	69%	67%	50%
Myanmar	19%	22%	33%	29%
Nepal	81%	81%	85%	79%
Netherlands	91%	88%	87%	90%
New Zealand	97%	96%	96%	94%
Nicaragua	72%	72%	74%	71%
Nigeria	64%	65%	71%	61%
Norway	90%	89%	85%	89%
Pakistan	60%	55%	63%	62%
Panama	75%	72%	71%	71%
Peru	76%	65%	69%	61%
Philippines	76%	81%	69%	70%
Poland	65%	46%	66%	56%
Portugal	81%	67%	80%	61%
Republic of Korea	80%	86%	86%	88%
Romania	73%	50%	73%	63%
Russia	52%	46%	60%	57%
Senegal	91%	88%	88%	85%
Serbia	81%	40%	60%	51%
Sierra Leone	73%	76%	69%	77%
Singapore	37%	38%	40%	44%
Slovenia	55%	27%	47%	23%
South Africa	83%	76%	81%	77%
Spain	72%	58%	76%	58%
Sri Lanka	55%	56%	65%	61%
Sweden	91%	86%	86%	86%
Tanzania	75%	66%	69%	63%
Thailand	84%	76%	78%	70%
Tunisia	89%	86%	87%	86%
Turkey	49%	54%	62%	48%
Uganda	32%	36%	34%	37%
Ukraine	42%	68%	23%	30%
United Arab Emirates	32%	44%	45%	48%
United Kingdom	86%	80%	84%	82%
United States	84%	75%	79%	77%
Uruguay	89%	78%	89%	77%
Uzbekistan	58%	5%	52%	32%
Vietnam	48%	45%	45%	55%
Zambia	41%	26%	47%	42%
Zimbabwe	15%	18%	21%	20%

0%

100%

data not available

*Egypt and Venezuela have been omitted from this chart due to lack of significant data

Freedom of Assembly and Association

Freedom of assembly is also necessary for robust civic participation. The following chart presents the percentage of respondents who answered "Strongly agree" or "Agree" to the following statements: a) people can freely join any (unforbidden) political organization they want, b) people can freely join together with others to draw attention to an issue or sign a petition, c) people can freely attend community meetings, d) people in this neighborhood can get together with others and present their concerns to local government officials.

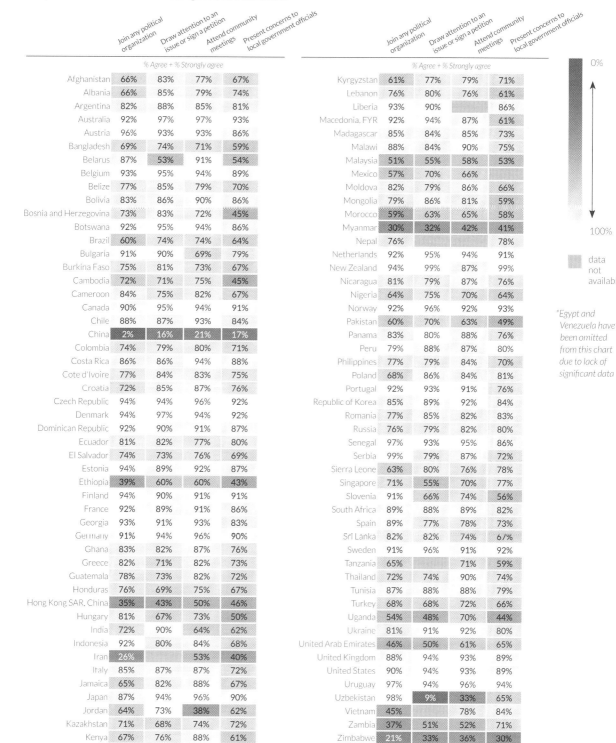

	Join any political organization	Draw attention to an issue or sign a petition	Attend community meetings	Present concerns to local government officials
% Agree + % Strongly agree				
Afghanistan	66%	83%	77%	67%
Albania	66%	85%	79%	74%
Argentina	82%	88%	85%	81%
Australia	92%	97%	97%	93%
Austria	96%	93%	93%	86%
Bangladesh	69%	74%	71%	59%
Belarus	87%	53%	91%	54%
Belgium	93%	95%	94%	89%
Belize	77%	85%	79%	70%
Bolivia	83%	86%	90%	86%
Bosnia and Herzegovina	73%	83%	72%	45%
Botswana	92%	95%	94%	86%
Brazil	60%	74%	74%	64%
Bulgaria	91%	90%	69%	79%
Burkina Faso	75%	81%	73%	67%
Cambodia	72%	71%	75%	45%
Cameroon	84%	75%	82%	67%
Canada	90%	95%	94%	91%
Chile	88%	87%	93%	84%
China	2%	16%	21%	17%
Colombia	74%	79%	80%	71%
Costa Rica	86%	86%	94%	88%
Cote d'Ivoire	77%	84%	83%	75%
Croatia	72%	85%	87%	76%
Czech Republic	94%	94%	96%	92%
Denmark	94%	97%	94%	92%
Dominican Republic	92%	90%	91%	87%
Ecuador	81%	82%	77%	80%
El Salvador	74%	73%	76%	69%
Estonia	94%	89%	92%	87%
Ethiopia	39%	60%	60%	43%
Finland	94%	90%	91%	91%
France	92%	89%	91%	86%
Georgia	93%	91%	93%	83%
Germany	91%	94%	96%	90%
Ghana	83%	82%	87%	76%
Greece	82%	71%	82%	73%
Guatemala	78%	73%	82%	72%
Honduras	76%	69%	75%	67%
Hong Kong SAR, China	35%	43%	50%	46%
Hungary	81%	67%	73%	50%
India	72%	90%	64%	62%
Indonesia	92%	80%	84%	68%
Iran	26%		53%	40%
Italy	85%	87%	87%	72%
Jamaica	65%	82%	88%	67%
Japan	87%	94%	96%	90%
Jordan	64%	73%	38%	62%
Kazakhstan	71%	68%	74%	72%
Kenya	67%	76%	88%	61%
Kyrgyzstan	61%	77%	79%	71%
Lebanon	76%	80%	76%	61%
Liberia	93%	90%		86%
Macedonia, FYR	92%	94%	87%	61%
Madagascar	85%	84%	85%	73%
Malawi	88%	84%	90%	75%
Malaysia	51%	55%	58%	53%
Mexico	57%	70%	66%	
Moldova	82%	79%	86%	66%
Mongolia	79%	86%	81%	59%
Morocco	59%	63%	65%	58%
Myanmar	30%	32%	42%	41%
Nepal	76%			78%
Netherlands	92%	95%	94%	91%
New Zealand	94%	99%	87%	99%
Nicaragua	81%	79%	87%	76%
Nigeria	64%	75%	70%	64%
Norway	92%	96%	92%	93%
Pakistan	60%	70%	63%	49%
Panama	83%	80%	88%	76%
Peru	79%	88%	87%	80%
Philippines	77%	79%	84%	70%
Poland	68%	86%	84%	81%
Portugal	92%	93%	91%	76%
Republic of Korea	85%	89%	92%	84%
Romania	77%	85%	82%	83%
Russia	76%	79%	82%	80%
Senegal	97%	93%	95%	86%
Serbia	99%	79%	87%	72%
Sierra Leone	63%	80%	76%	78%
Singapore	71%	55%	70%	77%
Slovenia	91%	66%	74%	56%
South Africa	89%	88%	89%	82%
Spain	89%	77%	78%	73%
Sri Lanka	82%	82%	74%	67%
Sweden	91%	96%	91%	92%
Tanzania	65%		71%	59%
Thailand	72%	74%	90%	74%
Tunisia	87%	88%	88%	79%
Turkey	68%	68%	72%	66%
Uganda	54%	48%	70%	44%
Ukraine	81%	91%	92%	80%
United Arab Emirates	46%	50%	61%	65%
United Kingdom	88%	94%	93%	89%
United States	90%	94%	93%	89%
Uruguay	97%	94%	96%	94%
Uzbekistan	98%	9%	33%	65%
Vietnam	45%		78%	84%
Zambia	37%	51%	52%	71%
Zimbabwe	21%	33%	36%	30%

0%

100%

data not available

*Egypt and Venezuela have been omitted from this chart due to lack of significant data

Perception of Police Discrimination

In recent years, news reports and investigations have put a spotlight on the treatment of criminal suspects by police in Europe and North America. The findings of these reports often focus on the disparate treatment suspects receive based on their personal characteristics. The chart below presents the hypothetical case of two equally suspected people being detained for the same crime and asks people whether they believe certain characteristics would put a suspect at a disadvantage. In nearly all Western European and North American countries, a majority of respondents believe that being of a different ethnic group than the police officers involved or being a foreigner would put suspects at a disadvantage.

Imagine the local police detain two people equally suspected of committing a crime. In your opinion, which of the following characteristics would place one of them at a disadvantage?

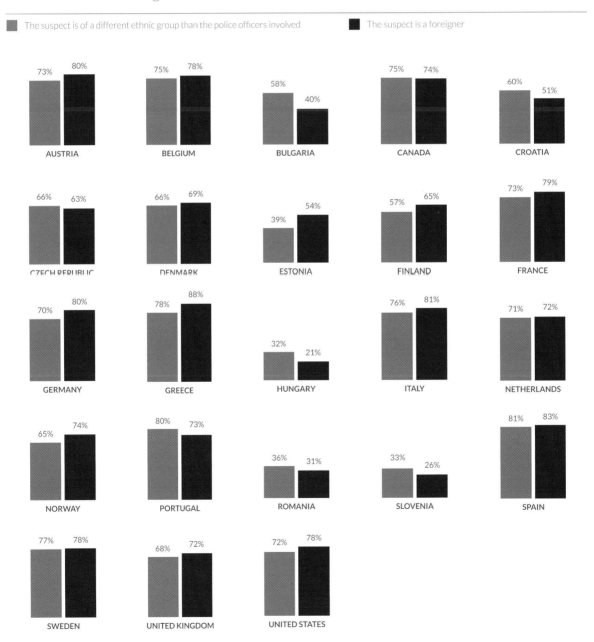

Crime Victimization by Region

In each indexed country, the World Justice Project asked 1,000 people living in the three largest cities if they or anyone in their households had been a victim of burglary, armed robbery, extortion, or homicide in the past three years. The regional averages of these responses are presented in the chart below. Sub-Saharan Africa and Latin America & the Caribbean report the highest rates of victimization, while the East Asia & the Pacific region reports the lowest.

During the past three years, did you or anyone in your household experience a(n):

■ Burglary   ■ Armed Robbery (individual only)   ■ Extortion   ■ Homicide

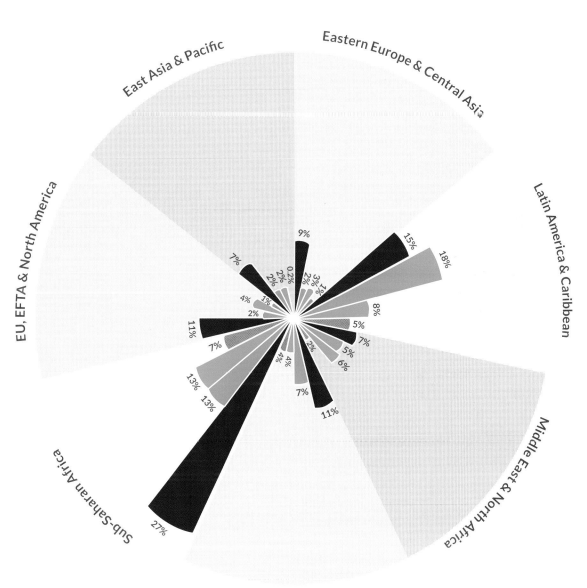

Vigilante Justice

Resorting to intimidation or violence to resolve disputes or seek redress demonstrates citizens' lack of trust in their formal or informal justice system's ability to effectively enforce codified laws and procedures, often due to perceived problems with capacity or corruption. When citizens take matters into their own hands, equal protection and due process mandates are often violated. The map below presents regional perceptions on the likely outcomes of a situation in which a criminal is apprehended by neighbors after committing a serious crime.

Assume that a criminal is apprehended by your neighbors after committing a serious crime. Which of the following two situations is more likely to happen?

a. The criminal gets beaten by the neighbors

b. The criminal is turned over to the authorities without harm

EU, EFTA & North America
26%
% The criminal gets beaten by the neighbors

30%
% The criminal gets beaten by the neighbors

Eastern Europe & Central Asia
35%
% The criminal gets beaten by the neighbors

Middle East & North Africa

East Asia & Pacific
26%
% The criminal gets beaten by the neighbors

Sub-Saharan Africa
58%
% The criminal gets beaten by the neighbors

South Asia
57%
% The criminal gets beaten by the neighbors

Latin America & Caribbean
56%
% The criminal gets beaten by the neighbors

Perceptions of Regulatory Enforcement

Around the world, environmental regulations vary widely due to differences in polices, institutional environments, and political choices. Whatever those differences may be, regulations are futile if they are not properly enforced by authorities. Ensuring compliance with regulations is thus a key feature of the rule of law. The infographic below presents the people's view in each region of the likely outcomes of a situation in which a company is found to be polluting beyond legally permitted levels.

Assume that the environment protection agency in your country notifies an industrial plant that it is polluting a river beyond the legally permitted levels. Which of the following outcomes is most likely?

a. The company complies with the law (either voluntarily or through court orders, fines, and other sanctions)

b. The company bribes or influences the authorities to ignore the violation

c. Absolutely nothing happens

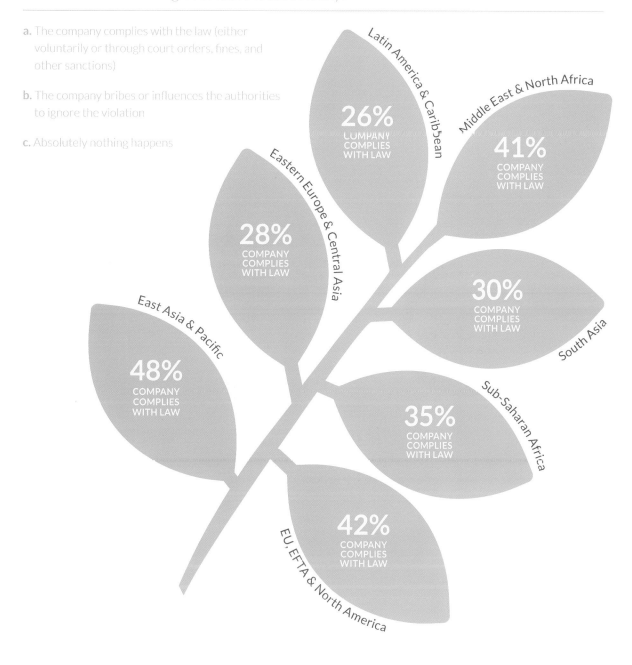

The Global Experience with Civil Justice

Around the world, people's ability to use legal channels to resolve their disputes is often impeded by obstacles such as financial barriers, complex procedures, corrupt personnel, the influence of powerful actors in judicial decision-making, a lack of knowledge, disempowerment, or exclusion. The following chart presents the aggregated experiences of nearly 12,000 people who, in the last three years, faced a conflict with someone who refused to fulfill a contract or pay a debt.

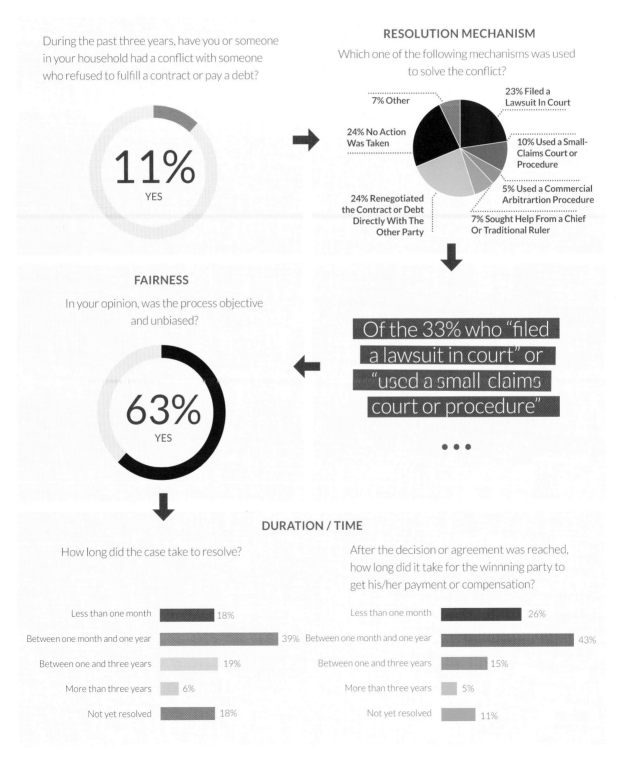

During the past three years, have you or someone in your household had a conflict with someone who refused to fulfill a contract or pay a debt?

11% YES

RESOLUTION MECHANISM

Which one of the following mechanisms was used to solve the conflict?

- 7% Other
- 23% Filed a Lawsuit In Court
- 24% No Action Was Taken
- 10% Used a Small-Claims Court or Procedure
- 5% Used a Commercial Arbitrartion Procedure
- 24% Renegotiated the Contract or Debt Directly With The Other Party
- 7% Sought Help From a Chief Or Traditional Ruler

FAIRNESS

In your opinion, was the process objective and unbiased?

63% YES

Of the 33% who "filed a lawsuit in court" or "used a small claims court or procedure"

· · ·

DURATION / TIME

How long did the case take to resolve?

Less than one month	18%
Between one month and one year	39%
Between one and three years	19%
More than three years	6%
Not yet resolved	18%

After the decision or agreement was reached, how long did it take for the winnning party to get his/her payment or compensation?

Less than one month	26%
Between one month and one year	43%
Between one and three years	15%
More than three years	5%
Not yet resolved	11%

LEGAL ASSISTANCE

Did you or your household member receive legal assistance during this process?

64%
YES

If yes, from whom?

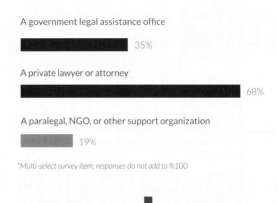

A government legal assistance office
35%

A private lawyer or attorney
68%

A paralegal, NGO, or other support organization
19%

Multi-select survey item, responses do not add to %100

If not, why not?

I did not think I needed a lawyer — 51%
I could not afford a lawyer — 27%
I did not know who to call — 46%
Other — 13%
Language or cultural problems — 14%

Multi-select survey item, responses do not add to %100

In your opinion, how expensive were the attorney's fees?

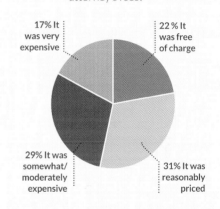

17% It was very expensive
22% It was free of charge
29% It was somewhat/moderately expensive
31% It was reasonably priced

SATISFACTION

Regardless of the outcome, please tell us how you feel about the way the process was handled

 61% the process was fair

 69% the process was slow

 54% the process was too expensive

CORRUPTION

At any stage of the judicial process, did the following officers ask you, or expect you, to pay a bribe?

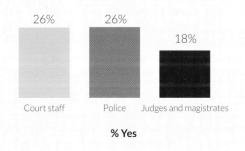

26% — Court staff
26% — Police
18% — Judges and magistrates

% Yes

Problems Facing Access to Civil Court Systems

The table below presents the findings from the 2015 Qualified Respondents Questionnaire (QRQ), which includes the opinions of over 2,500 legal academics and practitioners.

How important are the following factors in influencing people's decisions on whether or not to go to court to resolve a dispute in the city where you live?

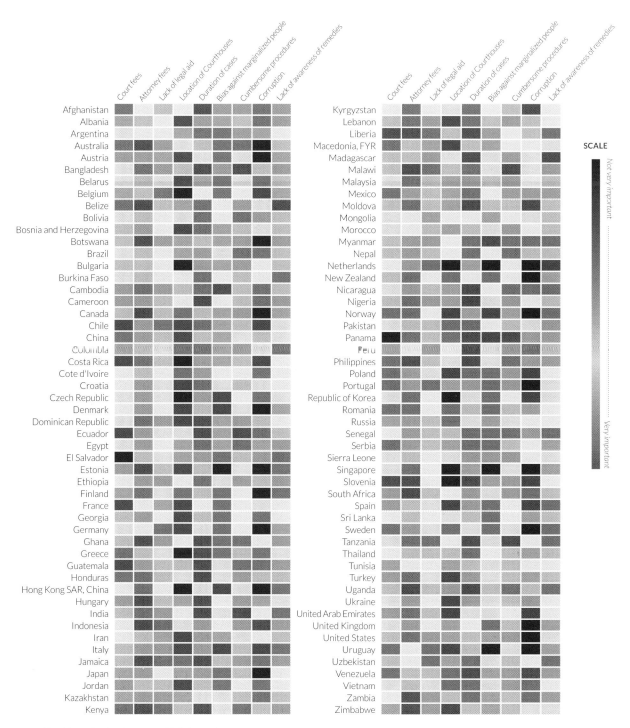

Problems Facing Civil Court Systems

FACTOR 7: Civil Justice

The table below presents the findings from the 2015 Qualified Respondents Questionnaire (QRQ), which includes the opinions of over 2,500 legal academics and practitioners.

How serious are the following problems in civil and commercial courts in the city where you live?

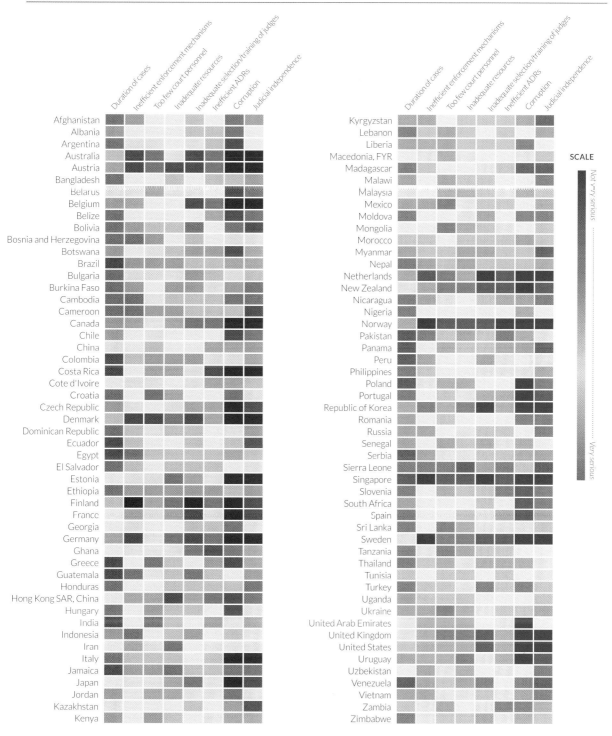

Problems Facing Criminal Investigation Systems

The table below presents the findings from the 2015 Qualified Respondents Questionnaire (QRQ), which includes the opinions of over 2,500 legal academics and practitioners.

How significant are the following problems for the criminal investigative service (prosecutors, investigators, judicial police officers, etc.) in the city where you live?

Problems Facing Criminal Justice Systems

The table below presents the findings from the 2015 Qualified Respondents Questionnaire (QRQ), which includes the opinions of over 2,500 legal academics and practitioners.

How significant are the following problems in criminal courts in the city where you live?

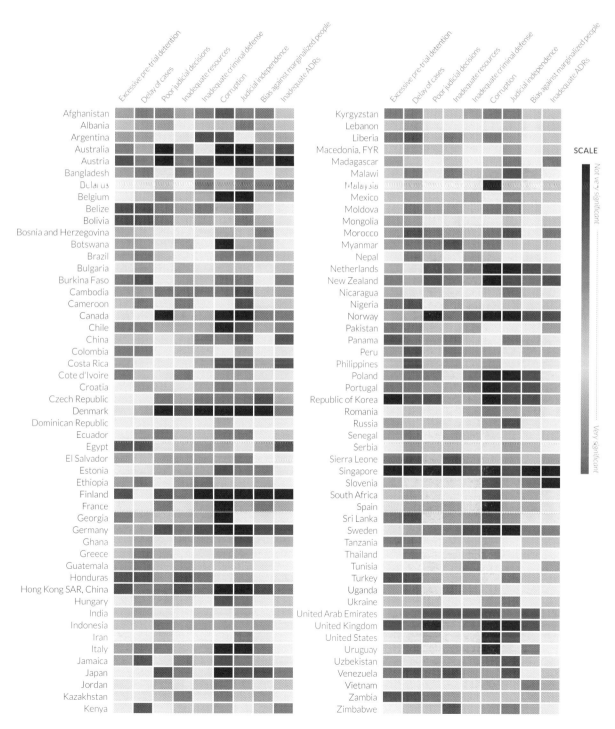

Perceptions of Police Accountability

FACTOR 8: Criminal Justice

The police occupy an important position in upholding the rule of law, and play a powerful role in interactions between average citizens and the formal justice system. Nonetheless, police officers are not above the law they serve. The following table presents perceptions of respondents on police performance in the following areas: 1) whether police act according to the law, 2) whether police respect the basic rights of suspects, and 3) whether police are punished for violating the law.

	Police act according to the law	Police respect the basic rights of suspects	Police are punished for violating the law
	%Always/Often		
Afghanistan	67%	50%	47%
Albania	73%	49%	73%
Argentina	39%	36%	24%
Australia	94%	90%	70%
Austria	92%	87%	58%
Bangladesh	25%	26%	18%
Belarus	37%	63%	54%
Belgium	93%	91%	62%
Belize	58%	48%	41%
Bolivia	19%	22%	19%
Bosnia and Herzegovina	88%	79%	73%
Botswana	90%	84%	82%
Brazil	22%	21%	24%
Bulgaria	63%	58%	30%
Burkina Faso	74%	65%	58%
Cambodia	28%	30%	22%
Cameroon	38%	30%	50%
Canada	88%	82%	58%
Chile	70%	60%	58%
China	89%	88%	93%
Colombia	48%	39%	42%
Costa Rica	79%	74%	67%
Cote d'Ivoire	63%	51%	61%
Croatia	63%	42%	66%
Czech Republic	91%	85%	47%
Denmark	94%	93%	75%
Dominican Republic	56%	48%	60%
Ecuador	62%	55%	52%
Egypt	39%	29%	48%
El Salvador	63%	56%	55%
Estonia	96%	91%	73%
Ethiopia	57%	58%	56%
Finland	95%	91%	79%
France	89%	84%	60%
Georgia	78%	57%	74%
Germany	89%	86%	52%
Ghana	39%	43%	54%
Greece	77%	57%	29%
Guatemala	50%	53%	61%
Honduras	59%	55%	54%
Hong Kong SAR, China	95%	95%	100%
Hungary	66%	64%	49%
India	48%	50%	54%
Indonesia	54%	47%	58%
Iran	67%	56%	55%
Italy	83%	72%	38%
Jamaica	35%	23%	32%
Japan	100%	97%	99%
Jordan	83%	65%	66%
Kazakhstan	41%	25%	30%
Kenya	27%	23%	36%

	Police act according to the law	Police respect the basic rights of suspects	Police are punished for violating the law
	%Always/Often		
Kyrgyzstan	39%	31%	36%
Lebanon	62%	43%	52%
Liberia	43%	30%	56%
Macedonia, FYR	66%	68%	42%
Madagascar	23%	21%	43%
Malawi	32%	33%	44%
Malaysia	92%	90%	92%
Mexico	24%	25%	25%
Moldova	44%	56%	43%
Mongolia	60%	39%	49%
Morocco	79%	72%	73%
Myanmar	98%	76%	89%
Nepal	78%	55%	63%
Netherlands	89%	88%	66%
New Zealand	100%	100%	99%
Nicaragua	66%	59%	61%
Nigeria	21%	23%	24%
Norway	95%	92%	75%
Pakistan	31%	13%	19%
Panama	79%	72%	64%
Peru	31%	30%	24%
Philippines	98%	83%	94%
Poland	62%	34%	65%
Portugal	88%	82%	61%
Republic of Korea	100%	96%	98%
Romania	65%	52%	59%
Russia	55%	35%	48%
Senegal	69%	63%	65%
Serbia	52%	66%	54%
Sierra Leone	70%	63%	60%
Singapore	93%	87%	91%
Slovenia	65%	60%	47%
South Africa	58%	59%	59%
Spain	88%	82%	49%
Sri Lanka	49%	40%	49%
Sweden	93%	89%	51%
Tanzania	58%	43%	52%
Thailand	96%	84%	95%
Tunisia	55%	39%	46%
Turkey	59%	46%	57%
Uganda	35%	28%	33%
Ukraine	31%	51%	37%
United Arab Emirates	100%	99%	89%
United Kingdom	91%	84%	63%
United States	83%	75%	53%
Uruguay	81%	73%	73%
Uzbekistan	36%	26%	58%
Venezuela	34%	28%	32%
Vietnam	79%	69%	71%
Zambia	53%	43%	48%
Zimbabwe	41%	26%	33%

0%

100%

Rule of Law Trends

The *WJP Rule of Law Index 2015* features analysis of whether a country's primary rule of law indicators experienced significant change over the past year. An arrow pointing up indicates a statistically significant improvement, while an arrow pointing down represents a statistically significant decline. A detailed explanation of these measures can be found in the Methodology section of this report.

Rule of Law Trends

COUNTRY/TERRITORY	CONSTRAINTS ON GOVERNMENT POWERS	ABSENCE OF CORRUPTION	OPEN GOVERNMENT	FUNDAMENTAL RIGHTS	ORDER & SECURITY	REGULATORY ENFORCEMENT	CIVIL JUSTICE	CRIMINAL JUSTICE
Afghanistan	—	—	—	—	—	—	—	—
Albania	—	—	—	—	—	—	—	—
Argentina	—	—	—	—	—	—	—	—
Australia	—	—	—	—	—	—	—	—
Austria	—	—	—	—	—	—	—	—
Bangladesh	—	—	—	—	—	—	—	—
Belarus	—	—	—	—	—	—	—	▲
Belgium	—	—	—	—	—	—	—	—
Belize	—	—	—	—	—	—	—	—
Bolivia	—	—	—	—	—	—	—	—
Bosnia and Herzegovina	—	—	—	—	—	—	—	—
Botswana	▼	—	—	—	—	—	—	—
Brazil	▼	—	—	▼	—	▼	—	—
Bulgaria	—	—	—	—	—	—	—	—
Burkina Faso	—	▼	—	—	—	—	▼	—
Cambodia	—	—	—	—	▼	—	▼	—
Cameroon					▼			
Canada	▼	—	—	—	—	—	—	—
Chile	—	—	—	—	—	—	—	—
China	—	—	—	—	▼	▲	▲	—
Colombia	—	—	—	—	—	—	—	—
Costa Rica	—	—	—	—	—	—	—	—
Cote d'Ivoire	—	—	—	—	—	—	▲	—
Croatia	—	—	—	—	—	—	—	—
Czech Republic	—	—	—	—	▲	—	—	—
Denmark	—	—	—	—	—	—	—	—
Dominican Republic	—	—	—	—	—	—	—	—
Ecuador	—	—	—	—	—	—	—	—
Egypt	—	—	—	—	—	▼	—	—
El Salvador	—	—	—	—	—	—	—	—
Estonia	—	—	—	—	—	—	—	—
Ethiopia	—	—	—	▼	—	—	—	—
Finland	—	—	—	—	—	—	—	—
France	—	—	—	—	—	—	—	—
Georgia	▲	—	—	▲	—	—	—	—
Germany	—	—	—	—	—	—	—	—
Ghana	—	—	—	—	—	—	—	—
Greece	—	—	—	—	—	—	—	—
Guatemala	—	—	—	—	—	—	—	—
Honduras	—	—	—	—	—	—	—	—
Hong Kong SAR, China	—	—	—	—	—	—	—	—
Hungary	▼	▼	—	—	—	▼	—	—
India	—	—	—	—	▲	—	—	—
Indonesia	—	—	—	—	—	—	—	—
Iran	—	—	—	—	—	—	—	—
Italy	—	—	—	—	—	—	—	—
Jamaica	—	▲	—	—	—	—	—	—
Japan	—	—	—	—	—	—	—	—
Jordan	—	—	—	—	—	—	—	—

COUNTRY/TERRITORY	CONTRAINTS ON GOVERNMENT POWERS	ABSENCE OF CORRUPTION	OPEN GOVERNMENT	FUNDAMENTAL RIGHTS	ORDER & SECURITY	REGULATORY ENFORCEMENT	CIVIL JUSTICE	CRIMINAL JUSTICE
Kazakhstan	–	–	–	▼	–	–	–	–
Kenya	–	–	–	–	▼	–	–	–
Kyrgyzstan	–	–	–	–	–	–	–	–
Lebanon	–	–	–	–	▼	–	–	–
Liberia	–	–	–	–	–	–	–	–
Macedonia, FYR	▼	–	–	▼	–	▼	–	–
Madagascar	–	–	–	–	–	–	–	–
Malawi	▲	–	–	–	▼	▲	–	–
Malaysia	–	–	–	–	–	–	–	–
Mexico	▼	▼	–	–	–	–	–	–
Moldova	–	–	–	–	–	–	–	–
Mongolia	–	–	–	–	–	–	–	–
Morocco	–	▲	–	–	–	–	–	–
Myanmar	–	–	–	–	▲	–	–	–
Nepal	–	–	–	–	–	–	–	–
Netherlands	–	–	–	–	–	–	–	–
New Zealand	▼	–	–	–	–	–	–	–
Nicaragua	–	–	–	▼	–	▼	–	–
Nigeria	–	–	–	–	–	–	–	–
Norway	–	–	–	–	–	–	–	–
Pakistan	–	▲	–	–	–	–	–	–
Panama	▲	▲	–	–	–	▲	▲	–
Peru	–	–	–	▼	–	–	–	–
Philippines	–	–	–	–	–	–	–	–
Poland	▲	–	–	–	–	–	–	–
Portugal	–	▲	–	–	–	–	–	–
Republic of Korea	–	–	–	–	–	–	–	–
Romania	–	–	–	–	–	–	–	–
Russia	–	–	–	–	–	–	–	–
Senegal	▲	▲	–	–	–	–	–	–
Serbia	–	–	–	▼	–	▼	–	▼
Sierra Leone	–	–	–	–	–	–	–	–
Singapore	–	–	–	–	–	▲	▲	–
Slovenia	–	–	–	–	–	–	–	–
South Africa	–	–	–	–	–	–	–	▲
Spain	–	–	–	–	–	–	–	–
Sri Lanka	▼	–	–	▼	–	–	–	–
Sweden	–	–	–	–	–	–	–	–
Tanzania	–	–	–	–	–	–	–	–
Thailand	–	–	–	▼	–	–	–	–
Tunisia	▲	–	–	–	–	–	–	–
Turkey	▼	▼	–	▼	–	–	–	–
Uganda	▼	–	–	–	–	–	–	–
Ukraine	–	▲	–	–	▼	–	–	–
United Arab Emirates	–	▲	–	–	–	–	–	–
United Kingdom	–	–	–	–	–	–	–	–
United States	–	–	–	–	–	–	–	–
Uruguay	–	–	–	–	–	–	–	–
Uzbekistan	–	–	–	–	–	–	–	–
Venezuela	–	–	–	–	–	–	–	–
Vietnam	–	–	–	–	–	–	–	–
Zambia	–	–	–	–	–	–	–	–
Zimbabwe	–	–	–	–	–	–	–	–

Country Profiles

This section presents profiles for the 102 countries and jurisdictions included in the *WJP Rule of Law Index 2015* report.

How to Read the Country Profiles

Each country profile presents the featured country's scores for each of the WJP Rule of Law Index's factors and sub-factors, and draws comparisons between the scores of the featured country and the scores of other indexed countries that share regional and income level similarities. The scores range between 0 and 1, where 1 signifies the highest score (high rule of law adherence) and 0 signifies the lowest score (low rule of law adherence). The country profiles consist of four sections, outlined below.

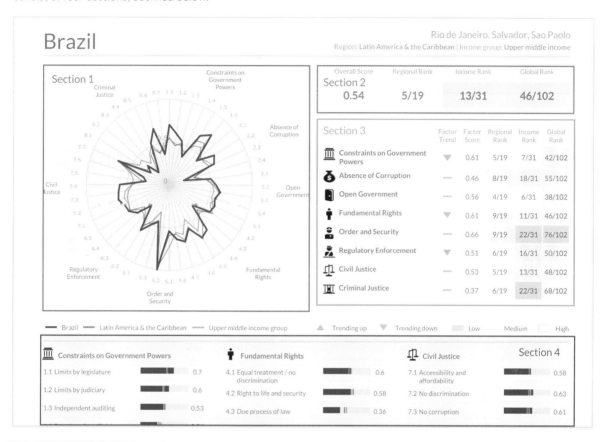

1 Displays the country's disaggregated scores for each of the sub-factors that compose the WJP Rule of Law Index. Each of the 44 sub-factors is represented by a gray line drawn from the center to the periphery of the circle. The center of the circle corresponds to the worst possible score for each sub-factor (0), and the outer edge of the circle marks the best possible score for each sub-factor (1).

The featured country's scores are shown in purple. The average score of the country's region is shown in orange. The average score of the country's income group is shown in green.

2 Displays the country's overall rule of law score, along with its overall global, income and regional ranks. The overall rule of law score is calculated by taking the simple average of the eight individual factors listed in the table in Section 3 of the country profile.

3 Displays the featured country's individual factor scores, along with the global, regional and income group rankings. The distribution of scores for the global rank, regional rank, and income rank is spread amongst three tiers – high, medium, and low as indicated by the color of the box in which the score is found.

It also features upward and downward arrows to illustrate whether the rule of law in a country changed in the past year. Further information about the statistical procedure to construct these arrows can be found in the "Methodology" section of this report.

4 Presents the individual sub-factor scores under-lying each of the factors listed in Section 3 of the country profile. The featured country's score is represented by the purple bar and labeled at the end of the bar. The average score of the country's region is represented by the orange line. The average score of the country's income group is represented by the green line. Each sub-factor score is scaled between 0 and 1, where 1 is the highest score and 0 is the lowest score.

Afghanistan

	Overall Score	Regional Rank	Income Rank	Global Rank
	0.35	6/6	15/15	101/102

		Factor Trend	Factor Score	Regional Rank	Income Rank	Global Rank
🏛	Constraints on Government Powers	—	0.44	5/6	9/15	82/102
💰	Absence of Corruption	—	0.23	6/6	15/15	102/102
📱	Open Government	—	0.43	6/6	8/15	89/102
🧍	Fundamental Rights	—	0.38	6/6	12/15	95/102
👮	Order and Security	—	0.42	5/6	15/15	100/102
🔧	Regulatory Enforcement	—	0.36	5/6	12/15	97/102
⚖	Civil Justice	—	0.32	6/6	14/15	101/102
🏛	Criminal Justice	—	0.24	6/6	15/15	100/102

— Afghanistan   — South Asia   — Low income group   ▲ Trending up   ▼ Trending down   ▨ Low   ▨ Medium   ☐ High

🏛 Constraints on Government Powers

1.1 Limits by legislature	0.59
1.2 Limits by judiciary	0.34
1.3 Independent auditing	0.4
1.4 Sanctions for official misconduct	0.3
1.5 Non-governmental checks	0.59
1.6 Lawful transition of power	0.42

💰 Absence of Corruption

2.1 No corruption in the executive branch	0.34
2.2 No corruption in the judiciary	0.08
2.3 No corruption in the police/military	0.31
2.4 No corruption in the legislature	0.18

📱 Open Government

3.1 Publicized laws and government data	0.37
3.2 Right to information	0.39
3.3 Civic participation	0.59
3.4 Complaint mechanisms	0.36

🧍 Fundamental Rights

4.1 Equal treatment / no discrimination	0.31
4.2 Right to life and security	0.33
4.3 Due process of law	0.27
4.4 Freedom of expression	0.6
4.5 Freedom of religion	0.42
4.6 Right to privacy	0.23
4.7 Freedom of association	0.65
4.8 Labor rights	0.25

👮 Order and Security

5.1 Absence of crime	0.68
5.2 Absence of civil conflict	0.26
5.3 Absence of violent redress	0.33

🔧 Regulatory Enforcement

6.1 Effective regulatory enforcement	0.35
6.2 No improper influence	0.31
6.3 No unreasonable delay	0.42
6.4 Respect for due process	0.26
6.5 No expropriation w/out adequate compensation	0.49

⚖ Civil Justice

7.1 Accessibility and affordability	0.37
7.2 No discrimination	0.11
7.3 No corruption	0.1
7.4 No improper gov. influence	0.33
7.5 No unreasonable delay	0.42
7.6 Effective enforcement	0.47
7.7 Impartial and effective ADRs	0.43

🏛 Criminal Justice

8.1 Effective investigations	0.35
8.2 Timely and effective adjudication	0.35
8.3 Effective correctional system	0.21
8.4 No discrimination	0.13
8.5 No corruption	0.22
8.6 No improper gov. influence	0.2
8.7 Due process of law	0.27

Albania

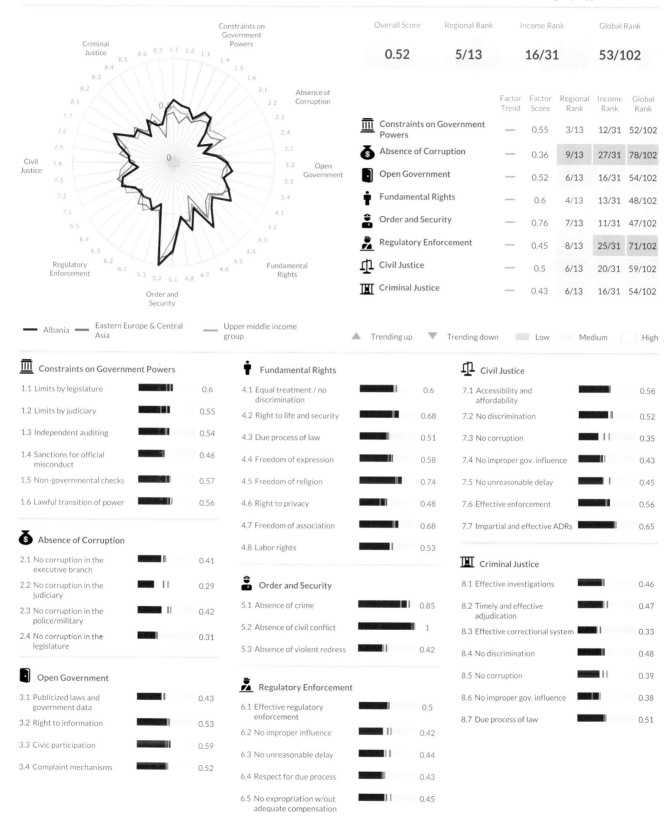

	Overall Score	Regional Rank	Income Rank	Global Rank
	0.52	**5/13**	**16/31**	**53/102**

	Factor Trend	Factor Score	Regional Rank	Income Rank	Global Rank
🏛 Constraints on Government Powers	—	0.55	3/13	12/31	52/102
💰 Absence of Corruption	—	0.36	9/13	27/31	78/102
🚪 Open Government	—	0.52	6/13	16/31	54/102
👤 Fundamental Rights	—	0.6	4/13	13/31	48/102
👤 Order and Security	—	0.76	7/13	11/31	47/102
🗞 Regulatory Enforcement	—	0.45	8/13	25/31	71/102
⚖ Civil Justice	—	0.5	6/13	20/31	59/102
🏛 Criminal Justice	—	0.43	6/13	16/31	54/102

— Albania   — Eastern Europe & Central Asia   — Upper middle income group

▲ Trending up   ▼ Trending down   ░ Low   ▒ Medium   ☐ High

🏛 Constraints on Government Powers

1.1 Limits by legislature		0.6
1.2 Limits by judiciary		0.55
1.3 Independent auditing		0.54
1.4 Sanctions for official misconduct		0.46
1.5 Non-governmental checks		0.57
1.6 Lawful transition of power		0.56

💰 Absence of Corruption

2.1 No corruption in the executive branch		0.41
2.2 No corruption in the judiciary		0.29
2.3 No corruption in the police/military		0.42
2.4 No corruption in the legislature		0.31

🚪 Open Government

3.1 Publicized laws and government data		0.43
3.2 Right to information		0.53
3.3 Civic participation		0.59
3.4 Complaint mechanisms		0.52

👤 Fundamental Rights

4.1 Equal treatment / no discrimination		0.6
4.2 Right to life and security		0.68
4.3 Due process of law		0.51
4.4 Freedom of expression		0.58
4.5 Freedom of religion		0.74
4.6 Right to privacy		0.48
4.7 Freedom of association		0.68
4.8 Labor rights		0.53

👤 Order and Security

5.1 Absence of crime		0.85
5.2 Absence of civil conflict		1
5.3 Absence of violent redress		0.42

🗞 Regulatory Enforcement

6.1 Effective regulatory enforcement		0.5
6.2 No improper influence		0.42
6.3 No unreasonable delay		0.44
6.4 Respect for due process		0.43
6.5 No expropriation w/out adequate compensation		0.45

⚖ Civil Justice

7.1 Accessibility and affordability		0.56
7.2 No discrimination		0.52
7.3 No corruption		0.35
7.4 No improper gov. influence		0.43
7.5 No unreasonable delay		0.45
7.6 Effective enforcement		0.56
7.7 Impartial and effective ADRs		0.65

🏛 Criminal Justice

8.1 Effective investigations		0.46
8.2 Timely and effective adjudication		0.47
8.3 Effective correctional system		0.33
8.4 No discrimination		0.48
8.5 No corruption		0.39
8.6 No improper gov. influence		0.38
8.7 Due process of law		0.51

Argentina

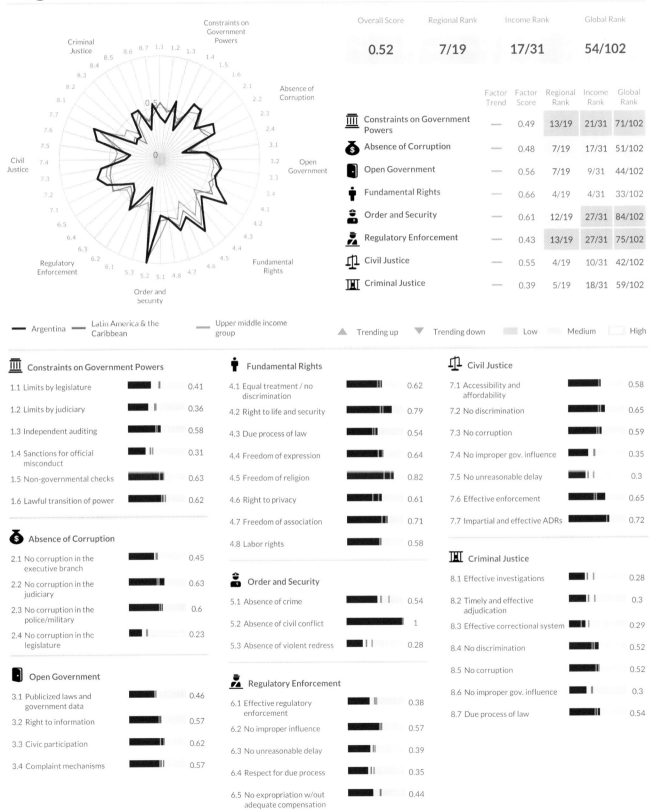

	Overall Score	Regional Rank	Income Rank	Global Rank
	0.52	7/19	17/31	54/102

	Factor Trend	Factor Score	Regional Rank	Income Rank	Global Rank
Constraints on Government Powers	—	0.49	13/19	21/31	71/102
Absence of Corruption	—	0.48	7/19	17/31	51/102
Open Government	—	0.56	7/19	9/31	44/102
Fundamental Rights	—	0.66	4/19	4/31	33/102
Order and Security	—	0.61	12/19	27/31	84/102
Regulatory Enforcement	—	0.43	13/19	27/31	75/102
Civil Justice	—	0.55	4/19	10/31	42/102
Criminal Justice	—	0.39	5/19	18/31	59/102

Legend: ▬ Argentina ▬ Latin America & the Caribbean ▬ Upper middle income group   ▲ Trending up   ▼ Trending down   ▨ Low   ▨ Medium   ☐ High

Constraints on Government Powers

1.1 Limits by legislature	0.41
1.2 Limits by judiciary	0.36
1.3 Independent auditing	0.58
1.4 Sanctions for official misconduct	0.31
1.5 Non-governmental checks	0.63
1.6 Lawful transition of power	0.62

Absence of Corruption

2.1 No corruption in the executive branch	0.45
2.2 No corruption in the judiciary	0.63
2.3 No corruption in the police/military	0.6
2.4 No corruption in the legislature	0.23

Open Government

3.1 Publicized laws and government data	0.46
3.2 Right to information	0.57
3.3 Civic participation	0.62
3.4 Complaint mechanisms	0.57

Fundamental Rights

4.1 Equal treatment / no discrimination	0.62
4.2 Right to life and security	0.79
4.3 Due process of law	0.54
4.4 Freedom of expression	0.64
4.5 Freedom of religion	0.82
4.6 Right to privacy	0.61
4.7 Freedom of association	0.71
4.8 Labor rights	0.58

Order and Security

5.1 Absence of crime	0.54
5.2 Absence of civil conflict	1
5.3 Absence of violent redress	0.28

Regulatory Enforcement

6.1 Effective regulatory enforcement	0.38
6.2 No improper influence	0.57
6.3 No unreasonable delay	0.39
6.4 Respect for due process	0.35
6.5 No expropriation w/out adequate compensation	0.44

Civil Justice

7.1 Accessibility and affordability	0.58
7.2 No discrimination	0.65
7.3 No corruption	0.59
7.4 No improper gov. influence	0.35
7.5 No unreasonable delay	0.3
7.6 Effective enforcement	0.65
7.7 Impartial and effective ADRs	0.72

Criminal Justice

8.1 Effective investigations	0.28
8.2 Timely and effective adjudication	0.3
8.3 Effective correctional system	0.29
8.4 No discrimination	0.52
8.5 No corruption	0.52
8.6 No improper gov. influence	0.3
8.7 Due process of law	0.54

Complete country profiles available at: data.worldjusticeproject.org

Australia

	Overall Score	Regional Rank	Income Rank	Global Rank
	0.8	3/15	10/31	10/102

		Factor Trend	Factor Score	Regional Rank	Income Rank	Global Rank
🏛	Constraints on Government Powers	—	0.83	2/15	9/31	9/102
💰	Absence of Corruption	—	0.84	4/15	9/31	9/102
📖	Open Government	—	0.74	2/15	9/31	9/102
👤	Fundamental Rights	—	0.82	2/15	10/31	10/102
👮	Order and Security	—	0.89	5/15	12/31	13/102
⚖	Regulatory Enforcement	—	0.81	3/15	8/31	8/102
⚖	Civil Justice	—	0.74	6/15	15/31	15/102
🏛	Criminal Justice	—	0.77	4/15	10/31	10/102

— Australia   — East Asia & Pacific   — High income group   ▲ Trending up   ▼ Trending down   ░ Low   Medium   High

🏛 Constraints on Government Powers

1.1 Limits by legislature	0.86
1.2 Limits by judiciary	0.87
1.3 Independent auditing	0.68
1.4 Sanctions for official misconduct	0.79
1.5 Non-governmental checks	0.84
1.6 Lawful transition of power	0.93

💰 Absence of Corruption

2.1 No corruption in the executive branch	0.8
2.2 No corruption in the judiciary	0.94
2.3 No corruption in the police/military	0.93
2.4 No corruption in the legislature	0.7

📖 Open Government

3.1 Publicized laws and government data	0.64
3.2 Right to information	0.7
3.3 Civic participation	0.8
3.4 Complaint mechanisms	0.82

👤 Fundamental Rights

4.1 Equal treatment / no discrimination	0.63
4.2 Right to life and security	0.9
4.3 Due process of law	0.8
4.4 Freedom of expression	0.85
4.5 Freedom of religion	0.88
4.6 Right to privacy	0.88
4.7 Freedom of association	0.89
4.8 Labor rights	0.73

👮 Order and Security

5.1 Absence of crime	0.91
5.2 Absence of civil conflict	1
5.3 Absence of violent redress	0.75

⚖ Regulatory Enforcement

6.1 Effective regulatory enforcement	0.78
6.2 No improper influence	0.92
6.3 No unreasonable delay	0.77
6.4 Respect for due process	0.73
6.5 No expropriation w/out adequate compensation	0.83

⚖ Civil Justice

7.1 Accessibility and affordability	0.5
7.2 No discrimination	0.54
7.3 No corruption	0.92
7.4 No improper gov. influence	0.91
7.5 No unreasonable delay	0.59
7.6 Effective enforcement	0.81
7.7 Impartial and effective ADRs	0.9

🏛 Criminal Justice

8.1 Effective investigations	0.68
8.2 Timely and effective adjudication	0.76
8.3 Effective correctional system	0.71
8.4 No discrimination	0.57
8.5 No corruption	0.88
8.6 No improper gov. influence	0.96
8.7 Due process of law	0.8

Austria

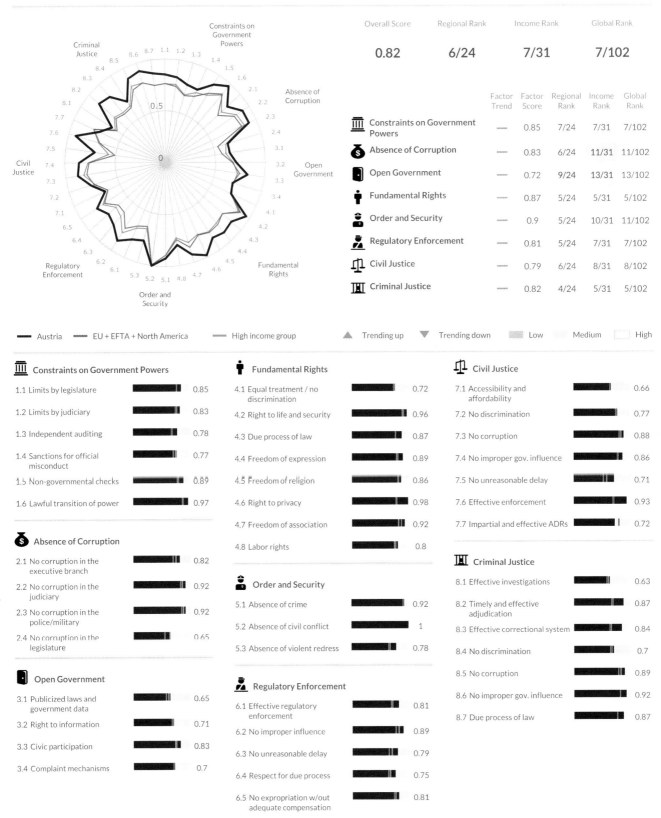

	Overall Score	Regional Rank	Income Rank	Global Rank
	0.82	6/24	7/31	7/102

		Factor Trend	Factor Score	Regional Rank	Income Rank	Global Rank
🏛	Constraints on Government Powers	—	0.85	7/24	7/31	7/102
💰	Absence of Corruption	—	0.83	6/24	11/31	11/102
📱	Open Government	—	0.72	9/24	13/31	13/102
👤	Fundamental Rights	—	0.87	5/24	5/31	5/102
👮	Order and Security	—	0.9	5/24	10/31	11/102
🗄	Regulatory Enforcement	—	0.81	5/24	7/31	7/102
⚖	Civil Justice	—	0.79	6/24	8/31	8/102
🏛	Criminal Justice	—	0.82	4/24	5/31	5/102

— Austria   ╍╍ EU + EFTA + North America   — High income group   ▲ Trending up   ▼ Trending down   ▨ Low   Medium   ☐ High

🏛 Constraints on Government Powers

1.1 Limits by legislature	0.85
1.2 Limits by judiciary	0.83
1.3 Independent auditing	0.78
1.4 Sanctions for official misconduct	0.77
1.5 Non-governmental checks	0.89
1.6 Lawful transition of power	0.97

💰 Absence of Corruption

2.1 No corruption in the executive branch	0.82
2.2 No corruption in the judiciary	0.92
2.3 No corruption in the police/military	0.92
2.4 No corruption in the legislature	0.65

📱 Open Government

3.1 Publicized laws and government data	0.65
3.2 Right to information	0.71
3.3 Civic participation	0.83
3.4 Complaint mechanisms	0.7

👤 Fundamental Rights

4.1 Equal treatment / no discrimination	0.72
4.2 Right to life and security	0.96
4.3 Due process of law	0.87
4.4 Freedom of expression	0.89
4.5 Freedom of religion	0.86
4.6 Right to privacy	0.98
4.7 Freedom of association	0.92
4.8 Labor rights	0.8

👮 Order and Security

5.1 Absence of crime	0.92
5.2 Absence of civil conflict	1
5.3 Absence of violent redress	0.78

🗄 Regulatory Enforcement

6.1 Effective regulatory enforcement	0.81
6.2 No improper influence	0.89
6.3 No unreasonable delay	0.79
6.4 Respect for due process	0.75
6.5 No expropriation w/out adequate compensation	0.81

⚖ Civil Justice

7.1 Accessibility and affordability	0.66
7.2 No discrimination	0.77
7.3 No corruption	0.88
7.4 No improper gov. influence	0.86
7.5 No unreasonable delay	0.71
7.6 Effective enforcement	0.93
7.7 Impartial and effective ADRs	0.72

🏛 Criminal Justice

8.1 Effective investigations	0.63
8.2 Timely and effective adjudication	0.87
8.3 Effective correctional system	0.84
8.4 No discrimination	0.7
8.5 No corruption	0.89
8.6 No improper gov. influence	0.92
8.7 Due process of law	0.87

Complete country profiles available at: data.worldjusticeproject.org

Bangladesh

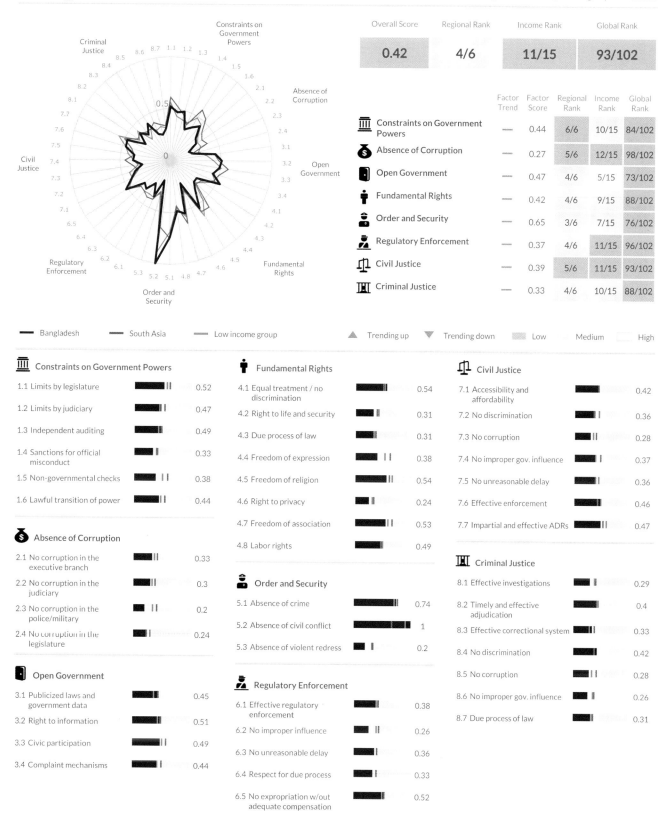

	Overall Score	Regional Rank	Income Rank	Global Rank
	0.42	4/6	11/15	93/102

	Factor Trend	Factor Score	Regional Rank	Income Rank	Global Rank
🏛 Constraints on Government Powers	—	0.44	6/6	10/15	84/102
💰 Absence of Corruption	—	0.27	5/6	12/15	98/102
📖 Open Government	—	0.47	4/6	5/15	73/102
👤 Fundamental Rights	—	0.42	4/6	9/15	88/102
👮 Order and Security	—	0.65	3/6	7/15	76/102
🚜 Regulatory Enforcement	—	0.37	4/6	11/15	96/102
⚖ Civil Justice	—	0.39	5/6	11/15	93/102
🏛 Criminal Justice	—	0.33	4/6	10/15	88/102

— Bangladesh — South Asia — Low income group ▲ Trending up ▼ Trending down ▨ Low Medium High

🏛 Constraints on Government Powers

1.1 Limits by legislature	0.52
1.2 Limits by judiciary	0.47
1.3 Independent auditing	0.49
1.4 Sanctions for official misconduct	0.33
1.5 Non-governmental checks	0.38
1.6 Lawful transition of power	0.44

💰 Absence of Corruption

2.1 No corruption in the executive branch	0.33
2.2 No corruption in the judiciary	0.3
2.3 No corruption in the police/military	0.2
2.4 No corruption in the legislature	0.24

📖 Open Government

3.1 Publicized laws and government data	0.45
3.2 Right to information	0.51
3.3 Civic participation	0.49
3.4 Complaint mechanisms	0.44

👤 Fundamental Rights

4.1 Equal treatment / no discrimination	0.54
4.2 Right to life and security	0.31
4.3 Due process of law	0.31
4.4 Freedom of expression	0.38
4.5 Freedom of religion	0.54
4.6 Right to privacy	0.24
4.7 Freedom of association	0.53
4.8 Labor rights	0.49

👮 Order and Security

5.1 Absence of crime	0.74
5.2 Absence of civil conflict	1
5.3 Absence of violent redress	0.2

🚜 Regulatory Enforcement

6.1 Effective regulatory enforcement	0.38
6.2 No improper influence	0.26
6.3 No unreasonable delay	0.36
6.4 Respect for due process	0.33
6.5 No expropriation w/out adequate compensation	0.52

⚖ Civil Justice

7.1 Accessibility and affordability	0.42
7.2 No discrimination	0.36
7.3 No corruption	0.28
7.4 No improper gov. influence	0.37
7.5 No unreasonable delay	0.36
7.6 Effective enforcement	0.46
7.7 Impartial and effective ADRs	0.47

🏛 Criminal Justice

8.1 Effective investigations	0.29
8.2 Timely and effective adjudication	0.4
8.3 Effective correctional system	0.33
8.4 No discrimination	0.42
8.5 No corruption	0.28
8.6 No improper gov. influence	0.26
8.7 Due process of law	0.31

Belarus

	Overall Score	Regional Rank	Income Rank	Global Rank
	0.53	4/13	15/31	50/102

	Factor Trend	Factor Score	Regional Rank	Income Rank	Global Rank
Constraints on Government Powers	—	0.35	12/13	30/31	97/102
Absence of Corruption	—	0.5	3/13	11/31	43/102
Open Government	—	0.46	10/13	24/31	78/102
Fundamental Rights	—	0.46	10/13	26/31	82/102
Order and Security	—	0.81	4/13	4/31	29/102
Regulatory Enforcement	—	0.55	2/13	4/31	34/102
Civil Justice	—	0.62	2/13	3/31	30/102
Criminal Justice	▲	0.48	3/13	10/31	43/102

— Belarus   Eastern Europe & Central Asia   Upper middle income group

▲ Trending up   ▼ Trending down   Low   Medium   High

Constraints on Government Powers

1.1 Limits by legislature	0.27
1.2 Limits by judiciary	0.32
1.3 Independent auditing	0.4
1.4 Sanctions for official misconduct	0.56
1.5 Non-governmental checks	0.23
1.6 Lawful transition of power	0.33

Absence of Corruption

2.1 No corruption in the executive branch	0.46
2.2 No corruption in the judiciary	0.61
2.3 No corruption in the police/military	0.6
2.4 No corruption in the legislature	0.34

Open Government

3.1 Publicized laws and government data	0.41
3.2 Right to information	0.5
3.3 Civic participation	0.36
3.4 Complaint mechanisms	0.55

Fundamental Rights

4.1 Equal treatment / no discrimination	0.76
4.2 Right to life and security	0.45
4.3 Due process of law	0.5
4.4 Freedom of expression	0.23
4.5 Freedom of religion	0.61
4.6 Right to privacy	0.23
4.7 Freedom of association	0.36
4.8 Labor rights	0.56

Order and Security

5.1 Absence of crime	0.91
5.2 Absence of civil conflict	1
5.3 Absence of violent redress	0.53

Regulatory Enforcement

6.1 Effective regulatory enforcement	0.59
6.2 No improper influence	0.55
6.3 No unreasonable delay	0.67
6.4 Respect for due process	0.56
6.5 No expropriation w/out adequate compensation	0.4

Civil Justice

7.1 Accessibility and affordability	0.53
7.2 No discrimination	0.73
7.3 No corruption	0.62
7.4 No improper gov. influence	0.33
7.5 No unreasonable delay	0.75
7.6 Effective enforcement	0.69
7.7 Impartial and effective ADRs	0.69

Criminal Justice

8.1 Effective investigations	0.54
8.2 Timely and effective adjudication	0.55
8.3 Effective correctional system	0.42
8.4 No discrimination	0.7
8.5 No corruption	0.48
8.6 No improper gov. influence	0.18
8.7 Due process of law	0.5

Belgium

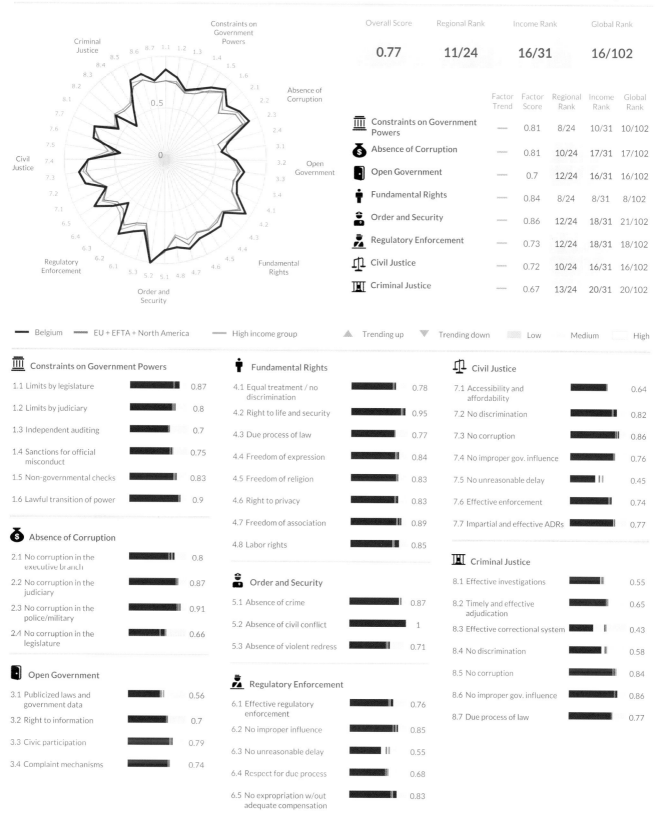

	Overall Score	Regional Rank	Income Rank	Global Rank
	0.77	**11/24**	**16/31**	**16/102**

		Factor Trend	Factor Score	Regional Rank	Income Rank	Global Rank
🏛	Constraints on Government Powers	—	0.81	8/24	10/31	10/102
💰	Absence of Corruption	—	0.81	10/24	17/31	17/102
📱	Open Government	—	0.7	12/24	16/31	16/102
👤	Fundamental Rights	—	0.84	8/24	8/31	8/102
👮	Order and Security	—	0.86	12/24	18/31	21/102
📊	Regulatory Enforcement	—	0.73	12/24	18/31	18/102
⚖	Civil Justice	—	0.72	10/24	16/31	16/102
🏛	Criminal Justice	—	0.67	13/24	20/31	20/102

— Belgium — EU + EFTA + North America — High income group ▲ Trending up ▼ Trending down ▦ Low Medium High

🏛 Constraints on Government Powers

1.1 Limits by legislature	0.87
1.2 Limits by judiciary	0.8
1.3 Independent auditing	0.7
1.4 Sanctions for official misconduct	0.75
1.5 Non-governmental checks	0.83
1.6 Lawful transition of power	0.9

💰 Absence of Corruption

2.1 No corruption in the executive branch	0.8
2.2 No corruption in the judiciary	0.87
2.3 No corruption in the police/military	0.91
2.4 No corruption in the legislature	0.66

📱 Open Government

3.1 Publicized laws and government data	0.56
3.2 Right to information	0.7
3.3 Civic participation	0.79
3.4 Complaint mechanisms	0.74

👤 Fundamental Rights

4.1 Equal treatment / no discrimination	0.78
4.2 Right to life and security	0.95
4.3 Due process of law	0.77
4.4 Freedom of expression	0.84
4.5 Freedom of religion	0.83
4.6 Right to privacy	0.83
4.7 Freedom of association	0.89
4.8 Labor rights	0.85

👮 Order and Security

5.1 Absence of crime	0.87
5.2 Absence of civil conflict	1
5.3 Absence of violent redress	0.71

📊 Regulatory Enforcement

6.1 Effective regulatory enforcement	0.76
6.2 No improper influence	0.85
6.3 No unreasonable delay	0.55
6.4 Respect for due process	0.68
6.5 No expropriation w/out adequate compensation	0.83

⚖ Civil Justice

7.1 Accessibility and affordability	0.64
7.2 No discrimination	0.82
7.3 No corruption	0.86
7.4 No improper gov. influence	0.76
7.5 No unreasonable delay	0.45
7.6 Effective enforcement	0.74
7.7 Impartial and effective ADRs	0.77

🏛 Criminal Justice

8.1 Effective investigations	0.55
8.2 Timely and effective adjudication	0.65
8.3 Effective correctional system	0.43
8.4 No discrimination	0.58
8.5 No corruption	0.84
8.6 No improper gov. influence	0.86
8.7 Due process of law	0.77

Belize

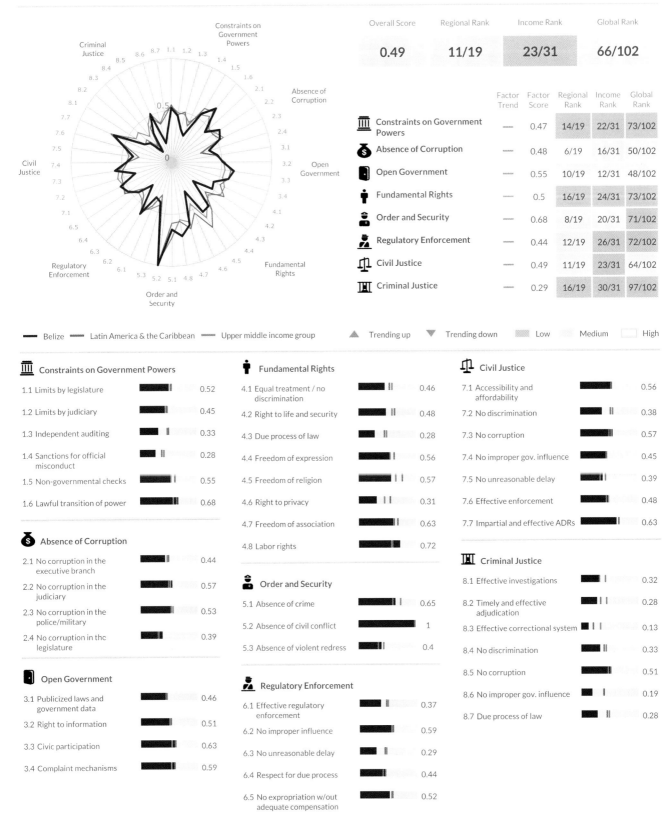

	Overall Score	Regional Rank	Income Rank	Global Rank
	0.49	**11/19**	**23/31**	**66/102**

	Factor Trend	Factor Score	Regional Rank	Income Rank	Global Rank
🏛 Constraints on Government Powers	—	0.47	14/19	22/31	73/102
💰 Absence of Corruption	—	0.48	6/19	16/31	50/102
📖 Open Government	—	0.55	10/19	12/31	48/102
🧍 Fundamental Rights	—	0.5	16/19	24/31	73/102
👮 Order and Security	—	0.68	8/19	20/31	71/102
🗜 Regulatory Enforcement	—	0.44	12/19	26/31	72/102
⚖ Civil Justice	—	0.49	11/19	23/31	64/102
🏛 Criminal Justice	—	0.29	16/19	30/31	97/102

— Belize   Latin America & the Caribbean   Upper middle income group   ▲ Trending up   ▼ Trending down   Low   Medium   High

🏛 Constraints on Government Powers

1.1 Limits by legislature	0.52
1.2 Limits by judiciary	0.45
1.3 Independent auditing	0.33
1.4 Sanctions for official misconduct	0.28
1.5 Non-governmental checks	0.55
1.6 Lawful transition of power	0.68

💰 Absence of Corruption

2.1 No corruption in the executive branch	0.44
2.2 No corruption in the judiciary	0.57
2.3 No corruption in the police/military	0.53
2.4 No corruption in the legislature	0.39

📖 Open Government

3.1 Publicized laws and government data	0.46
3.2 Right to information	0.51
3.3 Civic participation	0.63
3.4 Complaint mechanisms	0.59

🧍 Fundamental Rights

4.1 Equal treatment / no discrimination	0.46
4.2 Right to life and security	0.48
4.3 Due process of law	0.28
4.4 Freedom of expression	0.56
4.5 Freedom of religion	0.57
4.6 Right to privacy	0.31
4.7 Freedom of association	0.63
4.8 Labor rights	0.72

👮 Order and Security

5.1 Absence of crime	0.65
5.2 Absence of civil conflict	1
5.3 Absence of violent redress	0.4

🗜 Regulatory Enforcement

6.1 Effective regulatory enforcement	0.37
6.2 No improper influence	0.59
6.3 No unreasonable delay	0.29
6.4 Respect for due process	0.44
6.5 No expropriation w/out adequate compensation	0.52

⚖ Civil Justice

7.1 Accessibility and affordability	0.56
7.2 No discrimination	0.38
7.3 No corruption	0.57
7.4 No improper gov. influence	0.45
7.5 No unreasonable delay	0.39
7.6 Effective enforcement	0.48
7.7 Impartial and effective ADRs	0.63

🏛 Criminal Justice

8.1 Effective investigations	0.32
8.2 Timely and effective adjudication	0.28
8.3 Effective correctional system	0.13
8.4 No discrimination	0.33
8.5 No corruption	0.51
8.6 No improper gov. influence	0.19
8.7 Due process of law	0.28

Complete country profiles available at: data.worldjusticeproject.org

Bolivia

La Paz, Santa Cruz, Cochabamba
Region: **Latin America & the Caribbean** | Income group: **Lower middle income**

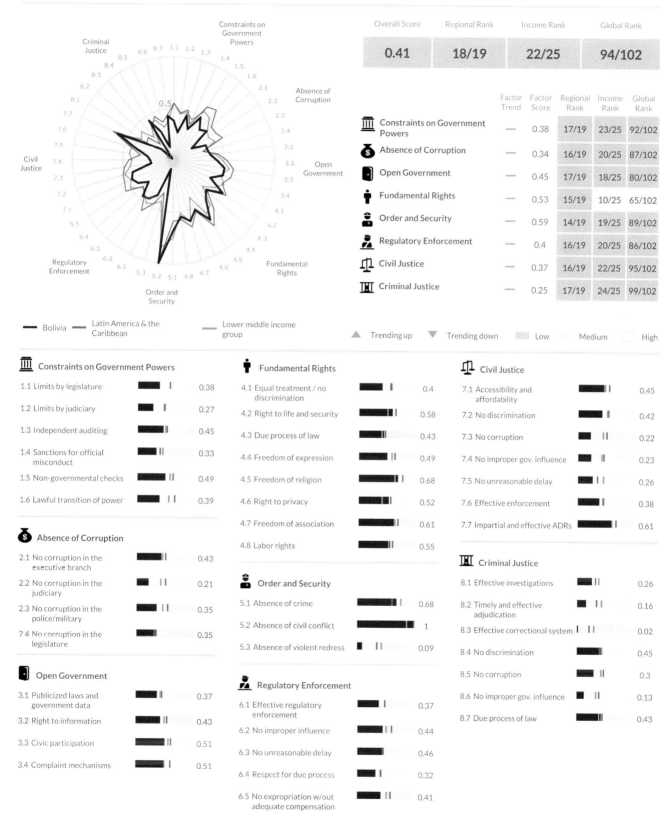

	Overall Score	Regional Rank	Income Rank	Global Rank
	0.41	18/19	22/25	94/102

		Factor Trend	Factor Score	Regional Rank	Income Rank	Global Rank
🏛	Constraints on Government Powers	—	0.38	17/19	23/25	92/102
💰	Absence of Corruption	—	0.34	16/19	20/25	87/102
📱	Open Government	—	0.45	17/19	18/25	80/102
🧍	Fundamental Rights	—	0.53	15/19	10/25	65/102
👮	Order and Security	—	0.59	14/19	19/25	89/102
🕵	Regulatory Enforcement	—	0.4	16/19	20/25	86/102
⚖	Civil Justice	—	0.37	16/19	22/25	95/102
🏛	Criminal Justice	—	0.25	17/19	24/25	99/102

— Bolivia — Latin America & the Caribbean — Lower middle income group

▲ Trending up   ▼ Trending down   Low   Medium   High

🏛 Constraints on Government Powers

1.1 Limits by legislature	0.38
1.2 Limits by judiciary	0.27
1.3 Independent auditing	0.45
1.4 Sanctions for official misconduct	0.33
1.5 Non-governmental checks	0.49
1.6 Lawful transition of power	0.39

💰 Absence of Corruption

2.1 No corruption in the executive branch	0.43
2.2 No corruption in the judiciary	0.21
2.3 No corruption in the police/military	0.35
2.4 No corruption in the legislature	0.35

📱 Open Government

3.1 Publicized laws and government data	0.37
3.2 Right to information	0.43
3.3 Civic participation	0.51
3.4 Complaint mechanisms	0.51

🧍 Fundamental Rights

4.1 Equal treatment / no discrimination	0.4
4.2 Right to life and security	0.58
4.3 Due process of law	0.43
4.4 Freedom of expression	0.49
4.5 Freedom of religion	0.68
4.6 Right to privacy	0.52
4.7 Freedom of association	0.61
4.8 Labor rights	0.55

👮 Order and Security

5.1 Absence of crime	0.68
5.2 Absence of civil conflict	1
5.3 Absence of violent redress	0.09

🕵 Regulatory Enforcement

6.1 Effective regulatory enforcement	0.37
6.2 No improper influence	0.44
6.3 No unreasonable delay	0.46
6.4 Respect for due process	0.32
6.5 No expropriation w/out adequate compensation	0.41

⚖ Civil Justice

7.1 Accessibility and affordability	0.45
7.2 No discrimination	0.42
7.3 No corruption	0.22
7.4 No improper gov. influence	0.23
7.5 No unreasonable delay	0.26
7.6 Effective enforcement	0.38
7.7 Impartial and effective ADRs	0.61

🏛 Criminal Justice

8.1 Effective investigations	0.26
8.2 Timely and effective adjudication	0.16
8.3 Effective correctional system	0.02
8.4 No discrimination	0.45
8.5 No corruption	0.3
8.6 No improper gov. influence	0.13
8.7 Due process of law	0.43

Bosnia and Herzegovina

Sarajevo, Tuzla, Banja Luka
Region: **Eastern Europe & Central Asia** | Income group: **Upper middle income**

	Overall Score	Regional Rank	Income Rank	Global Rank
	0.57	2/13	7/31	40/102

	Factor Trend	Factor Score	Regional Rank	Income Rank	Global Rank
Constraints on Government Powers	—	0.57	2/13	9/31	46/102
Absence of Corruption	—	0.43	7/13	21/31	61/102
Open Government	—	0.59	2/13	3/31	31/102
Fundamental Rights	—	0.66	1/13	6/31	35/102
Order and Security	—	0.72	10/13	15/31	55/102
Regulatory Enforcement	—	0.53	3/13	9/31	41/102
Civil Justice	—	0.52	4/13	15/31	51/102
Criminal Justice	—	0.51	2/13	7/31	37/102

Legend: — Bosnia and Herzegovina — Eastern Europe & Central Asia — Upper middle income group   ▲ Trending up   ▼ Trending down   Low   Medium   High

Constraints on Government Powers

1.1 Limits by legislature	0.65
1.2 Limits by judiciary	0.58
1.3 Independent auditing	0.5
1.4 Sanctions for official misconduct	0.47
1.5 Non-governmental checks	0.6
1.6 Lawful transition of power	0.63

Absence of Corruption

2.1 No corruption in the executive branch	0.4
2.2 No corruption in the judiciary	0.57
2.3 No corruption in the police/military	0.54
2.4 No corruption in the legislature	0.22

Open Government

3.1 Publicized laws and government data	0.53
3.2 Right to information	0.68
3.3 Civic participation	0.58
3.4 Complaint mechanisms	0.57

Fundamental Rights

4.1 Equal treatment / no discrimination	0.62
4.2 Right to life and security	0.78
4.3 Due process of law	0.64
4.4 Freedom of expression	0.61
4.5 Freedom of religion	0.66
4.6 Right to privacy	0.58
4.7 Freedom of association	0.68
4.8 Labor rights	0.67

Order and Security

5.1 Absence of crime	0.86
5.2 Absence of civil conflict	1
5.3 Absence of violent redress	0.31

Regulatory Enforcement

6.1 Effective regulatory enforcement	0.46
6.2 No improper influence	0.4
6.3 No unreasonable delay	0.51
6.4 Respect for due process	0.61
6.5 No expropriation w/out adequate compensation	0.64

Civil Justice

7.1 Accessibility and affordability	0.57
7.2 No discrimination	0.68
7.3 No corruption	0.59
7.4 No improper gov. influence	0.49
7.5 No unreasonable delay	0.38
7.6 Effective enforcement	0.26
7.7 Impartial and effective ADRs	0.64

Criminal Justice

8.1 Effective investigations	0.45
8.2 Timely and effective adjudication	0.58
8.3 Effective correctional system	0.37
8.4 No discrimination	0.59
8.5 No corruption	0.53
8.6 No improper gov. influence	0.4
8.7 Due process of law	0.64

Botswana

	Overall Score	Regional Rank	Income Rank	Global Rank
	0.64	**1/18**	**2/31**	**31/102**

		Factor Trend	Factor Score	Regional Rank	Income Rank	Global Rank
🏛	Constraints on Government Powers	▼	0.63	3/18	2/31	32/102
💰	Absence of Corruption	—	0.65	1/18	2/31	29/102
	Open Government	—	0.57	2/18	5/31	35/102
🧍	Fundamental Rights	—	0.56	6/18	16/31	55/102
	Order and Security	—	0.81	1/18	3/31	28/102
	Regulatory Enforcement	—	0.66	1/18	1/31	22/102
⚖	Civil Justice	—	0.61	1/18	5/31	33/102
	Criminal Justice	—	0.61	1/18	1/31	27/102

— Botswana — Sub-Saharan Africa — Upper middle income group   ▲ Trending up   ▼ Trending down   Low   Medium   High

🏛 Constraints on Government Powers

1.1 Limits by legislature	0.74
1.2 Limits by judiciary	0.75
1.3 Independent auditing	0.41
1.4 Sanctions for official misconduct	0.59
1.5 Non-governmental checks	0.61
1.6 Lawful transition of power	0.7

💰 Absence of Corruption

2.1 No corruption in the executive branch	0.67
2.2 No corruption in the judiciary	0.79
2.3 No corruption in the police/military	0.72
2.4 No corruption in the legislature	0.44

Open Government

3.1 Publicized laws and government data	0.44
3.2 Right to information	0.49
3.3 Civic participation	0.72
3.4 Complaint mechanisms	0.63

🧍 Fundamental Rights

4.1 Equal treatment / no discrimination	0.58
4.2 Right to life and security	0.53
4.3 Due process of law	0.54
4.4 Freedom of expression	0.61
4.5 Freedom of religion	0.65
4.6 Right to privacy	0.28
4.7 Freedom of association	0.7
4.8 Labor rights	0.61

Order and Security

5.1 Absence of crime	0.8
5.2 Absence of civil conflict	1
5.3 Absence of violent redress	0.64

Regulatory Enforcement

6.1 Effective regulatory enforcement	0.66
6.2 No improper influence	0.78
6.3 No unreasonable delay	0.54
6.4 Respect for due process	0.51
6.5 No expropriation w/out adequate compensation	0.81

⚖ Civil Justice

7.1 Accessibility and affordability	0.47
7.2 No discrimination	0.44
7.3 No corruption	0.83
7.4 No improper gov. influence	0.62
7.5 No unreasonable delay	0.55
7.6 Effective enforcement	0.61
7.7 Impartial and effective ADRs	0.76

Criminal Justice

8.1 Effective investigations	0.63
8.2 Timely and effective adjudication	0.53
8.3 Effective correctional system	0.54
8.4 No discrimination	0.61
8.5 No corruption	0.83
8.6 No improper gov. influence	0.59
8.7 Due process of law	0.54

Brazil

Rio de Janeiro, Salvador, Sao Paolo
Region: **Latin America & the Caribbean** | Income group: **Upper middle income**

	Overall Score	Regional Rank	Income Rank	Global Rank
	0.54	5/19	13/31	46/102

	Factor Trend	Factor Score	Regional Rank	Income Rank	Global Rank
Constraints on Government Powers	▼	0.61	5/19	7/31	42/102
Absence of Corruption	—	0.46	8/19	18/31	55/102
Open Government	—	0.56	4/19	6/31	38/102
Fundamental Rights	▼	0.61	9/19	11/31	46/102
Order and Security	—	0.66	9/19	22/31	75/102
Regulatory Enforcement	▼	0.51	6/19	16/31	50/102
Civil Justice	—	0.53	5/19	13/31	48/102
Criminal Justice	—	0.37	6/19	22/31	68/102

— Brazil — Latin America & the Caribbean — Upper middle income group ▲ Trending up ▼ Trending down ▒ Low ▒ Medium ☐ High

Constraints on Government Powers

1.1 Limits by legislature		0.7
1.2 Limits by judiciary		0.6
1.3 Independent auditing		0.53
1.4 Sanctions for official misconduct		0.36
1.5 Non-governmental checks		0.68
1.6 Lawful transition of power		0.77

Absence of Corruption

2.1 No corruption in the executive branch		0.43
2.2 No corruption in the judiciary		0.64
2.3 No corruption in the police/military		0.59
2.4 No corruption in the legislature		0.18

Open Government

3.1 Publicized laws and government data		0.5
3.2 Right to information		0.56
3.3 Civic participation		0.62
3.4 Complaint mechanisms		0.57

Fundamental Rights

4.1 Equal treatment / no discrimination		0.6
4.2 Right to life and security		0.58
4.3 Due process of law		0.36
4.4 Freedom of expression		0.69
4.5 Freedom of religion		0.73
4.6 Right to privacy		0.56
4.7 Freedom of association		0.69
4.8 Labor rights		0.64

Order and Security

5.1 Absence of crime		0.54
5.2 Absence of civil conflict		1
5.3 Absence of violent redress		0.45

Regulatory Enforcement

6.1 Effective regulatory enforcement		0.51
6.2 No improper influence		0.63
6.3 No unreasonable delay		0.32
6.4 Respect for due process		0.5
6.5 No expropriation w/out adequate compensation		0.57

Civil Justice

7.1 Accessibility and affordability		0.58
7.2 No discrimination		0.63
7.3 No corruption		0.61
7.4 No improper gov. influence		0.59
7.5 No unreasonable delay		0.28
7.6 Effective enforcement		0.32
7.7 Impartial and effective ADRs		0.67

Criminal Justice

8.1 Effective investigations		0.26
8.2 Timely and effective adjudication		0.34
8.3 Effective correctional system		0.19
8.4 No discrimination		0.26
8.5 No corruption		0.53
8.6 No improper gov. influence		0.68
8.7 Due process of law		0.36

 Complete country profiles available at: data.worldjusticeproject.org

Bulgaria

Sofia, Plovdiv, Varna

Region: **EU + EFTA + North America** | Income group: **Upper middle income**

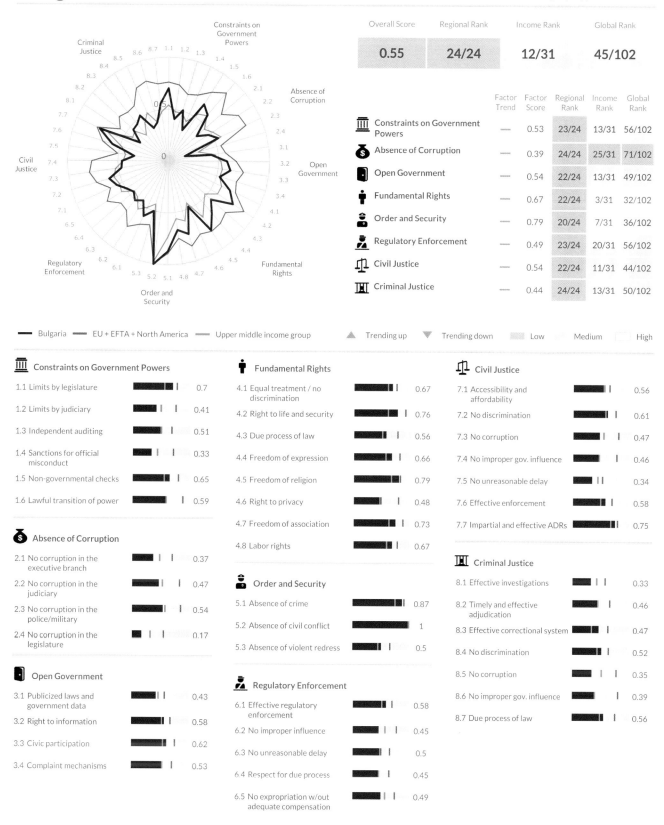

	Overall Score	Regional Rank	Income Rank	Global Rank
	0.55	24/24	12/31	45/102

		Factor Trend	Factor Score	Regional Rank	Income Rank	Global Rank
🏛	Constraints on Government Powers	—	0.53	23/24	13/31	56/102
💰	Absence of Corruption	—	0.39	24/24	25/31	71/102
📱	Open Government	—	0.54	22/24	13/31	49/102
👤	Fundamental Rights	—	0.67	22/24	3/31	32/102
👮	Order and Security	—	0.79	20/24	7/31	36/102
📋	Regulatory Enforcement	—	0.49	23/24	20/31	56/102
⚖	Civil Justice	—	0.54	22/24	11/31	44/102
🏛	Criminal Justice	—	0.44	24/24	13/31	50/102

— Bulgaria — EU + EFTA + North America — Upper middle income group ▲ Trending up ▼ Trending down ▒ Low Medium High

🏛 Constraints on Government Powers

1.1 Limits by legislature	0.7
1.2 Limits by judiciary	0.41
1.3 Independent auditing	0.51
1.4 Sanctions for official misconduct	0.33
1.5 Non-governmental checks	0.65
1.6 Lawful transition of power	0.59

💰 Absence of Corruption

2.1 No corruption in the executive branch	0.37
2.2 No corruption in the judiciary	0.47
2.3 No corruption in the police/military	0.54
2.4 No corruption in the legislature	0.17

📱 Open Government

3.1 Publicized laws and government data	0.43
3.2 Right to information	0.58
3.3 Civic participation	0.62
3.4 Complaint mechanisms	0.53

👤 Fundamental Rights

4.1 Equal treatment / no discrimination	0.67
4.2 Right to life and security	0.76
4.3 Due process of law	0.56
4.4 Freedom of expression	0.66
4.5 Freedom of religion	0.79
4.6 Right to privacy	0.48
4.7 Freedom of association	0.73
4.8 Labor rights	0.67

👮 Order and Security

5.1 Absence of crime	0.87
5.2 Absence of civil conflict	1
5.3 Absence of violent redress	0.5

📋 Regulatory Enforcement

6.1 Effective regulatory enforcement	0.58
6.2 No improper influence	0.45
6.3 No unreasonable delay	0.5
6.4 Respect for due process	0.45
6.5 No expropriation w/out adequate compensation	0.49

⚖ Civil Justice

7.1 Accessibility and affordability	0.56
7.2 No discrimination	0.61
7.3 No corruption	0.47
7.4 No improper gov. influence	0.46
7.5 No unreasonable delay	0.34
7.6 Effective enforcement	0.58
7.7 Impartial and effective ADRs	0.75

🏛 Criminal Justice

8.1 Effective investigations	0.33
8.2 Timely and effective adjudication	0.46
8.3 Effective correctional system	0.47
8.4 No discrimination	0.52
8.5 No corruption	0.35
8.6 No improper gov. influence	0.39
8.7 Due process of law	0.56

Burkina Faso

	Overall Score	Regional Rank	Income Rank	Global Rank
	0.47	9/18	4/15	78/102

	Factor Trend	Factor Score	Regional Rank	Income Rank	Global Rank
Constraints on Government Powers	—	0.41	15/18	11/15	86/102
Absence of Corruption	▼	0.38	8/18	4/15	73/102
Open Government	—	0.43	12/18	9/15	90/102
Fundamental Rights	—	0.55	7/18	4/15	58/102
Order and Security	—	0.69	7/18	5/15	67/102
Regulatory Enforcement	—	0.46	6/18	2/15	67/102
Civil Justice	▼	0.47	10/18	4/15	70/102
Criminal Justice	—	0.36	10/18	5/15	70/102

— Burkina Faso   ···· Sub-Saharan Africa   — Low income group   ▲ Trending up   ▼ Trending down   Low   Medium   High

Constraints on Government Powers

1.1 Limits by legislature	0.42
1.2 Limits by judiciary	0.36
1.3 Independent auditing	0.41
1.4 Sanctions for official misconduct	0.24
1.5 Non-governmental checks	0.53
1.6 Lawful transition of power	0.51

Absence of Corruption

2.1 No corruption in the executive branch	0.4
2.2 No corruption in the judiciary	0.49
2.3 No corruption in the police/military	0.48
2.4 No corruption in the legislature	0.14

Open Government

3.1 Publicized laws and government data	0.28
3.2 Right to information	0.38
3.3 Civic participation	0.57
3.4 Complaint mechanisms	0.48

Fundamental Rights

4.1 Equal treatment / no discrimination	0.66
4.2 Right to life and security	0.47
4.3 Due process of law	0.41
4.4 Freedom of expression	0.54
4.5 Freedom of religion	0.75
4.6 Right to privacy	0.29
4.7 Freedom of association	0.68
4.8 Labor rights	0.61

Order and Security

5.1 Absence of crime	0.8
5.2 Absence of civil conflict	1
5.3 Absence of violent redress	0.27

Regulatory Enforcement

6.1 Effective regulatory enforcement	0.4
6.2 No improper influence	0.53
6.3 No unreasonable delay	0.36
6.4 Respect for due process	0.38
6.5 No expropriation w/out adequate compensation	0.61

Civil Justice

7.1 Accessibility and affordability	0.39
7.2 No discrimination	0.54
7.3 No corruption	0.45
7.4 No improper gov. influence	0.46
7.5 No unreasonable delay	0.47
7.6 Effective enforcement	0.3
7.7 Impartial and effective ADRs	0.68

Criminal Justice

8.1 Effective investigations	0.32
8.2 Timely and effective adjudication	0.49
8.3 Effective correctional system	0.27
8.4 No discrimination	0.45
8.5 No corruption	0.39
8.6 No improper gov. influence	0.23
8.7 Due process of law	0.41

Complete country profiles available at: data.worldjusticeproject.org

Cambodia

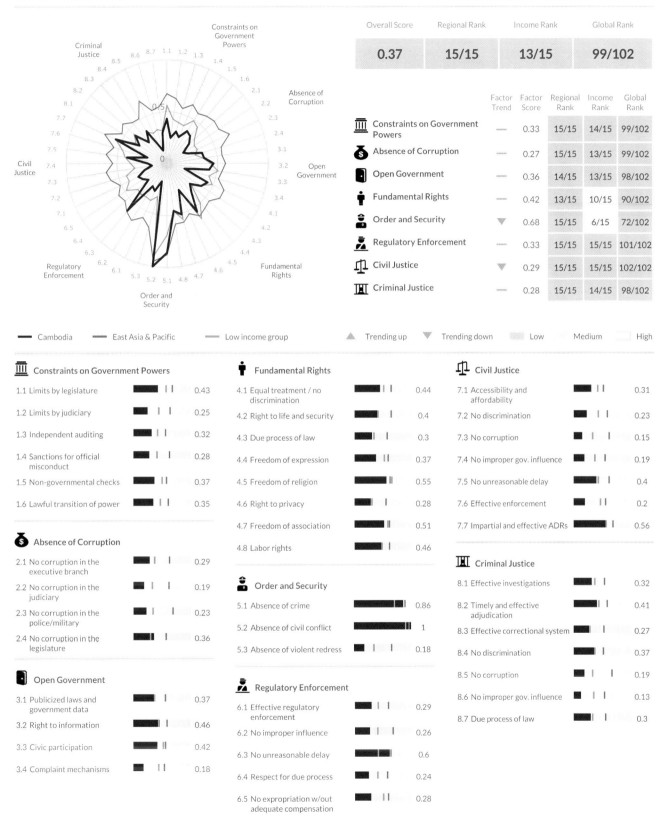

	Overall Score	Regional Rank	Income Rank	Global Rank
	0.37	15/15	13/15	99/102

		Factor Trend	Factor Score	Regional Rank	Income Rank	Global Rank
🏛	Constraints on Government Powers	—	0.33	15/15	14/15	99/102
💰	Absence of Corruption	—	0.27	15/15	13/15	99/102
📱	Open Government	—	0.36	14/15	13/15	98/102
👤	Fundamental Rights	—	0.42	13/15	10/15	90/102
👮	Order and Security	▼	0.68	15/15	6/15	72/102
👷	Regulatory Enforcement	—	0.33	15/15	15/15	101/102
⚖	Civil Justice	▼	0.29	15/15	15/15	102/102
🏛	Criminal Justice	—	0.28	15/15	14/15	98/102

— Cambodia — East Asia & Pacific — Low income group   ▲ Trending up ▼ Trending down   Low   Medium   High

🏛 Constraints on Government Powers

1.1 Limits by legislature	0.43
1.2 Limits by judiciary	0.25
1.3 Independent auditing	0.32
1.4 Sanctions for official misconduct	0.28
1.5 Non-governmental checks	0.37
1.6 Lawful transition of power	0.35

💰 Absence of Corruption

2.1 No corruption in the executive branch	0.29
2.2 No corruption in the judiciary	0.19
2.3 No corruption in the police/military	0.23
2.4 No corruption in the legislature	0.36

📱 Open Government

3.1 Publicized laws and government data	0.37
3.2 Right to information	0.46
3.3 Civic participation	0.42
3.4 Complaint mechanisms	0.18

👤 Fundamental Rights

4.1 Equal treatment / no discrimination	0.44
4.2 Right to life and security	0.4
4.3 Due process of law	0.3
4.4 Freedom of expression	0.37
4.5 Freedom of religion	0.55
4.6 Right to privacy	0.28
4.7 Freedom of association	0.51
4.8 Labor rights	0.46

👮 Order and Security

5.1 Absence of crime	0.86
5.2 Absence of civil conflict	1
5.3 Absence of violent redress	0.18

👷 Regulatory Enforcement

6.1 Effective regulatory enforcement	0.29
6.2 No improper influence	0.26
6.3 No unreasonable delay	0.6
6.4 Respect for due process	0.24
6.5 No expropriation w/out adequate compensation	0.28

⚖ Civil Justice

7.1 Accessibility and affordability	0.31
7.2 No discrimination	0.23
7.3 No corruption	0.15
7.4 No improper gov. influence	0.19
7.5 No unreasonable delay	0.4
7.6 Effective enforcement	0.2
7.7 Impartial and effective ADRs	0.56

🏛 Criminal Justice

8.1 Effective investigations	0.32
8.2 Timely and effective adjudication	0.41
8.3 Effective correctional system	0.27
8.4 No discrimination	0.37
8.5 No corruption	0.19
8.6 No improper gov. influence	0.13
8.7 Due process of law	0.3

Cameroon

	Overall Score	Regional Rank	Income Rank	Global Rank
	0.4	17/18	24/25	97/102

	Factor Trend	Factor Score	Regional Rank	Income Rank	Global Rank
🏛 Constraints on Government Powers	—	0.44	14/18	20/25	83/102
💰 Absence of Corruption	—	0.25	18/18	25/25	101/102
📱 Open Government	—	0.39	16/18	24/25	95/102
👤 Fundamental Rights	—	0.5	10/18	15/25	74/102
👮 Order and Security	▼	0.54	17/18	23/25	98/102
📋 Regulatory Enforcement	—	0.39	14/18	23/25	92/102
⚖ Civil Justice	—	0.37	17/18	23/25	96/102
🏛 Criminal Justice	—	0.32	17/18	21/25	91/102

— Cameroon   — Sub-Saharan Africa   — Lower middle income group   ▲ Trending up   ▼ Trending down   Low   Medium   High

🏛 Constraints on Government Powers

1.1 Limits by legislature	0.38
1.2 Limits by judiciary	0.35
1.3 Independent auditing	0.54
1.4 Sanctions for official misconduct	0.43
1.5 Non-governmental checks	0.12
1.6 Lawful transition of power	0.45

💰 Absence of Corruption

2.1 No corruption in the executive branch	0.3
2.2 No corruption in the judiciary	0.25
2.3 No corruption in the police/military	0.24
2.4 No corruption in the legislature	0.19

📱 Open Government

3.1 Publicized laws and government data	0.37
3.2 Right to information	0.4
3.3 Civic participation	0.51
3.4 Complaint mechanisms	0.28

👤 Fundamental Rights

4.1 Equal treatment / no discrimination	0.47
4.2 Right to life and security	0.47
4.3 Due process of law	0.37
4.4 Freedom of expression	0.49
4.5 Freedom of religion	0.67
4.6 Right to privacy	0.42
4.7 Freedom of association	0.62
4.8 Labor rights	0.45

👮 Order and Security

5.1 Absence of crime	0.62
5.2 Absence of civil conflict	0.75
5.3 Absence of violent redress	0.24

📋 Regulatory Enforcement

6.1 Effective regulatory enforcement	0.42
6.2 No improper influence	0.37
6.3 No unreasonable delay	0.26
6.4 Respect for due process	0.38
6.5 No expropriation w/out adequate compensation	0.53

⚖ Civil Justice

7.1 Accessibility and affordability	0.4
7.2 No discrimination	0.43
7.3 No corruption	0.27
7.4 No improper gov. influence	0.3
7.5 No unreasonable delay	0.34
7.6 Effective enforcement	0.28
7.7 Impartial and effective ADRs	0.53

🏛 Criminal Justice

8.1 Effective investigations	0.38
8.2 Timely and effective adjudication	0.45
8.3 Effective correctional system	0.17
8.4 No discrimination	0.46
8.5 No corruption	0.25
8.6 No improper gov. influence	0.13
8.7 Due process of law	0.37

Canada

Toronto, Montreal, Vancouver
Region: **EU + EFTA + North America** | Income group: **High income**

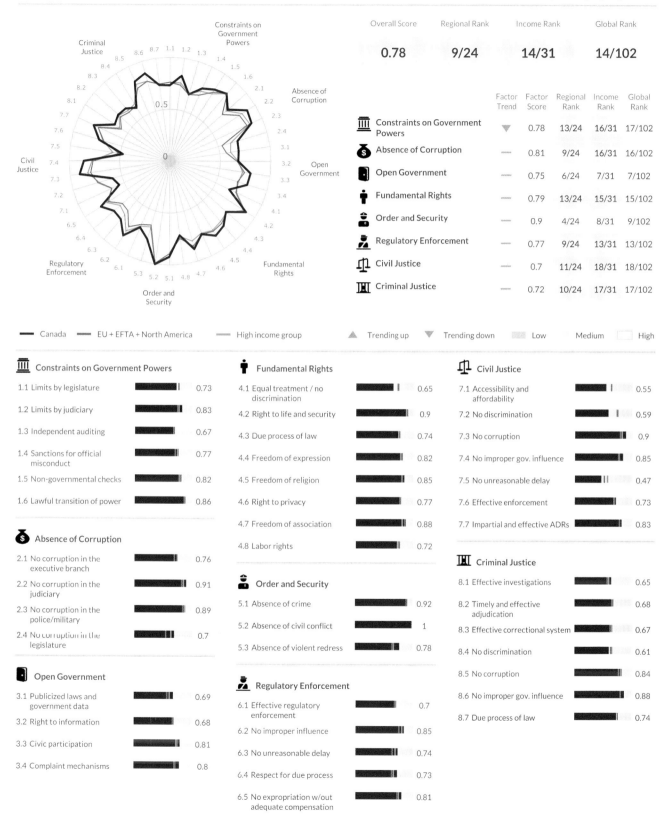

	Overall Score	Regional Rank	Income Rank	Global Rank
	0.78	**9/24**	**14/31**	**14/102**

		Factor Trend	Factor Score	Regional Rank	Income Rank	Global Rank
🏛	Constraints on Government Powers	▼	0.78	13/24	16/31	17/102
💰	Absence of Corruption	—	0.81	9/24	16/31	16/102
📱	Open Government	—	0.75	6/24	7/31	7/102
👤	Fundamental Rights	—	0.79	13/24	15/31	15/102
👮	Order and Security	—	0.9	4/24	8/31	9/102
🕵	Regulatory Enforcement	—	0.77	9/24	13/31	13/102
⚖	Civil Justice	—	0.7	11/24	18/31	18/102
🏛	Criminal Justice	—	0.72	10/24	17/31	17/102

— Canada — EU + EFTA + North America — High income group ▲ Trending up ▼ Trending down ░ Low Medium ☐ High

🏛 Constraints on Government Powers

1.1 Limits by legislature	0.73
1.2 Limits by judiciary	0.83
1.3 Independent auditing	0.67
1.4 Sanctions for official misconduct	0.77
1.5 Non-governmental checks	0.82
1.6 Lawful transition of power	0.86

💰 Absence of Corruption

2.1 No corruption in the executive branch	0.76
2.2 No corruption in the judiciary	0.91
2.3 No corruption in the police/military	0.89
2.4 No corruption in the legislature	0.7

📱 Open Government

3.1 Publicized laws and government data	0.69
3.2 Right to information	0.68
3.3 Civic participation	0.81
3.4 Complaint mechanisms	0.8

👤 Fundamental Rights

4.1 Equal treatment / no discrimination	0.65
4.2 Right to life and security	0.9
4.3 Due process of law	0.74
4.4 Freedom of expression	0.82
4.5 Freedom of religion	0.85
4.6 Right to privacy	0.77
4.7 Freedom of association	0.88
4.8 Labor rights	0.72

👮 Order and Security

5.1 Absence of crime	0.92
5.2 Absence of civil conflict	1
5.3 Absence of violent redress	0.78

🕵 Regulatory Enforcement

6.1 Effective regulatory enforcement	0.7
6.2 No improper influence	0.85
6.3 No unreasonable delay	0.74
6.4 Respect for due process	0.73
6.5 No expropriation w/out adequate compensation	0.81

⚖ Civil Justice

7.1 Accessibility and affordability	0.55
7.2 No discrimination	0.59
7.3 No corruption	0.9
7.4 No improper gov. influence	0.85
7.5 No unreasonable delay	0.47
7.6 Effective enforcement	0.73
7.7 Impartial and effective ADRs	0.83

🏛 Criminal Justice

8.1 Effective investigations	0.65
8.2 Timely and effective adjudication	0.68
8.3 Effective correctional system	0.67
8.4 No discrimination	0.61
8.5 No corruption	0.84
8.6 No improper gov. influence	0.88
8.7 Due process of law	0.74

Chile

	Overall Score	Regional Rank	Income Rank	Global Rank
	0.68	3/19	25/31	26/102

	Factor Trend	Factor Score	Regional Rank	Income Rank	Global Rank
Constraints on Government Powers	—	0.74	3/19	22/31	23/102
Absence of Corruption	—	0.72	2/19	22/31	23/102
Open Government	—	0.68	1/19	18/31	18/102
Fundamental Rights	—	0.74	3/19	23/31	24/102
Order and Security	—	0.7	2/19	30/31	60/102
Regulatory Enforcement	—	0.65	2/19	22/31	23/102
Civil Justice	—	0.61	3/19	27/31	32/102
Criminal Justice	—	0.56	2/19	28/31	32/102

— Chile ···· Latin America & the Caribbean — High income group ▲ Trending up ▼ Trending down ▨ Low Medium ☐ High

Constraints on Government Powers

1.1 Limits by legislature		0.73
1.2 Limits by judiciary		0.63
1.3 Independent auditing		0.74
1.4 Sanctions for official misconduct		0.65
1.5 Non-governmental checks		0.79
1.6 Lawful transition of power		0.91

Absence of Corruption

2.1 No corruption in the executive branch		0.74
2.2 No corruption in the judiciary		0.75
2.3 No corruption in the police/military		0.86
2.4 No corruption in the legislature		0.52

Open Government

3.1 Publicized laws and government data		0.54
3.2 Right to information		0.69
3.3 Civic participation		0.73
3.4 Complaint mechanisms		0.76

Fundamental Rights

4.1 Equal treatment / no discrimination		0.51
4.2 Right to life and security		0.85
4.3 Due process of law		0.62
4.4 Freedom of expression		0.79
4.5 Freedom of religion		0.81
4.6 Right to privacy		0.86
4.7 Freedom of association		0.83
4.8 Labor rights		0.66

Order and Security

5.1 Absence of crime		0.78
5.2 Absence of civil conflict		1
5.3 Absence of violent redress		0.33

Regulatory Enforcement

6.1 Effective regulatory enforcement		0.6
6.2 No improper influence		0.73
6.3 No unreasonable delay		0.73
6.4 Respect for due process		0.45
6.5 No expropriation w/out adequate compensation		0.75

Civil Justice

7.1 Accessibility and affordability		0.66
7.2 No discrimination		0.54
7.3 No corruption		0.65
7.4 No improper gov. influence		0.74
7.5 No unreasonable delay		0.42
7.6 Effective enforcement		0.55
7.7 Impartial and effective ADRs		0.72

Criminal Justice

8.1 Effective investigations		0.43
8.2 Timely and effective adjudication		0.57
8.3 Effective correctional system		0.26
8.4 No discrimination		0.55
8.5 No corruption		0.73
8.6 No improper gov. influence		0.79
8.7 Due process of law		0.62

China

Shanghai, Beijing, Guangzhou
Region: **East Asia & Pacific** | Income group: **Upper middle income**

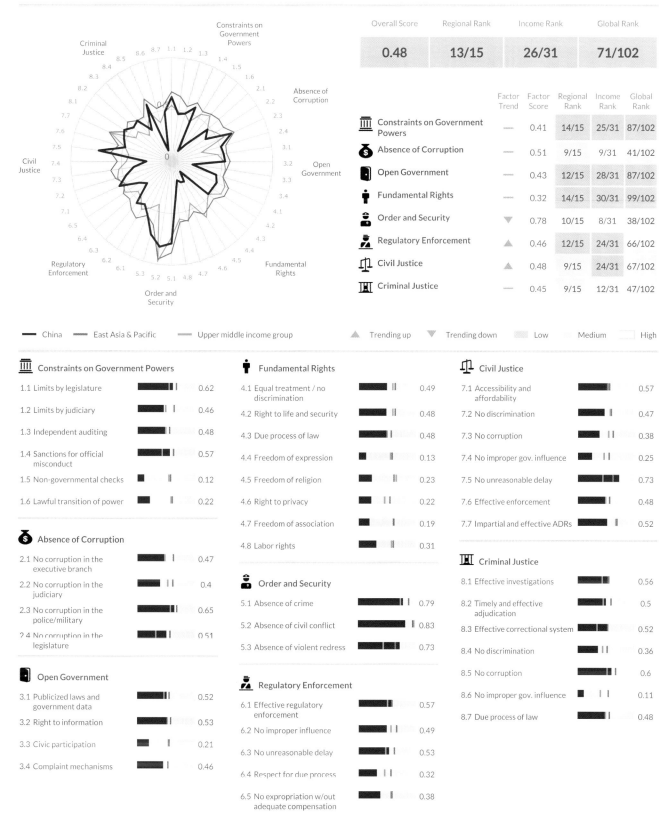

	Overall Score	Regional Rank	Income Rank	Global Rank
	0.48	13/15	26/31	71/102

		Factor Trend	Factor Score	Regional Rank	Income Rank	Global Rank
🏛	Constraints on Government Powers	—	0.41	14/15	25/31	87/102
💰	Absence of Corruption	—	0.51	9/15	9/31	41/102
📱	Open Government	—	0.43	12/15	28/31	87/102
🧍	Fundamental Rights	—	0.32	14/15	30/31	99/102
👮	Order and Security	▼	0.78	10/15	8/31	38/102
🛠	Regulatory Enforcement	▲	0.46	12/15	24/31	66/102
⚖	Civil Justice	▲	0.48	9/15	24/31	67/102
🏛	Criminal Justice	—	0.45	9/15	12/31	47/102

— China — East Asia & Pacific — Upper middle income group   ▲ Trending up   ▼ Trending down   Low   Medium   High

🏛 Constraints on Government Powers

1.1 Limits by legislature	0.62
1.2 Limits by judiciary	0.46
1.3 Independent auditing	0.48
1.4 Sanctions for official misconduct	0.57
1.5 Non-governmental checks	0.12
1.6 Lawful transition of power	0.22

💰 Absence of Corruption

2.1 No corruption in the executive branch	0.47
2.2 No corruption in the judiciary	0.4
2.3 No corruption in the police/military	0.65
2.4 No corruption in the legislature	0.51

📱 Open Government

3.1 Publicized laws and government data	0.52
3.2 Right to information	0.53
3.3 Civic participation	0.21
3.4 Complaint mechanisms	0.46

🧍 Fundamental Rights

4.1 Equal treatment / no discrimination	0.49
4.2 Right to life and security	0.48
4.3 Due process of law	0.48
4.4 Freedom of expression	0.13
4.5 Freedom of religion	0.23
4.6 Right to privacy	0.22
4.7 Freedom of association	0.19
4.8 Labor rights	0.31

👮 Order and Security

5.1 Absence of crime	0.79
5.2 Absence of civil conflict	0.83
5.3 Absence of violent redress	0.73

🛠 Regulatory Enforcement

6.1 Effective regulatory enforcement	0.57
6.2 No improper influence	0.49
6.3 No unreasonable delay	0.53
6.4 Respect for due process	0.32
6.5 No expropriation w/out adequate compensation	0.38

⚖ Civil Justice

7.1 Accessibility and affordability	0.57
7.2 No discrimination	0.47
7.3 No corruption	0.38
7.4 No improper gov. influence	0.25
7.5 No unreasonable delay	0.73
7.6 Effective enforcement	0.48
7.7 Impartial and effective ADRs	0.52

🏛 Criminal Justice

8.1 Effective investigations	0.56
8.2 Timely and effective adjudication	0.5
8.3 Effective correctional system	0.52
8.4 No discrimination	0.36
8.5 No corruption	0.6
8.6 No improper gov. influence	0.11
8.7 Due process of law	0.48

Colombia

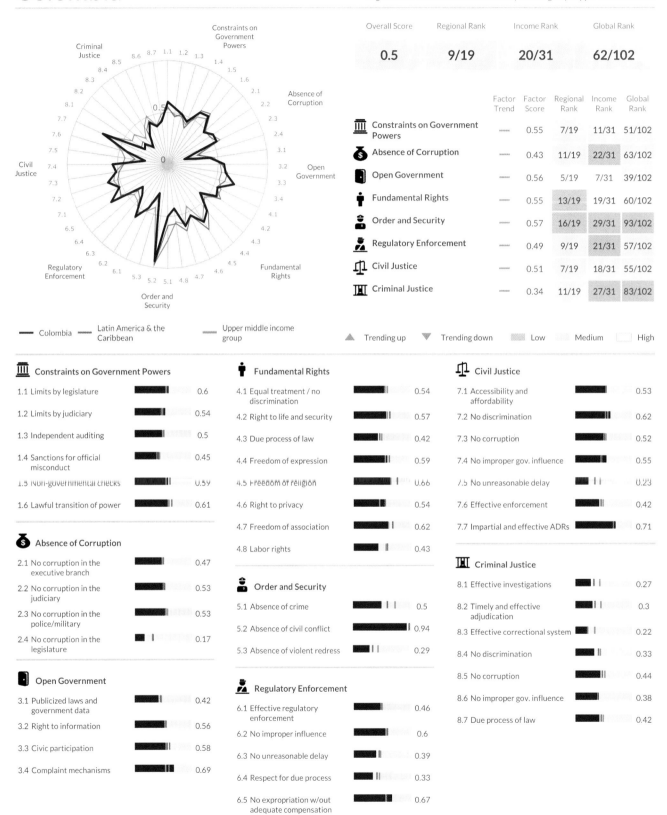

	Overall Score	Regional Rank	Income Rank	Global Rank
	0.5	**9/19**	**20/31**	**62/102**

	Factor Trend	Factor Score	Regional Rank	Income Rank	Global Rank
🏛 Constraints on Government Powers	—	0.55	7/19	11/31	51/102
💰 Absence of Corruption	—	0.43	11/19	22/31	63/102
📱 Open Government	—	0.56	5/19	7/31	39/102
👤 Fundamental Rights	—	0.55	13/19	19/31	60/102
👮 Order and Security	—	0.57	16/19	29/31	93/102
📋 Regulatory Enforcement	—	0.49	9/19	21/31	57/102
⚖ Civil Justice	—	0.51	7/19	18/31	55/102
🏛 Criminal Justice	—	0.34	11/19	27/31	83/102

— Colombia   — Latin America & the Caribbean   — Upper middle income group

▲ Trending up   ▼ Trending down   ▨ Low   Medium   High

🏛 Constraints on Government Powers

1.1 Limits by legislature	0.6
1.2 Limits by judiciary	0.54
1.3 Independent auditing	0.5
1.4 Sanctions for official misconduct	0.45
1.5 Non-governmental checks	0.59
1.6 Lawful transition of power	0.61

💰 Absence of Corruption

2.1 No corruption in the executive branch	0.47
2.2 No corruption in the judiciary	0.53
2.3 No corruption in the police/military	0.53
2.4 No corruption in the legislature	0.17

📱 Open Government

3.1 Publicized laws and government data	0.42
3.2 Right to information	0.56
3.3 Civic participation	0.58
3.4 Complaint mechanisms	0.69

👤 Fundamental Rights

4.1 Equal treatment / no discrimination	0.54
4.2 Right to life and security	0.57
4.3 Due process of law	0.42
4.4 Freedom of expression	0.59
4.5 Freedom of religion	0.66
4.6 Right to privacy	0.54
4.7 Freedom of association	0.62
4.8 Labor rights	0.43

👮 Order and Security

5.1 Absence of crime	0.5
5.2 Absence of civil conflict	0.94
5.3 Absence of violent redress	0.29

📋 Regulatory Enforcement

6.1 Effective regulatory enforcement	0.46
6.2 No improper influence	0.6
6.3 No unreasonable delay	0.39
6.4 Respect for due process	0.33
6.5 No expropriation w/out adequate compensation	0.67

⚖ Civil Justice

7.1 Accessibility and affordability	0.53
7.2 No discrimination	0.62
7.3 No corruption	0.52
7.4 No improper gov. influence	0.55
7.5 No unreasonable delay	0.23
7.6 Effective enforcement	0.42
7.7 Impartial and effective ADRs	0.71

🏛 Criminal Justice

8.1 Effective investigations	0.27
8.2 Timely and effective adjudication	0.3
8.3 Effective correctional system	0.22
8.4 No discrimination	0.33
8.5 No corruption	0.44
8.6 No improper gov. influence	0.38
8.7 Due process of law	0.42

Costa Rica

San Jose, Alajuela, Cartago
Region: **Latin America & the Caribbean** | Income group: **Upper middle income**

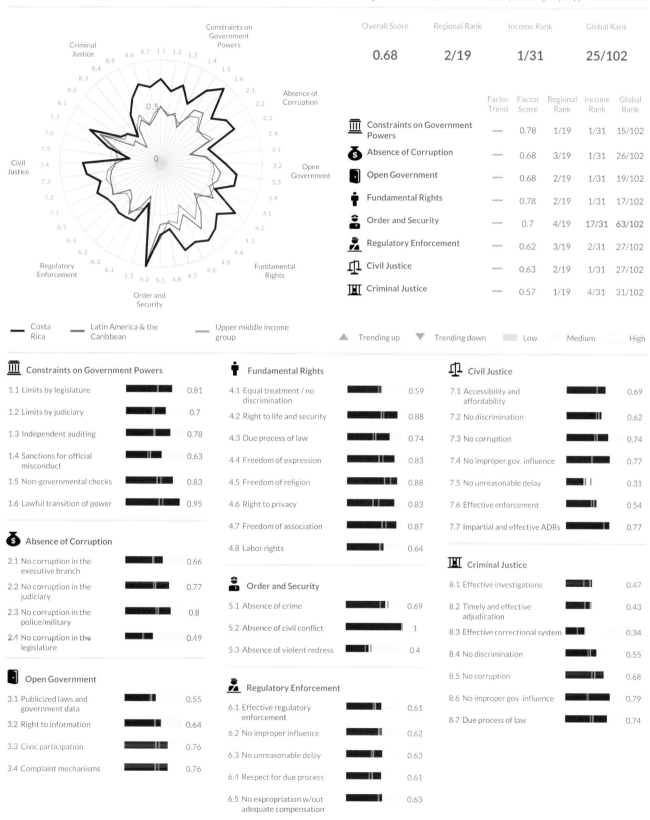

		Overall Score	Regional Rank	Income Rank	Global Rank
		0.68	**2/19**	**1/31**	**25/102**

		Factor Trend	Factor Score	Regional Rank	Income Rank	Global Rank
🏛	Constraints on Government Powers	—	0.78	1/19	1/31	15/102
💰	Absence of Corruption	—	0.68	3/19	1/31	26/102
📱	Open Government	—	0.68	2/19	1/31	19/102
👤	Fundamental Rights	—	0.78	2/19	1/31	17/102
👮	Order and Security	—	0.7	4/19	17/31	63/102
📊	Regulatory Enforcement	—	0.62	3/19	2/31	27/102
⚖	Civil Justice	—	0.63	2/19	1/31	27/102
🏛	Criminal Justice	—	0.57	1/19	4/31	31/102

Legend: — Costa Rica — Latin America & the Caribbean — Upper middle income group

▲ Trending up   ▼ Trending down   ▒ Low   Medium   High

🏛 Constraints on Government Powers

1.1 Limits by legislature	0.81
1.2 Limits by judiciary	0.7
1.3 Independent auditing	0.78
1.4 Sanctions for official misconduct	0.63
1.5 Non-governmental checks	0.83
1.6 Lawful transition of power	0.95

💰 Absence of Corruption

2.1 No corruption in the executive branch	0.66
2.2 No corruption in the judiciary	0.77
2.3 No corruption in the police/military	0.8
2.4 No corruption in the legislature	0.49

📱 Open Government

3.1 Publicized laws and government data	0.55
3.2 Right to information	0.64
3.3 Civic participation	0.76
3.4 Complaint mechanisms	0.76

👤 Fundamental Rights

4.1 Equal treatment / no discrimination	0.59
4.2 Right to life and security	0.88
4.3 Due process of law	0.74
4.4 Freedom of expression	0.83
4.5 Freedom of religion	0.88
4.6 Right to privacy	0.83
4.7 Freedom of association	0.87
4.8 Labor rights	0.64

👮 Order and Security

5.1 Absence of crime	0.69
5.2 Absence of civil conflict	1
5.3 Absence of violent redress	0.4

📊 Regulatory Enforcement

6.1 Effective regulatory enforcement	0.61
6.2 No improper influence	0.62
6.3 No unreasonable delay	0.63
6.4 Respect for due process	0.61
6.5 No expropriation w/out adequate compensation	0.63

⚖ Civil Justice

7.1 Accessibility and affordability	0.69
7.2 No discrimination	0.62
7.3 No corruption	0.74
7.4 No improper gov. influence	0.77
7.5 No unreasonable delay	0.31
7.6 Effective enforcement	0.54
7.7 Impartial and effective ADRs	0.77

🏛 Criminal Justice

8.1 Effective investigations	0.47
8.2 Timely and effective adjudication	0.43
8.3 Effective correctional system	0.34
8.4 No discrimination	0.55
8.5 No corruption	0.68
8.6 No improper gov. influence	0.79
8.7 Due process of law	0.74

Cote d'Ivoire

	Overall Score	Regional Rank	Income Rank	Global Rank
	0.47	8/18	16/25	76/102

	Factor Trend	Factor Score	Regional Rank	Income Rank	Global Rank
Constraints on Government Powers	—	0.47	12/18	15/25	72/102
Absence of Corruption	—	0.4	6/18	12/25	69/102
Open Government	—	0.4	14/18	23/25	93/102
Fundamental Rights	—	0.47	12/18	17/25	79/102
Order and Security	—	0.63	8/18	17/25	77/102
Regulatory Enforcement	—	0.46	5/18	10/25	65/102
Civil Justice	▲	0.54	4/18	4/25	43/102
Criminal Justice	—	0.38	7/18	10/25	64/102

— Cote d'Ivoire — Sub-Saharan Africa — Lower middle income group   ▲ Trending up ▼ Trending down   Low Medium High

Constraints on Government Powers

1.1 Limits by legislature	0.51
1.2 Limits by judiciary	0.43
1.3 Independent auditing	0.52
1.4 Sanctions for official misconduct	0.41
1.5 Non-governmental checks	0.49
1.6 Lawful transition of power	0.47

Absence of Corruption

2.1 No corruption in the executive branch	0.41
2.2 No corruption in the judiciary	0.42
2.3 No corruption in the police/military	0.49
2.4 No corruption in the legislature	0.3

Open Government

3.1 Publicized laws and government data	0.26
3.2 Right to information	0.38
3.3 Civic participation	0.56
3.4 Complaint mechanisms	0.4

Fundamental Rights

4.1 Equal treatment / no discrimination	0.62
4.2 Right to life and security	0.27
4.3 Due process of law	0.33
4.4 Freedom of expression	0.5
4.5 Freedom of religion	0.67
4.6 Right to privacy	0.2
4.7 Freedom of association	0.64
4.8 Labor rights	0.57

Order and Security

5.1 Absence of crime	0.78
5.2 Absence of civil conflict	0.75
5.3 Absence of violent redress	0.37

Regulatory Enforcement

6.1 Effective regulatory enforcement	0.4
6.2 No improper influence	0.49
6.3 No unreasonable delay	0.42
6.4 Respect for due process	0.34
6.5 No expropriation w/out adequate compensation	0.65

Civil Justice

7.1 Accessibility and affordability	0.55
7.2 No discrimination	0.58
7.3 No corruption	0.46
7.4 No improper gov. influence	0.43
7.5 No unreasonable delay	0.63
7.6 Effective enforcement	0.54
7.7 Impartial and effective ADRs	0.63

Criminal Justice

8.1 Effective investigations	0.25
8.2 Timely and effective adjudication	0.5
8.3 Effective correctional system	0.37
8.4 No discrimination	0.45
8.5 No corruption	0.38
8.6 No improper gov. influence	0.39
8.7 Due process of law	0.33

    Complete country profiles available at: data.worldjusticeproject.org

Croatia

	Overall Score	Regional Rank	Income Rank	Global Rank
	0.6	22/24	30/31	35/102

		Factor Trend	Factor Score	Regional Rank	Income Rank	Global Rank
🏛	Constraints on Government Powers	—	0.59	22/24	29/31	44/102
💰	Absence of Corruption	—	0.54	21/24	30/31	35/102
📱	Open Government	—	0.58	20/24	28/31	33/102
🧍	Fundamental Rights	—	0.67	21/24	28/31	31/102
👮	Order and Security	—	0.81	18/24	24/31	31/102
⚖	Regulatory Enforcement	—	0.48	24/24	30/31	60/102
⚖	Civil Justice	—	0.54	23/24	30/31	45/102
🏛	Criminal Justice	—	0.58	21/24	27/31	29/102

— Croatia   — EU + EFTA + North America   — High income group   ▲ Trending up   ▼ Trending down   ░ Low   Medium   High

🏛 Constraints on Government Powers

1.1 Limits by legislature	0.61
1.2 Limits by judiciary	0.48
1.3 Independent auditing	0.58
1.4 Sanctions for official misconduct	0.54
1.5 Non-governmental checks	0.61
1.6 Lawful transition of power	0.73

💰 Absence of Corruption

2.1 No corruption in the executive branch	0.46
2.2 No corruption in the judiciary	0.62
2.3 No corruption in the police/military	0.69
2.4 No corruption in the legislature	0.39

📱 Open Government

3.1 Publicized laws and government data	0.48
3.2 Right to information	0.63
3.3 Civic participation	0.63
3.4 Complaint mechanisms	0.57

🧍 Fundamental Rights

4.1 Equal treatment / no discrimination	0.64
4.2 Right to life and security	0.77
4.3 Due process of law	0.62
4.4 Freedom of expression	0.63
4.5 Freedom of religion	0.68
4.6 Right to privacy	0.51
4.7 Freedom of association	0.76
4.8 Labor rights	0.78

👮 Order and Security

5.1 Absence of crime	0.97
5.2 Absence of civil conflict	1
5.3 Absence of violent redress	0.45

⚖ Regulatory Enforcement

6.1 Effective regulatory enforcement	0.55
6.2 No improper influence	0.49
6.3 No unreasonable delay	0.39
6.4 Respect for due process	0.46
6.5 No expropriation w/out adequate compensation	0.53

⚖ Civil Justice

7.1 Accessibility and affordability	0.63
7.2 No discrimination	0.57
7.3 No corruption	0.55
7.4 No improper gov. influence	0.56
7.5 No unreasonable delay	0.21
7.6 Effective enforcement	0.51
7.7 Impartial and effective ADRs	0.73

🏛 Criminal Justice

8.1 Effective investigations	0.7
8.2 Timely and effective adjudication	0.6
8.3 Effective correctional system	0.47
8.4 No discrimination	0.52
8.5 No corruption	0.59
8.6 No improper gov. influence	0.59
8.7 Due process of law	0.62

Czech Republic

	Overall Score	Regional Rank	Income Rank	Global Rank
	0.72	14/24	20/31	20/102

		Factor Trend	Factor Score	Regional Rank	Income Rank	Global Rank
🏛	Constraints on Government Powers	—	0.74	16/24	23/31	24/102
💰	Absence of Corruption	—	0.66	16/24	25/31	27/102
📖	Open Government	—	0.64	15/24	21/31	22/102
👤	Fundamental Rights	—	0.8	11/24	13/31	13/102
👮	Order and Security	▲	0.89	6/24	11/31	12/102
🏭	Regulatory Enforcement	—	0.63	14/24	23/31	24/102
⚖	Civil Justice	—	0.69	13/24	20/31	20/102
🏛	Criminal Justice	—	0.69	12/24	19/31	19/102

— Czech Republic   — EU + EFTA + North America   — High income group   ▲ Trending up   ▼ Trending down   ▨ Low   Medium   High

🏛 Constraints on Government Powers

1.1 Limits by legislature	0.75
1.2 Limits by judiciary	0.68
1.3 Independent auditing	0.72
1.4 Sanctions for official misconduct	0.66
1.5 Non-governmental checks	0.78
1.6 Lawful transition of power	0.83

💰 Absence of Corruption

2.1 No corruption in the executive branch	0.6
2.2 No corruption in the judiciary	0.74
2.3 No corruption in the police/military	0.84
2.4 No corruption in the legislature	0.46

📖 Open Government

3.1 Publicized laws and government data	0.47
3.2 Right to information	0.7
3.3 Civic participation	0.75
3.4 Complaint mechanisms	0.66

👤 Fundamental Rights

4.1 Equal treatment / no discrimination	0.77
4.2 Right to life and security	0.92
4.3 Due process of law	0.8
4.4 Freedom of expression	0.78
4.5 Freedom of religion	0.74
4.6 Right to privacy	0.83
4.7 Freedom of association	0.84
4.8 Labor rights	0.68

👮 Order and Security

5.1 Absence of crime	0.87
5.2 Absence of civil conflict	1
5.3 Absence of violent redress	0.8

🏭 Regulatory Enforcement

6.1 Effective regulatory enforcement	0.65
6.2 No improper influence	0.73
6.3 No unreasonable delay	0.51
6.4 Respect for due process	0.57
6.5 No expropriation w/out adequate compensation	0.69

⚖ Civil Justice

7.1 Accessibility and affordability	0.68
7.2 No discrimination	0.85
7.3 No corruption	0.73
7.4 No improper gov. influence	0.72
7.5 No unreasonable delay	0.4
7.6 Effective enforcement	0.69
7.7 Impartial and effective ADRs	0.75

🏛 Criminal Justice

8.1 Effective investigations	0.54
8.2 Timely and effective adjudication	0.71
8.3 Effective correctional system	0.6
8.4 No discrimination	0.73
8.5 No corruption	0.72
8.6 No improper gov. influence	0.74
8.7 Due process of law	0.8

Denmark

Copenhagen, Arhus, Odense
Region: **EU + EFTA + North America** | Income group: **High income**

	Overall Score	Regional Rank	Income Rank	Global Rank
	0.87	**1/24**	**1/31**	**1/102**

		Factor Trend	Factor Score	Regional Rank	Income Rank	Global Rank
🏛	Constraints on Government Powers	—	0.92	1/24	1/31	1/102
💰	Absence of Corruption	—	0.96	1/24	1/31	1/102
📖	Open Government	—	0.78	3/24	4/31	4/102
👤	Fundamental Rights	—	0.91	2/24	2/31	2/102
👮	Order and Security	—	0.92	1/24	2/31	2/102
🗂	Regulatory Enforcement	—	0.81	4/24	6/31	6/102
⚖	Civil Justice	—	0.83	3/24	4/31	4/102
🏛	Criminal Justice	—	0.84	2/24	2/31	2/102

— Denmark   — EU + EFTA + North America   — High income group   ▲ Trending up   ▼ Trending down   ▨ Low   Medium   High

🏛 Constraints on Government Powers

1.1 Limits by legislature	0.9
1.2 Limits by judiciary	0.96
1.3 Independent auditing	0.79
1.4 Sanctions for official misconduct	0.92
1.5 Non-governmental checks	0.97
1.6 Lawful transition of power	0.98

💰 Absence of Corruption

2.1 No corruption in the executive branch	0.92
2.2 No corruption in the judiciary	0.97
2.3 No corruption in the police/military	0.97
2.4 No corruption in the legislature	0.96

📖 Open Government

3.1 Publicized laws and government data	0.68
3.2 Right to information	0.72
3.3 Civic participation	0.89
3.4 Complaint mechanisms	0.84

👤 Fundamental Rights

4.1 Equal treatment / no discrimination	0.81
4.2 Right to life and security	0.94
4.3 Due process of law	0.89
4.4 Freedom of expression	0.97
4.5 Freedom of religion	0.87
4.6 Right to privacy	0.87
4.7 Freedom of association	0.97
4.8 Labor rights	0.93

👮 Order and Security

5.1 Absence of crime	0.92
5.2 Absence of civil conflict	1
5.3 Absence of violent redress	0.84

🗂 Regulatory Enforcement

6.1 Effective regulatory enforcement	0.8
6.2 No improper influence	0.93
6.3 No unreasonable delay	0.79
6.4 Respect for due process	0.73
6.5 No expropriation w/out adequate compensation	0.81

⚖ Civil Justice

7.1 Accessibility and affordability	0.73
7.2 No discrimination	0.9
7.3 No corruption	0.96
7.4 No improper gov. influence	0.93
7.5 No unreasonable delay	0.61
7.6 Effective enforcement	0.81
7.7 Impartial and effective ADRs	0.87

🏛 Criminal Justice

8.1 Effective investigations	0.67
8.2 Timely and effective adjudication	0.78
8.3 Effective correctional system	0.83
8.4 No discrimination	0.77
8.5 No corruption	0.97
8.6 No improper gov. influence	0.96
8.7 Due process of law	0.89

Dominican Republic

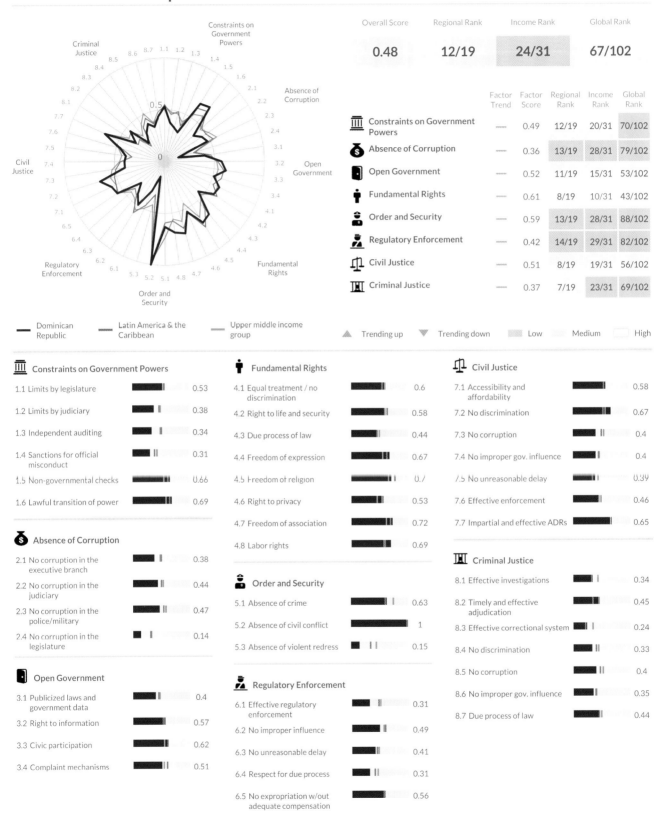

	Overall Score	Regional Rank	Income Rank	Global Rank
	0.48	12/19	24/31	67/102

	Factor Trend	Factor Score	Regional Rank	Income Rank	Global Rank
Constraints on Government Powers	—	0.49	12/19	20/31	70/102
Absence of Corruption	—	0.36	13/19	28/31	79/102
Open Government	—	0.52	11/19	15/31	53/102
Fundamental Rights	—	0.61	8/19	10/31	43/102
Order and Security	—	0.59	13/19	28/31	88/102
Regulatory Enforcement	—	0.42	14/19	29/31	82/102
Civil Justice	—	0.51	8/19	19/31	56/102
Criminal Justice	—	0.37	7/19	23/31	69/102

— Dominican Republic   — Latin America & the Caribbean   — Upper middle income group

▲ Trending up   ▼ Trending down   ▨ Low   Medium   ☐ High

Constraints on Government Powers

1.1 Limits by legislature	0.53
1.2 Limits by judiciary	0.38
1.3 Independent auditing	0.34
1.4 Sanctions for official misconduct	0.31
1.5 Non-governmental checks	0.66
1.6 Lawful transition of power	0.69

Absence of Corruption

2.1 No corruption in the executive branch	0.38
2.2 No corruption in the judiciary	0.44
2.3 No corruption in the police/military	0.47
2.4 No corruption in the legislature	0.14

Open Government

3.1 Publicized laws and government data	0.4
3.2 Right to information	0.57
3.3 Civic participation	0.62
3.4 Complaint mechanisms	0.51

Fundamental Rights

4.1 Equal treatment / no discrimination	0.6
4.2 Right to life and security	0.58
4.3 Due process of law	0.44
4.4 Freedom of expression	0.67
4.5 Freedom of religion	0.7
4.6 Right to privacy	0.53
4.7 Freedom of association	0.72
4.8 Labor rights	0.69

Order and Security

5.1 Absence of crime	0.63
5.2 Absence of civil conflict	1
5.3 Absence of violent redress	0.15

Regulatory Enforcement

6.1 Effective regulatory enforcement	0.31
6.2 No improper influence	0.49
6.3 No unreasonable delay	0.41
6.4 Respect for due process	0.31
6.5 No expropriation w/out adequate compensation	0.56

Civil Justice

7.1 Accessibility and affordability	0.58
7.2 No discrimination	0.67
7.3 No corruption	0.4
7.4 No improper gov. influence	0.4
7.5 No unreasonable delay	0.39
7.6 Effective enforcement	0.46
7.7 Impartial and effective ADRs	0.65

Criminal Justice

8.1 Effective investigations	0.34
8.2 Timely and effective adjudication	0.45
8.3 Effective correctional system	0.24
8.4 No discrimination	0.33
8.5 No corruption	0.4
8.6 No improper gov. influence	0.35
8.7 Due process of law	0.44

Ecuador

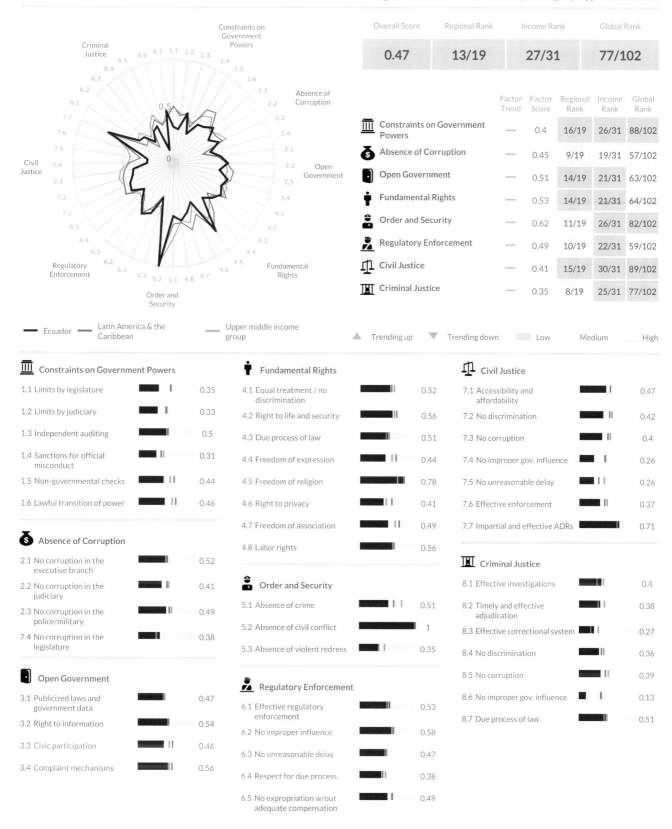

	Overall Score	Regional Rank	Income Rank	Global Rank
	0.47	13/19	27/31	77/102

		Factor Trend	Factor Score	Regional Rank	Income Rank	Global Rank
🏛	Constraints on Government Powers	—	0.4	16/19	26/31	88/102
💰	Absence of Corruption	—	0.45	9/19	19/31	57/102
📱	Open Government	—	0.51	14/19	21/31	63/102
👤	Fundamental Rights	—	0.53	14/19	21/31	64/102
👮	Order and Security	—	0.62	11/19	26/31	82/102
📋	Regulatory Enforcement	—	0.49	10/19	22/31	59/102
⚖	Civil Justice	—	0.41	15/19	30/31	89/102
🏛	Criminal Justice	—	0.35	8/19	25/31	77/102

— Ecuador — Latin America & the Caribbean — Upper middle income group

▲ Trending up ▼ Trending down ░ Low Medium High

🏛 Constraints on Government Powers

1.1 Limits by legislature		0.35
1.2 Limits by judiciary		0.33
1.3 Independent auditing		0.5
1.4 Sanctions for official misconduct		0.31
1.5 Non-governmental checks		0.44
1.6 Lawful transition of power		0.46

💰 Absence of Corruption

2.1 No corruption in the executive branch		0.52
2.2 No corruption in the judiciary		0.41
2.3 No corruption in the police/military		0.49
2.4 No corruption in the legislature		0.38

📱 Open Government

3.1 Publicized laws and government data		0.47
3.2 Right to information		0.54
3.3 Civic participation		0.46
3.4 Complaint mechanisms		0.56

👤 Fundamental Rights

4.1 Equal treatment / no discrimination		0.52
4.2 Right to life and security		0.56
4.3 Due process of law		0.51
4.4 Freedom of expression		0.44
4.5 Freedom of religion		0.78
4.6 Right to privacy		0.41
4.7 Freedom of association		0.49
4.8 Labor rights		0.56

👮 Order and Security

5.1 Absence of crime		0.51
5.2 Absence of civil conflict		1
5.3 Absence of violent redress		0.35

📋 Regulatory Enforcement

6.1 Effective regulatory enforcement		0.53
6.2 No improper influence		0.58
6.3 No unreasonable delay		0.47
6.4 Respect for due process		0.38
6.5 No expropriation w/out adequate compensation		0.49

⚖ Civil Justice

7.1 Accessibility and affordability		0.47
7.2 No discrimination		0.42
7.3 No corruption		0.4
7.4 No improper gov. influence		0.26
7.5 No unreasonable delay		0.26
7.6 Effective enforcement		0.37
7.7 Impartial and effective ADRs		0.71

🏛 Criminal Justice

8.1 Effective investigations		0.4
8.2 Timely and effective adjudication		0.38
8.3 Effective correctional system		0.27
8.4 No discrimination		0.36
8.5 No corruption		0.39
8.6 No improper gov. influence		0.13
8.7 Due process of law		0.51

Egypt

	Overall Score	Regional Rank	Income Rank	Global Rank
	0.44	6/7	19/25	86/102

	Factor Trend	Factor Score	Regional Rank	Income Rank	Global Rank
🏛 Constraints on Government Powers	—	0.39	6/7	22/25	91/102
💰 Absence of Corruption	—	0.47	5/7	5/25	52/102
📱 Open Government	—	0.42	6/7	22/25	91/102
👤 Fundamental Rights	—	0.32	6/7	25/25	98/102
👮 Order and Security	—	0.69	5/7	14/25	66/102
📋 Regulatory Enforcement	▼	0.39	7/7	24/25	93/102
⚖ Civil Justice	—	0.39	7/7	21/25	92/102
🏛 Criminal Justice	—	0.43	4/7	8/25	55/102

— Egypt   — Middle East & North Africa   — Lower middle income group   ▲ Trending up   ▼ Trending down   ▨ Low   ▨ Medium   ▢ High

🏛 Constraints on Government Powers

1.1 Limits by legislature		0.37
1.2 Limits by judiciary		0.5
1.3 Independent auditing		0.35
1.4 Sanctions for official misconduct		0.54
1.5 Non-governmental checks		0.21
1.6 Lawful transition of power		0.34

💰 Absence of Corruption

2.1 No corruption in the executive branch		0.48
2.2 No corruption in the judiciary		0.59
2.3 No corruption in the police/military		0.45
2.4 No corruption in the legislature		0.38

📱 Open Government

3.1 Publicized laws and government data		0.43
3.2 Right to information		0.41
3.3 Civic participation		0.52
3.4 Complaint mechanisms		0.34

👤 Fundamental Rights

4.1 Equal treatment / no discrimination		0.56
4.2 Right to life and security		0.3
4.3 Due process of law		0.28
4.4 Freedom of expression		0.22
4.5 Freedom of religion		0.29
4.6 Right to privacy		0.11
4.7 Freedom of association		0.46
4.8 Labor rights		0.31

👮 Order and Security

5.1 Absence of crime		0.84
5.2 Absence of civil conflict		0.92
5.3 Absence of violent redress		0.32

📋 Regulatory Enforcement

6.1 Effective regulatory enforcement		0.52
6.2 No improper influence		0.53
6.3 No unreasonable delay		0.02
6.4 Respect for due process		0.42
6.5 No expropriation w/out adequate compensation		0.47

⚖ Civil Justice

7.1 Accessibility and affordability		0.39
7.2 No discrimination		0.48
7.3 No corruption		0.63
7.4 No improper gov. influence		0.46
7.5 No unreasonable delay		0.3
7.6 Effective enforcement		0.16
7.7 Impartial and effective ADRs		0.35

🏛 Criminal Justice

8.1 Effective investigations		0.45
8.2 Timely and effective adjudication		0.44
8.3 Effective correctional system		0.31
8.4 No discrimination		0.5
8.5 No corruption		0.54
8.6 No improper gov. influence		0.46
8.7 Due process of law		0.28

El Salvador

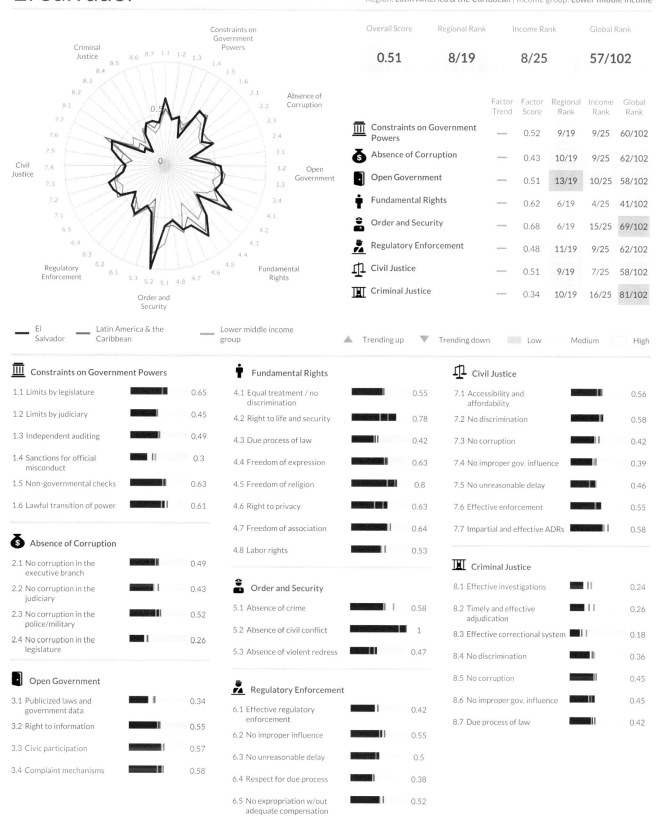

Overall Score	Regional Rank	Income Rank	Global Rank
0.51	8/19	8/25	57/102

		Factor Trend	Factor Score	Regional Rank	Income Rank	Global Rank
🏛	Constraints on Government Powers	—	0.52	9/19	9/25	60/102
💰	Absence of Corruption	—	0.43	10/19	9/25	62/102
📖	Open Government	—	0.51	13/19	10/25	58/102
👤	Fundamental Rights	—	0.62	6/19	4/25	41/102
👮	Order and Security	—	0.68	6/19	15/25	69/102
🗎	Regulatory Enforcement	—	0.48	11/19	9/25	62/102
⚖	Civil Justice	—	0.51	9/19	7/25	58/102
🏛	Criminal Justice	—	0.34	10/19	16/25	81/102

— El Salvador   — Latin America & the Caribbean   — Lower middle income group

▲ Trending up   ▼ Trending down   ▨ Low   Medium   High

🏛 Constraints on Government Powers

1.1 Limits by legislature	0.65
1.2 Limits by judiciary	0.45
1.3 Independent auditing	0.49
1.4 Sanctions for official misconduct	0.3
1.5 Non-governmental checks	0.63
1.6 Lawful transition of power	0.61

💰 Absence of Corruption

2.1 No corruption in the executive branch	0.49
2.2 No corruption in the judiciary	0.43
2.3 No corruption in the police/military	0.52
2.4 No corruption in the legislature	0.26

📖 Open Government

3.1 Publicized laws and government data	0.34
3.2 Right to information	0.55
3.3 Civic participation	0.57
3.4 Complaint mechanisms	0.58

👤 Fundamental Rights

4.1 Equal treatment / no discrimination	0.55
4.2 Right to life and security	0.78
4.3 Due process of law	0.42
4.4 Freedom of expression	0.63
4.5 Freedom of religion	0.8
4.6 Right to privacy	0.63
4.7 Freedom of association	0.64
4.8 Labor rights	0.53

👮 Order and Security

5.1 Absence of crime	0.58
5.2 Absence of civil conflict	1
5.3 Absence of violent redress	0.47

🗎 Regulatory Enforcement

6.1 Effective regulatory enforcement	0.42
6.2 No improper influence	0.55
6.3 No unreasonable delay	0.5
6.4 Respect for due process	0.38
6.5 No expropriation w/out adequate compensation	0.52

⚖ Civil Justice

7.1 Accessibility and affordability	0.56
7.2 No discrimination	0.58
7.3 No corruption	0.42
7.4 No improper gov. influence	0.39
7.5 No unreasonable delay	0.46
7.6 Effective enforcement	0.55
7.7 Impartial and effective ADRs	0.58

🏛 Criminal Justice

8.1 Effective investigations	0.24
8.2 Timely and effective adjudication	0.26
8.3 Effective correctional system	0.18
8.4 No discrimination	0.36
8.5 No corruption	0.45
8.6 No improper gov. influence	0.45
8.7 Due process of law	0.42

Estonia

	Overall Score	Regional Rank	Income Rank	Global Rank
	0.77	**10/24**	**15/31**	**15/102**

		Factor Trend	Factor Score	Regional Rank	Income Rank	Global Rank
🏛	Constraints on Government Powers	—	0.79	11/24	13/31	13/102
💰	Absence of Corruption	—	0.78	11/24	19/31	19/102
	Open Government	—	0.72	10/24	14/31	14/102
	Fundamental Rights	—	0.81	9/24	11/31	11/102
	Order and Security	—	0.88	8/24	15/31	16/102
	Regulatory Enforcement	—	0.75	10/24	16/31	16/102
⚖	Civil Justice	—	0.75	8/24	12/31	12/102
🏛	Criminal Justice	—	0.71	11/24	18/31	18/102

— Estonia   ⋯ EU + EFTA + North America   — High income group   ▲ Trending up   ▼ Trending down   ▒ Low   ░ Medium   ☐ High

🏛 Constraints on Government Powers

1.1 Limits by legislature	0.78
1.2 Limits by judiciary	0.81
1.3 Independent auditing	0.65
1.4 Sanctions for official misconduct	0.83
1.5 Non-governmental checks	0.79
1.6 Lawful transition of power	0.88

💰 Absence of Corruption

2.1 No corruption in the executive branch	0.71
2.2 No corruption in the judiciary	0.92
2.3 No corruption in the police/military	0.9
2.4 No corruption in the legislature	0.57

Open Government

3.1 Publicized laws and government data	0.62
3.2 Right to information	0.77
3.3 Civic participation	0.75
3.4 Complaint mechanisms	0.76

Fundamental Rights

4.1 Equal treatment / no discrimination	0.84
4.2 Right to life and security	0.92
4.3 Due process of law	0.77
4.4 Freedom of expression	0.79
4.5 Freedom of religion	0.85
4.6 Right to privacy	0.76
4.7 Freedom of association	0.84
4.8 Labor rights	0.72

Order and Security

5.1 Absence of crime	0.88
5.2 Absence of civil conflict	1
5.3 Absence of violent redress	0.74

Regulatory Enforcement

6.1 Effective regulatory enforcement	0.82
6.2 No improper influence	0.85
6.3 No unreasonable delay	0.75
6.4 Respect for due process	0.52
6.5 No expropriation w/out adequate compensation	0.8

⚖ Civil Justice

7.1 Accessibility and affordability	0.57
7.2 No discrimination	0.87
7.3 No corruption	0.88
7.4 No improper gov. influence	0.86
7.5 No unreasonable delay	0.63
7.6 Effective enforcement	0.66
7.7 Impartial and effective ADRs	0.8

🏛 Criminal Justice

8.1 Effective investigations	0.46
8.2 Timely and effective adjudication	0.65
8.3 Effective correctional system	0.68
8.4 No discrimination	0.7
8.5 No corruption	0.85
8.6 No improper gov. influence	0.84
8.7 Due process of law	0.77

Ethiopia

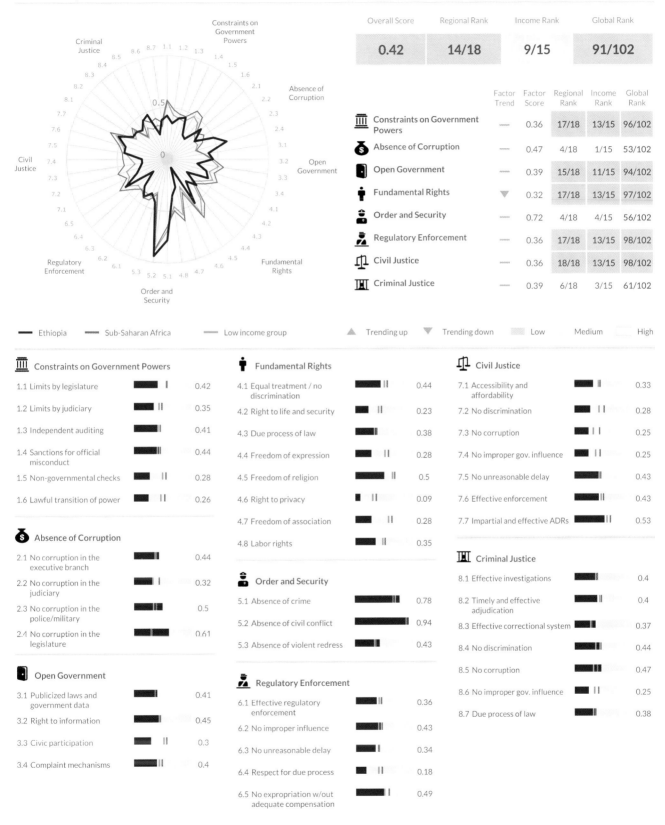

		Overall Score	Regional Rank	Income Rank	Global Rank
		0.42	14/18	9/15	91/102

		Factor Trend	Factor Score	Regional Rank	Income Rank	Global Rank
🏛	Constraints on Government Powers	—	0.36	17/18	13/15	96/102
💰	Absence of Corruption	—	0.47	4/18	1/15	53/102
📱	Open Government	—	0.39	15/18	11/15	94/102
👤	Fundamental Rights	▼	0.32	17/18	13/15	97/102
👮	Order and Security	—	0.72	4/18	4/15	56/102
🧑‍⚖	Regulatory Enforcement	—	0.36	17/18	13/15	98/102
⚖	Civil Justice	—	0.36	18/18	13/15	98/102
🏛	Criminal Justice	—	0.39	6/18	3/15	61/102

— Ethiopia   — Sub-Saharan Africa   — Low income group   ▲ Trending up   ▼ Trending down   Low   Medium   High

🏛 Constraints on Government Powers

1.1 Limits by legislature		0.42
1.2 Limits by judiciary		0.35
1.3 Independent auditing		0.41
1.4 Sanctions for official misconduct		0.44
1.5 Non-governmental checks		0.28
1.6 Lawful transition of power		0.26

💰 Absence of Corruption

2.1 No corruption in the executive branch		0.44
2.2 No corruption in the judiciary		0.32
2.3 No corruption in the police/military		0.5
2.4 No corruption in the legislature		0.61

📱 Open Government

3.1 Publicized laws and government data		0.41
3.2 Right to information		0.45
3.3 Civic participation		0.3
3.4 Complaint mechanisms		0.4

👤 Fundamental Rights

4.1 Equal treatment / no discrimination		0.44
4.2 Right to life and security		0.23
4.3 Due process of law		0.38
4.4 Freedom of expression		0.28
4.5 Freedom of religion		0.5
4.6 Right to privacy		0.09
4.7 Freedom of association		0.28
4.8 Labor rights		0.35

👮 Order and Security

5.1 Absence of crime		0.78
5.2 Absence of civil conflict		0.94
5.3 Absence of violent redress		0.43

🧑‍⚖ Regulatory Enforcement

6.1 Effective regulatory enforcement		0.36
6.2 No improper influence		0.43
6.3 No unreasonable delay		0.34
6.4 Respect for due process		0.18
6.5 No expropriation w/out adequate compensation		0.49

⚖ Civil Justice

7.1 Accessibility and affordability		0.33
7.2 No discrimination		0.28
7.3 No corruption		0.25
7.4 No improper gov. influence		0.25
7.5 No unreasonable delay		0.43
7.6 Effective enforcement		0.43
7.7 Impartial and effective ADRs		0.53

🏛 Criminal Justice

8.1 Effective investigations		0.4
8.2 Timely and effective adjudication		0.4
8.3 Effective correctional system		0.37
8.4 No discrimination		0.44
8.5 No corruption		0.47
8.6 No improper gov. influence		0.25
8.7 Due process of law		0.38

Finland

	Overall Score	Regional Rank	Income Rank	Global Rank
	0.85	4/24	4/31	4/102

	Factor Trend	Factor Score	Regional Rank	Income Rank	Global Rank
Constraints on Government Powers	—	0.88	2/24	2/31	2/102
Absence of Corruption	—	0.9	4/24	5/31	5/102
Open Government	—	0.76	5/24	6/31	6/102
Fundamental Rights	—	0.91	1/24	1/31	1/102
Order and Security	—	0.92	2/24	3/31	3/102
Regulatory Enforcement	—	0.79	6/24	9/31	9/102
Civil Justice	—	0.78	7/24	10/31	10/102
Criminal Justice	—	0.85	1/24	1/31	1/102

— Finland — EU + EFTA + North America — High income group ▲ Trending up ▼ Trending down ▨ Low ▨ Medium ▢ High

Constraints on Government Powers

1.1 Limits by legislature	0.86
1.2 Limits by judiciary	0.86
1.3 Independent auditing	0.8
1.4 Sanctions for official misconduct	0.9
1.5 Non governmental checks	0.71
1.6 Lawful transition of power	0.96

Absence of Corruption

2.1 No corruption in the executive branch	0.9
2.2 No corruption in the judiciary	0.95
2.3 No corruption in the police/military	0.96
2.4 No corruption in the legislature	0.79

Open Government

3.1 Publicized laws and government data	0.7
3.2 Right to information	0.71
3.3 Civic participation	0.83
3.4 Complaint mechanisms	0.79

Fundamental Rights

4.1 Equal treatment / no discrimination	0.87
4.2 Right to life and security	0.96
4.3 Due process of law	0.92
4.4 Freedom of expression	0.91
4.5 Freedom of religion	0.87
4.6 Right to privacy	1
4.7 Freedom of association	0.91
4.8 Labor rights	0.85

Order and Security

5.1 Absence of crime	0.92
5.2 Absence of civil conflict	1
5.3 Absence of violent redress	0.83

Regulatory Enforcement

6.1 Effective regulatory enforcement	0.77
6.2 No improper influence	0.9
6.3 No unreasonable delay	0.77
6.4 Respect for due process	0.76
6.5 No expropriation w/out adequate compensation	0.75

Civil Justice

7.1 Accessibility and affordability	0.59
7.2 No discrimination	0.86
7.3 No corruption	0.92
7.4 No improper gov. influence	0.87
7.5 No unreasonable delay	0.57
7.6 Effective enforcement	0.86
7.7 Impartial and effective ADRs	0.76

Criminal Justice

8.1 Effective investigations	0.67
8.2 Timely and effective adjudication	0.8
8.3 Effective correctional system	0.82
8.4 No discrimination	0.83
8.5 No corruption	0.93
8.6 No improper gov. influence	0.99
8.7 Due process of law	0.92

Complete country profiles available at: data.worldjusticeproject.org

France

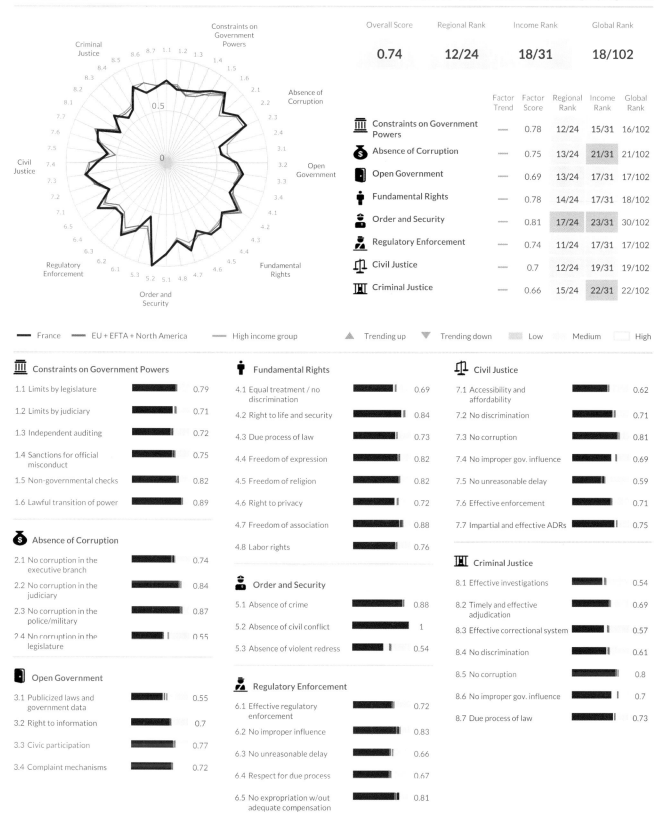

	Overall Score	Regional Rank	Income Rank	Global Rank
	0.74	12/24	18/31	18/102

		Factor Trend	Factor Score	Regional Rank	Income Rank	Global Rank
🏛	Constraints on Government Powers	—	0.78	12/24	15/31	16/102
💰	Absence of Corruption	—	0.75	13/24	21/31	21/102
📱	Open Government	—	0.69	13/24	17/31	17/102
🧍	Fundamental Rights	—	0.78	14/24	17/31	18/102
👮	Order and Security	—	0.81	17/24	23/31	30/102
📋	Regulatory Enforcement	—	0.74	11/24	17/31	17/102
⚖	Civil Justice	—	0.7	12/24	19/31	19/102
🏛	Criminal Justice	—	0.66	15/24	22/31	22/102

━━ France ━━ EU + EFTA + North America ━━ High income group ▲ Trending up ▼ Trending down ▨ Low Medium ☐ High

🏛 Constraints on Government Powers

1.1 Limits by legislature	0.79
1.2 Limits by judiciary	0.71
1.3 Independent auditing	0.72
1.4 Sanctions for official misconduct	0.75
1.5 Non-governmental checks	0.82
1.6 Lawful transition of power	0.89

💰 Absence of Corruption

2.1 No corruption in the executive branch	0.74
2.2 No corruption in the judiciary	0.84
2.3 No corruption in the police/military	0.87
2.4 No corruption in the legislature	0.55

📱 Open Government

3.1 Publicized laws and government data	0.55
3.2 Right to information	0.7
3.3 Civic participation	0.77
3.4 Complaint mechanisms	0.72

🧍 Fundamental Rights

4.1 Equal treatment / no discrimination	0.69
4.2 Right to life and security	0.84
4.3 Due process of law	0.73
4.4 Freedom of expression	0.82
4.5 Freedom of religion	0.82
4.6 Right to privacy	0.72
4.7 Freedom of association	0.88
4.8 Labor rights	0.76

👮 Order and Security

5.1 Absence of crime	0.88
5.2 Absence of civil conflict	1
5.3 Absence of violent redress	0.54

📋 Regulatory Enforcement

6.1 Effective regulatory enforcement	0.72
6.2 No improper influence	0.83
6.3 No unreasonable delay	0.66
6.4 Respect for due process	0.67
6.5 No expropriation w/out adequate compensation	0.81

⚖ Civil Justice

7.1 Accessibility and affordability	0.62
7.2 No discrimination	0.71
7.3 No corruption	0.81
7.4 No improper gov. influence	0.69
7.5 No unreasonable delay	0.59
7.6 Effective enforcement	0.71
7.7 Impartial and effective ADRs	0.75

🏛 Criminal Justice

8.1 Effective investigations	0.54
8.2 Timely and effective adjudication	0.69
8.3 Effective correctional system	0.57
8.4 No discrimination	0.61
8.5 No corruption	0.8
8.6 No improper gov. influence	0.7
8.7 Due process of law	0.73

Georgia

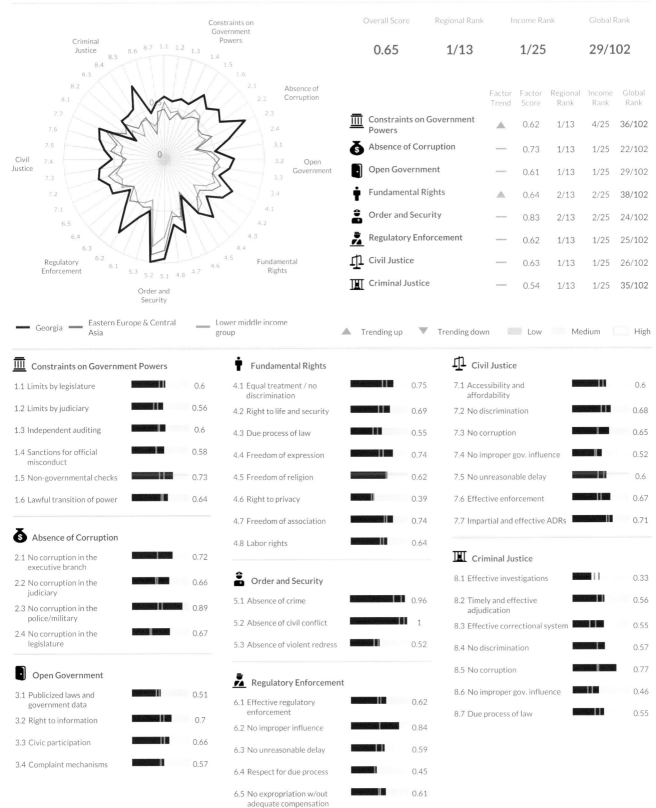

	Overall Score	Regional Rank	Income Rank	Global Rank
	0.65	1/13	1/25	29/102

	Factor Trend	Factor Score	Regional Rank	Income Rank	Global Rank
🏛 Constraints on Government Powers	▲	0.62	1/13	4/25	36/102
💰 Absence of Corruption	—	0.73	1/13	1/25	22/102
📱 Open Government	—	0.61	1/13	1/25	29/102
👤 Fundamental Rights	▲	0.64	2/13	2/25	38/102
👮 Order and Security	—	0.83	2/13	2/25	24/102
🧑‍💼 Regulatory Enforcement	—	0.62	1/13	1/25	25/102
⚖ Civil Justice	—	0.63	1/13	1/25	26/102
🏛 Criminal Justice	—	0.54	1/13	1/25	35/102

— Georgia ⋯ Eastern Europe & Central Asia — Lower middle income group ▲ Trending up ▼ Trending down ▨ Low ▨ Medium ☐ High

🏛 Constraints on Government Powers

1.1 Limits by legislature	0.6
1.2 Limits by judiciary	0.56
1.3 Independent auditing	0.6
1.4 Sanctions for official misconduct	0.58
1.5 Non-governmental checks	0.73
1.6 Lawful transition of power	0.64

💰 Absence of Corruption

2.1 No corruption in the executive branch	0.72
2.2 No corruption in the judiciary	0.66
2.3 No corruption in the police/military	0.89
2.4 No corruption in the legislature	0.67

📱 Open Government

3.1 Publicized laws and government data	0.51
3.2 Right to information	0.7
3.3 Civic participation	0.66
3.4 Complaint mechanisms	0.57

👤 Fundamental Rights

4.1 Equal treatment / no discrimination	0.75
4.2 Right to life and security	0.69
4.3 Due process of law	0.55
4.4 Freedom of expression	0.74
4.5 Freedom of religion	0.62
4.6 Right to privacy	0.39
4.7 Freedom of association	0.74
4.8 Labor rights	0.64

👮 Order and Security

5.1 Absence of crime	0.96
5.2 Absence of civil conflict	1
5.3 Absence of violent redress	0.52

🧑‍💼 Regulatory Enforcement

6.1 Effective regulatory enforcement	0.62
6.2 No improper influence	0.84
6.3 No unreasonable delay	0.59
6.4 Respect for due process	0.45
6.5 No expropriation w/out adequate compensation	0.61

⚖ Civil Justice

7.1 Accessibility and affordability	0.6
7.2 No discrimination	0.68
7.3 No corruption	0.65
7.4 No improper gov. influence	0.52
7.5 No unreasonable delay	0.6
7.6 Effective enforcement	0.67
7.7 Impartial and effective ADRs	0.71

🏛 Criminal Justice

8.1 Effective investigations	0.33
8.2 Timely and effective adjudication	0.56
8.3 Effective correctional system	0.55
8.4 No discrimination	0.57
8.5 No corruption	0.77
8.6 No improper gov. influence	0.46
8.7 Due process of law	0.55

Germany

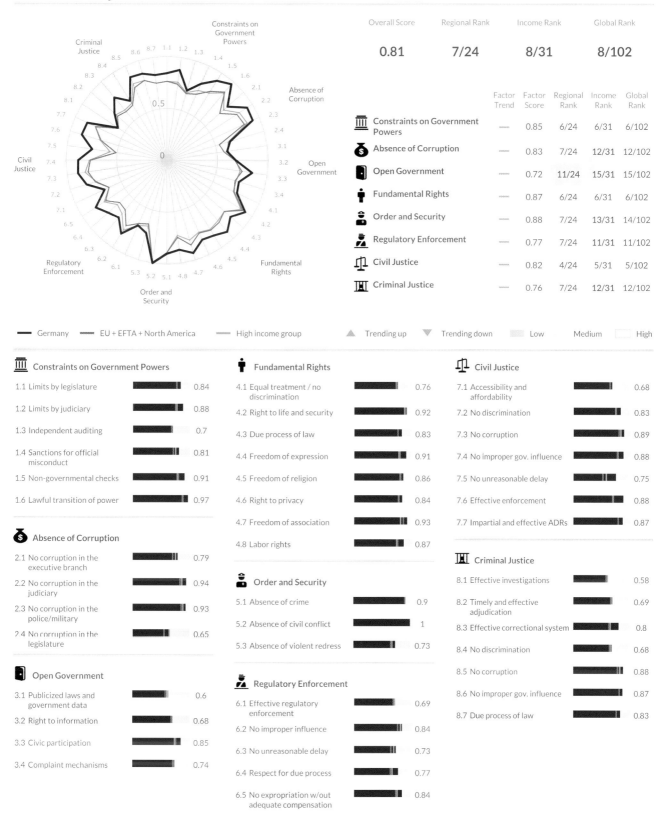

	Overall Score	Regional Rank	Income Rank	Global Rank
	0.81	**7/24**	**8/31**	**8/102**

		Factor Trend	Factor Score	Regional Rank	Income Rank	Global Rank
🏛	Constraints on Government Powers	—	0.85	6/24	6/31	6/102
💰	Absence of Corruption	—	0.83	7/24	12/31	12/102
📱	Open Government	—	0.72	11/24	15/31	15/102
👤	Fundamental Rights	—	0.87	6/24	6/31	6/102
👮	Order and Security	—	0.88	7/24	13/31	14/102
⚖	Regulatory Enforcement	—	0.77	7/24	11/31	11/102
⚖	Civil Justice	—	0.82	4/24	5/31	5/102
🏛	Criminal Justice	—	0.76	7/24	12/31	12/102

— Germany   — EU + EFTA + North America   — High income group   ▲ Trending up   ▼ Trending down   ▨ Low   Medium   ☐ High

🏛 Constraints on Government Powers

1.1 Limits by legislature	0.84
1.2 Limits by judiciary	0.88
1.3 Independent auditing	0.7
1.4 Sanctions for official misconduct	0.81
1.5 Non-governmental checks	0.91
1.6 Lawful transition of power	0.97

💰 Absence of Corruption

2.1 No corruption in the executive branch	0.79
2.2 No corruption in the judiciary	0.94
2.3 No corruption in the police/military	0.93
2.4 No corruption in the legislature	0.65

📱 Open Government

3.1 Publicized laws and government data	0.6
3.2 Right to information	0.68
3.3 Civic participation	0.85
3.4 Complaint mechanisms	0.74

👤 Fundamental Rights

4.1 Equal treatment / no discrimination	0.76
4.2 Right to life and security	0.92
4.3 Due process of law	0.83
4.4 Freedom of expression	0.91
4.5 Freedom of religion	0.86
4.6 Right to privacy	0.84
4.7 Freedom of association	0.93
4.8 Labor rights	0.87

👮 Order and Security

5.1 Absence of crime	0.9
5.2 Absence of civil conflict	1
5.3 Absence of violent redress	0.73

⚖ Regulatory Enforcement

6.1 Effective regulatory enforcement	0.69
6.2 No improper influence	0.84
6.3 No unreasonable delay	0.73
6.4 Respect for due process	0.77
6.5 No expropriation w/out adequate compensation	0.84

⚖ Civil Justice

7.1 Accessibility and affordability	0.68
7.2 No discrimination	0.83
7.3 No corruption	0.89
7.4 No improper gov. influence	0.88
7.5 No unreasonable delay	0.75
7.6 Effective enforcement	0.88
7.7 Impartial and effective ADRs	0.87

🏛 Criminal Justice

8.1 Effective investigations	0.58
8.2 Timely and effective adjudication	0.69
8.3 Effective correctional system	0.8
8.4 No discrimination	0.68
8.5 No corruption	0.88
8.6 No improper gov. influence	0.87
8.7 Due process of law	0.83

Ghana

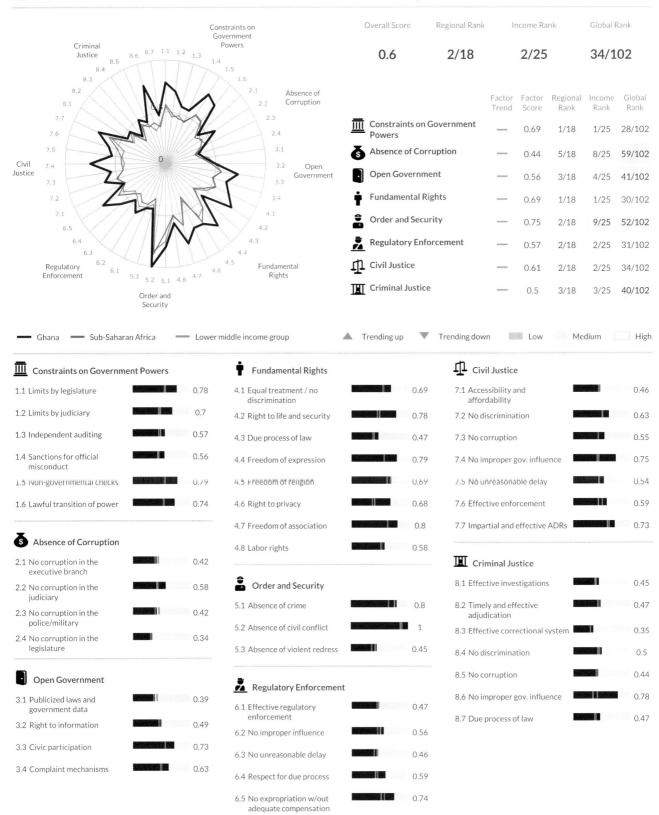

	Overall Score	Regional Rank	Income Rank	Global Rank
	0.6	2/18	2/25	34/102

	Factor Trend	Factor Score	Regional Rank	Income Rank	Global Rank
Constraints on Government Powers	—	0.69	1/18	1/25	28/102
Absence of Corruption	—	0.44	5/18	8/25	59/102
Open Government	—	0.56	3/18	4/25	41/102
Fundamental Rights	—	0.69	1/18	1/25	30/102
Order and Security	—	0.75	2/18	9/25	52/102
Regulatory Enforcement	—	0.57	2/18	2/25	31/102
Civil Justice	—	0.61	2/18	2/25	34/102
Criminal Justice	—	0.5	3/18	3/25	40/102

Legend: — Ghana — Sub-Saharan Africa — Lower middle income group ▲ Trending up ▼ Trending down ▨ Low ▨ Medium ☐ High

Constraints on Government Powers

1.1 Limits by legislature	0.78
1.2 Limits by judiciary	0.7
1.3 Independent auditing	0.57
1.4 Sanctions for official misconduct	0.56
1.5 Non-governmental checks	0.79
1.6 Lawful transition of power	0.74

Absence of Corruption

2.1 No corruption in the executive branch	0.42
2.2 No corruption in the judiciary	0.58
2.3 No corruption in the police/military	0.42
2.4 No corruption in the legislature	0.34

Open Government

3.1 Publicized laws and government data	0.39
3.2 Right to information	0.49
3.3 Civic participation	0.73
3.4 Complaint mechanisms	0.63

Fundamental Rights

4.1 Equal treatment / no discrimination	0.69
4.2 Right to life and security	0.78
4.3 Due process of law	0.47
4.4 Freedom of expression	0.79
4.5 Freedom of religion	0.69
4.6 Right to privacy	0.68
4.7 Freedom of association	0.8
4.8 Labor rights	0.58

Order and Security

5.1 Absence of crime	0.8
5.2 Absence of civil conflict	1
5.3 Absence of violent redress	0.45

Regulatory Enforcement

6.1 Effective regulatory enforcement	0.47
6.2 No improper influence	0.56
6.3 No unreasonable delay	0.46
6.4 Respect for due process	0.59
6.5 No expropriation w/out adequate compensation	0.74

Civil Justice

7.1 Accessibility and affordability	0.46
7.2 No discrimination	0.63
7.3 No corruption	0.55
7.4 No improper gov. influence	0.75
7.5 No unreasonable delay	0.54
7.6 Effective enforcement	0.59
7.7 Impartial and effective ADRs	0.73

Criminal Justice

8.1 Effective investigations	0.45
8.2 Timely and effective adjudication	0.47
8.3 Effective correctional system	0.35
8.4 No discrimination	0.5
8.5 No corruption	0.44
8.6 No improper gov. influence	0.78
8.7 Due process of law	0.47

Greece

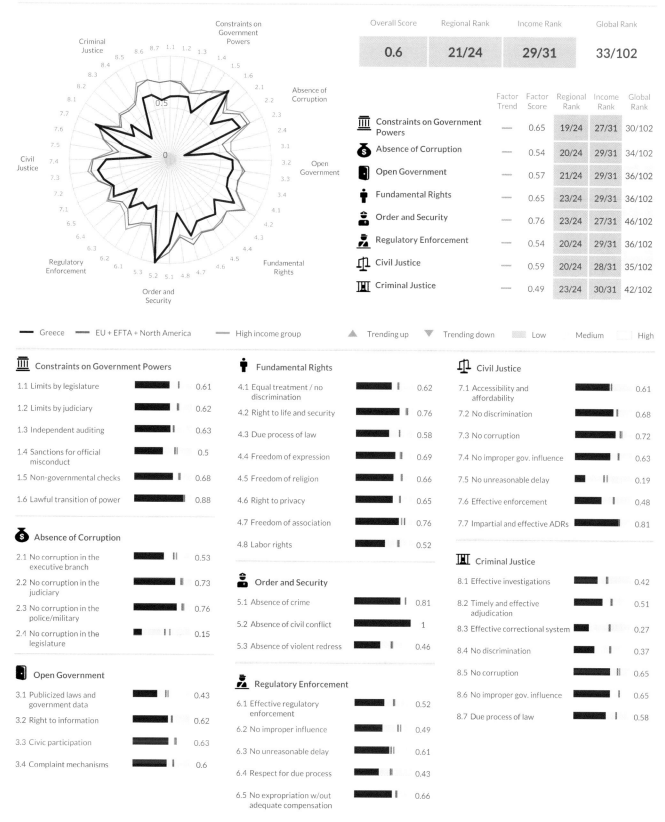

	Overall Score	Regional Rank	Income Rank	Global Rank
	0.6	21/24	29/31	33/102

	Factor Trend	Factor Score	Regional Rank	Income Rank	Global Rank
Constraints on Government Powers	—	0.65	19/24	27/31	30/102
Absence of Corruption	—	0.54	20/24	29/31	34/102
Open Government	—	0.57	21/24	29/31	36/102
Fundamental Rights	—	0.65	23/24	29/31	36/102
Order and Security	—	0.76	23/24	27/31	46/102
Regulatory Enforcement	—	0.54	20/24	29/31	36/102
Civil Justice	—	0.59	20/24	28/31	35/102
Criminal Justice	—	0.49	23/24	30/31	42/102

Legend: ▬ Greece   ▬ EU + EFTA + North America   ▬ High income group   ▲ Trending up   ▼ Trending down   Low   Medium   High

Constraints on Government Powers

1.1 Limits by legislature	0.61
1.2 Limits by judiciary	0.62
1.3 Independent auditing	0.63
1.4 Sanctions for official misconduct	0.5
1.5 Non-governmental checks	0.68
1.6 Lawful transition of power	0.88

Absence of Corruption

2.1 No corruption in the executive branch	0.53
2.2 No corruption in the judiciary	0.73
2.3 No corruption in the police/military	0.76
2.4 No corruption in the legislature	0.15

Open Government

3.1 Publicized laws and government data	0.43
3.2 Right to information	0.62
3.3 Civic participation	0.63
3.4 Complaint mechanisms	0.6

Fundamental Rights

4.1 Equal treatment / no discrimination	0.62
4.2 Right to life and security	0.76
4.3 Due process of law	0.58
4.4 Freedom of expression	0.69
4.5 Freedom of religion	0.66
4.6 Right to privacy	0.65
4.7 Freedom of association	0.76
4.8 Labor rights	0.52

Order and Security

5.1 Absence of crime	0.81
5.2 Absence of civil conflict	1
5.3 Absence of violent redress	0.46

Regulatory Enforcement

6.1 Effective regulatory enforcement	0.52
6.2 No improper influence	0.49
6.3 No unreasonable delay	0.61
6.4 Respect for due process	0.43
6.5 No expropriation w/out adequate compensation	0.66

Civil Justice

7.1 Accessibility and affordability	0.61
7.2 No discrimination	0.68
7.3 No corruption	0.72
7.4 No improper gov. influence	0.63
7.5 No unreasonable delay	0.19
7.6 Effective enforcement	0.48
7.7 Impartial and effective ADRs	0.81

Criminal Justice

8.1 Effective investigations	0.42
8.2 Timely and effective adjudication	0.51
8.3 Effective correctional system	0.27
8.4 No discrimination	0.37
8.5 No corruption	0.65
8.6 No improper gov. influence	0.65
8.7 Due process of law	0.58

Guatemala

Guatemala City, Quetzaltenango, Escuintla
Region: **Latin America & the Caribbean** | Income group: **Lower middle income**

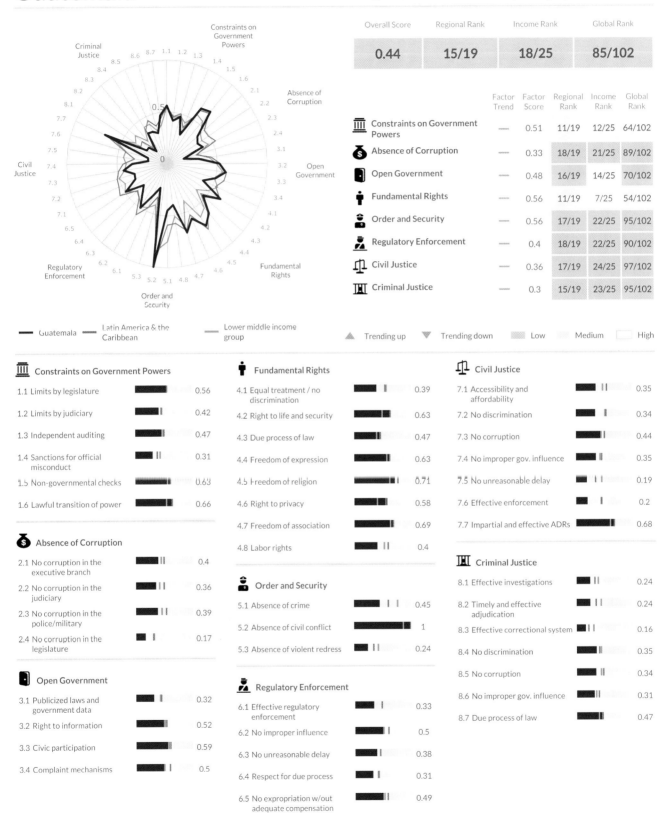

	Overall Score	Regional Rank	Income Rank	Global Rank
	0.44	15/19	18/25	85/102

		Factor Trend	Factor Score	Regional Rank	Income Rank	Global Rank
🏛	Constraints on Government Powers	—	0.51	11/19	12/25	64/102
💰	Absence of Corruption	—	0.33	18/19	21/25	89/102
📋	Open Government	—	0.48	16/19	14/25	70/102
👤	Fundamental Rights	—	0.56	11/19	7/25	54/102
👮	Order and Security	—	0.56	17/19	22/25	95/102
🗂	Regulatory Enforcement	—	0.4	18/19	22/25	90/102
⚖	Civil Justice	—	0.36	17/19	24/25	97/102
🏛	Criminal Justice	—	0.3	15/19	23/25	95/102

— Guatemala   — Latin America & the Caribbean   — Lower middle income group

▲ Trending up   ▼ Trending down   ▨ Low   Medium   □ High

🏛 Constraints on Government Powers

1.1 Limits by legislature	0.56
1.2 Limits by judiciary	0.42
1.3 Independent auditing	0.47
1.4 Sanctions for official misconduct	0.31
1.5 Non-governmental checks	0.63
1.6 Lawful transition of power	0.66

💰 Absence of Corruption

2.1 No corruption in the executive branch	0.4
2.2 No corruption in the judiciary	0.36
2.3 No corruption in the police/military	0.39
2.4 No corruption in the legislature	0.17

📋 Open Government

3.1 Publicized laws and government data	0.32
3.2 Right to information	0.52
3.3 Civic participation	0.59
3.4 Complaint mechanisms	0.5

👤 Fundamental Rights

4.1 Equal treatment / no discrimination	0.39
4.2 Right to life and security	0.63
4.3 Due process of law	0.47
4.4 Freedom of expression	0.63
4.5 Freedom of religion	0.71
4.6 Right to privacy	0.58
4.7 Freedom of association	0.69
4.8 Labor rights	0.4

👮 Order and Security

5.1 Absence of crime	0.45
5.2 Absence of civil conflict	1
5.3 Absence of violent redress	0.24

🗂 Regulatory Enforcement

6.1 Effective regulatory enforcement	0.33
6.2 No improper influence	0.5
6.3 No unreasonable delay	0.38
6.4 Respect for due process	0.31
6.5 No expropriation w/out adequate compensation	0.49

⚖ Civil Justice

7.1 Accessibility and affordability	0.35
7.2 No discrimination	0.34
7.3 No corruption	0.44
7.4 No improper gov. influence	0.35
7.5 No unreasonable delay	0.19
7.6 Effective enforcement	0.2
7.7 Impartial and effective ADRs	0.68

🏛 Criminal Justice

8.1 Effective investigations	0.24
8.2 Timely and effective adjudication	0.24
8.3 Effective correctional system	0.16
8.4 No discrimination	0.35
8.5 No corruption	0.34
8.6 No improper gov. influence	0.31
8.7 Due process of law	0.47

Complete country profiles available at: data.worldjusticeproject.org

Honduras

	Overall Score	Regional Rank	Income Rank	Global Rank
	0.42	17/19	21/25	90/102

		Factor Trend	Factor Score	Regional Rank	Income Rank	Global Rank
🏛	Constraints on Government Powers	—	0.45	15/19	19/25	80/102
💰	Absence of Corruption	—	0.34	14/19	19/25	85/102
📋	Open Government	—	0.49	15/19	13/25	66/102
👤	Fundamental Rights	—	0.45	18/19	19/25	85/102
👮	Order and Security	—	0.58	15/19	21/25	92/102
📊	Regulatory Enforcement	—	0.4	17/19	21/25	88/102
⚖	Civil Justice	—	0.45	12/19	16/25	80/102
🏛	Criminal Justice	—	0.21	18/19	25/25	101/102

— Honduras — Latin America & the Caribbean — Lower middle income group

▲ Trending up ▼ Trending down ░ Low Medium High

🏛 Constraints on Government Powers

1.1 Limits by legislature	0.51
1.2 Limits by judiciary	0.31
1.3 Independent auditing	0.46
1.4 Sanctions for official misconduct	0.39
1.5 Non-governmental checks	0.55
1.6 Lawful transition of power	0.46

💰 Absence of Corruption

2.1 No corruption in the executive branch	0.39
2.2 No corruption in the judiciary	0.37
2.3 No corruption in the police/military	0.36
2.4 No corruption in the legislature	0.25

📋 Open Government

3.1 Publicized laws and government data	0.42
3.2 Right to information	0.47
3.3 Civic participation	0.54
3.4 Complaint mechanisms	0.53

👤 Fundamental Rights

4.1 Equal treatment / no discrimination	0.35
4.2 Right to life and security	0.44
4.3 Due process of law	0.28
4.4 Freedom of expression	0.57
4.5 Freedom of religion	0.62
4.6 Right to privacy	0.34
4.7 Freedom of association	0.6
4.8 Labor rights	0.44

👮 Order and Security

5.1 Absence of crime	0.41
5.2 Absence of civil conflict	1
5.3 Absence of violent redress	0.31

📊 Regulatory Enforcement

6.1 Effective regulatory enforcement	0.33
6.2 No improper influence	0.46
6.3 No unreasonable delay	0.43
6.4 Respect for due process	0.25
6.5 No expropriation w/out adequate compensation	0.53

⚖ Civil Justice

7.1 Accessibility and affordability	0.52
7.2 No discrimination	0.34
7.3 No corruption	0.42
7.4 No improper gov. influence	0.26
7.5 No unreasonable delay	0.36
7.6 Effective enforcement	0.53
7.7 Impartial and effective ADRs	0.72

🏛 Criminal Justice

8.1 Effective investigations	0.14
8.2 Timely and effective adjudication	0.19
8.3 Effective correctional system	0.08
8.4 No discrimination	0.28
8.5 No corruption	0.34
8.6 No improper gov. influence	0.13
8.7 Due process of law	0.28

Hong Kong SAR, China

	Overall Score	Regional Rank	Income Rank	Global Rank
	0.76	6/15	17/31	17/102

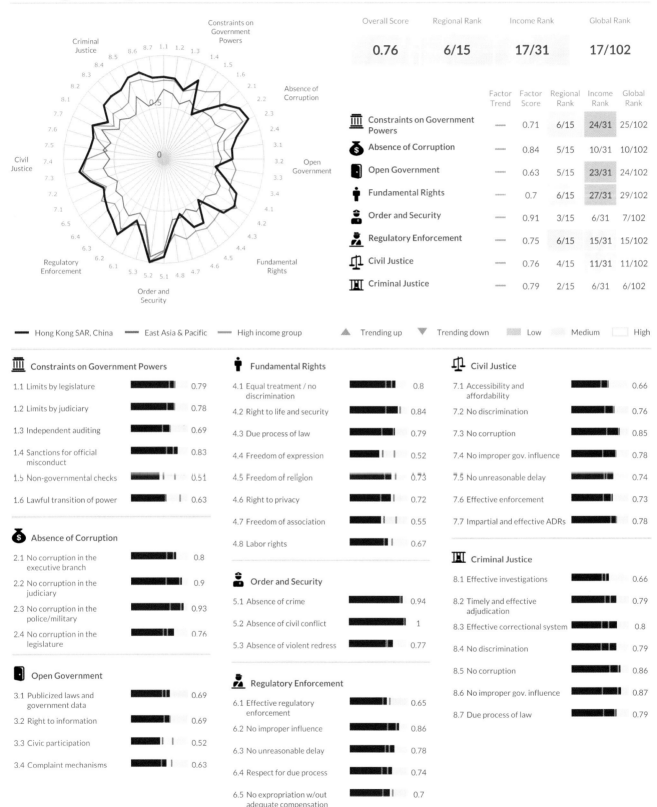

	Factor Trend	Factor Score	Regional Rank	Income Rank	Global Rank
Constraints on Government Powers	—	0.71	6/15	24/31	25/102
Absence of Corruption	—	0.84	5/15	10/31	10/102
Open Government	—	0.63	5/15	23/31	24/102
Fundamental Rights	—	0.7	6/15	27/31	29/102
Order and Security	—	0.91	3/15	6/31	7/102
Regulatory Enforcement	—	0.75	6/15	15/31	15/102
Civil Justice	—	0.76	4/15	11/31	11/102
Criminal Justice	—	0.79	2/15	6/31	6/102

— Hong Kong SAR, China   ▬ ▬ East Asia & Pacific   — High income group   ▲ Trending up   ▼ Trending down   ▒ Low   ░ Medium   ☐ High

Constraints on Government Powers

1.1 Limits by legislature	0.79
1.2 Limits by judiciary	0.78
1.3 Independent auditing	0.69
1.4 Sanctions for official misconduct	0.83
1.5 Non-governmental checks	0.51
1.6 Lawful transition of power	0.63

Absence of Corruption

2.1 No corruption in the executive branch	0.8
2.2 No corruption in the judiciary	0.9
2.3 No corruption in the police/military	0.93
2.4 No corruption in the legislature	0.76

Open Government

3.1 Publicized laws and government data	0.69
3.2 Right to information	0.69
3.3 Civic participation	0.52
3.4 Complaint mechanisms	0.63

Fundamental Rights

4.1 Equal treatment / no discrimination	0.8
4.2 Right to life and security	0.84
4.3 Due process of law	0.79
4.4 Freedom of expression	0.52
4.5 Freedom of religion	0.73
4.6 Right to privacy	0.72
4.7 Freedom of association	0.55
4.8 Labor rights	0.67

Order and Security

5.1 Absence of crime	0.94
5.2 Absence of civil conflict	1
5.3 Absence of violent redress	0.77

Regulatory Enforcement

6.1 Effective regulatory enforcement	0.65
6.2 No improper influence	0.86
6.3 No unreasonable delay	0.78
6.4 Respect for due process	0.74
6.5 No expropriation w/out adequate compensation	0.7

Civil Justice

7.1 Accessibility and affordability	0.66
7.2 No discrimination	0.76
7.3 No corruption	0.85
7.4 No improper gov. influence	0.78
7.5 No unreasonable delay	0.74
7.6 Effective enforcement	0.73
7.7 Impartial and effective ADRs	0.78

Criminal Justice

8.1 Effective investigations	0.66
8.2 Timely and effective adjudication	0.79
8.3 Effective correctional system	0.8
8.4 No discrimination	0.79
8.5 No corruption	0.86
8.6 No improper gov. influence	0.87
8.7 Due process of law	0.79

Hungary

Budapest, Debrecen, Szeged

Region: **EU + EFTA + North America** | Income group: **Upper middle income**

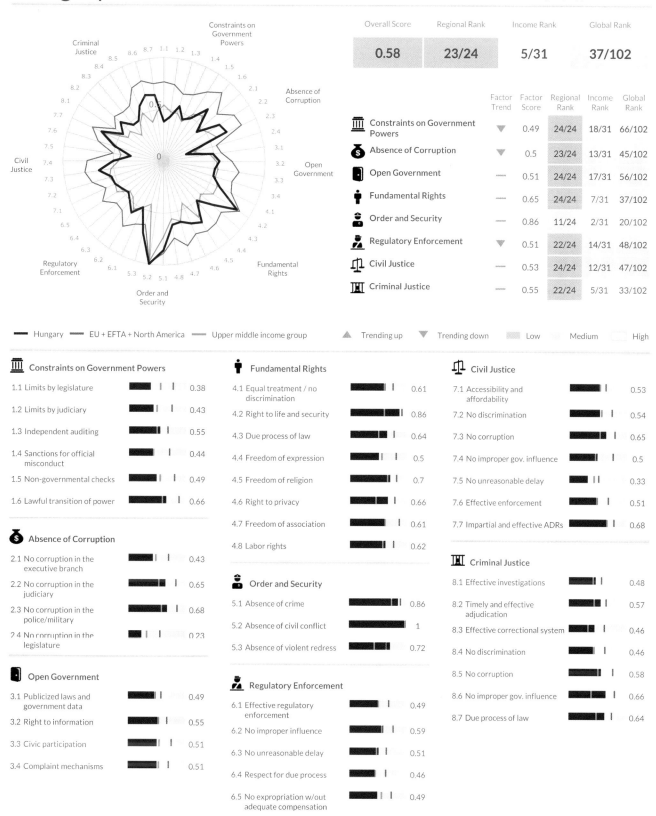

	Overall Score	Regional Rank	Income Rank	Global Rank
	0.58	23/24	5/31	37/102

		Factor Trend	Factor Score	Regional Rank	Income Rank	Global Rank
🏛	Constraints on Government Powers	▼	0.49	24/24	18/31	66/102
💰	Absence of Corruption	▼	0.5	23/24	13/31	45/102
📱	Open Government	—	0.51	24/24	17/31	56/102
👤	Fundamental Rights	—	0.65	24/24	7/31	37/102
👮	Order and Security	—	0.86	11/24	2/31	20/102
⚖	Regulatory Enforcement	▼	0.51	22/24	14/31	48/102
⚖	Civil Justice	—	0.53	24/24	12/31	47/102
🏛	Criminal Justice	—	0.55	22/24	5/31	33/102

— Hungary   — EU + EFTA + North America   — Upper middle income group   ▲ Trending up   ▼ Trending down   ▦ Low   Medium   High

🏛 Constraints on Government Powers

1.1 Limits by legislature	0.38
1.2 Limits by judiciary	0.43
1.3 Independent auditing	0.55
1.4 Sanctions for official misconduct	0.44
1.5 Non-governmental checks	0.49
1.6 Lawful transition of power	0.66

💰 Absence of Corruption

2.1 No corruption in the executive branch	0.43
2.2 No corruption in the judiciary	0.65
2.3 No corruption in the police/military	0.68
2.4 No corruption in the legislature	0.23

📱 Open Government

3.1 Publicized laws and government data	0.49
3.2 Right to information	0.55
3.3 Civic participation	0.51
3.4 Complaint mechanisms	0.51

👤 Fundamental Rights

4.1 Equal treatment / no discrimination	0.61
4.2 Right to life and security	0.86
4.3 Due process of law	0.64
4.4 Freedom of expression	0.5
4.5 Freedom of religion	0.7
4.6 Right to privacy	0.66
4.7 Freedom of association	0.61
4.8 Labor rights	0.62

👮 Order and Security

5.1 Absence of crime	0.86
5.2 Absence of civil conflict	1
5.3 Absence of violent redress	0.72

⚖ Regulatory Enforcement

6.1 Effective regulatory enforcement	0.49
6.2 No improper influence	0.59
6.3 No unreasonable delay	0.51
6.4 Respect for due process	0.46
6.5 No expropriation w/out adequate compensation	0.49

⚖ Civil Justice

7.1 Accessibility and affordability	0.53
7.2 No discrimination	0.54
7.3 No corruption	0.65
7.4 No improper gov. influence	0.5
7.5 No unreasonable delay	0.33
7.6 Effective enforcement	0.51
7.7 Impartial and effective ADRs	0.68

🏛 Criminal Justice

8.1 Effective investigations	0.48
8.2 Timely and effective adjudication	0.57
8.3 Effective correctional system	0.46
8.4 No discrimination	0.46
8.5 No corruption	0.58
8.6 No improper gov. influence	0.66
8.7 Due process of law	0.64

India

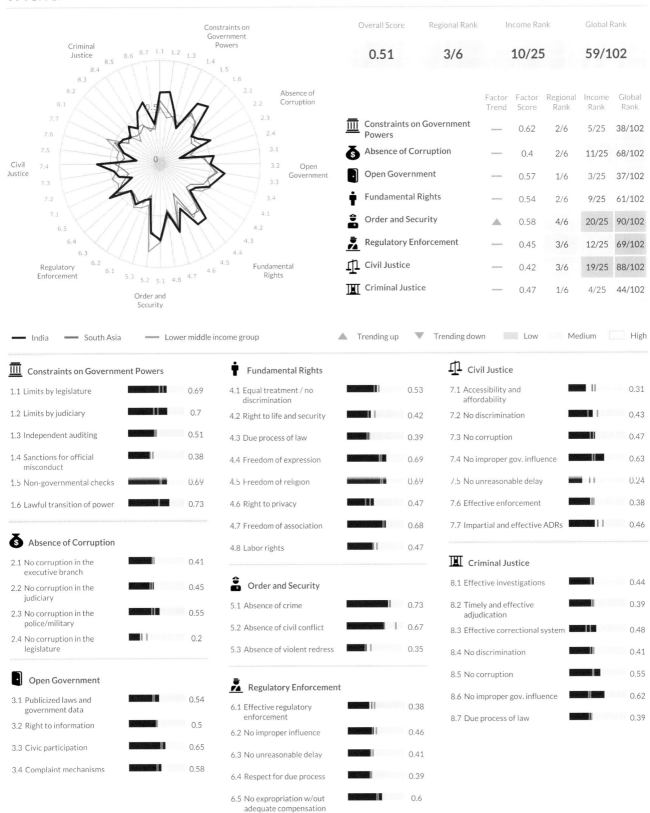

	Overall Score	Regional Rank	Income Rank	Global Rank
	0.51	3/6	10/25	59/102

		Factor Trend	Factor Score	Regional Rank	Income Rank	Global Rank
🏛	Constraints on Government Powers	—	0.62	2/6	5/25	38/102
💰	Absence of Corruption	—	0.4	2/6	11/25	68/102
📖	Open Government	—	0.57	1/6	3/25	37/102
👤	Fundamental Rights	—	0.54	2/6	9/25	61/102
👮	Order and Security	▲	0.58	4/6	20/25	90/102
📋	Regulatory Enforcement	—	0.45	3/6	12/25	69/102
⚖	Civil Justice	—	0.42	3/6	19/25	88/102
🏛	Criminal Justice	—	0.47	1/6	4/25	44/102

—— India   ···· South Asia   —— Lower middle income group   ▲ Trending up   ▼ Trending down   ▨ Low   Medium   ☐ High

🏛 Constraints on Government Powers

1.1 Limits by legislature	0.69
1.2 Limits by judiciary	0.7
1.3 Independent auditing	0.51
1.4 Sanctions for official misconduct	0.38
1.5 Non-governmental checks	0.69
1.6 Lawful transition of power	0.73

💰 Absence of Corruption

2.1 No corruption in the executive branch	0.41
2.2 No corruption in the judiciary	0.45
2.3 No corruption in the police/military	0.55
2.4 No corruption in the legislature	0.2

📖 Open Government

3.1 Publicized laws and government data	0.54
3.2 Right to information	0.5
3.3 Civic participation	0.65
3.4 Complaint mechanisms	0.58

👤 Fundamental Rights

4.1 Equal treatment / no discrimination	0.53
4.2 Right to life and security	0.42
4.3 Due process of law	0.39
4.4 Freedom of expression	0.69
4.5 Freedom of religion	0.69
4.6 Right to privacy	0.47
4.7 Freedom of association	0.68
4.8 Labor rights	0.47

👮 Order and Security

5.1 Absence of crime	0.73
5.2 Absence of civil conflict	0.67
5.3 Absence of violent redress	0.35

📋 Regulatory Enforcement

6.1 Effective regulatory enforcement	0.38
6.2 No improper influence	0.46
6.3 No unreasonable delay	0.41
6.4 Respect for due process	0.39
6.5 No expropriation w/out adequate compensation	0.6

⚖ Civil Justice

7.1 Accessibility and affordability	0.31
7.2 No discrimination	0.43
7.3 No corruption	0.47
7.4 No improper gov. influence	0.63
7.5 No unreasonable delay	0.24
7.6 Effective enforcement	0.38
7.7 Impartial and effective ADRs	0.46

🏛 Criminal Justice

8.1 Effective investigations	0.44
8.2 Timely and effective adjudication	0.39
8.3 Effective correctional system	0.48
8.4 No discrimination	0.41
8.5 No corruption	0.55
8.6 No improper gov. influence	0.62
8.7 Due process of law	0.39

Indonesia

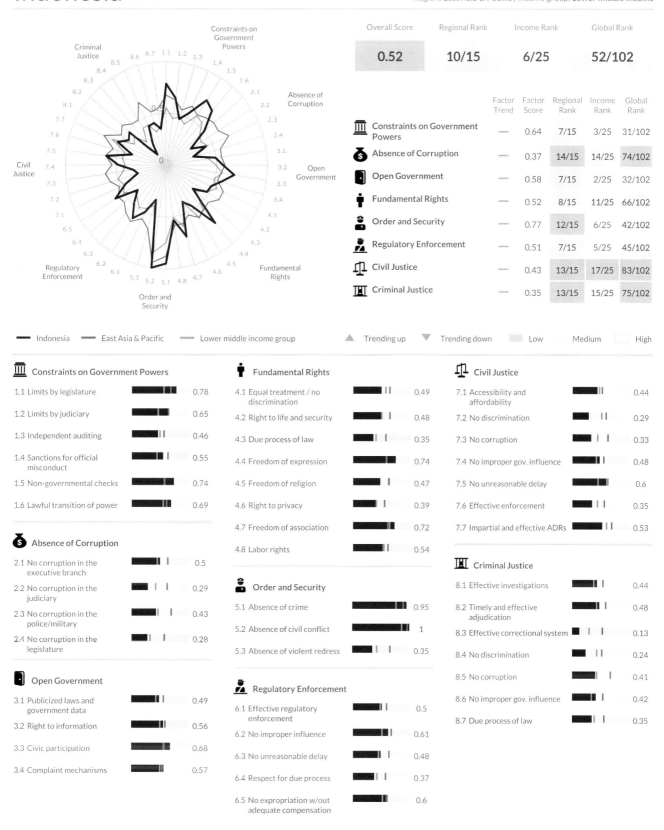

	Overall Score	Regional Rank	Income Rank	Global Rank
	0.52	10/15	6/25	52/102

		Factor Trend	Factor Score	Regional Rank	Income Rank	Global Rank
🏛	Constraints on Government Powers	—	0.64	7/15	3/25	31/102
💰	Absence of Corruption	—	0.37	14/15	14/25	74/102
📱	Open Government	—	0.58	7/15	2/25	32/102
👤	Fundamental Rights	—	0.52	8/15	11/25	66/102
👮	Order and Security	—	0.77	12/15	6/25	42/102
🛡	Regulatory Enforcement	—	0.51	7/15	5/25	45/102
⚖	Civil Justice	—	0.43	13/15	17/25	83/102
⚖	Criminal Justice	—	0.35	13/15	15/25	75/102

━━ Indonesia ━━ East Asia & Pacific ━━ Lower middle income group ▲ Trending up ▼ Trending down ▨ Low Medium High

🏛 Constraints on Government Powers

1.1 Limits by legislature	0.78
1.2 Limits by judiciary	0.65
1.3 Independent auditing	0.46
1.4 Sanctions for official misconduct	0.55
1.5 Non-governmental checks	0.74
1.6 Lawful transition of power	0.69

💰 Absence of Corruption

2.1 No corruption in the executive branch	0.5
2.2 No corruption in the judiciary	0.29
2.3 No corruption in the police/military	0.43
2.4 No corruption in the legislature	0.28

📱 Open Government

3.1 Publicized laws and government data	0.49
3.2 Right to information	0.56
3.3 Civic participation	0.68
3.4 Complaint mechanisms	0.57

👤 Fundamental Rights

4.1 Equal treatment / no discrimination	0.49
4.2 Right to life and security	0.48
4.3 Due process of law	0.35
4.4 Freedom of expression	0.74
4.5 Freedom of religion	0.47
4.6 Right to privacy	0.39
4.7 Freedom of association	0.72
4.8 Labor rights	0.54

👮 Order and Security

5.1 Absence of crime	0.95
5.2 Absence of civil conflict	1
5.3 Absence of violent redress	0.35

🛡 Regulatory Enforcement

6.1 Effective regulatory enforcement	0.5
6.2 No improper influence	0.61
6.3 No unreasonable delay	0.48
6.4 Respect for due process	0.37
6.5 No expropriation w/out adequate compensation	0.6

⚖ Civil Justice

7.1 Accessibility and affordability	0.44
7.2 No discrimination	0.29
7.3 No corruption	0.33
7.4 No improper gov. influence	0.48
7.5 No unreasonable delay	0.6
7.6 Effective enforcement	0.35
7.7 Impartial and effective ADRs	0.53

⚖ Criminal Justice

8.1 Effective investigations	0.44
8.2 Timely and effective adjudication	0.48
8.3 Effective correctional system	0.13
8.4 No discrimination	0.24
8.5 No corruption	0.41
8.6 No improper gov. influence	0.42
8.7 Due process of law	0.35

Iran

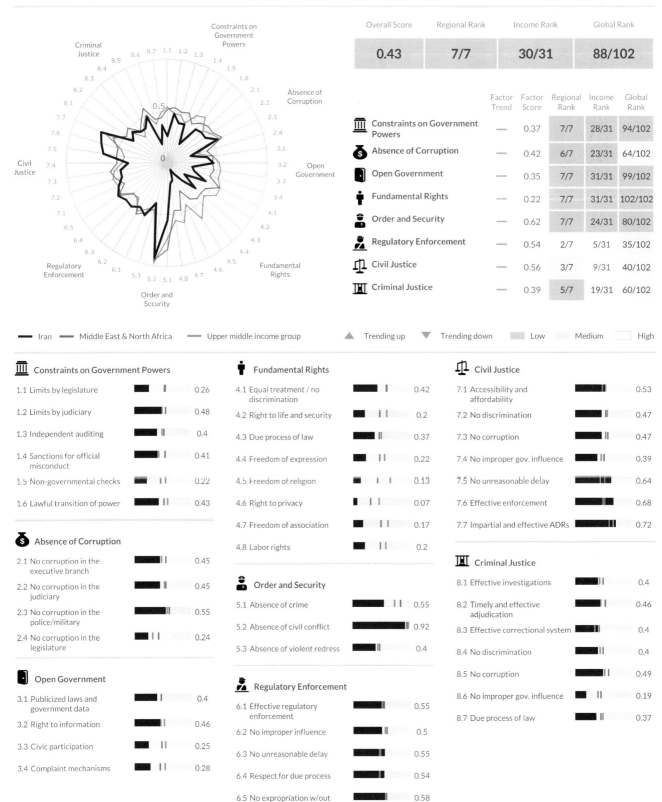

	Overall Score	Regional Rank	Income Rank	Global Rank
	0.43	7/7	30/31	88/102

		Factor Trend	Factor Score	Regional Rank	Income Rank	Global Rank
🏛	Constraints on Government Powers	—	0.37	7/7	28/31	94/102
💰	Absence of Corruption	—	0.42	6/7	23/31	64/102
📋	Open Government	—	0.35	7/7	31/31	99/102
👤	Fundamental Rights	—	0.22	7/7	31/31	102/102
👮	Order and Security	—	0.62	7/7	24/31	80/102
🗂	Regulatory Enforcement	—	0.54	2/7	5/31	35/102
⚖	Civil Justice	—	0.56	3/7	9/31	40/102
🏛	Criminal Justice	—	0.39	5/7	19/31	60/102

— Iran — Middle East & North Africa — Upper middle income group ▲ Trending up ▼ Trending down ▦ Low Medium ☐ High

🏛 Constraints on Government Powers

1.1 Limits by legislature		0.26
1.2 Limits by judiciary		0.48
1.3 Independent auditing		0.4
1.4 Sanctions for official misconduct		0.41
1.5 Non-governmental checks		0.22
1.6 Lawful transition of power		0.43

💰 Absence of Corruption

2.1 No corruption in the executive branch		0.45
2.2 No corruption in the judiciary		0.45
2.3 No corruption in the police/military		0.55
2.4 No corruption in the legislature		0.24

📋 Open Government

3.1 Publicized laws and government data		0.4
3.2 Right to information		0.46
3.3 Civic participation		0.25
3.4 Complaint mechanisms		0.28

👤 Fundamental Rights

4.1 Equal treatment / no discrimination		0.42
4.2 Right to life and security		0.2
4.3 Due process of law		0.37
4.4 Freedom of expression		0.22
4.5 Freedom of religion		0.13
4.6 Right to privacy		0.07
4.7 Freedom of association		0.17
4.8 Labor rights		0.2

👮 Order and Security

5.1 Absence of crime		0.55
5.2 Absence of civil conflict		0.92
5.3 Absence of violent redress		0.4

🗂 Regulatory Enforcement

6.1 Effective regulatory enforcement		0.55
6.2 No improper influence		0.5
6.3 No unreasonable delay		0.55
6.4 Respect for due process		0.54
6.5 No expropriation w/out adequate compensation		0.58

⚖ Civil Justice

7.1 Accessibility and affordability		0.53
7.2 No discrimination		0.47
7.3 No corruption		0.47
7.4 No improper gov. influence		0.39
7.5 No unreasonable delay		0.64
7.6 Effective enforcement		0.68
7.7 Impartial and effective ADRs		0.72

🏛 Criminal Justice

8.1 Effective investigations		0.4
8.2 Timely and effective adjudication		0.46
8.3 Effective correctional system		0.4
8.4 No discrimination		0.4
8.5 No corruption		0.49
8.6 No improper gov. influence		0.19
8.7 Due process of law		0.37

Italy

	Overall Score	Regional Rank	Income Rank	Global Rank
	0.64	19/24	28/31	30/102

		Factor Trend	Factor Score	Regional Rank	Income Rank	Global Rank
🏛	Constraints on Government Powers	—	0.69	18/24	26/31	27/102
💰	Absence of Corruption	—	0.59	19/24	28/31	33/102
📱	Open Government	—	0.61	18/24	26/31	28/102
👤	Fundamental Rights	—	0.74	18/24	22/31	23/102
👮	Order and Security	—	0.74	24/24	28/31	53/102
🏗	Regulatory Enforcement	—	0.56	19/24	28/31	32/102
⚖	Civil Justice	—	0.58	21/24	29/31	36/102
🏛	Criminal Justice	—	0.63	18/24	25/31	25/102

— Italy   — EU + EFTA + North America   — High income group   ▲ Trending up   ▼ Trending down   ▧ Low   ▨ Medium   ▢ High

🏛 Constraints on Government Powers

1.1 Limits by legislature	0.72
1.2 Limits by judiciary	0.7
1.3 Independent auditing	0.63
1.4 Sanctions for official misconduct	0.55
1.5 Non-governmental checks	0.74
1.6 Lawful transition of power	0.81

💰 Absence of Corruption

2.1 No corruption in the executive branch	0.55
2.2 No corruption in the judiciary	0.74
2.3 No corruption in the police/military	0.84
2.4 No corruption in the legislature	0.24

📱 Open Government

3.1 Publicized laws and government data	0.58
3.2 Right to information	0.59
3.3 Civic participation	0.69
3.4 Complaint mechanisms	0.58

👤 Fundamental Rights

4.1 Equal treatment / no discrimination	0.65
4.2 Right to life and security	0.91
4.3 Due process of law	0.69
4.4 Freedom of expression	0.75
4.5 Freedom of religion	0.79
4.6 Right to privacy	0.77
4.7 Freedom of association	0.82
4.8 Labor rights	0.58

👮 Order and Security

5.1 Absence of crime	0.83
5.2 Absence of civil conflict	1
5.3 Absence of violent redress	0.4

🏗 Regulatory Enforcement

6.1 Effective regulatory enforcement	0.56
6.2 No improper influence	0.66
6.3 No unreasonable delay	0.43
6.4 Respect for due process	0.53
6.5 No expropriation w/out adequate compensation	0.64

⚖ Civil Justice

7.1 Accessibility and affordability	0.62
7.2 No discrimination	0.61
7.3 No corruption	0.68
7.4 No improper gov. influence	0.72
7.5 No unreasonable delay	0.32
7.6 Effective enforcement	0.4
7.7 Impartial and effective ADRs	0.69

🏛 Criminal Justice

8.1 Effective investigations	0.51
8.2 Timely and effective adjudication	0.56
8.3 Effective correctional system	0.44
8.4 No discrimination	0.58
8.5 No corruption	0.73
8.6 No improper gov. influence	0.87
8.7 Due process of law	0.69

Jamaica

	Overall Score	Regional Rank	Income Rank	Global Rank
	0.56	4/19	9/31	42/102

	Factor Trend	Factor Score	Regional Rank	Income Rank	Global Rank
🏛 Constraints on Government Powers	—	0.61	4/19	6/31	41/102
💰 Absence of Corruption	▲	0.53	4/19	5/31	37/102
📗 Open Government	—	0.51	12/19	18/31	57/102
👤 Fundamental Rights	—	0.66	5/19	5/31	34/102
👮 Order and Security	—	0.69	5/19	18/31	64/102
👨‍💼 Regulatory Enforcement	—	0.53	5/19	8/31	40/102
⚖ Civil Justice	—	0.52	6/19	16/31	52/102
🏛 Criminal Justice	—	0.46	4/19	11/31	45/102

— Jamaica ···· Latin America & the Caribbean — Upper middle income group

▲ Trending up ▼ Trending down ▨ Low ░ Medium ☐ High

🏛 Constraints on Government Powers

1.1 Limits by legislature	0.68
1.2 Limits by judiciary	0.71
1.3 Independent auditing	0.4
1.4 Sanctions for official misconduct	0.46
1.5 Non-governmental checks	0.72
1.6 Lawful transition of power	0.7

💰 Absence of Corruption

2.1 No corruption in the executive branch	0.51
2.2 No corruption in the judiciary	0.63
2.3 No corruption in the police/military	0.63
2.4 No corruption in the legislature	0.36

📗 Open Government

3.1 Publicized laws and government data	0.38
3.2 Right to information	0.48
3.3 Civic participation	0.65
3.4 Complaint mechanisms	0.53

👤 Fundamental Rights

4.1 Equal treatment / no discrimination	0.64
4.2 Right to life and security	0.57
4.3 Due process of law	0.44
4.4 Freedom of expression	0.73
4.5 Freedom of religion	0.91
4.6 Right to privacy	0.61
4.7 Freedom of association	0.77
4.8 Labor rights	0.59

👮 Order and Security

5.1 Absence of crime	0.8
5.2 Absence of civil conflict	1
5.3 Absence of violent redress	0.29

👨‍💼 Regulatory Enforcement

6.1 Effective regulatory enforcement	0.5
6.2 No improper influence	0.71
6.3 No unreasonable delay	0.35
6.4 Respect for due process	0.44
6.5 No expropriation w/out adequate compensation	0.64

⚖ Civil Justice

7.1 Accessibility and affordability	0.47
7.2 No discrimination	0.48
7.3 No corruption	0.68
7.4 No improper gov. influence	0.7
7.5 No unreasonable delay	0.33
7.6 Effective enforcement	0.35
7.7 Impartial and effective ADRs	0.6

🏛 Criminal Justice

8.1 Effective investigations	0.4
8.2 Timely and effective adjudication	0.41
8.3 Effective correctional system	0.23
8.4 No discrimination	0.33
8.5 No corruption	0.62
8.6 No improper gov. influence	0.75
8.7 Due process of law	0.44

Japan

Tokyo, Yokohama, Osaka
Region: **East Asia & Pacific** | Income group: **High income**

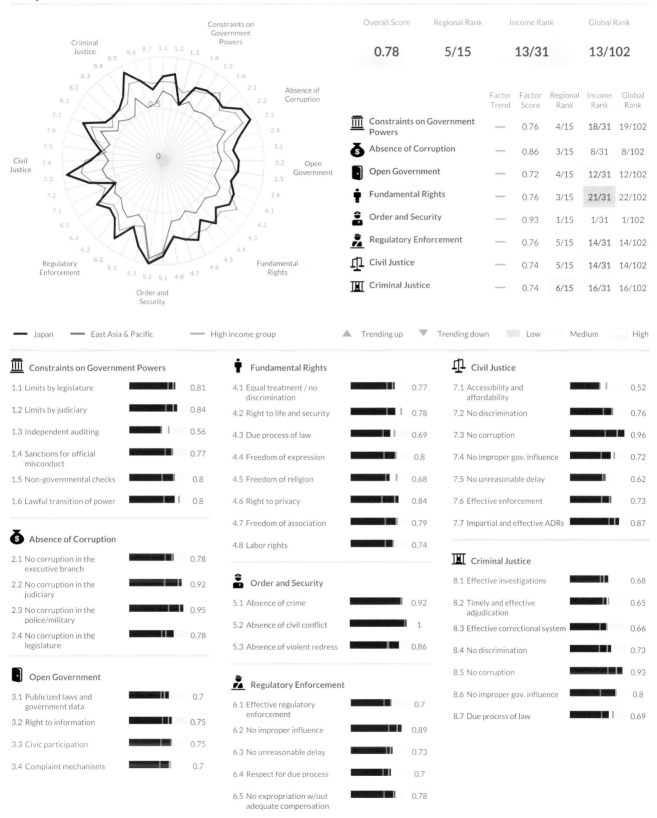

	Overall Score	Regional Rank	Income Rank	Global Rank
	0.78	**5/15**	**13/31**	**13/102**

		Factor Trend	Factor Score	Regional Rank	Income Rank	Global Rank
🏛	Constraints on Government Powers	—	0.76	4/15	18/31	19/102
💰	Absence of Corruption	—	0.86	3/15	8/31	8/102
📖	Open Government	—	0.72	4/15	12/31	12/102
👤	Fundamental Rights	—	0.76	3/15	21/31	22/102
👮	Order and Security	—	0.93	1/15	1/31	1/102
👨‍⚖	Regulatory Enforcement	—	0.76	5/15	14/31	14/102
⚖	Civil Justice	—	0.74	5/15	14/31	14/102
🏛	Criminal Justice	—	0.74	6/15	16/31	16/102

— Japan   ▬ East Asia & Pacific   — High income group   ▲ Trending up   ▼ Trending down   ▓ Low   Medium   High

🏛 Constraints on Government Powers

1.1 Limits by legislature	0.81
1.2 Limits by judiciary	0.84
1.3 Independent auditing	0.56
1.4 Sanctions for official misconduct	0.77
1.5 Non-governmental checks	0.8
1.6 Lawful transition of power	0.8

💰 Absence of Corruption

2.1 No corruption in the executive branch	0.78
2.2 No corruption in the judiciary	0.92
2.3 No corruption in the police/military	0.95
2.4 No corruption in the legislature	0.78

📖 Open Government

3.1 Publicized laws and government data	0.7
3.2 Right to information	0.75
3.3 Civic participation	0.75
3.4 Complaint mechanisms	0.7

👤 Fundamental Rights

4.1 Equal treatment / no discrimination	0.77
4.2 Right to life and security	0.78
4.3 Due process of law	0.69
4.4 Freedom of expression	0.8
4.5 Freedom of religion	0.68
4.6 Right to privacy	0.84
4.7 Freedom of association	0.79
4.8 Labor rights	0.74

👮 Order and Security

5.1 Absence of crime	0.92
5.2 Absence of civil conflict	1
5.3 Absence of violent redress	0.86

👨‍⚖ Regulatory Enforcement

6.1 Effective regulatory enforcement	0.7
6.2 No improper influence	0.89
6.3 No unreasonable delay	0.73
6.4 Respect for due process	0.7
6.5 No expropriation w/out adequate compensation	0.78

⚖ Civil Justice

7.1 Accessibility and affordability	0.52
7.2 No discrimination	0.76
7.3 No corruption	0.96
7.4 No improper gov. influence	0.72
7.5 No unreasonable delay	0.62
7.6 Effective enforcement	0.73
7.7 Impartial and effective ADRs	0.87

🏛 Criminal Justice

8.1 Effective investigations	0.68
8.2 Timely and effective adjudication	0.65
8.3 Effective correctional system	0.66
8.4 No discrimination	0.73
8.5 No corruption	0.93
8.6 No improper gov. influence	0.8
8.7 Due process of law	0.69

Jordan

Amman, Irbid, Zarqa

Region: **Middle East & North Africa** | Income group: **Upper middle income**

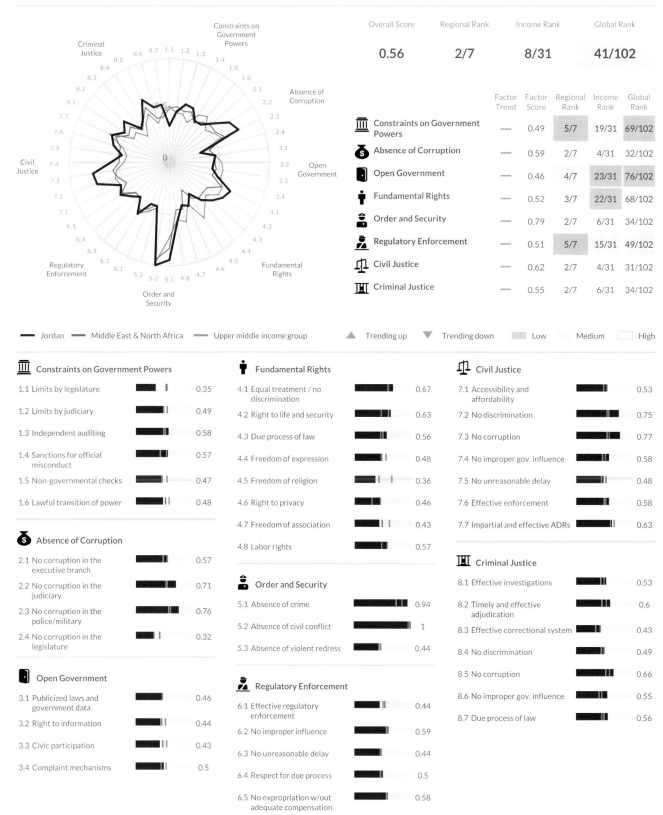

	Overall Score	Regional Rank	Income Rank	Global Rank
	0.56	2/7	8/31	41/102

	Factor Trend	Factor Score	Regional Rank	Income Rank	Global Rank
Constraints on Government Powers	—	0.49	5/7	19/31	69/102
Absence of Corruption	—	0.59	2/7	4/31	32/102
Open Government	—	0.46	4/7	23/31	76/102
Fundamental Rights	—	0.52	3/7	22/31	68/102
Order and Security	—	0.79	2/7	6/31	34/102
Regulatory Enforcement	—	0.51	5/7	15/31	49/102
Civil Justice	—	0.62	2/7	4/31	31/102
Criminal Justice	—	0.55	2/7	6/31	34/102

— Jordan — Middle East & North Africa — Upper middle income group ▲ Trending up ▼ Trending down ▨ Low ▨ Medium ▢ High

Constraints on Government Powers

1.1 Limits by legislature	0.35
1.2 Limits by judiciary	0.49
1.3 Independent auditing	0.58
1.4 Sanctions for official misconduct	0.57
1.5 Non-governmental checks	0.47
1.6 Lawful transition of power	0.48

Absence of Corruption

2.1 No corruption in the executive branch	0.57
2.2 No corruption in the judiciary	0.71
2.3 No corruption in the police/military	0.76
2.4 No corruption in the legislature	0.32

Open Government

3.1 Publicized laws and government data	0.46
3.2 Right to information	0.44
3.3 Civic participation	0.43
3.4 Complaint mechanisms	0.5

Fundamental Rights

4.1 Equal treatment / no discrimination	0.67
4.2 Right to life and security	0.63
4.3 Due process of law	0.56
4.4 Freedom of expression	0.48
4.5 Freedom of religion	0.36
4.6 Right to privacy	0.46
4.7 Freedom of association	0.43
4.8 Labor rights	0.57

Order and Security

5.1 Absence of crime	0.94
5.2 Absence of civil conflict	1
5.3 Absence of violent redress	0.44

Regulatory Enforcement

6.1 Effective regulatory enforcement	0.44
6.2 No improper influence	0.59
6.3 No unreasonable delay	0.44
6.4 Respect for due process	0.5
6.5 No expropriation w/out adequate compensation	0.58

Civil Justice

7.1 Accessibility and affordability	0.53
7.2 No discrimination	0.75
7.3 No corruption	0.77
7.4 No improper gov. influence	0.58
7.5 No unreasonable delay	0.48
7.6 Effective enforcement	0.58
7.7 Impartial and effective ADRs	0.63

Criminal Justice

8.1 Effective investigations	0.53
8.2 Timely and effective adjudication	0.6
8.3 Effective correctional system	0.43
8.4 No discrimination	0.49
8.5 No corruption	0.66
8.6 No improper gov. influence	0.55
8.7 Due process of law	0.56

Complete country profiles available at: data.worldjusticeproject.org

Kazakhstan

Almaty, Astana, Shymkent
Region: **Eastern Europe & Central Asia** | Income group: **Upper middle income**

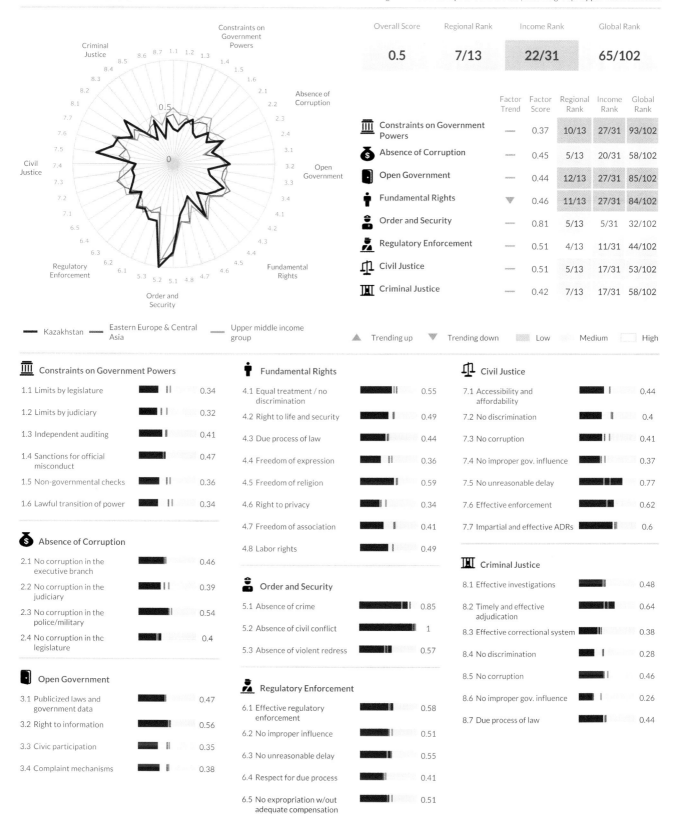

	Overall Score	Regional Rank	Income Rank	Global Rank
	0.5	7/13	22/31	65/102

		Factor Trend	Factor Score	Regional Rank	Income Rank	Global Rank
🏛	Constraints on Government Powers	—	0.37	10/13	27/31	93/102
💰	Absence of Corruption	—	0.45	5/13	20/31	58/102
📖	Open Government	—	0.44	12/13	27/31	85/102
👤	Fundamental Rights	▼	0.46	11/13	27/31	84/102
👮	Order and Security	—	0.81	5/13	5/31	32/102
🛡	Regulatory Enforcement	—	0.51	4/13	11/31	44/102
⚖	Civil Justice	—	0.51	5/13	17/31	53/102
⚖	Criminal Justice	—	0.42	7/13	17/31	58/102

— Kazakhstan   — Eastern Europe & Central Asia   — Upper middle income group

▲ Trending up   ▼ Trending down   ▦ Low   Medium   ☐ High

🏛 Constraints on Government Powers

1.1 Limits by legislature	0.34
1.2 Limits by judiciary	0.32
1.3 Independent auditing	0.41
1.4 Sanctions for official misconduct	0.47
1.5 Non-governmental checks	0.36
1.6 Lawful transition of power	0.34

💰 Absence of Corruption

2.1 No corruption in the executive branch	0.46
2.2 No corruption in the judiciary	0.39
2.3 No corruption in the police/military	0.54
2.4 No corruption in the legislature	0.4

📖 Open Government

3.1 Publicized laws and government data	0.47
3.2 Right to information	0.56
3.3 Civic participation	0.35
3.4 Complaint mechanisms	0.38

👤 Fundamental Rights

4.1 Equal treatment / no discrimination	0.55
4.2 Right to life and security	0.49
4.3 Due process of law	0.44
4.4 Freedom of expression	0.36
4.5 Freedom of religion	0.59
4.6 Right to privacy	0.34
4.7 Freedom of association	0.41
4.8 Labor rights	0.49

👮 Order and Security

5.1 Absence of crime	0.85
5.2 Absence of civil conflict	1
5.3 Absence of violent redress	0.57

🛡 Regulatory Enforcement

6.1 Effective regulatory enforcement	0.58
6.2 No improper influence	0.51
6.3 No unreasonable delay	0.55
6.4 Respect for due process	0.41
6.5 No expropriation w/out adequate compensation	0.51

⚖ Civil Justice

7.1 Accessibility and affordability	0.44
7.2 No discrimination	0.4
7.3 No corruption	0.41
7.4 No improper gov. influence	0.37
7.5 No unreasonable delay	0.77
7.6 Effective enforcement	0.62
7.7 Impartial and effective ADRs	0.6

⚖ Criminal Justice

8.1 Effective investigations	0.48
8.2 Timely and effective adjudication	0.64
8.3 Effective correctional system	0.38
8.4 No discrimination	0.28
8.5 No corruption	0.46
8.6 No improper gov. influence	0.26
8.7 Due process of law	0.44

Kenya

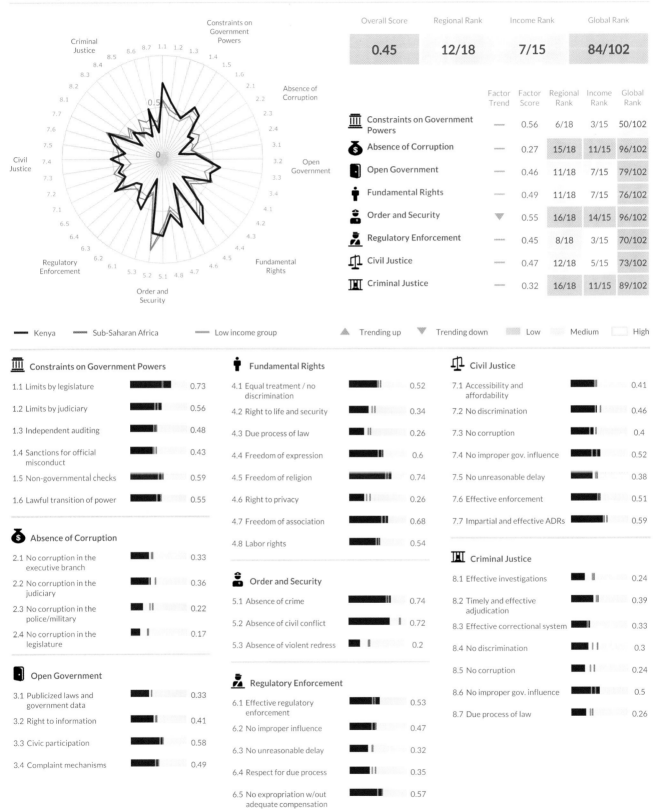

	Overall Score	Regional Rank	Income Rank	Global Rank
	0.45	12/18	7/15	84/102

		Factor Trend	Factor Score	Regional Rank	Income Rank	Global Rank
🏛	Constraints on Government Powers	—	0.56	6/18	3/15	50/102
💰	Absence of Corruption	—	0.27	15/18	11/15	96/102
📋	Open Government	—	0.46	11/18	7/15	79/102
👤	Fundamental Rights	—	0.49	11/18	7/15	76/102
👮	Order and Security	▼	0.55	16/18	14/15	96/102
🗂	Regulatory Enforcement	⋯	0.45	8/18	3/15	70/102
⚖	Civil Justice	—	0.47	12/18	5/15	73/102
🏛	Criminal Justice	—	0.32	16/18	11/15	89/102

━━ Kenya　　━━ Sub-Saharan Africa　　━━ Low income group　　▲ Trending up　　▼ Trending down　　Low　　Medium　　High

🏛 Constraints on Government Powers

1.1 Limits by legislature	0.73
1.2 Limits by judiciary	0.56
1.3 Independent auditing	0.48
1.4 Sanctions for official misconduct	0.43
1.5 Non-governmental checks	0.59
1.6 Lawful transition of power	0.55

💰 Absence of Corruption

2.1 No corruption in the executive branch	0.33
2.2 No corruption in the judiciary	0.36
2.3 No corruption in the police/military	0.22
2.4 No corruption in the legislature	0.17

📋 Open Government

3.1 Publicized laws and government data	0.33
3.2 Right to information	0.41
3.3 Civic participation	0.58
3.4 Complaint mechanisms	0.49

👤 Fundamental Rights

4.1 Equal treatment / no discrimination	0.52
4.2 Right to life and security	0.34
4.3 Due process of law	0.26
4.4 Freedom of expression	0.6
4.5 Freedom of religion	0.74
4.6 Right to privacy	0.26
4.7 Freedom of association	0.68
4.8 Labor rights	0.54

👮 Order and Security

5.1 Absence of crime	0.74
5.2 Absence of civil conflict	0.72
5.3 Absence of violent redress	0.2

🗂 Regulatory Enforcement

6.1 Effective regulatory enforcement	0.53
6.2 No improper influence	0.47
6.3 No unreasonable delay	0.32
6.4 Respect for due process	0.35
6.5 No expropriation w/out adequate compensation	0.57

⚖ Civil Justice

7.1 Accessibility and affordability	0.41
7.2 No discrimination	0.46
7.3 No corruption	0.4
7.4 No improper gov. influence	0.52
7.5 No unreasonable delay	0.38
7.6 Effective enforcement	0.51
7.7 Impartial and effective ADRs	0.59

🏛 Criminal Justice

8.1 Effective investigations	0.24
8.2 Timely and effective adjudication	0.39
8.3 Effective correctional system	0.33
8.4 No discrimination	0.3
8.5 No corruption	0.24
8.6 No improper gov. influence	0.5
8.7 Due process of law	0.26

Kyrgyzstan

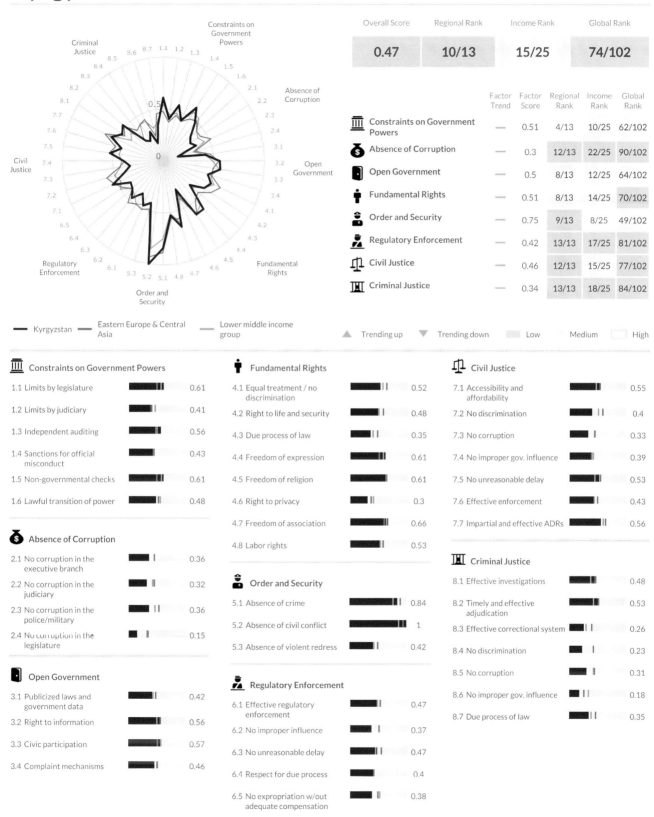

	Overall Score	Regional Rank	Income Rank	Global Rank
	0.47	10/13	15/25	74/102

		Factor Trend	Factor Score	Regional Rank	Income Rank	Global Rank
🏛	Constraints on Government Powers	—	0.51	4/13	10/25	62/102
💰	Absence of Corruption	—	0.3	12/13	22/25	90/102
📱	Open Government	—	0.5	8/13	12/25	64/102
🧍	Fundamental Rights	—	0.51	8/13	14/25	70/102
👮	Order and Security	—	0.75	9/13	8/25	49/102
💼	Regulatory Enforcement	—	0.42	13/13	17/25	81/102
⚖	Civil Justice	—	0.46	12/13	15/25	77/102
🏛	Criminal Justice	—	0.34	13/13	18/25	84/102

— Kyrgyzstan — Eastern Europe & Central Asia — Lower middle income group

▲ Trending up ▼ Trending down ▒ Low Medium ☐ High

🏛 Constraints on Government Powers

1.1 Limits by legislature	0.61
1.2 Limits by judiciary	0.41
1.3 Independent auditing	0.56
1.4 Sanctions for official misconduct	0.43
1.5 Non-governmental checks	0.61
1.6 Lawful transition of power	0.48

💰 Absence of Corruption

2.1 No corruption in the executive branch	0.36
2.2 No corruption in the judiciary	0.32
2.3 No corruption in the police/military	0.36
2.4 No corruption in the legislature	0.15

📱 Open Government

3.1 Publicized laws and government data	0.42
3.2 Right to information	0.56
3.3 Civic participation	0.57
3.4 Complaint mechanisms	0.46

🧍 Fundamental Rights

4.1 Equal treatment / no discrimination	0.52
4.2 Right to life and security	0.48
4.3 Due process of law	0.35
4.4 Freedom of expression	0.61
4.5 Freedom of religion	0.61
4.6 Right to privacy	0.3
4.7 Freedom of association	0.66
4.8 Labor rights	0.53

👮 Order and Security

5.1 Absence of crime	0.84
5.2 Absence of civil conflict	1
5.3 Absence of violent redress	0.42

💼 Regulatory Enforcement

6.1 Effective regulatory enforcement	0.47
6.2 No improper influence	0.37
6.3 No unreasonable delay	0.47
6.4 Respect for due process	0.4
6.5 No expropriation w/out adequate compensation	0.38

⚖ Civil Justice

7.1 Accessibility and affordability	0.55
7.2 No discrimination	0.4
7.3 No corruption	0.33
7.4 No improper gov. influence	0.39
7.5 No unreasonable delay	0.53
7.6 Effective enforcement	0.43
7.7 Impartial and effective ADRs	0.56

🏛 Criminal Justice

8.1 Effective investigations	0.48
8.2 Timely and effective adjudication	0.53
8.3 Effective correctional system	0.26
8.4 No discrimination	0.23
8.5 No corruption	0.31
8.6 No improper gov. influence	0.18
8.7 Due process of law	0.35

Lebanon

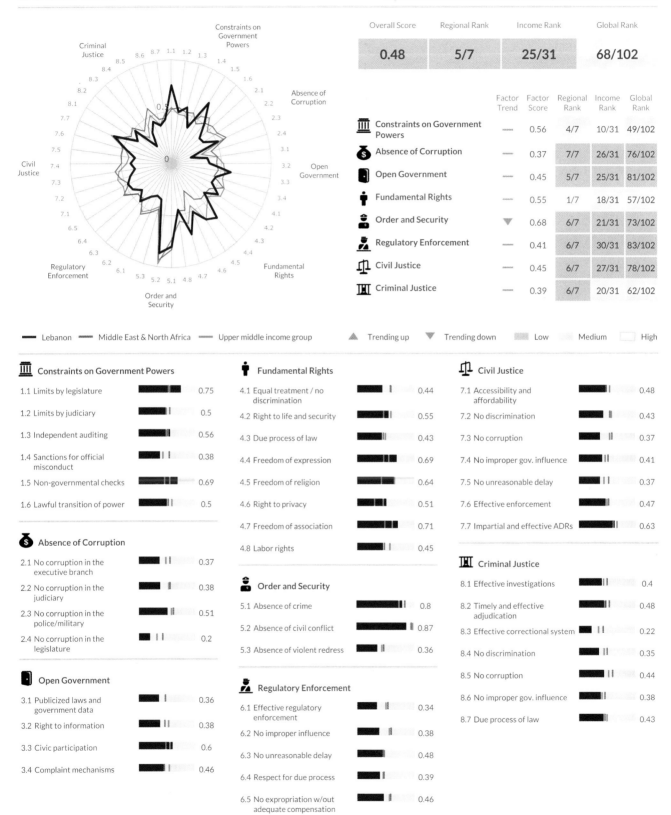

	Overall Score	Regional Rank	Income Rank	Global Rank
	0.48	5/7	25/31	68/102

		Factor Trend	Factor Score	Regional Rank	Income Rank	Global Rank
🏛	Constraints on Government Powers	—	0.56	4/7	10/31	49/102
💰	Absence of Corruption	—	0.37	7/7	26/31	76/102
📖	Open Government	—	0.45	5/7	25/31	81/102
👤	Fundamental Rights	—	0.55	1/7	18/31	57/102
👮	Order and Security	▼	0.68	6/7	21/31	73/102
🧑‍💼	Regulatory Enforcement	—	0.41	6/7	30/31	83/102
⚖	Civil Justice	—	0.45	6/7	27/31	78/102
🏛	Criminal Justice	—	0.39	6/7	20/31	62/102

— Lebanon   — Middle East & North Africa   — Upper middle income group   ▲ Trending up   ▼ Trending down   ▨ Low   ▨ Medium   ☐ High

🏛 Constraints on Government Powers

1.1 Limits by legislature	0.75
1.2 Limits by judiciary	0.5
1.3 Independent auditing	0.56
1.4 Sanctions for official misconduct	0.38
1.5 Non-governmental checks	0.69
1.6 Lawful transition of power	0.5

💰 Absence of Corruption

2.1 No corruption in the executive branch	0.37
2.2 No corruption in the judiciary	0.38
2.3 No corruption in the police/military	0.51
2.4 No corruption in the legislature	0.2

📖 Open Government

3.1 Publicized laws and government data	0.36
3.2 Right to information	0.38
3.3 Civic participation	0.6
3.4 Complaint mechanisms	0.46

👤 Fundamental Rights

4.1 Equal treatment / no discrimination	0.44
4.2 Right to life and security	0.55
4.3 Due process of law	0.43
4.4 Freedom of expression	0.69
4.5 Freedom of religion	0.64
4.6 Right to privacy	0.51
4.7 Freedom of association	0.71
4.8 Labor rights	0.45

👮 Order and Security

5.1 Absence of crime	0.8
5.2 Absence of civil conflict	0.87
5.3 Absence of violent redress	0.36

🧑‍💼 Regulatory Enforcement

6.1 Effective regulatory enforcement	0.34
6.2 No improper influence	0.38
6.3 No unreasonable delay	0.48
6.4 Respect for due process	0.39
6.5 No expropriation w/out adequate compensation	0.46

⚖ Civil Justice

7.1 Accessibility and affordability	0.48
7.2 No discrimination	0.43
7.3 No corruption	0.37
7.4 No improper gov. influence	0.41
7.5 No unreasonable delay	0.37
7.6 Effective enforcement	0.47
7.7 Impartial and effective ADRs	0.63

🏛 Criminal Justice

8.1 Effective investigations	0.4
8.2 Timely and effective adjudication	0.48
8.3 Effective correctional system	0.22
8.4 No discrimination	0.35
8.5 No corruption	0.44
8.6 No improper gov. influence	0.38
8.7 Due process of law	0.43

Liberia

Region: **Sub-Saharan Africa** | Income group: **Low income**

	Overall Score	Regional Rank	Income Rank	Global Rank
	0.45	11/18	6/15	83/102

		Factor Trend	Factor Score	Regional Rank	Income Rank	Global Rank
🏛	Constraints on Government Powers	—	0.54	7/18	4/15	54/102
💰	Absence of Corruption	—	0.28	14/18	10/15	94/102
📱	Open Government	—	0.48	7/18	4/15	71/102
👤	Fundamental Rights	—	0.58	5/18	2/15	50/102
👮	Order and Security	—	0.57	15/18	13/15	94/102
🗄	Regulatory Enforcement	—	0.37	16/18	10/15	95/102
⚖	Civil Justice	—	0.44	14/18	7/15	81/102
🏛	Criminal Justice	—	0.32	18/18	12/15	92/102

— Liberia — Sub-Saharan Africa — Low income group ▲ Trending up ▼ Trending down ▒ Low ▒ Medium ☐ High

🏛 Constraints on Government Powers

1.1 Limits by legislature	0.7
1.2 Limits by judiciary	0.49
1.3 Independent auditing	0.28
1.4 Sanctions for official misconduct	0.32
1.5 Non-governmental checks	0.74
1.6 Lawful transition of power	0.69

💰 Absence of Corruption

2.1 No corruption in the executive branch	0.33
2.2 No corruption in the judiciary	0.28
2.3 No corruption in the police/military	0.31
2.4 No corruption in the legislature	0.19

📱 Open Government

3.1 Publicized laws and government data	0.35
3.2 Right to information	0.44
3.3 Civic participation	0.66
3.4 Complaint mechanisms	0.47

👤 Fundamental Rights

4.1 Equal treatment / no discrimination	0.48
4.2 Right to life and security	0.54
4.3 Due process of law	0.3
4.4 Freedom of expression	0.74
4.5 Freedom of religion	0.82
4.6 Right to privacy	0.53
4.7 Freedom of association	0.74
4.8 Labor rights	0.47

👮 Order and Security

5.1 Absence of crime	0.63
5.2 Absence of civil conflict	0.83
5.3 Absence of violent redress	0.26

🗄 Regulatory Enforcement

6.1 Effective regulatory enforcement	0.41
6.2 No improper influence	0.34
6.3 No unreasonable delay	0.33
6.4 Respect for due process	0.42
6.5 No expropriation w/out adequate compensation	0.36

⚖ Civil Justice

7.1 Accessibility and affordability	0.39
7.2 No discrimination	0.36
7.3 No corruption	0.3
7.4 No improper gov. influence	0.44
7.5 No unreasonable delay	0.46
7.6 Effective enforcement	0.63
7.7 Impartial and effective ADRs	0.52

🏛 Criminal Justice

8.1 Effective investigations	0.3
8.2 Timely and effective adjudication	0.38
8.3 Effective correctional system	0.22
8.4 No discrimination	0.38
8.5 No corruption	0.27
8.6 No improper gov. influence	0.35
8.7 Due process of law	0.3

Macedonia, FYR

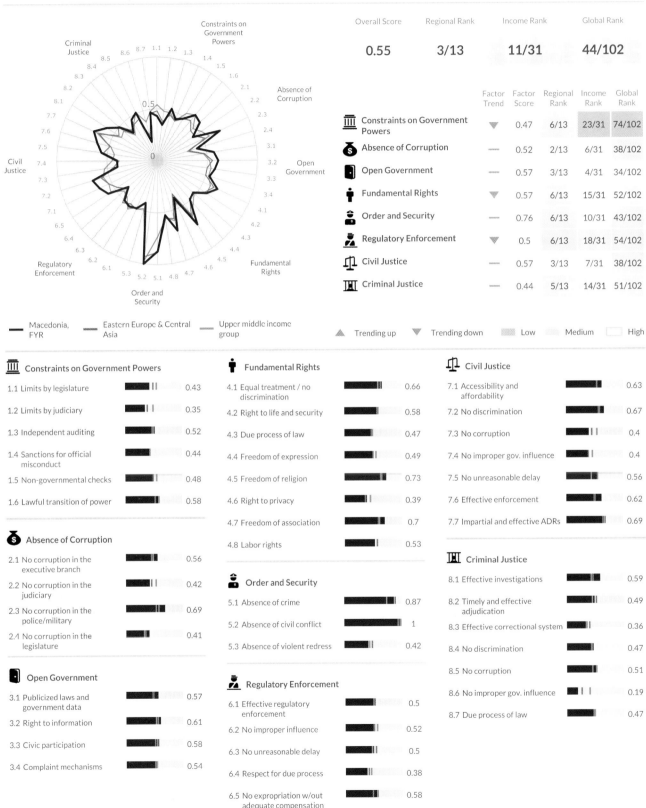

	Overall Score	Regional Rank	Income Rank	Global Rank
	0.55	3/13	11/31	44/102

	Factor Trend	Factor Score	Regional Rank	Income Rank	Global Rank
🏛 Constraints on Government Powers	▼	0.47	6/13	23/31	74/102
💰 Absence of Corruption	—	0.52	2/13	6/31	38/102
📖 Open Government	—	0.57	3/13	4/31	34/102
🧍 Fundamental Rights	▼	0.57	6/13	15/31	52/102
👮 Order and Security	—	0.76	6/13	10/31	43/102
⚖ Regulatory Enforcement	▼	0.5	6/13	18/31	54/102
⚖ Civil Justice	—	0.57	3/13	7/31	38/102
🏛 Criminal Justice	—	0.44	5/13	14/31	51/102

—— Macedonia, FYR —— Eastern Europe & Central Asia —— Upper middle income group

▲ Trending up ▼ Trending down ▨ Low ▨ Medium ▢ High

🏛 Constraints on Government Powers

1.1 Limits by legislature	0.43
1.2 Limits by judiciary	0.35
1.3 Independent auditing	0.52
1.4 Sanctions for official misconduct	0.44
1.5 Non-governmental checks	0.48
1.6 Lawful transition of power	0.58

💰 Absence of Corruption

2.1 No corruption in the executive branch	0.56
2.2 No corruption in the judiciary	0.42
2.3 No corruption in the police/military	0.69
2.4 No corruption in the legislature	0.41

📖 Open Government

3.1 Publicized laws and government data	0.57
3.2 Right to information	0.61
3.3 Civic participation	0.58
3.4 Complaint mechanisms	0.54

🧍 Fundamental Rights

4.1 Equal treatment / no discrimination	0.66
4.2 Right to life and security	0.58
4.3 Due process of law	0.47
4.4 Freedom of expression	0.49
4.5 Freedom of religion	0.73
4.6 Right to privacy	0.39
4.7 Freedom of association	0.7
4.8 Labor rights	0.53

👮 Order and Security

5.1 Absence of crime	0.87
5.2 Absence of civil conflict	1
5.3 Absence of violent redress	0.42

⚖ Regulatory Enforcement

6.1 Effective regulatory enforcement	0.5
6.2 No improper influence	0.52
6.3 No unreasonable delay	0.5
6.4 Respect for due process	0.38
6.5 No expropriation w/out adequate compensation	0.58

⚖ Civil Justice

7.1 Accessibility and affordability	0.63
7.2 No discrimination	0.67
7.3 No corruption	0.4
7.4 No improper gov. influence	0.4
7.5 No unreasonable delay	0.56
7.6 Effective enforcement	0.62
7.7 Impartial and effective ADRs	0.69

🏛 Criminal Justice

8.1 Effective investigations	0.59
8.2 Timely and effective adjudication	0.49
8.3 Effective correctional system	0.36
8.4 No discrimination	0.47
8.5 No corruption	0.51
8.6 No improper gov. influence	0.19
8.7 Due process of law	0.47

Madagascar

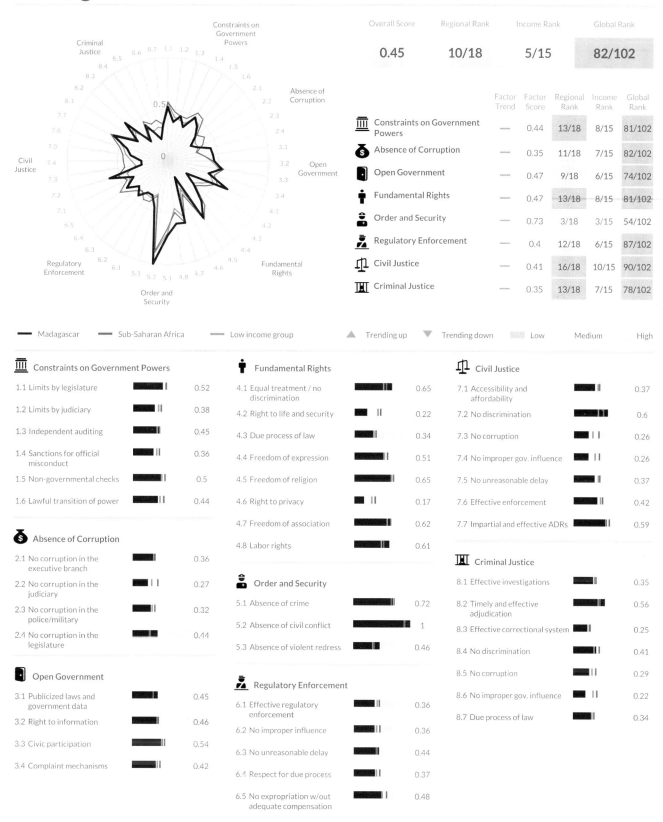

	Overall Score	Regional Rank	Income Rank	Global Rank
	0.45	10/18	5/15	82/102

	Factor Trend	Factor Score	Regional Rank	Income Rank	Global Rank
Constraints on Government Powers	—	0.44	13/18	8/15	81/102
Absence of Corruption	—	0.35	11/18	7/15	82/102
Open Government	—	0.47	9/18	6/15	74/102
Fundamental Rights	—	0.47	13/18	8/15	81/102
Order and Security	—	0.73	3/18	3/15	54/102
Regulatory Enforcement	—	0.4	12/18	6/15	87/102
Civil Justice	—	0.41	16/18	10/15	90/102
Criminal Justice	—	0.35	13/18	7/15	78/102

—— Madagascar　　—— Sub-Saharan Africa　　—— Low income group　　▲ Trending up　　▼ Trending down　　Low　　Medium　　High

Constraints on Government Powers

1.1 Limits by legislature	0.52
1.2 Limits by judiciary	0.38
1.3 Independent auditing	0.45
1.4 Sanctions for official misconduct	0.36
1.5 Non-governmental checks	0.5
1.6 Lawful transition of power	0.44

Absence of Corruption

2.1 No corruption in the executive branch	0.36
2.2 No corruption in the judiciary	0.27
2.3 No corruption in the police/military	0.32
2.4 No corruption in the legislature	0.44

Open Government

3.1 Publicized laws and government data	0.45
3.2 Right to information	0.46
3.3 Civic participation	0.54
3.4 Complaint mechanisms	0.42

Fundamental Rights

4.1 Equal treatment / no discrimination	0.65
4.2 Right to life and security	0.22
4.3 Due process of law	0.34
4.4 Freedom of expression	0.51
4.5 Freedom of religion	0.65
4.6 Right to privacy	0.17
4.7 Freedom of association	0.62
4.8 Labor rights	0.61

Order and Security

5.1 Absence of crime	0.72
5.2 Absence of civil conflict	1
5.3 Absence of violent redress	0.46

Regulatory Enforcement

6.1 Effective regulatory enforcement	0.36
6.2 No improper influence	0.36
6.3 No unreasonable delay	0.44
6.4 Respect for due process	0.37
6.5 No expropriation w/out adequate compensation	0.48

Civil Justice

7.1 Accessibility and affordability	0.37
7.2 No discrimination	0.6
7.3 No corruption	0.26
7.4 No improper gov. influence	0.26
7.5 No unreasonable delay	0.37
7.6 Effective enforcement	0.42
7.7 Impartial and effective ADRs	0.59

Criminal Justice

8.1 Effective investigations	0.35
8.2 Timely and effective adjudication	0.56
8.3 Effective correctional system	0.25
8.4 No discrimination	0.41
8.5 No corruption	0.29
8.6 No improper gov. influence	0.22
8.7 Due process of law	0.34

Malawi

	Overall Score	Regional Rank	Income Rank	Global Rank
	0.5	5/18	2/15	61/102

	Factor Trend	Factor Score	Regional Rank	Income Rank	Global Rank
Constraints on Government Powers	▲	0.57	5/18	2/15	47/102
Absence of Corruption	—	0.36	10/18	6/15	80/102
Open Government	—	0.5	6/18	3/15	65/102
Fundamental Rights	—	0.59	4/18	1/15	49/102
Order and Security	▼	0.61	11/18	9/15	83/102
Regulatory Enforcement	▲	0.44	9/18	4/15	73/102
Civil Justice	—	0.52	6/18	1/15	50/102
Criminal Justice	—	0.45	4/18	1/15	48/102

— Malawi   **—** Sub-Saharan Africa   **—** Low income group   ▲ Trending up   ▼ Trending down   Low   Medium   High

Constraints on Government Powers

1.1 Limits by legislature	0.65
1.2 Limits by judiciary	0.63
1.3 Independent auditing	0.41
1.4 Sanctions for official misconduct	0.5
1.5 Non-governmental checks	0.68
1.6 Lawful transition of power	0.56

Absence of Corruption

2.1 No corruption in the executive branch	0.32
2.2 No corruption in the judiciary	0.49
2.3 No corruption in the police/military	0.32
2.4 No corruption in the legislature	0.29

Open Government

3.1 Publicized laws and government data	0.36
3.2 Right to information	0.38
3.3 Civic participation	0.71
3.4 Complaint mechanisms	0.54

Fundamental Rights

4.1 Equal treatment / no discrimination	0.49
4.2 Right to life and security	0.62
4.3 Due process of law	0.34
4.4 Freedom of expression	0.68
4.5 Freedom of religion	0.79
4.6 Right to privacy	0.52
4.7 Freedom of association	0.79
4.8 Labor rights	0.47

Order and Security

5.1 Absence of crime	0.58
5.2 Absence of civil conflict	1
5.3 Absence of violent redress	0.26

Regulatory Enforcement

6.1 Effective regulatory enforcement	0.43
6.2 No improper influence	0.33
6.3 No unreasonable delay	0.33
6.4 Respect for due process	0.47
6.5 No expropriation w/out adequate compensation	0.65

Civil Justice

7.1 Accessibility and affordability	0.45
7.2 No discrimination	0.53
7.3 No corruption	0.53
7.4 No improper gov. influence	0.45
7.5 No unreasonable delay	0.4
7.6 Effective enforcement	0.57
7.7 Impartial and effective ADRs	0.71

Criminal Justice

8.1 Effective investigations	0.39
8.2 Timely and effective adjudication	0.48
8.3 Effective correctional system	0.24
8.4 No discrimination	0.48
8.5 No corruption	0.43
8.6 No improper gov. influence	0.77
8.7 Due process of law	0.34

Malaysia

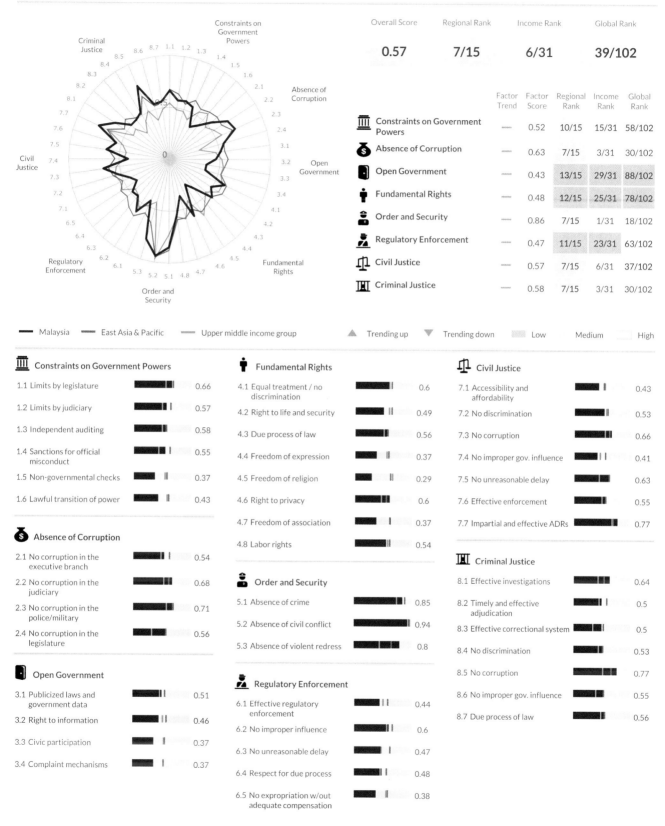

Overall Score	Regional Rank	Income Rank	Global Rank
0.57	7/15	6/31	39/102

		Factor Trend	Factor Score	Regional Rank	Income Rank	Global Rank
🏛	Constraints on Government Powers	—	0.52	10/15	15/31	58/102
💰	Absence of Corruption	—	0.63	7/15	3/31	30/102
📖	Open Government	—	0.43	13/15	29/31	88/102
👤	Fundamental Rights	—	0.48	12/15	25/31	78/102
👮	Order and Security	—	0.86	7/15	1/31	18/102
👷	Regulatory Enforcement	—	0.47	11/15	23/31	63/102
⚖	Civil Justice	—	0.57	7/15	6/31	37/102
🏛	Criminal Justice	—	0.58	7/15	3/31	30/102

— Malaysia — East Asia & Pacific — Upper middle income group ▲ Trending up ▼ Trending down ▨ Low Medium High

🏛 Constraints on Government Powers

1.1 Limits by legislature	0.66
1.2 Limits by judiciary	0.57
1.3 Independent auditing	0.58
1.4 Sanctions for official misconduct	0.55
1.5 Non-governmental checks	0.37
1.6 Lawful transition of power	0.43

💰 Absence of Corruption

2.1 No corruption in the executive branch	0.54
2.2 No corruption in the judiciary	0.68
2.3 No corruption in the police/military	0.71
2.4 No corruption in the legislature	0.56

📖 Open Government

3.1 Publicized laws and government data	0.51
3.2 Right to information	0.46
3.3 Civic participation	0.37
3.4 Complaint mechanisms	0.37

👤 Fundamental Rights

4.1 Equal treatment / no discrimination	0.6
4.2 Right to life and security	0.49
4.3 Due process of law	0.56
4.4 Freedom of expression	0.37
4.5 Freedom of religion	0.29
4.6 Right to privacy	0.6
4.7 Freedom of association	0.37
4.8 Labor rights	0.54

👮 Order and Security

5.1 Absence of crime	0.85
5.2 Absence of civil conflict	0.94
5.3 Absence of violent redress	0.8

👷 Regulatory Enforcement

6.1 Effective regulatory enforcement	0.44
6.2 No improper influence	0.6
6.3 No unreasonable delay	0.47
6.4 Respect for due process	0.48
6.5 No expropriation w/out adequate compensation	0.38

⚖ Civil Justice

7.1 Accessibility and affordability	0.43
7.2 No discrimination	0.53
7.3 No corruption	0.66
7.4 No improper gov. influence	0.41
7.5 No unreasonable delay	0.63
7.6 Effective enforcement	0.55
7.7 Impartial and effective ADRs	0.77

🏛 Criminal Justice

8.1 Effective investigations	0.64
8.2 Timely and effective adjudication	0.5
8.3 Effective correctional system	0.5
8.4 No discrimination	0.53
8.5 No corruption	0.77
8.6 No improper gov. influence	0.55
8.7 Due process of law	0.56

Mexico

Mexico City, Guadalajara, Monterrey
Region: **Latin America & the Caribbean** | Income group: **Upper middle income**

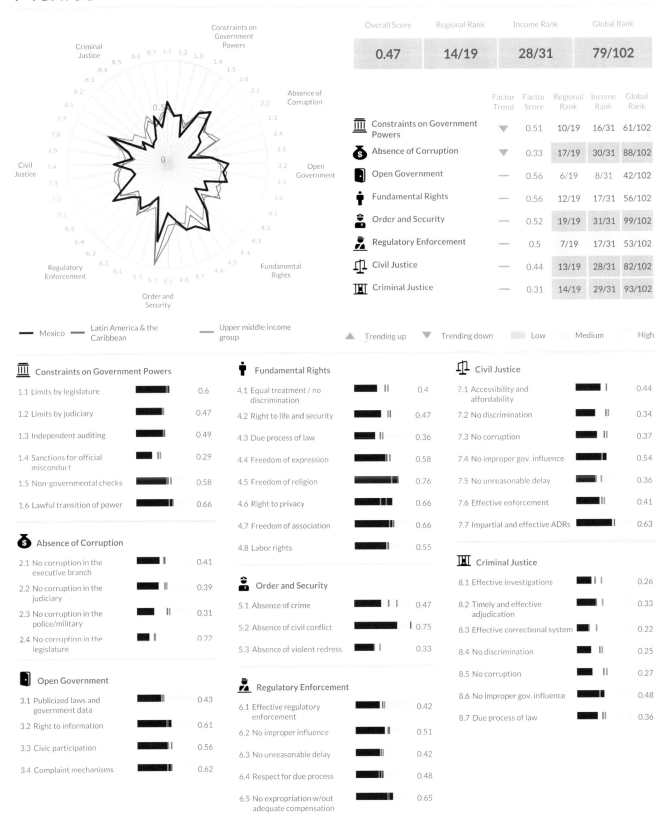

	Overall Score	Regional Rank	Income Rank	Global Rank
	0.47	14/19	28/31	79/102

		Factor Trend	Factor Score	Regional Rank	Income Rank	Global Rank
🏛	Constraints on Government Powers	▼	0.51	10/19	16/31	61/102
💰	Absence of Corruption	▼	0.33	17/19	30/31	88/102
📋	Open Government	—	0.56	6/19	8/31	42/102
👤	Fundamental Rights	—	0.56	12/19	17/31	56/102
👮	Order and Security	—	0.52	19/19	31/31	99/102
🧑‍💼	Regulatory Enforcement	—	0.5	7/19	17/31	53/102
⚖	Civil Justice	—	0.44	13/19	28/31	82/102
🏛	Criminal Justice	—	0.31	14/19	29/31	93/102

— Mexico — Latin America & the Caribbean — Upper middle income group

▲ Trending up ▼ Trending down ░ Low Medium High

🏛 Constraints on Government Powers

1.1 Limits by legislature	0.6
1.2 Limits by judiciary	0.47
1.3 Independent auditing	0.49
1.4 Sanctions for official misconduct	0.29
1.5 Non-governmental checks	0.58
1.6 Lawful transition of power	0.66

💰 Absence of Corruption

2.1 No corruption in the executive branch	0.41
2.2 No corruption in the judiciary	0.39
2.3 No corruption in the police/military	0.31
2.4 No corruption in the legislature	0.22

📋 Open Government

3.1 Publicized laws and government data	0.43
3.2 Right to information	0.61
3.3 Civic participation	0.56
3.4 Complaint mechanisms	0.62

👤 Fundamental Rights

4.1 Equal treatment / no discrimination	0.4
4.2 Right to life and security	0.47
4.3 Due process of law	0.36
4.4 Freedom of expression	0.58
4.5 Freedom of religion	0.76
4.6 Right to privacy	0.66
4.7 Freedom of association	0.66
4.8 Labor rights	0.55

👮 Order and Security

5.1 Absence of crime	0.47
5.2 Absence of civil conflict	0.75
5.3 Absence of violent redress	0.33

🧑‍💼 Regulatory Enforcement

6.1 Effective regulatory enforcement	0.42
6.2 No improper influence	0.51
6.3 No unreasonable delay	0.42
6.4 Respect for due process	0.48
6.5 No expropriation w/out adequate compensation	0.65

⚖ Civil Justice

7.1 Accessibility and affordability	0.44
7.2 No discrimination	0.34
7.3 No corruption	0.37
7.4 No improper gov. influence	0.54
7.5 No unreasonable delay	0.36
7.6 Effective enforcement	0.41
7.7 Impartial and effective ADRs	0.63

🏛 Criminal Justice

8.1 Effective investigations	0.26
8.2 Timely and effective adjudication	0.33
8.3 Effective correctional system	0.22
8.4 No discrimination	0.25
8.5 No corruption	0.27
8.6 No improper gov. influence	0.48
8.7 Due process of law	0.36

Complete country profiles available at: data.worldjusticeproject.org

Moldova

	Overall Score	Regional Rank	Income Rank	Global Rank
	0.48	8/13	12/25	69/102

	Factor Trend	Factor Score	Regional Rank	Income Rank	Global Rank
🏛 Constraints on Government Powers	—	0.45	8/13	18/25	79/102
💰 Absence of Corruption	—	0.28	13/13	23/25	93/102
🚪 Open Government	—	0.55	5/13	6/25	46/102
👤 Fundamental Rights	—	0.55	7/13	8/25	59/102
👮 Order and Security	—	0.82	3/13	3/25	25/102
🕵 Regulatory Enforcement	—	0.42	11/13	15/25	79/102
⚖ Civil Justice	—	0.43	13/13	18/25	84/102
🏛 Criminal Justice	—	0.34	12/13	17/25	82/102

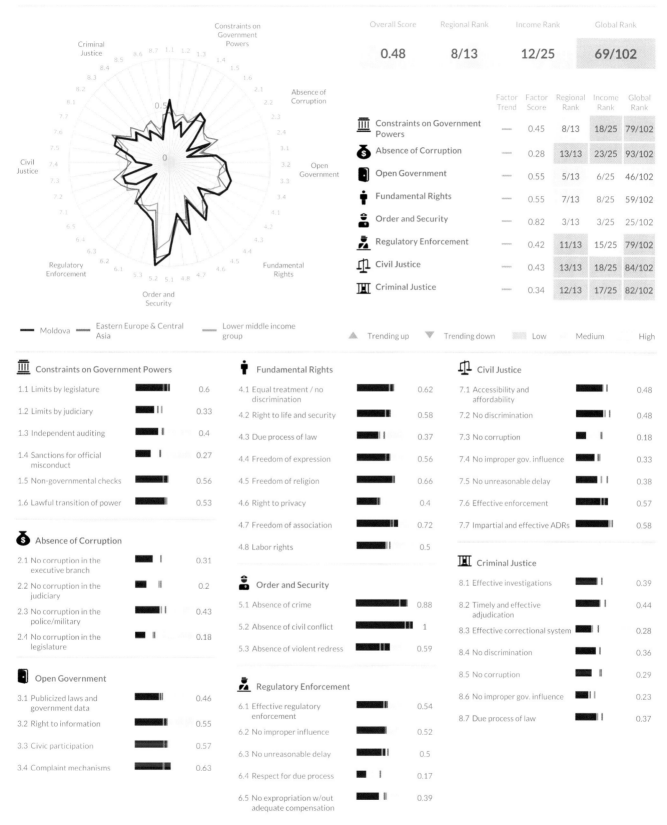

— Moldova — Eastern Europe & Central Asia — Lower middle income group

▲ Trending up ▼ Trending down ▨ Low Medium High

🏛 Constraints on Government Powers

1.1 Limits by legislature		0.6
1.2 Limits by judiciary		0.33
1.3 Independent auditing		0.4
1.4 Sanctions for official misconduct		0.27
1.5 Non-governmental checks		0.56
1.6 Lawful transition of power		0.53

💰 Absence of Corruption

2.1 No corruption in the executive branch		0.31
2.2 No corruption in the judiciary		0.2
2.3 No corruption in the police/military		0.43
2.4 No corruption in the legislature		0.18

🚪 Open Government

3.1 Publicized laws and government data		0.46
3.2 Right to information		0.55
3.3 Civic participation		0.57
3.4 Complaint mechanisms		0.63

👤 Fundamental Rights

4.1 Equal treatment / no discrimination		0.62
4.2 Right to life and security		0.58
4.3 Due process of law		0.37
4.4 Freedom of expression		0.56
4.5 Freedom of religion		0.66
4.6 Right to privacy		0.4
4.7 Freedom of association		0.72
4.8 Labor rights		0.5

👮 Order and Security

5.1 Absence of crime		0.88
5.2 Absence of civil conflict		1
5.3 Absence of violent redress		0.59

🕵 Regulatory Enforcement

6.1 Effective regulatory enforcement		0.54
6.2 No improper influence		0.52
6.3 No unreasonable delay		0.5
6.4 Respect for due process		0.17
6.5 No expropriation w/out adequate compensation		0.39

⚖ Civil Justice

7.1 Accessibility and affordability		0.48
7.2 No discrimination		0.48
7.3 No corruption		0.18
7.4 No improper gov. influence		0.33
7.5 No unreasonable delay		0.38
7.6 Effective enforcement		0.57
7.7 Impartial and effective ADRs		0.58

🏛 Criminal Justice

8.1 Effective investigations		0.39
8.2 Timely and effective adjudication		0.44
8.3 Effective correctional system		0.28
8.4 No discrimination		0.36
8.5 No corruption		0.29
8.6 No improper gov. influence		0.23
8.7 Due process of law		0.37

Mongolia

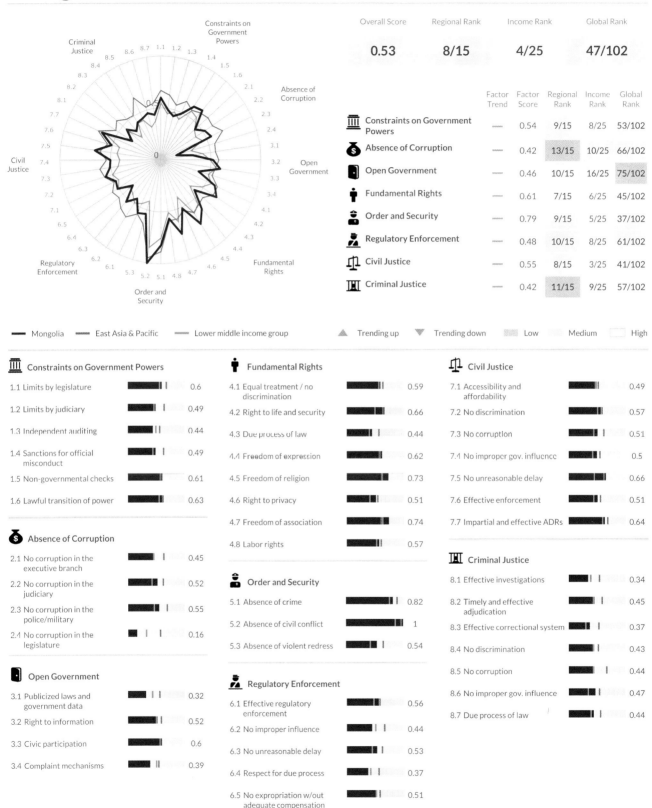

	Overall Score	Regional Rank	Income Rank	Global Rank
	0.53	**8/15**	**4/25**	**47/102**

	Factor Trend	Factor Score	Regional Rank	Income Rank	Global Rank
Constraints on Government Powers	—	0.54	9/15	8/25	53/102
Absence of Corruption	—	0.42	13/15	10/25	66/102
Open Government	—	0.46	10/15	16/25	75/102
Fundamental Rights	—	0.61	7/15	6/25	45/102
Order and Security	—	0.79	9/15	5/25	37/102
Regulatory Enforcement	—	0.48	10/15	8/25	61/102
Civil Justice	—	0.55	8/15	3/25	41/102
Criminal Justice	—	0.42	11/15	9/25	57/102

— Mongolia   ·· East Asia & Pacific   — Lower middle income group   ▲ Trending up   ▼ Trending down   Low   Medium   High

Constraints on Government Powers

1.1 Limits by legislature	0.6
1.2 Limits by judiciary	0.49
1.3 Independent auditing	0.44
1.4 Sanctions for official misconduct	0.49
1.5 Non-governmental checks	0.61
1.6 Lawful transition of power	0.63

Absence of Corruption

2.1 No corruption in the executive branch	0.45
2.2 No corruption in the judiciary	0.52
2.3 No corruption in the police/military	0.55
2.4 No corruption in the legislature	0.16

Open Government

3.1 Publicized laws and government data	0.32
3.2 Right to information	0.52
3.3 Civic participation	0.6
3.4 Complaint mechanisms	0.39

Fundamental Rights

4.1 Equal treatment / no discrimination	0.59
4.2 Right to life and security	0.66
4.3 Due process of law	0.44
4.4 Freedom of expression	0.62
4.5 Freedom of religion	0.73
4.6 Right to privacy	0.51
4.7 Freedom of association	0.74
4.8 Labor rights	0.57

Order and Security

5.1 Absence of crime	0.82
5.2 Absence of civil conflict	1
5.3 Absence of violent redress	0.54

Regulatory Enforcement

6.1 Effective regulatory enforcement	0.56
6.2 No improper influence	0.44
6.3 No unreasonable delay	0.53
6.4 Respect for due process	0.37
6.5 No expropriation w/out adequate compensation	0.51

Civil Justice

7.1 Accessibility and affordability	0.49
7.2 No discrimination	0.57
7.3 No corruption	0.51
7.4 No improper gov. influence	0.5
7.5 No unreasonable delay	0.66
7.6 Effective enforcement	0.51
7.7 Impartial and effective ADRs	0.64

Criminal Justice

8.1 Effective investigations	0.34
8.2 Timely and effective adjudication	0.45
8.3 Effective correctional system	0.37
8.4 No discrimination	0.43
8.5 No corruption	0.44
8.6 No improper gov. influence	0.47
8.7 Due process of law	0.44

Morocco

Casablanca, Rabat, Marrakesh

Region: **Middle East & North Africa** | Income group: **Lower middle income**

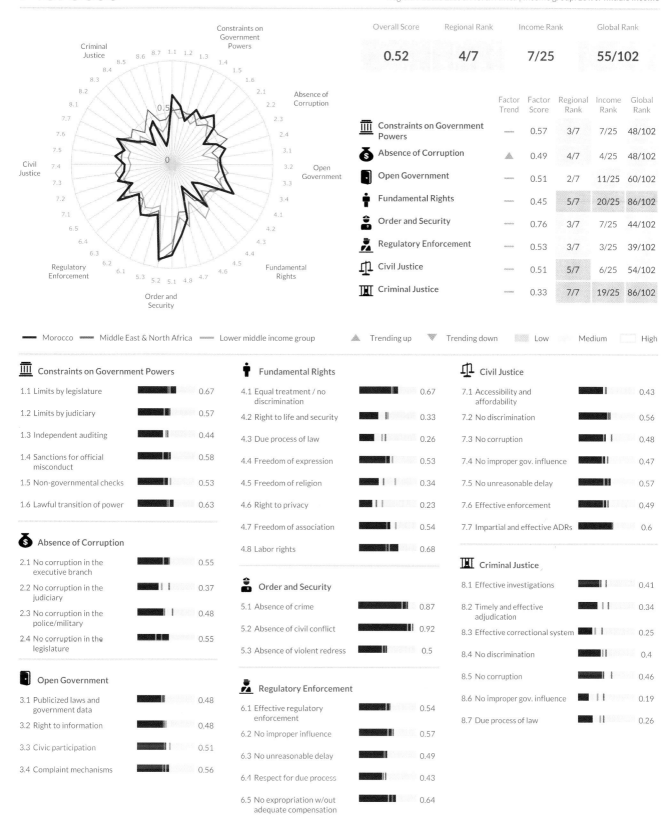

	Overall Score	Regional Rank	Income Rank	Global Rank
	0.52	**4/7**	**7/25**	**55/102**

	Factor Trend	Factor Score	Regional Rank	Income Rank	Global Rank
Constraints on Government Powers	—	0.57	3/7	7/25	48/102
Absence of Corruption	▲	0.49	4/7	4/25	48/102
Open Government	—	0.51	2/7	11/25	60/102
Fundamental Rights	—	0.45	5/7	20/25	86/102
Order and Security	—	0.76	3/7	7/25	44/102
Regulatory Enforcement	—	0.53	3/7	3/25	39/102
Civil Justice	—	0.51	5/7	6/25	54/102
Criminal Justice	—	0.33	7/7	19/25	86/102

— Morocco — Middle East & North Africa — Lower middle income group   ▲ Trending up   ▼ Trending down   Low   Medium   High

Constraints on Government Powers

1.1 Limits by legislature	0.67
1.2 Limits by judiciary	0.57
1.3 Independent auditing	0.44
1.4 Sanctions for official misconduct	0.58
1.5 Non-governmental checks	0.53
1.6 Lawful transition of power	0.63

Absence of Corruption

2.1 No corruption in the executive branch	0.55
2.2 No corruption in the judiciary	0.37
2.3 No corruption in the police/military	0.48
2.4 No corruption in the legislature	0.55

Open Government

3.1 Publicized laws and government data	0.48
3.2 Right to information	0.48
3.3 Civic participation	0.51
3.4 Complaint mechanisms	0.56

Fundamental Rights

4.1 Equal treatment / no discrimination	0.67
4.2 Right to life and security	0.33
4.3 Due process of law	0.26
4.4 Freedom of expression	0.53
4.5 Freedom of religion	0.34
4.6 Right to privacy	0.23
4.7 Freedom of association	0.54
4.8 Labor rights	0.68

Order and Security

5.1 Absence of crime	0.87
5.2 Absence of civil conflict	0.92
5.3 Absence of violent redress	0.5

Regulatory Enforcement

6.1 Effective regulatory enforcement	0.54
6.2 No improper influence	0.57
6.3 No unreasonable delay	0.49
6.4 Respect for due process	0.43
6.5 No expropriation w/out adequate compensation	0.64

Civil Justice

7.1 Accessibility and affordability	0.43
7.2 No discrimination	0.56
7.3 No corruption	0.48
7.4 No improper gov. influence	0.47
7.5 No unreasonable delay	0.57
7.6 Effective enforcement	0.49
7.7 Impartial and effective ADRs	0.6

Criminal Justice

8.1 Effective investigations	0.41
8.2 Timely and effective adjudication	0.34
8.3 Effective correctional system	0.25
8.4 No discrimination	0.4
8.5 No corruption	0.46
8.6 No improper gov. influence	0.19
8.7 Due process of law	0.26

Myanmar

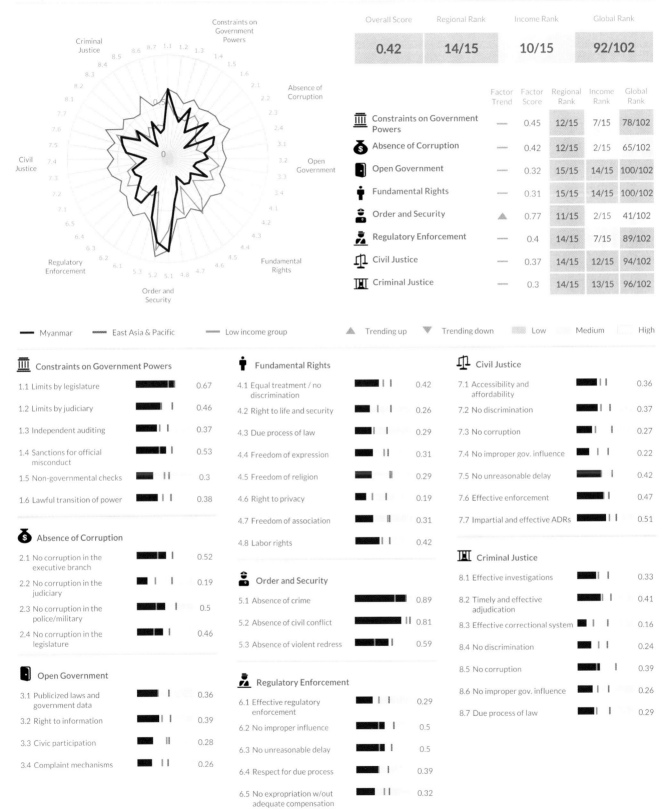

	Overall Score	Regional Rank	Income Rank	Global Rank
	0.42	14/15	10/15	92/102

		Factor Trend	Factor Score	Regional Rank	Income Rank	Global Rank
🏛	Constraints on Government Powers	—	0.45	12/15	7/15	78/102
💰	Absence of Corruption	—	0.42	12/15	2/15	65/102
📖	Open Government	—	0.32	15/15	14/15	100/102
👤	Fundamental Rights	—	0.31	15/15	14/15	100/102
👮	Order and Security	▲	0.77	11/15	2/15	41/102
🗄	Regulatory Enforcement	—	0.4	14/15	7/15	89/102
⚖	Civil Justice	—	0.37	14/15	12/15	94/102
🏛	Criminal Justice	—	0.3	14/15	13/15	96/102

— Myanmar   — East Asia & Pacific   — Low income group   ▲ Trending up   ▼ Trending down   ░ Low   Medium   High

🏛 Constraints on Government Powers

1.1 Limits by legislature	0.67
1.2 Limits by judiciary	0.46
1.3 Independent auditing	0.37
1.4 Sanctions for official misconduct	0.53
1.5 Non-governmental checks	0.3
1.6 Lawful transition of power	0.38

💰 Absence of Corruption

2.1 No corruption in the executive branch	0.52
2.2 No corruption in the judiciary	0.19
2.3 No corruption in the police/military	0.5
2.4 No corruption in the legislature	0.46

📖 Open Government

3.1 Publicized laws and government data	0.36
3.2 Right to information	0.39
3.3 Civic participation	0.28
3.4 Complaint mechanisms	0.26

👤 Fundamental Rights

4.1 Equal treatment / no discrimination	0.42
4.2 Right to life and security	0.26
4.3 Due process of law	0.29
4.4 Freedom of expression	0.31
4.5 Freedom of religion	0.29
4.6 Right to privacy	0.19
4.7 Freedom of association	0.31
4.8 Labor rights	0.42

👮 Order and Security

5.1 Absence of crime	0.89
5.2 Absence of civil conflict	0.81
5.3 Absence of violent redress	0.59

🗄 Regulatory Enforcement

6.1 Effective regulatory enforcement	0.29
6.2 No improper influence	0.5
6.3 No unreasonable delay	0.5
6.4 Respect for due process	0.39
6.5 No expropriation w/out adequate compensation	0.32

⚖ Civil Justice

7.1 Accessibility and affordability	0.36
7.2 No discrimination	0.37
7.3 No corruption	0.27
7.4 No improper gov. influence	0.22
7.5 No unreasonable delay	0.42
7.6 Effective enforcement	0.47
7.7 Impartial and effective ADRs	0.51

🏛 Criminal Justice

8.1 Effective investigations	0.33
8.2 Timely and effective adjudication	0.41
8.3 Effective correctional system	0.16
8.4 No discrimination	0.24
8.5 No corruption	0.39
8.6 No improper gov. influence	0.26
8.7 Due process of law	0.29

Complete country profiles available at: data.worldjusticeproject.org

Nepal

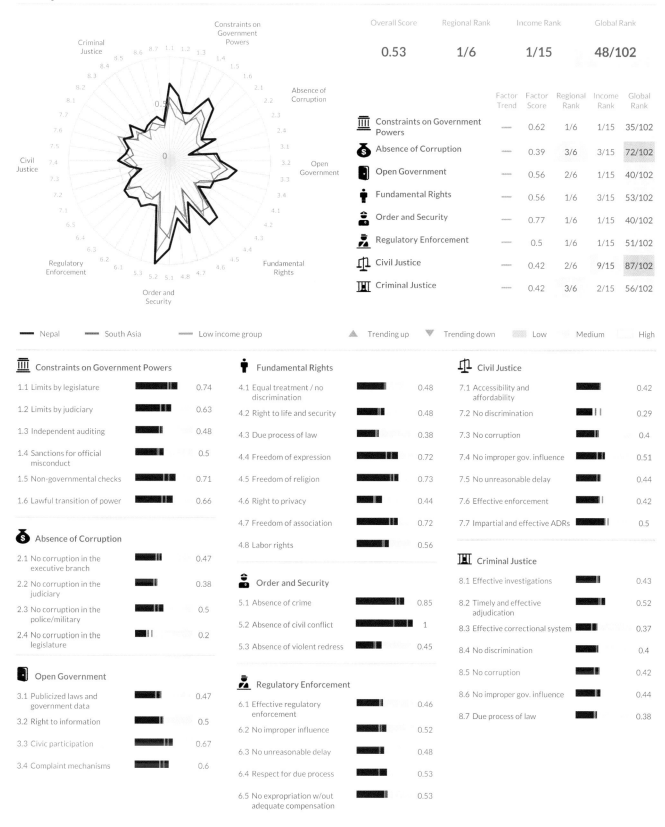

	Overall Score	Regional Rank	Income Rank	Global Rank
	0.53	1/6	1/15	48/102

		Factor Trend	Factor Score	Regional Rank	Income Rank	Global Rank
🏛	Constraints on Government Powers	—	0.62	1/6	1/15	35/102
💰	Absence of Corruption	—	0.39	3/6	3/15	72/102
📱	Open Government	—	0.56	2/6	1/15	40/102
👤	Fundamental Rights	—	0.56	1/6	3/15	53/102
👮	Order and Security	—	0.77	1/6	1/15	40/102
🗂	Regulatory Enforcement	—	0.5	1/6	1/15	51/102
⚖	Civil Justice	—	0.42	2/6	9/15	87/102
🏛	Criminal Justice	—	0.42	3/6	2/15	56/102

— Nepal   — South Asia   — Low income group   ▲ Trending up   ▼ Trending down   ▒ Low   Medium   High

🏛 Constraints on Government Powers

1.1 Limits by legislature		0.74
1.2 Limits by judiciary		0.63
1.3 Independent auditing		0.48
1.4 Sanctions for official misconduct		0.5
1.5 Non-governmental checks		0.71
1.6 Lawful transition of power		0.66

💰 Absence of Corruption

2.1 No corruption in the executive branch		0.47
2.2 No corruption in the judiciary		0.38
2.3 No corruption in the police/military		0.5
2.4 No corruption in the legislature		0.2

📱 Open Government

3.1 Publicized laws and government data		0.47
3.2 Right to information		0.5
3.3 Civic participation		0.67
3.4 Complaint mechanisms		0.6

👤 Fundamental Rights

4.1 Equal treatment / no discrimination		0.48
4.2 Right to life and security		0.48
4.3 Due process of law		0.38
4.4 Freedom of expression		0.72
4.5 Freedom of religion		0.73
4.6 Right to privacy		0.44
4.7 Freedom of association		0.72
4.8 Labor rights		0.56

👮 Order and Security

5.1 Absence of crime		0.85
5.2 Absence of civil conflict		1
5.3 Absence of violent redress		0.45

🗂 Regulatory Enforcement

6.1 Effective regulatory enforcement		0.46
6.2 No improper influence		0.52
6.3 No unreasonable delay		0.48
6.4 Respect for due process		0.53
6.5 No expropriation w/out adequate compensation		0.53

⚖ Civil Justice

7.1 Accessibility and affordability		0.42
7.2 No discrimination		0.29
7.3 No corruption		0.4
7.4 No improper gov. influence		0.51
7.5 No unreasonable delay		0.44
7.6 Effective enforcement		0.42
7.7 Impartial and effective ADRs		0.5

🏛 Criminal Justice

8.1 Effective investigations		0.43
8.2 Timely and effective adjudication		0.52
8.3 Effective correctional system		0.37
8.4 No discrimination		0.4
8.5 No corruption		0.42
8.6 No improper gov. influence		0.44
8.7 Due process of law		0.38

Netherlands

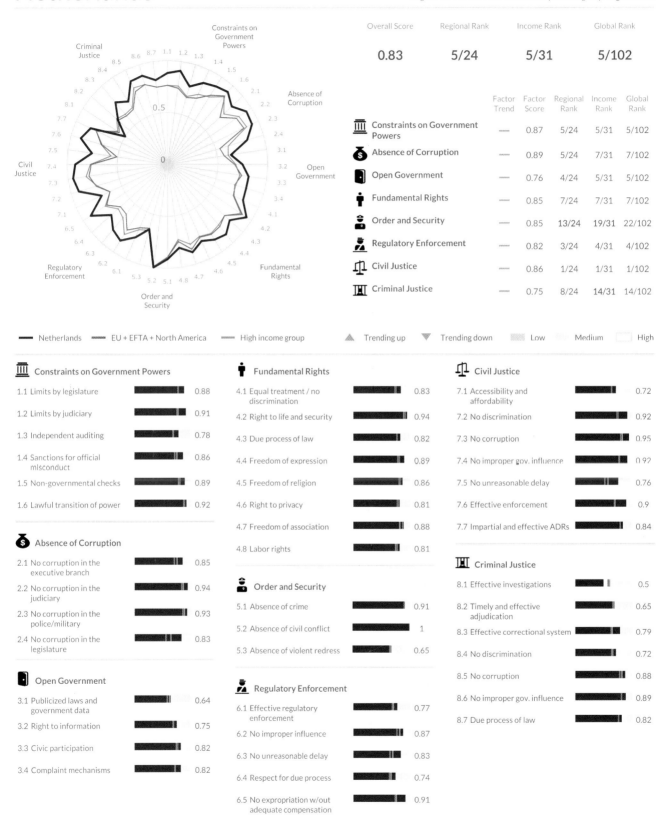

	Overall Score	Regional Rank	Income Rank	Global Rank
	0.83	5/24	5/31	5/102

	Factor Trend	Factor Score	Regional Rank	Income Rank	Global Rank
Constraints on Government Powers	—	0.87	5/24	5/31	5/102
Absence of Corruption	—	0.89	5/24	7/31	7/102
Open Government	—	0.76	4/24	5/31	5/102
Fundamental Rights	—	0.85	7/24	7/31	7/102
Order and Security	—	0.85	13/24	19/31	22/102
Regulatory Enforcement	—	0.82	3/24	4/31	4/102
Civil Justice	—	0.86	1/24	1/31	1/102
Criminal Justice	—	0.75	8/24	14/31	14/102

Legend: ▬ Netherlands ▬ EU + EFTA + North America ▬ High income group ▲ Trending up ▼ Trending down ▨ Low ▨ Medium ☐ High

⛪ Constraints on Government Powers

1.1 Limits by legislature	0.88
1.2 Limits by judiciary	0.91
1.3 Independent auditing	0.78
1.4 Sanctions for official misconduct	0.86
1.5 Non-governmental checks	0.89
1.6 Lawful transition of power	0.92

💰 Absence of Corruption

2.1 No corruption in the executive branch	0.85
2.2 No corruption in the judiciary	0.94
2.3 No corruption in the police/military	0.93
2.4 No corruption in the legislature	0.83

📱 Open Government

3.1 Publicized laws and government data	0.64
3.2 Right to information	0.75
3.3 Civic participation	0.82
3.4 Complaint mechanisms	0.82

👤 Fundamental Rights

4.1 Equal treatment / no discrimination	0.83
4.2 Right to life and security	0.94
4.3 Due process of law	0.82
4.4 Freedom of expression	0.89
4.5 Freedom of religion	0.86
4.6 Right to privacy	0.81
4.7 Freedom of association	0.88
4.8 Labor rights	0.81

👮 Order and Security

5.1 Absence of crime	0.91
5.2 Absence of civil conflict	1
5.3 Absence of violent redress	0.65

🛂 Regulatory Enforcement

6.1 Effective regulatory enforcement	0.77
6.2 No improper influence	0.87
6.3 No unreasonable delay	0.83
6.4 Respect for due process	0.74
6.5 No expropriation w/out adequate compensation	0.91

⚖ Civil Justice

7.1 Accessibility and affordability	0.72
7.2 No discrimination	0.92
7.3 No corruption	0.95
7.4 No improper gov. influence	0.92
7.5 No unreasonable delay	0.76
7.6 Effective enforcement	0.9
7.7 Impartial and effective ADRs	0.84

🏛 Criminal Justice

8.1 Effective investigations	0.5
8.2 Timely and effective adjudication	0.65
8.3 Effective correctional system	0.79
8.4 No discrimination	0.72
8.5 No corruption	0.88
8.6 No improper gov. influence	0.89
8.7 Due process of law	0.82

New Zealand

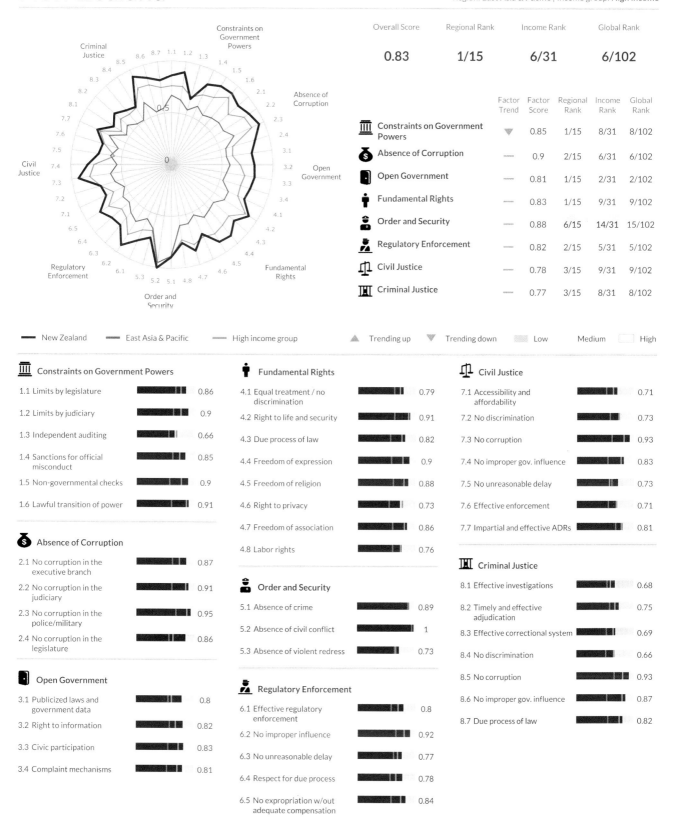

	Overall Score	Regional Rank	Income Rank	Global Rank
	0.83	1/15	6/31	6/102

		Factor Trend	Factor Score	Regional Rank	Income Rank	Global Rank
🏛	Constraints on Government Powers	▼	0.85	1/15	8/31	8/102
💰	Absence of Corruption	—	0.9	2/15	6/31	6/102
🚪	Open Government	—	0.81	1/15	2/31	2/102
👤	Fundamental Rights	—	0.83	1/15	9/31	9/102
👮	Order and Security	—	0.88	6/15	14/31	15/102
👷	Regulatory Enforcement	—	0.82	2/15	5/31	5/102
⚖	Civil Justice	—	0.78	3/15	9/31	9/102
🏛	Criminal Justice	—	0.77	3/15	8/31	8/102

— New Zealand   — East Asia & Pacific   — High income group   ▲ Trending up   ▼ Trending down   ▒ Low   Medium   ☐ High

🏛 Constraints on Government Powers

1.1 Limits by legislature	0.86
1.2 Limits by judiciary	0.9
1.3 Independent auditing	0.66
1.4 Sanctions for official misconduct	0.85
1.5 Non-governmental checks	0.9
1.6 Lawful transition of power	0.91

💰 Absence of Corruption

2.1 No corruption in the executive branch	0.87
2.2 No corruption in the judiciary	0.91
2.3 No corruption in the police/military	0.95
2.4 No corruption in the legislature	0.86

🚪 Open Government

3.1 Publicized laws and government data	0.8
3.2 Right to information	0.82
3.3 Civic participation	0.83
3.4 Complaint mechanisms	0.81

👤 Fundamental Rights

4.1 Equal treatment / no discrimination	0.79
4.2 Right to life and security	0.91
4.3 Due process of law	0.82
4.4 Freedom of expression	0.9
4.5 Freedom of religion	0.88
4.6 Right to privacy	0.73
4.7 Freedom of association	0.86
4.8 Labor rights	0.76

👮 Order and Security

5.1 Absence of crime	0.89
5.2 Absence of civil conflict	1
5.3 Absence of violent redress	0.73

👷 Regulatory Enforcement

6.1 Effective regulatory enforcement	0.8
6.2 No improper influence	0.92
6.3 No unreasonable delay	0.77
6.4 Respect for due process	0.78
6.5 No expropriation w/out adequate compensation	0.84

⚖ Civil Justice

7.1 Accessibility and affordability	0.71
7.2 No discrimination	0.73
7.3 No corruption	0.93
7.4 No improper gov. influence	0.83
7.5 No unreasonable delay	0.73
7.6 Effective enforcement	0.71
7.7 Impartial and effective ADRs	0.81

🏛 Criminal Justice

8.1 Effective investigations	0.68
8.2 Timely and effective adjudication	0.75
8.3 Effective correctional system	0.69
8.4 No discrimination	0.66
8.5 No corruption	0.93
8.6 No improper gov. influence	0.87
8.7 Due process of law	0.82

Nicaragua

Overall Score	Regional Rank	Income Rank	Global Rank
0.43	16/19	20/25	89/102

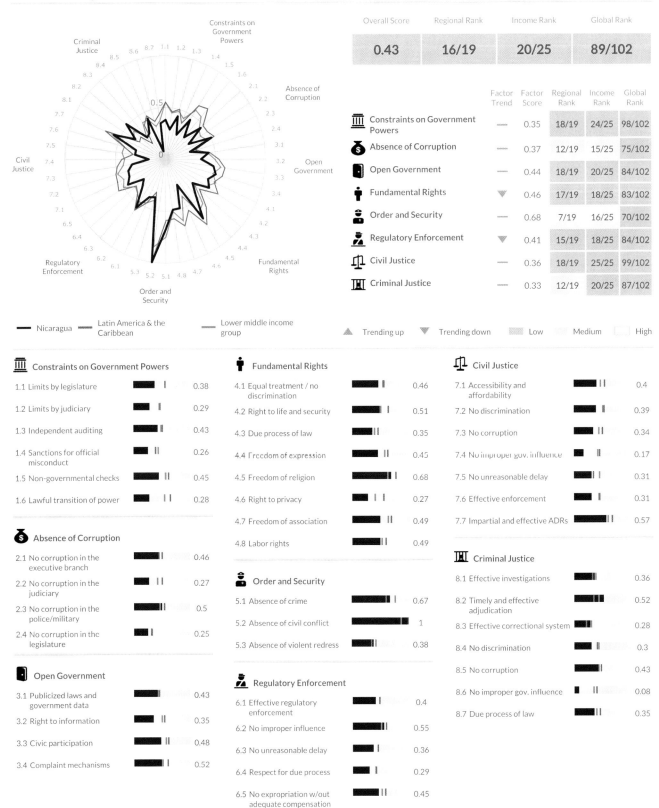

	Factor Trend	Factor Score	Regional Rank	Income Rank	Global Rank
Constraints on Government Powers	—	0.35	18/19	24/25	98/102
Absence of Corruption	—	0.37	12/19	15/25	75/102
Open Government	—	0.44	18/19	20/25	84/102
Fundamental Rights	▼	0.46	17/19	18/25	83/102
Order and Security	—	0.68	7/19	16/25	70/102
Regulatory Enforcement	▼	0.41	15/19	18/25	84/102
Civil Justice	—	0.36	18/19	25/25	99/102
Criminal Justice	—	0.33	12/19	20/25	87/102

— Nicaragua — Latin America & the Caribbean — Lower middle income group ▲ Trending up ▼ Trending down Low Medium High

Constraints on Government Powers

1.1 Limits by legislature	0.38
1.2 Limits by judiciary	0.29
1.3 Independent auditing	0.43
1.4 Sanctions for official misconduct	0.26
1.5 Non-governmental checks	0.45
1.6 Lawful transition of power	0.28

Absence of Corruption

2.1 No corruption in the executive branch	0.46
2.2 No corruption in the judiciary	0.27
2.3 No corruption in the police/military	0.5
2.4 No corruption in the legislature	0.25

Open Government

3.1 Publicized laws and government data	0.43
3.2 Right to information	0.35
3.3 Civic participation	0.48
3.4 Complaint mechanisms	0.52

Fundamental Rights

4.1 Equal treatment / no discrimination	0.46
4.2 Right to life and security	0.51
4.3 Due process of law	0.35
4.4 Freedom of expression	0.45
4.5 Freedom of religion	0.68
4.6 Right to privacy	0.27
4.7 Freedom of association	0.49
4.8 Labor rights	0.49

Order and Security

5.1 Absence of crime	0.67
5.2 Absence of civil conflict	1
5.3 Absence of violent redress	0.38

Regulatory Enforcement

6.1 Effective regulatory enforcement	0.4
6.2 No improper influence	0.55
6.3 No unreasonable delay	0.36
6.4 Respect for due process	0.29
6.5 No expropriation w/out adequate compensation	0.45

Civil Justice

7.1 Accessibility and affordability	0.4
7.2 No discrimination	0.39
7.3 No corruption	0.34
7.4 No improper gov. influence	0.17
7.5 No unreasonable delay	0.31
7.6 Effective enforcement	0.31
7.7 Impartial and effective ADRs	0.57

Criminal Justice

8.1 Effective investigations	0.36
8.2 Timely and effective adjudication	0.52
8.3 Effective correctional system	0.28
8.4 No discrimination	0.3
8.5 No corruption	0.43
8.6 No improper gov. influence	0.08
8.7 Due process of law	0.35

Nigeria

Lagos, Oyo, Kano
Region: Sub-Saharan Africa | Income group: Lower middle income

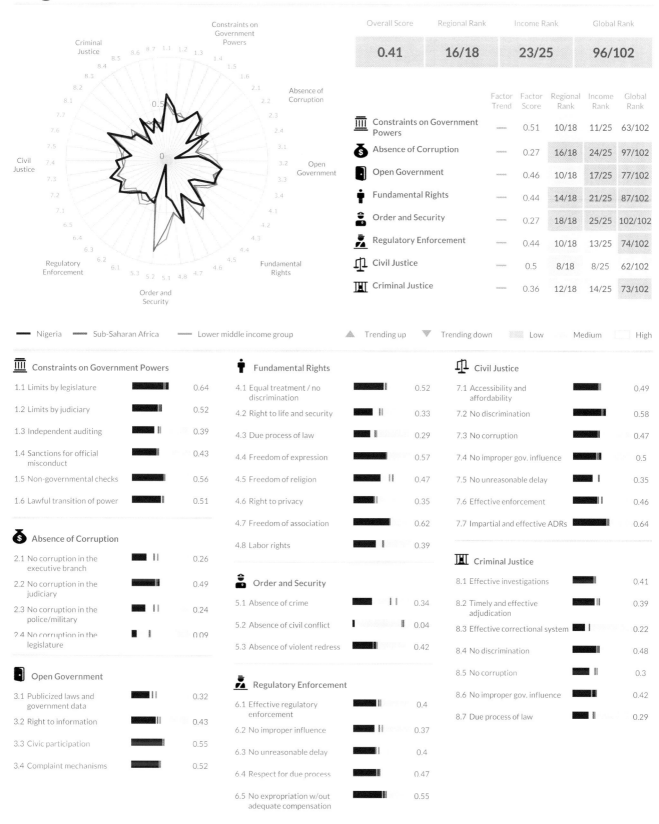

	Overall Score	Regional Rank	Income Rank	Global Rank
	0.41	16/18	23/25	96/102

	Factor Trend	Factor Score	Regional Rank	Income Rank	Global Rank
Constraints on Government Powers	—	0.51	10/18	11/25	63/102
Absence of Corruption	—	0.27	16/18	24/25	97/102
Open Government	—	0.46	10/18	17/25	77/102
Fundamental Rights	—	0.44	14/18	21/25	87/102
Order and Security	—	0.27	18/18	25/25	102/102
Regulatory Enforcement	—	0.44	10/18	13/25	74/102
Civil Justice	—	0.5	8/18	8/25	62/102
Criminal Justice	—	0.36	12/18	14/25	73/102

— Nigeria — Sub-Saharan Africa — Lower middle income group ▲ Trending up ▼ Trending down ▨ Low Medium High

Constraints on Government Powers

1.1 Limits by legislature	0.64
1.2 Limits by judiciary	0.52
1.3 Independent auditing	0.39
1.4 Sanctions for official misconduct	0.43
1.5 Non-governmental checks	0.56
1.6 Lawful transition of power	0.51

Absence of Corruption

2.1 No corruption in the executive branch	0.26
2.2 No corruption in the judiciary	0.49
2.3 No corruption in the police/military	0.24
2.4 No corruption in the legislature	0.09

Open Government

3.1 Publicized laws and government data	0.32
3.2 Right to information	0.43
3.3 Civic participation	0.55
3.4 Complaint mechanisms	0.52

Fundamental Rights

4.1 Equal treatment / no discrimination	0.52
4.2 Right to life and security	0.33
4.3 Due process of law	0.29
4.4 Freedom of expression	0.57
4.5 Freedom of religion	0.47
4.6 Right to privacy	0.35
4.7 Freedom of association	0.62
4.8 Labor rights	0.39

Order and Security

5.1 Absence of crime	0.34
5.2 Absence of civil conflict	0.04
5.3 Absence of violent redress	0.42

Regulatory Enforcement

6.1 Effective regulatory enforcement	0.4
6.2 No improper influence	0.37
6.3 No unreasonable delay	0.4
6.4 Respect for due process	0.47
6.5 No expropriation w/out adequate compensation	0.55

Civil Justice

7.1 Accessibility and affordability	0.49
7.2 No discrimination	0.58
7.3 No corruption	0.47
7.4 No improper gov. influence	0.5
7.5 No unreasonable delay	0.35
7.6 Effective enforcement	0.46
7.7 Impartial and effective ADRs	0.64

Criminal Justice

8.1 Effective investigations	0.41
8.2 Timely and effective adjudication	0.39
8.3 Effective correctional system	0.22
8.4 No discrimination	0.48
8.5 No corruption	0.3
8.6 No improper gov. influence	0.42
8.7 Due process of law	0.29

Norway

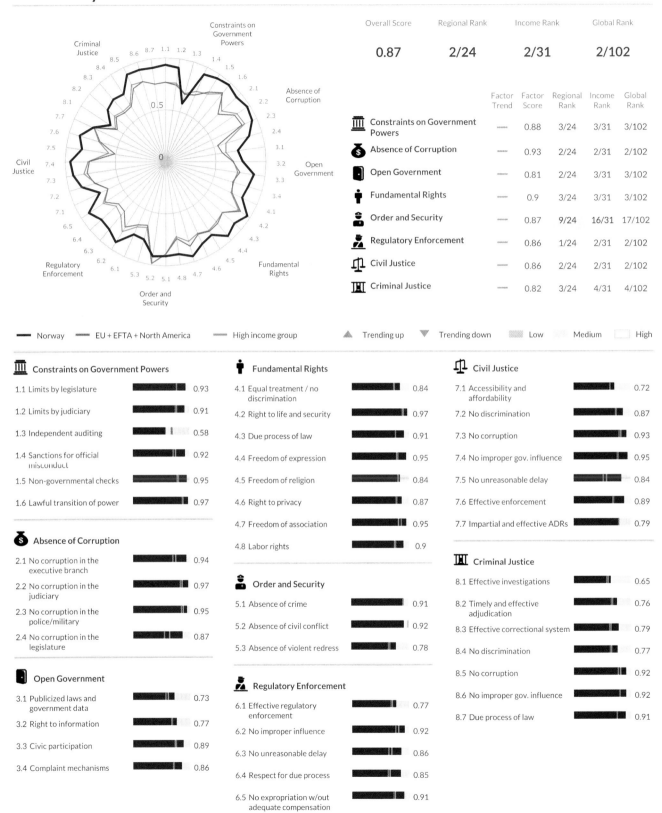

	Overall Score	Regional Rank	Income Rank	Global Rank
	0.87	2/24	2/31	2/102

	Factor Trend	Factor Score	Regional Rank	Income Rank	Global Rank
Constraints on Government Powers	—	0.88	3/24	3/31	3/102
Absence of Corruption	—	0.93	2/24	2/31	2/102
Open Government	—	0.81	2/24	3/31	3/102
Fundamental Rights	—	0.9	3/24	3/31	3/102
Order and Security	—	0.87	9/24	16/31	17/102
Regulatory Enforcement	—	0.86	1/24	2/31	2/102
Civil Justice	—	0.86	2/24	2/31	2/102
Criminal Justice	—	0.82	3/24	4/31	4/102

Legend: Norway | EU + EFTA + North America | High income group | ▲ Trending up | ▼ Trending down | Low | Medium | High

Constraints on Government Powers

1.1 Limits by legislature	0.93
1.2 Limits by judiciary	0.91
1.3 Independent auditing	0.58
1.4 Sanctions for official misconduct	0.92
1.5 Non-governmental checks	0.95
1.6 Lawful transition of power	0.97

Absence of Corruption

2.1 No corruption in the executive branch	0.94
2.2 No corruption in the judiciary	0.97
2.3 No corruption in the police/military	0.95
2.4 No corruption in the legislature	0.87

Open Government

3.1 Publicized laws and government data	0.73
3.2 Right to information	0.77
3.3 Civic participation	0.89
3.4 Complaint mechanisms	0.86

Fundamental Rights

4.1 Equal treatment / no discrimination	0.84
4.2 Right to life and security	0.97
4.3 Due process of law	0.91
4.4 Freedom of expression	0.95
4.5 Freedom of religion	0.84
4.6 Right to privacy	0.87
4.7 Freedom of association	0.95
4.8 Labor rights	0.9

Order and Security

5.1 Absence of crime	0.91
5.2 Absence of civil conflict	0.92
5.3 Absence of violent redress	0.78

Regulatory Enforcement

6.1 Effective regulatory enforcement	0.77
6.2 No improper influence	0.92
6.3 No unreasonable delay	0.86
6.4 Respect for due process	0.85
6.5 No expropriation w/out adequate compensation	0.91

Civil Justice

7.1 Accessibility and affordability	0.72
7.2 No discrimination	0.87
7.3 No corruption	0.93
7.4 No improper gov. influence	0.95
7.5 No unreasonable delay	0.84
7.6 Effective enforcement	0.89
7.7 Impartial and effective ADRs	0.79

Criminal Justice

8.1 Effective investigations	0.65
8.2 Timely and effective adjudication	0.76
8.3 Effective correctional system	0.79
8.4 No discrimination	0.77
8.5 No corruption	0.92
8.6 No improper gov. influence	0.92
8.7 Due process of law	0.91

Pakistan

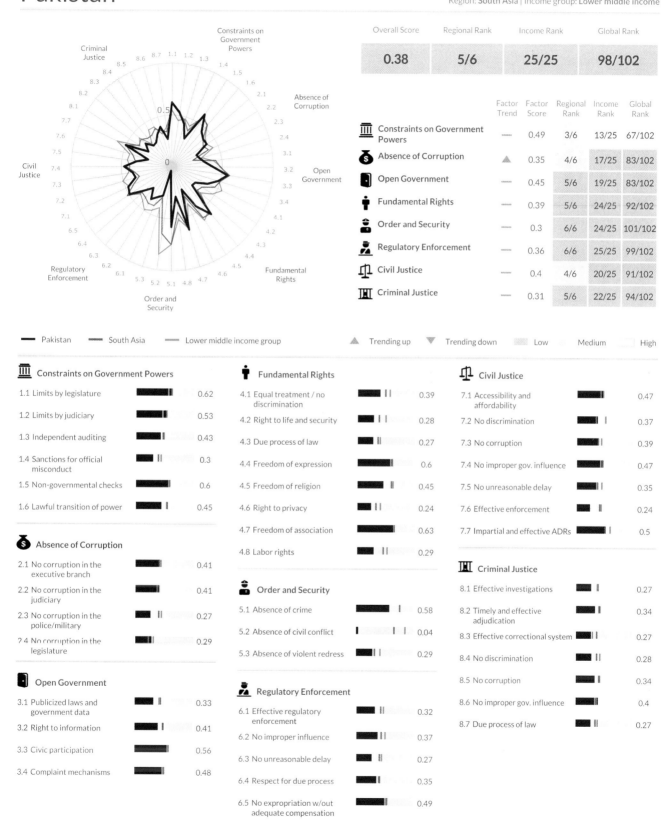

	Overall Score	Regional Rank	Income Rank	Global Rank
	0.38	5/6	25/25	98/102

		Factor Trend	Factor Score	Regional Rank	Income Rank	Global Rank
🏛	Constraints on Government Powers	—	0.49	3/6	13/25	67/102
💰	Absence of Corruption	▲	0.35	4/6	17/25	83/102
📱	Open Government	—	0.45	5/6	19/25	83/102
👤	Fundamental Rights	—	0.39	5/6	24/25	92/102
👮	Order and Security	—	0.3	6/6	24/25	101/102
🔧	Regulatory Enforcement	—	0.36	6/6	25/25	99/102
⚖	Civil Justice	—	0.4	4/6	20/25	91/102
🏛	Criminal Justice	—	0.31	5/6	22/25	94/102

━━ Pakistan   ━━ South Asia   ━━ Lower middle income group   ▲ Trending up   ▼ Trending down   ▨ Low   Medium   High

🏛 Constraints on Government Powers

1.1 Limits by legislature	0.62
1.2 Limits by judiciary	0.53
1.3 Independent auditing	0.43
1.4 Sanctions for official misconduct	0.3
1.5 Non-governmental checks	0.6
1.6 Lawful transition of power	0.45

💰 Absence of Corruption

2.1 No corruption in the executive branch	0.41
2.2 No corruption in the judiciary	0.41
2.3 No corruption in the police/military	0.27
2.4 No corruption in the legislature	0.29

📱 Open Government

3.1 Publicized laws and government data	0.33
3.2 Right to information	0.41
3.3 Civic participation	0.56
3.4 Complaint mechanisms	0.48

👤 Fundamental Rights

4.1 Equal treatment / no discrimination	0.39
4.2 Right to life and security	0.28
4.3 Due process of law	0.27
4.4 Freedom of expression	0.6
4.5 Freedom of religion	0.45
4.6 Right to privacy	0.24
4.7 Freedom of association	0.63
4.8 Labor rights	0.29

👮 Order and Security

5.1 Absence of crime	0.58
5.2 Absence of civil conflict	0.04
5.3 Absence of violent redress	0.29

🔧 Regulatory Enforcement

6.1 Effective regulatory enforcement	0.32
6.2 No improper influence	0.37
6.3 No unreasonable delay	0.27
6.4 Respect for due process	0.35
6.5 No expropriation w/out adequate compensation	0.49

⚖ Civil Justice

7.1 Accessibility and affordability	0.47
7.2 No discrimination	0.37
7.3 No corruption	0.39
7.4 No improper gov. influence	0.47
7.5 No unreasonable delay	0.35
7.6 Effective enforcement	0.24
7.7 Impartial and effective ADRs	0.5

🏛 Criminal Justice

8.1 Effective investigations	0.27
8.2 Timely and effective adjudication	0.34
8.3 Effective correctional system	0.27
8.4 No discrimination	0.28
8.5 No corruption	0.34
8.6 No improper gov. influence	0.4
8.7 Due process of law	0.27

Panama

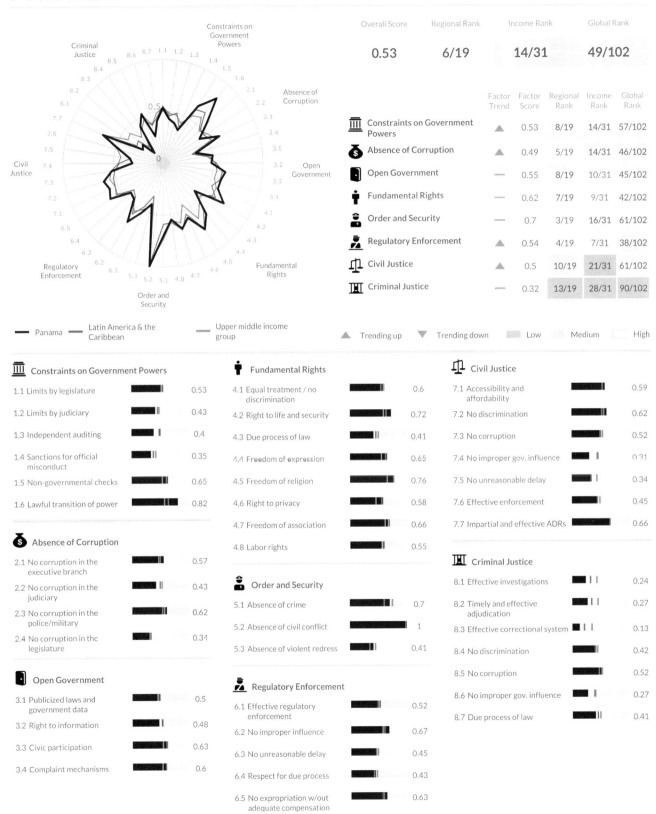

Panama City, San Miguelito, David

Region: **Latin America & the Caribbean** | Income group: **Upper middle income**

	Overall Score	Regional Rank	Income Rank	Global Rank
	0.53	6/19	14/31	49/102

	Factor Trend	Factor Score	Regional Rank	Income Rank	Global Rank
🏛 Constraints on Government Powers	▲	0.53	8/19	14/31	57/102
💰 Absence of Corruption	▲	0.49	5/19	14/31	46/102
📖 Open Government	—	0.55	8/19	10/31	45/102
👤 Fundamental Rights	—	0.62	7/19	9/31	42/102
👮 Order and Security	—	0.7	3/19	16/31	61/102
🛡 Regulatory Enforcement	▲	0.54	4/19	7/31	38/102
⚖ Civil Justice	▲	0.5	10/19	21/31	61/102
🏛 Criminal Justice	—	0.32	13/19	28/31	90/102

Legend: ▬ Panama ▬ Latin America & the Caribbean ▬ Upper middle income group ▲ Trending up ▼ Trending down ▨ Low Medium High

🏛 Constraints on Government Powers

1.1 Limits by legislature	0.53
1.2 Limits by judiciary	0.43
1.3 Independent auditing	0.4
1.4 Sanctions for official misconduct	0.35
1.5 Non-governmental checks	0.65
1.6 Lawful transition of power	0.82

💰 Absence of Corruption

2.1 No corruption in the executive branch	0.57
2.2 No corruption in the judiciary	0.43
2.3 No corruption in the police/military	0.62
2.4 No corruption in the legislature	0.34

📖 Open Government

3.1 Publicized laws and government data	0.5
3.2 Right to information	0.48
3.3 Civic participation	0.63
3.4 Complaint mechanisms	0.6

👤 Fundamental Rights

4.1 Equal treatment / no discrimination	0.6
4.2 Right to life and security	0.72
4.3 Due process of law	0.41
4.4 Freedom of expression	0.65
4.5 Freedom of religion	0.76
4.6 Right to privacy	0.58
4.7 Freedom of association	0.66
4.8 Labor rights	0.55

👮 Order and Security

5.1 Absence of crime	0.7
5.2 Absence of civil conflict	1
5.3 Absence of violent redress	0.41

🛡 Regulatory Enforcement

6.1 Effective regulatory enforcement	0.52
6.2 No improper influence	0.67
6.3 No unreasonable delay	0.45
6.4 Respect for due process	0.43
6.5 No expropriation w/out adequate compensation	0.63

⚖ Civil Justice

7.1 Accessibility and affordability	0.59
7.2 No discrimination	0.62
7.3 No corruption	0.52
7.4 No improper gov. influence	0.31
7.5 No unreasonable delay	0.34
7.6 Effective enforcement	0.45
7.7 Impartial and effective ADRs	0.66

🏛 Criminal Justice

8.1 Effective investigations	0.24
8.2 Timely and effective adjudication	0.27
8.3 Effective correctional system	0.13
8.4 No discrimination	0.42
8.5 No corruption	0.52
8.6 No improper gov. influence	0.27
8.7 Due process of law	0.41

Complete country profiles available at: data.worldjusticeproject.org

Peru

	Overall Score	Regional Rank	Income Rank	Global Rank
	0.5	10/19	21/31	63/102

	Factor Trend	Factor Score	Regional Rank	Income Rank	Global Rank
Constraints on Government Powers	—	0.6	6/19	8/31	43/102
Absence of Corruption	—	0.34	15/19	29/31	86/102
Open Government	—	0.55	9/19	11/31	47/102
Fundamental Rights	▼	0.6	10/19	12/31	47/102
Order and Security	—	0.63	10/19	23/31	79/102
Regulatory Enforcement	—	0.5	8/19	19/31	55/102
Civil Justice	—	0.43	14/19	29/31	86/102
Criminal Justice	—	0.34	9/19	26/31	79/102

— Peru — Latin America & the Caribbean — Upper middle income group   ▲ Trending up   ▼ Trending down   Low   Medium   High

Constraints on Government Powers

1.1 Limits by legislature		0.63
1.2 Limits by judiciary		0.46
1.3 Independent auditing		0.63
1.4 Sanctions for official misconduct		0.42
1.5 Non-governmental checks		0.68
1.6 Lawful transition of power		0.77

Absence of Corruption

2.1 No corruption in the executive branch		0.48
2.2 No corruption in the judiciary		0.37
2.3 No corruption in the police/military		0.36
2.4 No corruption in the legislature		0.16

Open Government

3.1 Publicized laws and government data		0.39
3.2 Right to information		0.55
3.3 Civic participation		0.65
3.4 Complaint mechanisms		0.63

Fundamental Rights

4.1 Equal treatment / no discrimination		0.54
4.2 Right to life and security		0.64
4.3 Due process of law		0.46
4.4 Freedom of expression		0.68
4.5 Freedom of religion		0.72
4.6 Right to privacy		0.52
4.7 Freedom of association		0.73
4.8 Labor rights		0.53

Order and Security

5.1 Absence of crime		0.55
5.2 Absence of civil conflict		1
5.3 Absence of violent redress		0.33

Regulatory Enforcement

6.1 Effective regulatory enforcement		0.44
6.2 No improper influence		0.53
6.3 No unreasonable delay		0.43
6.4 Respect for due process		0.44
6.5 No expropriation w/out adequate compensation		0.63

Civil Justice

7.1 Accessibility and affordability		0.43
7.2 No discrimination		0.48
7.3 No corruption		0.35
7.4 No improper gov. influence		0.44
7.5 No unreasonable delay		0.27
7.6 Effective enforcement		0.37
7.7 Impartial and effective ADRs		0.64

Criminal Justice

8.1 Effective investigations		0.31
8.2 Timely and effective adjudication		0.23
8.3 Effective correctional system		0.18
8.4 No discrimination		0.52
8.5 No corruption		0.3
8.6 No improper gov. influence		0.38
8.7 Due process of law		0.46

Philippines

	Overall Score	Regional Rank	Income Rank	Global Rank
	0.53	9/15	5/25	51/102

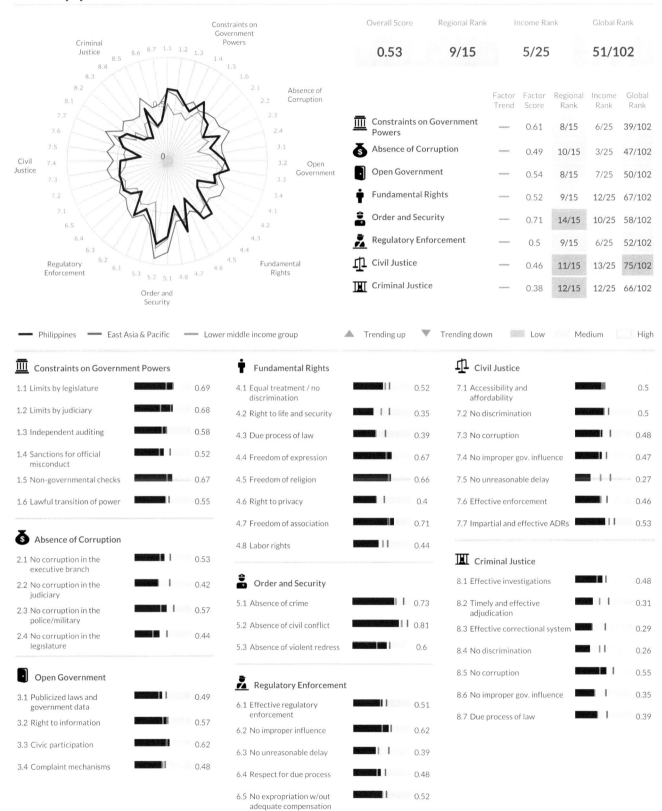

	Factor Trend	Factor Score	Regional Rank	Income Rank	Global Rank
Constraints on Government Powers	—	0.61	8/15	6/25	39/102
Absence of Corruption	—	0.49	10/15	3/25	47/102
Open Government	—	0.54	8/15	7/25	50/102
Fundamental Rights	—	0.52	9/15	12/25	67/102
Order and Security	—	0.71	14/15	10/25	58/102
Regulatory Enforcement	—	0.5	9/15	6/25	52/102
Civil Justice	—	0.46	11/15	13/25	75/102
Criminal Justice	—	0.38	12/15	12/25	66/102

— Philippines — East Asia & Pacific — Lower middle income group   ▲ Trending up   ▼ Trending down   ▨ Low   Medium   ☐ High

Constraints on Government Powers

1.1 Limits by legislature		0.69
1.2 Limits by judiciary		0.68
1.3 Independent auditing		0.58
1.4 Sanctions for official misconduct		0.52
1.5 Non-governmental checks		0.67
1.6 Lawful transition of power		0.55

Absence of Corruption

2.1 No corruption in the executive branch		0.53
2.2 No corruption in the judiciary		0.42
2.3 No corruption in the police/military		0.57
2.4 No corruption in the legislature		0.44

Open Government

3.1 Publicized laws and government data		0.49
3.2 Right to information		0.57
3.3 Civic participation		0.62
3.4 Complaint mechanisms		0.48

Fundamental Rights

4.1 Equal treatment / no discrimination		0.52
4.2 Right to life and security		0.35
4.3 Due process of law		0.39
4.4 Freedom of expression		0.67
4.5 Freedom of religion		0.66
4.6 Right to privacy		0.4
4.7 Freedom of association		0.71
4.8 Labor rights		0.44

Order and Security

5.1 Absence of crime		0.73
5.2 Absence of civil conflict		0.81
5.3 Absence of violent redress		0.6

Regulatory Enforcement

6.1 Effective regulatory enforcement		0.51
6.2 No improper influence		0.62
6.3 No unreasonable delay		0.39
6.4 Respect for due process		0.48
6.5 No expropriation w/out adequate compensation		0.52

Civil Justice

7.1 Accessibility and affordability		0.5
7.2 No discrimination		0.5
7.3 No corruption		0.48
7.4 No improper gov. influence		0.47
7.5 No unreasonable delay		0.27
7.6 Effective enforcement		0.46
7.7 Impartial and effective ADRs		0.53

Criminal Justice

8.1 Effective investigations		0.48
8.2 Timely and effective adjudication		0.31
8.3 Effective correctional system		0.29
8.4 No discrimination		0.26
8.5 No corruption		0.55
8.6 No improper gov. influence		0.35
8.7 Due process of law		0.39

Poland

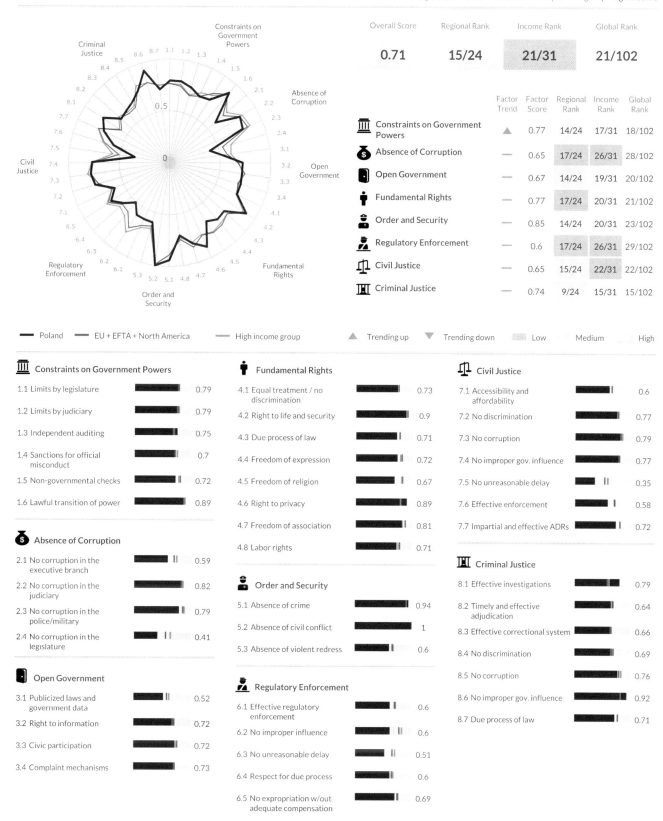

	Overall Score	Regional Rank	Income Rank	Global Rank
	0.71	**15/24**	**21/31**	**21/102**

	Factor Trend	Factor Score	Regional Rank	Income Rank	Global Rank
🏛 Constraints on Government Powers	▲	0.77	14/24	17/31	18/102
💰 Absence of Corruption	—	0.65	17/24	26/31	28/102
📱 Open Government	—	0.67	14/24	19/31	20/102
🧍 Fundamental Rights	—	0.77	17/24	20/31	21/102
👮 Order and Security	—	0.85	14/24	20/31	23/102
Regulatory Enforcement	—	0.6	17/24	26/31	29/102
⚖ Civil Justice	—	0.65	15/24	22/31	22/102
Criminal Justice	—	0.74	9/24	15/31	15/102

— Poland   — EU + EFTA + North America   — High income group   ▲ Trending up   ▼ Trending down   Low   Medium   High

🏛 Constraints on Government Powers

1.1 Limits by legislature	0.79
1.2 Limits by judiciary	0.79
1.3 Independent auditing	0.75
1.4 Sanctions for official misconduct	0.7
1.5 Non-governmental checks	0.72
1.6 Lawful transition of power	0.89

💰 Absence of Corruption

2.1 No corruption in the executive branch	0.59
2.2 No corruption in the judiciary	0.82
2.3 No corruption in the police/military	0.79
2.4 No corruption in the legislature	0.41

📱 Open Government

3.1 Publicized laws and government data	0.52
3.2 Right to information	0.72
3.3 Civic participation	0.72
3.4 Complaint mechanisms	0.73

🧍 Fundamental Rights

4.1 Equal treatment / no discrimination	0.73
4.2 Right to life and security	0.9
4.3 Due process of law	0.71
4.4 Freedom of expression	0.72
4.5 Freedom of religion	0.67
4.6 Right to privacy	0.89
4.7 Freedom of association	0.81
4.8 Labor rights	0.71

👮 Order and Security

5.1 Absence of crime	0.94
5.2 Absence of civil conflict	1
5.3 Absence of violent redress	0.6

Regulatory Enforcement

6.1 Effective regulatory enforcement	0.6
6.2 No improper influence	0.6
6.3 No unreasonable delay	0.51
6.4 Respect for due process	0.6
6.5 No expropriation w/out adequate compensation	0.69

⚖ Civil Justice

7.1 Accessibility and affordability	0.6
7.2 No discrimination	0.77
7.3 No corruption	0.79
7.4 No improper gov. influence	0.77
7.5 No unreasonable delay	0.35
7.6 Effective enforcement	0.58
7.7 Impartial and effective ADRs	0.72

Criminal Justice

8.1 Effective investigations	0.79
8.2 Timely and effective adjudication	0.64
8.3 Effective correctional system	0.66
8.4 No discrimination	0.69
8.5 No corruption	0.76
8.6 No improper gov. influence	0.92
8.7 Due process of law	0.71

Portugal

	Overall Score	Regional Rank	Income Rank	Global Rank
	0.7	16/24	23/31	23/102

	Factor Trend	Factor Score	Regional Rank	Income Rank	Global Rank
Constraints on Government Powers	—	0.79	10/24	12/31	12/102
Absence of Corruption	▲	0.71	14/24	23/31	24/102
Open Government	—	0.64	16/24	22/31	23/102
Fundamental Rights	—	0.8	10/24	12/31	12/102
Order and Security	—	0.76	22/24	26/31	45/102
Regulatory Enforcement	—	0.57	18/24	27/31	30/102
Civil Justice	—	0.65	16/24	23/31	23/102
Criminal Justice	—	0.67	14/24	21/31	21/102

— Portugal   — EU + EFTA + North America   — High income group   ▲ Trending up   ▼ Trending down   Low   Medium   High

Constraints on Government Powers

1.1 Limits by legislature	0.79
1.2 Limits by judiciary	0.76
1.3 Independent auditing	0.79
1.4 Sanctions for official misconduct	0.65
1.5 Non-governmental checks	0.82
1.6 Lawful transition of power	0.95

Absence of Corruption

2.1 No corruption in the executive branch	0.68
2.2 No corruption in the judiciary	0.81
2.3 No corruption in the police/military	0.91
2.4 No corruption in the legislature	0.45

Open Government

3.1 Publicized laws and government data	0.49
3.2 Right to information	0.64
3.3 Civic participation	0.76
3.4 Complaint mechanisms	0.67

Fundamental Rights

4.1 Equal treatment / no discrimination	0.73
4.2 Right to life and security	0.93
4.3 Due process of law	0.71
4.4 Freedom of expression	0.82
4.5 Freedom of religion	0.9
4.6 Right to privacy	0.72
4.7 Freedom of association	0.9
4.8 Labor rights	0.68

Order and Security

5.1 Absence of crime	0.88
5.2 Absence of civil conflict	1
5.3 Absence of violent redress	0.39

Regulatory Enforcement

6.1 Effective regulatory enforcement	0.63
6.2 No improper influence	0.75
6.3 No unreasonable delay	0.45
6.4 Respect for due process	0.4
6.5 No expropriation w/out adequate compensation	0.61

Civil Justice

7.1 Accessibility and affordability	0.63
7.2 No discrimination	0.81
7.3 No corruption	0.77
7.4 No improper gov. influence	0.76
7.5 No unreasonable delay	0.34
7.6 Effective enforcement	0.49
7.7 Impartial and effective ADRs	0.77

Criminal Justice

8.1 Effective investigations	0.47
8.2 Timely and effective adjudication	0.46
8.3 Effective correctional system	0.63
8.4 No discrimination	0.68
8.5 No corruption	0.8
8.6 No improper gov. influence	0.94
8.7 Due process of law	0.71

Republic of Korea

	Overall Score	Regional Rank	Income Rank	Global Rank
	0.79	4/15	11/31	11/102

		Factor Trend	Factor Score	Regional Rank	Income Rank	Global Rank
🏛	Constraints on Government Powers	—	0.79	3/15	14/31	14/102
💰	Absence of Corruption	—	0.82	6/15	14/31	14/102
📱	Open Government	—	0.73	3/15	10/31	10/102
👤	Fundamental Rights	—	0.73	4/15	24/31	25/102
👮	Order and Security	—	0.9	4/15	9/31	10/102
👮	Regulatory Enforcement	—	0.78	4/15	10/31	10/102
⚖	Civil Justice	—	0.8	2/15	7/31	7/102
🏛	Criminal Justice	—	0.76	5/15	13/31	13/102

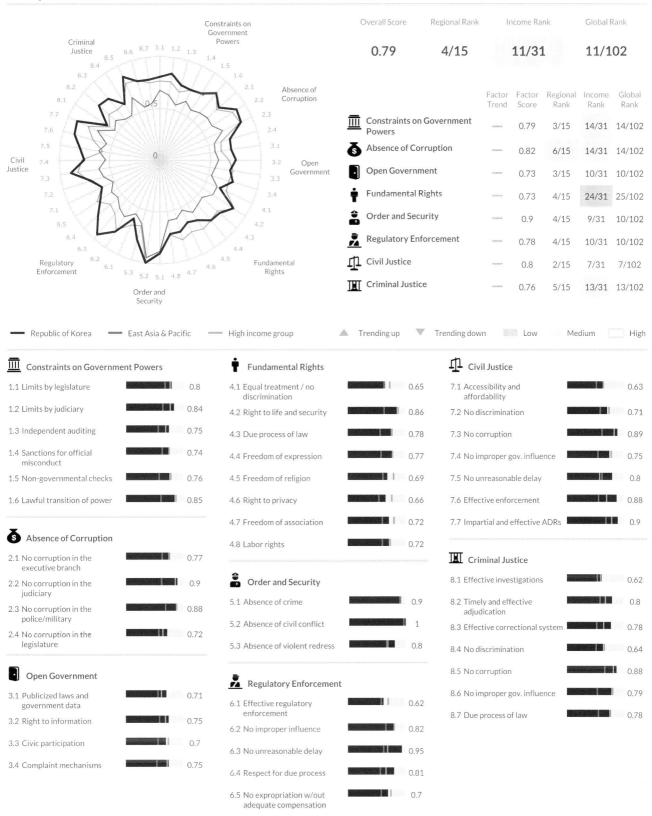

— Republic of Korea   — East Asia & Pacific   — High income group   ▲ Trending up   ▼ Trending down   ▦ Low   ▦ Medium   ☐ High

🏛 Constraints on Government Powers

1.1 Limits by legislature	0.8
1.2 Limits by judiciary	0.84
1.3 Independent auditing	0.75
1.4 Sanctions for official misconduct	0.74
1.5 Non-governmental checks	0.76
1.6 Lawful transition of power	0.85

💰 Absence of Corruption

2.1 No corruption in the executive branch	0.77
2.2 No corruption in the judiciary	0.9
2.3 No corruption in the police/military	0.88
2.4 No corruption in the legislature	0.72

📱 Open Government

3.1 Publicized laws and government data	0.71
3.2 Right to information	0.75
3.3 Civic participation	0.7
3.4 Complaint mechanisms	0.75

👤 Fundamental Rights

4.1 Equal treatment / no discrimination	0.65
4.2 Right to life and security	0.86
4.3 Due process of law	0.78
4.4 Freedom of expression	0.77
4.5 Freedom of religion	0.69
4.6 Right to privacy	0.66
4.7 Freedom of association	0.72
4.8 Labor rights	0.72

👮 Order and Security

5.1 Absence of crime	0.9
5.2 Absence of civil conflict	1
5.3 Absence of violent redress	0.8

👮 Regulatory Enforcement

6.1 Effective regulatory enforcement	0.62
6.2 No improper influence	0.82
6.3 No unreasonable delay	0.95
6.4 Respect for due process	0.81
6.5 No expropriation w/out adequate compensation	0.7

⚖ Civil Justice

7.1 Accessibility and affordability	0.63
7.2 No discrimination	0.71
7.3 No corruption	0.89
7.4 No improper gov. influence	0.75
7.5 No unreasonable delay	0.8
7.6 Effective enforcement	0.88
7.7 Impartial and effective ADRs	0.9

🏛 Criminal Justice

8.1 Effective investigations	0.62
8.2 Timely and effective adjudication	0.8
8.3 Effective correctional system	0.78
8.4 No discrimination	0.64
8.5 No corruption	0.88
8.6 No improper gov. influence	0.79
8.7 Due process of law	0.78

Romania

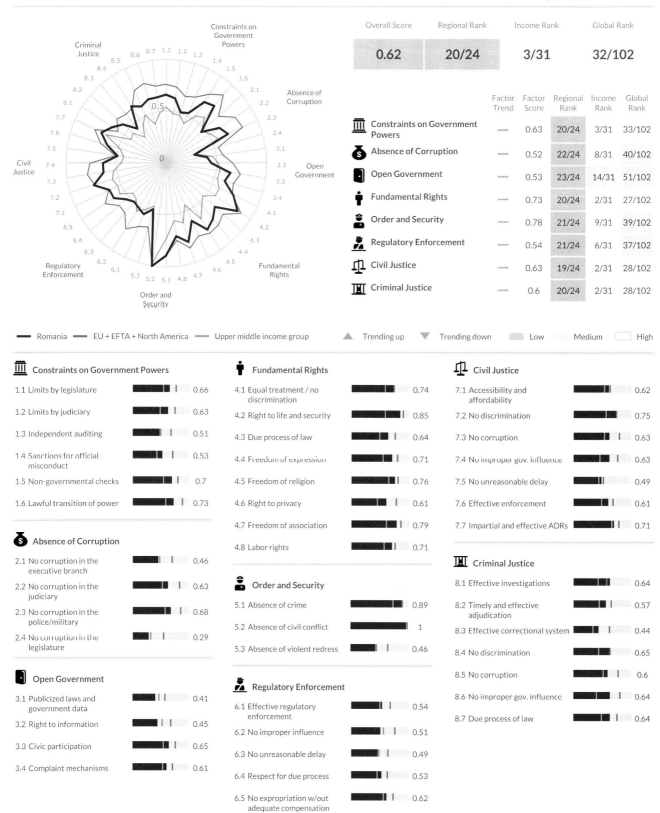

	Overall Score	Regional Rank	Income Rank	Global Rank
	0.62	20/24	3/31	32/102

	Factor Trend	Factor Score	Regional Rank	Income Rank	Global Rank
🏛 Constraints on Government Powers	—	0.63	20/24	3/31	33/102
💰 Absence of Corruption	—	0.52	22/24	8/31	40/102
📱 Open Government	—	0.53	23/24	14/31	51/102
👤 Fundamental Rights	—	0.73	20/24	2/31	27/102
👮 Order and Security	—	0.78	21/24	9/31	39/102
👷 Regulatory Enforcement	—	0.54	21/24	6/31	37/102
⚖ Civil Justice	—	0.63	19/24	2/31	28/102
🏛 Criminal Justice	—	0.6	20/24	2/31	28/102

━━ Romania ━━ EU + EFTA + North America ━━ Upper middle income group ▲ Trending up ▼ Trending down ▦ Low ▦ Medium ▢ High

🏛 Constraints on Government Powers

1.1 Limits by legislature	0.66
1.2 Limits by judiciary	0.63
1.3 Independent auditing	0.51
1.4 Sanctions for official misconduct	0.53
1.5 Non-governmental checks	0.7
1.6 Lawful transition of power	0.73

💰 Absence of Corruption

2.1 No corruption in the executive branch	0.46
2.2 No corruption in the judiciary	0.63
2.3 No corruption in the police/military	0.68
2.4 No corruption in the legislature	0.29

📱 Open Government

3.1 Publicized laws and government data	0.41
3.2 Right to information	0.45
3.3 Civic participation	0.65
3.4 Complaint mechanisms	0.61

👤 Fundamental Rights

4.1 Equal treatment / no discrimination	0.74
4.2 Right to life and security	0.85
4.3 Due process of law	0.64
4.4 Freedom of expression	0.71
4.5 Freedom of religion	0.76
4.6 Right to privacy	0.61
4.7 Freedom of association	0.79
4.8 Labor rights	0.71

👮 Order and Security

5.1 Absence of crime	0.89
5.2 Absence of civil conflict	1
5.3 Absence of violent redress	0.46

👷 Regulatory Enforcement

6.1 Effective regulatory enforcement	0.54
6.2 No improper influence	0.51
6.3 No unreasonable delay	0.49
6.4 Respect for due process	0.53
6.5 No expropriation w/out adequate compensation	0.62

⚖ Civil Justice

7.1 Accessibility and affordability	0.62
7.2 No discrimination	0.75
7.3 No corruption	0.63
7.4 No improper gov. influence	0.63
7.5 No unreasonable delay	0.49
7.6 Effective enforcement	0.61
7.7 Impartial and effective ADRs	0.71

🏛 Criminal Justice

8.1 Effective investigations	0.64
8.2 Timely and effective adjudication	0.57
8.3 Effective correctional system	0.44
8.4 No discrimination	0.65
8.5 No corruption	0.6
8.6 No improper gov. influence	0.64
8.7 Due process of law	0.64

Russia

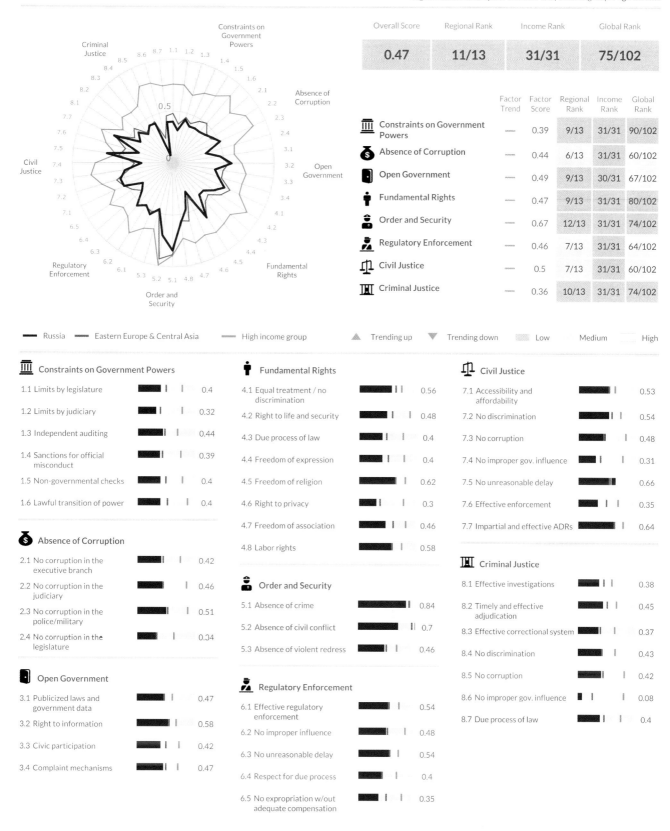

	Overall Score	Regional Rank	Income Rank	Global Rank
	0.47	11/13	31/31	75/102

		Factor Trend	Factor Score	Regional Rank	Income Rank	Global Rank
🏛	Constraints on Government Powers	—	0.39	9/13	31/31	90/102
💰	Absence of Corruption	—	0.44	6/13	31/31	60/102
📱	Open Government	—	0.49	9/13	30/31	67/102
👤	Fundamental Rights	—	0.47	9/13	31/31	80/102
	Order and Security	—	0.67	12/13	31/31	74/102
	Regulatory Enforcement	—	0.46	7/13	31/31	64/102
⚖	Civil Justice	—	0.5	7/13	31/31	60/102
	Criminal Justice	—	0.36	10/13	31/31	74/102

— Russia **—** Eastern Europe & Central Asia **—** High income group ▲ Trending up ▼ Trending down Low Medium High

🏛 Constraints on Government Powers

1.1 Limits by legislature		0.4
1.2 Limits by judiciary		0.32
1.3 Independent auditing		0.44
1.4 Sanctions for official misconduct		0.39
1.5 Non-governmental checks		0.4
1.6 Lawful transition of power		0.4

💰 Absence of Corruption

2.1 No corruption in the executive branch		0.42
2.2 No corruption in the judiciary		0.46
2.3 No corruption in the police/military		0.51
2.4 No corruption in the legislature		0.34

📱 Open Government

3.1 Publicized laws and government data		0.47
3.2 Right to information		0.58
3.3 Civic participation		0.42
3.4 Complaint mechanisms		0.47

👤 Fundamental Rights

4.1 Equal treatment / no discrimination		0.56
4.2 Right to life and security		0.48
4.3 Due process of law		0.4
4.4 Freedom of expression		0.4
4.5 Freedom of religion		0.62
4.6 Right to privacy		0.3
4.7 Freedom of association		0.46
4.8 Labor rights		0.58

Order and Security

5.1 Absence of crime		0.84
5.2 Absence of civil conflict		0.7
5.3 Absence of violent redress		0.46

Regulatory Enforcement

6.1 Effective regulatory enforcement		0.54
6.2 No improper influence		0.48
6.3 No unreasonable delay		0.54
6.4 Respect for due process		0.4
6.5 No expropriation w/out adequate compensation		0.35

⚖ Civil Justice

7.1 Accessibility and affordability		0.53
7.2 No discrimination		0.54
7.3 No corruption		0.48
7.4 No improper gov. influence		0.31
7.5 No unreasonable delay		0.66
7.6 Effective enforcement		0.35
7.7 Impartial and effective ADRs		0.64

Criminal Justice

8.1 Effective investigations		0.38
8.2 Timely and effective adjudication		0.45
8.3 Effective correctional system		0.37
8.4 No discrimination		0.43
8.5 No corruption		0.42
8.6 No improper gov. influence		0.08
8.7 Due process of law		0.4

Senegal

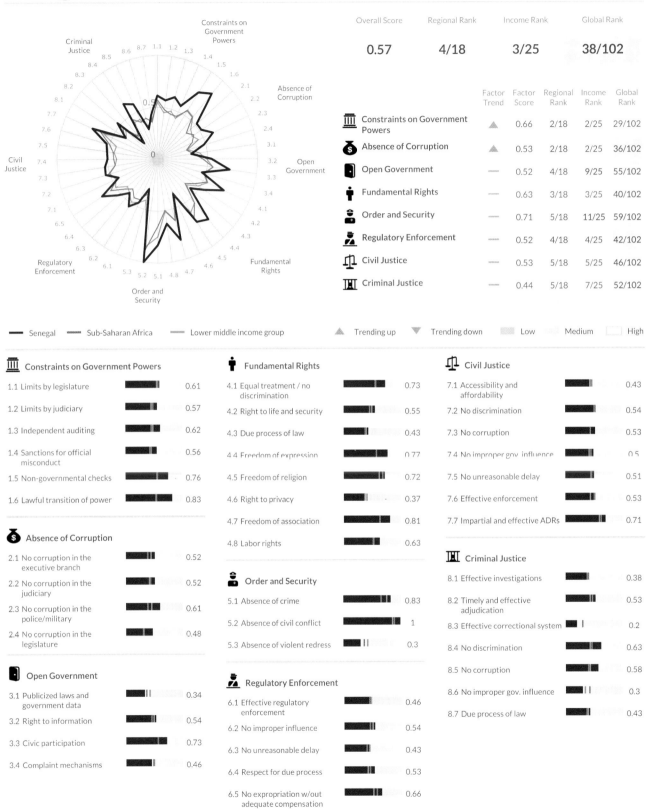

	Overall Score	Regional Rank	Income Rank	Global Rank
	0.57	4/18	3/25	38/102

		Factor Trend	Factor Score	Regional Rank	Income Rank	Global Rank
🏛	Constraints on Government Powers	▲	0.66	2/18	2/25	29/102
💰	Absence of Corruption	▲	0.53	2/18	2/25	36/102
📖	Open Government	—	0.52	4/18	9/25	55/102
🧍	Fundamental Rights	—	0.63	3/18	3/25	40/102
👮	Order and Security	—	0.71	5/18	11/25	59/102
🗂	Regulatory Enforcement	—	0.52	4/18	4/25	42/102
⚖	Civil Justice	—	0.53	5/18	5/25	46/102
🏛	Criminal Justice	—	0.44	5/18	7/25	52/102

— Senegal　— Sub-Saharan Africa　— Lower middle income group　▲ Trending up　▼ Trending down　■ Low　Medium　□ High

🏛 Constraints on Government Powers

1.1 Limits by legislature	0.61
1.2 Limits by judiciary	0.57
1.3 Independent auditing	0.62
1.4 Sanctions for official misconduct	0.56
1.5 Non-governmental checks	0.76
1.6 Lawful transition of power	0.83

💰 Absence of Corruption

2.1 No corruption in the executive branch	0.52
2.2 No corruption in the judiciary	0.52
2.3 No corruption in the police/military	0.61
2.4 No corruption in the legislature	0.48

📖 Open Government

3.1 Publicized laws and government data	0.34
3.2 Right to information	0.54
3.3 Civic participation	0.73
3.4 Complaint mechanisms	0.46

🧍 Fundamental Rights

4.1 Equal treatment / no discrimination	0.73
4.2 Right to life and security	0.55
4.3 Due process of law	0.43
4.4 Freedom of expression	0.77
4.5 Freedom of religion	0.72
4.6 Right to privacy	0.37
4.7 Freedom of association	0.81
4.8 Labor rights	0.63

👮 Order and Security

5.1 Absence of crime	0.83
5.2 Absence of civil conflict	1
5.3 Absence of violent redress	0.3

🗂 Regulatory Enforcement

6.1 Effective regulatory enforcement	0.46
6.2 No improper influence	0.54
6.3 No unreasonable delay	0.43
6.4 Respect for due process	0.53
6.5 No expropriation w/out adequate compensation	0.66

⚖ Civil Justice

7.1 Accessibility and affordability	0.43
7.2 No discrimination	0.54
7.3 No corruption	0.53
7.4 No improper gov. influence	0.5
7.5 No unreasonable delay	0.51
7.6 Effective enforcement	0.53
7.7 Impartial and effective ADRs	0.71

🏛 Criminal Justice

8.1 Effective investigations	0.38
8.2 Timely and effective adjudication	0.53
8.3 Effective correctional system	0.2
8.4 No discrimination	0.63
8.5 No corruption	0.58
8.6 No improper gov. influence	0.3
8.7 Due process of law	0.43

Serbia

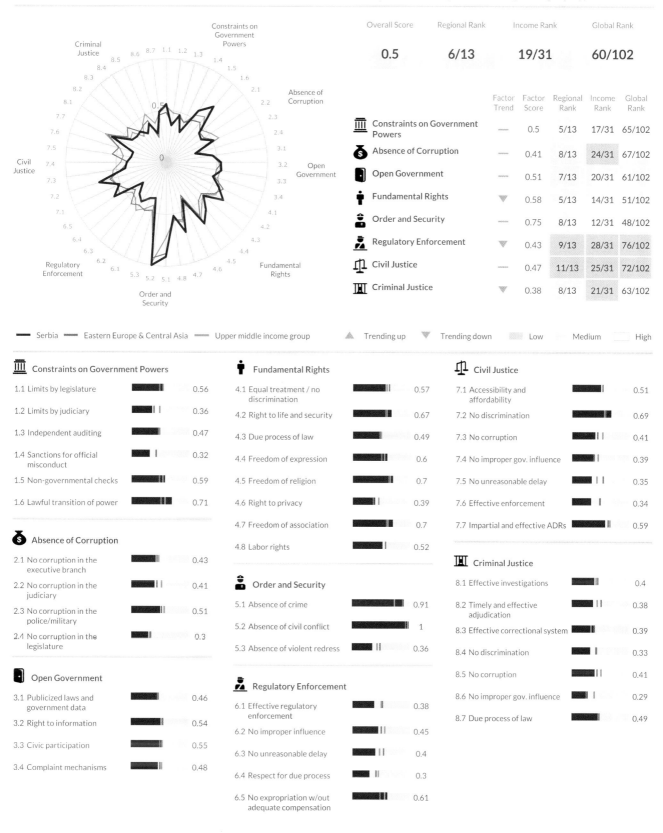

	Overall Score	Regional Rank	Income Rank	Global Rank
	0.5	6/13	19/31	60/102

		Factor Trend	Factor Score	Regional Rank	Income Rank	Global Rank
🏛	Constraints on Government Powers	—	0.5	5/13	17/31	65/102
💰	Absence of Corruption	—	0.41	8/13	24/31	67/102
📱	Open Government	—	0.51	7/13	20/31	61/102
👤	Fundamental Rights	▼	0.58	5/13	14/31	51/102
👮	Order and Security	—	0.75	8/13	12/31	48/102
🗂	Regulatory Enforcement	▼	0.43	9/13	28/31	76/102
⚖	Civil Justice	—	0.47	11/13	25/31	72/102
🏛	Criminal Justice	▼	0.38	8/13	21/31	63/102

— Serbia — Eastern Europe & Central Asia — Upper middle income group   ▲ Trending up   ▼ Trending down   Low   Medium   High

🏛 Constraints on Government Powers

1.1 Limits by legislature	0.56
1.2 Limits by judiciary	0.36
1.3 Independent auditing	0.47
1.4 Sanctions for official misconduct	0.32
1.5 Non-governmental checks	0.59
1.6 Lawful transition of power	0.71

💰 Absence of Corruption

2.1 No corruption in the executive branch	0.43
2.2 No corruption in the judiciary	0.41
2.3 No corruption in the police/military	0.51
2.4 No corruption in the legislature	0.3

📱 Open Government

3.1 Publicized laws and government data	0.46
3.2 Right to information	0.54
3.3 Civic participation	0.55
3.4 Complaint mechanisms	0.48

👤 Fundamental Rights

4.1 Equal treatment / no discrimination	0.57
4.2 Right to life and security	0.67
4.3 Due process of law	0.49
4.4 Freedom of expression	0.6
4.5 Freedom of religion	0.7
4.6 Right to privacy	0.39
4.7 Freedom of association	0.7
4.8 Labor rights	0.52

👮 Order and Security

5.1 Absence of crime	0.91
5.2 Absence of civil conflict	1
5.3 Absence of violent redress	0.36

🗂 Regulatory Enforcement

6.1 Effective regulatory enforcement	0.38
6.2 No improper influence	0.45
6.3 No unreasonable delay	0.4
6.4 Respect for due process	0.3
6.5 No expropriation w/out adequate compensation	0.61

⚖ Civil Justice

7.1 Accessibility and affordability	0.51
7.2 No discrimination	0.69
7.3 No corruption	0.41
7.4 No improper gov. influence	0.39
7.5 No unreasonable delay	0.35
7.6 Effective enforcement	0.34
7.7 Impartial and effective ADRs	0.59

🏛 Criminal Justice

8.1 Effective investigations	0.4
8.2 Timely and effective adjudication	0.38
8.3 Effective correctional system	0.39
8.4 No discrimination	0.33
8.5 No corruption	0.41
8.6 No improper gov. influence	0.29
8.7 Due process of law	0.49

Sierra Leone

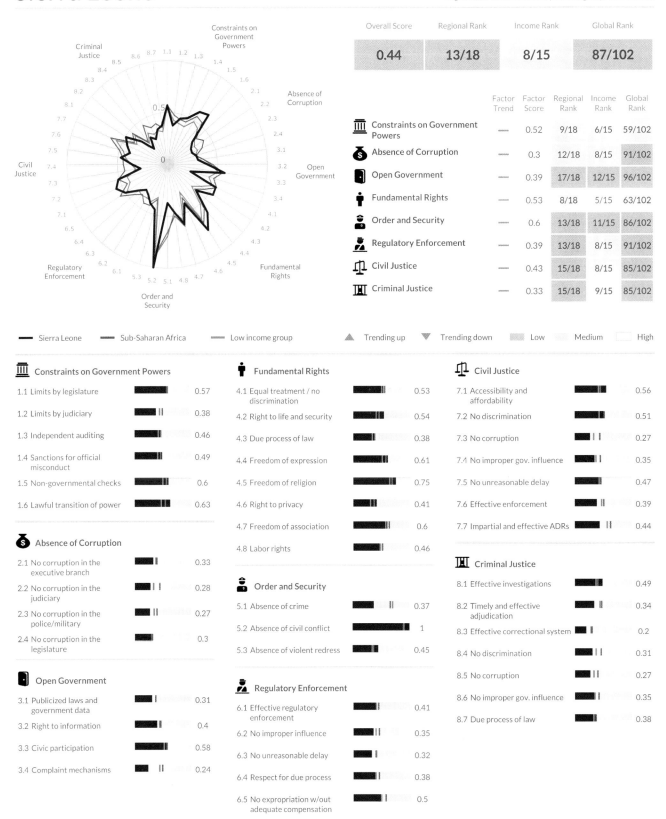

	Overall Score	Regional Rank	Income Rank	Global Rank
	0.44	13/18	8/15	87/102

	Factor Trend	Factor Score	Regional Rank	Income Rank	Global Rank
Constraints on Government Powers	—	0.52	9/18	6/15	59/102
Absence of Corruption	—	0.3	12/18	8/15	91/102
Open Government	—	0.39	17/18	12/15	96/102
Fundamental Rights	—	0.53	8/18	5/15	63/102
Order and Security	—	0.6	13/18	11/15	86/102
Regulatory Enforcement	—	0.39	13/18	8/15	91/102
Civil Justice	—	0.43	15/18	8/15	85/102
Criminal Justice	—	0.33	15/18	9/15	85/102

Legend: ▬ Sierra Leone ▬ Sub-Saharan Africa ▬ Low income group ▲ Trending up ▼ Trending down ░ Low ▒ Medium ☐ High

Constraints on Government Powers

1.1 Limits by legislature	0.57
1.2 Limits by judiciary	0.38
1.3 Independent auditing	0.46
1.4 Sanctions for official misconduct	0.49
1.5 Non-governmental checks	0.6
1.6 Lawful transition of power	0.63

Absence of Corruption

2.1 No corruption in the executive branch	0.33
2.2 No corruption in the judiciary	0.28
2.3 No corruption in the police/military	0.27
2.4 No corruption in the legislature	0.3

Open Government

3.1 Publicized laws and government data	0.31
3.2 Right to information	0.4
3.3 Civic participation	0.58
3.4 Complaint mechanisms	0.24

Fundamental Rights

4.1 Equal treatment / no discrimination	0.53
4.2 Right to life and security	0.54
4.3 Due process of law	0.38
4.4 Freedom of expression	0.61
4.5 Freedom of religion	0.75
4.6 Right to privacy	0.41
4.7 Freedom of association	0.6
4.8 Labor rights	0.46

Order and Security

5.1 Absence of crime	0.37
5.2 Absence of civil conflict	1
5.3 Absence of violent redress	0.45

Regulatory Enforcement

6.1 Effective regulatory enforcement	0.41
6.2 No improper influence	0.35
6.3 No unreasonable delay	0.32
6.4 Respect for due process	0.38
6.5 No expropriation w/out adequate compensation	0.5

Civil Justice

7.1 Accessibility and affordability	0.56
7.2 No discrimination	0.51
7.3 No corruption	0.27
7.4 No improper gov. influence	0.35
7.5 No unreasonable delay	0.47
7.6 Effective enforcement	0.39
7.7 Impartial and effective ADRs	0.44

Criminal Justice

8.1 Effective investigations	0.49
8.2 Timely and effective adjudication	0.34
8.3 Effective correctional system	0.2
8.4 No discrimination	0.31
8.5 No corruption	0.27
8.6 No improper gov. influence	0.35
8.7 Due process of law	0.38

Singapore

	Overall Score	Regional Rank	Income Rank	Global Rank
	0.81	2/15	9/31	9/102

		Factor Trend	Factor Score	Regional Rank	Income Rank	Global Rank
🏛	Constraints on Government Powers	—	0.76	5/15	21/31	22/102
Ⓢ	Absence of Corruption	—	0.93	1/15	3/31	3/102
▯	Open Government	—	0.63	6/15	24/31	25/102
👤	Fundamental Rights	—	0.72	5/15	26/31	28/102
👮	Order and Security	—	0.91	2/15	4/31	4/102
👷	Regulatory Enforcement	▲	0.86	1/15	1/31	1/102
⚖	Civil Justice	▲	0.84	1/15	3/31	3/102
🏛	Criminal Justice	—	0.82	1/15	3/31	3/102

Legend: — Singapore — East Asia & Pacific — High income group | ▲ Trending up ▼ Trending down | Low Medium High

🏛 Constraints on Government Powers

1.1 Limits by legislature — 0.69
1.2 Limits by judiciary — 0.82
1.3 Independent auditing — 0.65
1.4 Sanctions for official misconduct — 0.92
1.5 Non-governmental checks — 0.59
1.6 Lawful transition of power — 0.88

💰 Absence of Corruption

2.1 No corruption in the executive branch — 0.92
2.2 No corruption in the judiciary — 0.92
2.3 No corruption in the police/military — 0.93
2.4 No corruption in the legislature — 0.95

▯ Open Government

3.1 Publicized laws and government data — 0.68
3.2 Right to information — 0.58
3.3 Civic participation — 0.55
3.4 Complaint mechanisms — 0.7

👤 Fundamental Rights

4.1 Equal treatment / no discrimination — 0.85
4.2 Right to life and security — 0.85
4.3 Due process of law — 0.74
4.4 Freedom of expression — 0.59
4.5 Freedom of religion — 0.78
4.6 Right to privacy — 0.62
4.7 Freedom of association — 0.56
4.8 Labor rights — 0.74

👮 Order and Security

5.1 Absence of crime — 0.94
5.2 Absence of civil conflict — 1
5.3 Absence of violent redress — 0.79

👷 Regulatory Enforcement

6.1 Effective regulatory enforcement — 0.8
6.2 No improper influence — 0.96
6.3 No unreasonable delay — 0.83
6.4 Respect for due process — 0.92
6.5 No expropriation w/out adequate compensation — 0.81

⚖ Civil Justice

7.1 Accessibility and affordability — 0.66
7.2 No discrimination — 0.97
7.3 No corruption — 0.89
7.4 No improper gov. influence — 0.84
7.5 No unreasonable delay — 0.93
7.6 Effective enforcement — 0.88
7.7 Impartial and effective ADRs — 0.74

🏛 Criminal Justice

8.1 Effective investigations — 0.68
8.2 Timely and effective adjudication — 0.85
8.3 Effective correctional system — 0.97
8.4 No discrimination — 0.85
8.5 No corruption — 0.92
8.6 No improper gov. influence — 0.74
8.7 Due process of law — 0.74

Slovenia

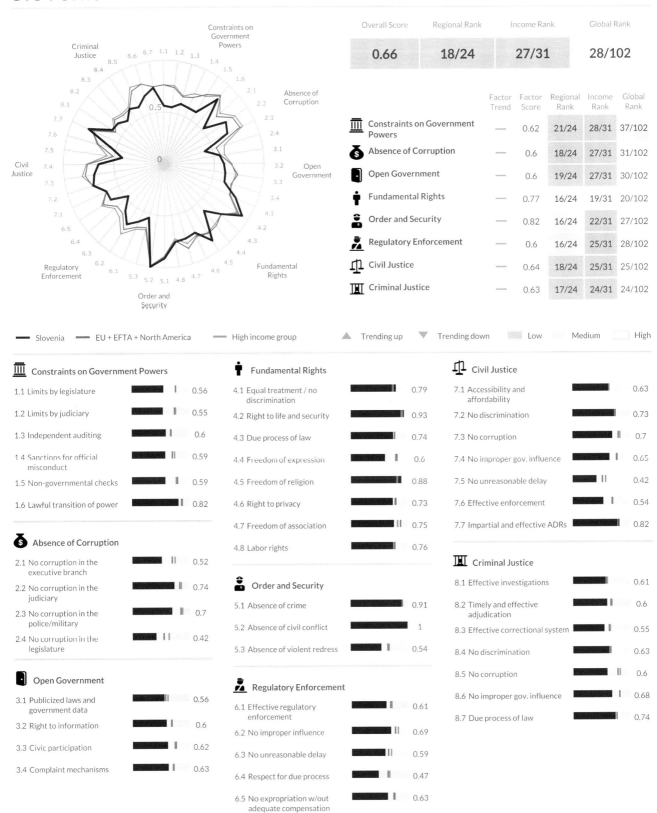

	Overall Score	Regional Rank	Income Rank	Global Rank
	0.66	18/24	27/31	28/102

		Factor Trend	Factor Score	Regional Rank	Income Rank	Global Rank
🏛	Constraints on Government Powers	—	0.62	21/24	28/31	37/102
💰	Absence of Corruption	—	0.6	18/24	27/31	31/102
🚪	Open Government	—	0.6	19/24	27/31	30/102
👤	Fundamental Rights	—	0.77	16/24	19/31	20/102
👮	Order and Security	—	0.82	16/24	22/31	27/102
👷	Regulatory Enforcement	—	0.6	16/24	25/31	28/102
⚖	Civil Justice	—	0.64	18/24	25/31	25/102
🏛	Criminal Justice	—	0.63	17/24	24/31	24/102

— Slovenia   — EU + EFTA + North America   — High income group   ▲ Trending up   ▼ Trending down   ▨ Low   Medium   High

🏛 Constraints on Government Powers

1.1 Limits by legislature		0.56
1.2 Limits by judiciary		0.55
1.3 Independent auditing		0.6
1.4 Sanctions for official misconduct		0.59
1.5 Non-governmental checks		0.59
1.6 Lawful transition of power		0.82

💰 Absence of Corruption

2.1 No corruption in the executive branch		0.52
2.2 No corruption in the judiciary		0.74
2.3 No corruption in the police/military		0.7
2.4 No corruption in the legislature		0.42

🚪 Open Government

3.1 Publicized laws and government data		0.56
3.2 Right to information		0.6
3.3 Civic participation		0.62
3.4 Complaint mechanisms		0.63

👤 Fundamental Rights

4.1 Equal treatment / no discrimination		0.79
4.2 Right to life and security		0.93
4.3 Due process of law		0.74
4.4 Freedom of expression		0.6
4.5 Freedom of religion		0.88
4.6 Right to privacy		0.73
4.7 Freedom of association		0.75
4.8 Labor rights		0.76

👮 Order and Security

5.1 Absence of crime		0.91
5.2 Absence of civil conflict		1
5.3 Absence of violent redress		0.54

👷 Regulatory Enforcement

6.1 Effective regulatory enforcement		0.61
6.2 No improper influence		0.69
6.3 No unreasonable delay		0.59
6.4 Respect for due process		0.47
6.5 No expropriation w/out adequate compensation		0.63

⚖ Civil Justice

7.1 Accessibility and affordability		0.63
7.2 No discrimination		0.73
7.3 No corruption		0.7
7.4 No improper gov. influence		0.65
7.5 No unreasonable delay		0.42
7.6 Effective enforcement		0.54
7.7 Impartial and effective ADRs		0.82

🏛 Criminal Justice

8.1 Effective investigations		0.61
8.2 Timely and effective adjudication		0.6
8.3 Effective correctional system		0.55
8.4 No discrimination		0.63
8.5 No corruption		0.6
8.6 No improper gov. influence		0.68
8.7 Due process of law		0.74

Complete country profiles available at: data.worldjusticeproject.org

South Africa

	Overall Score	Regional Rank	Income Rank	Global Rank
	0.58	**3/18**	**4/31**	**36/102**

	Factor Trend	Factor Score	Regional Rank	Income Rank	Global Rank
🏛 Constraints on Government Powers	—	0.61	4/18	5/31	40/102
💰 Absence of Corruption	—	0.51	3/18	10/31	42/102
📱 Open Government	—	0.62	1/18	2/31	27/102
👤 Fundamental Rights	—	0.63	2/18	8/31	39/102
👮 Order and Security	—	0.62	10/18	25/31	81/102
📋 Regulatory Enforcement	—	0.55	3/18	3/31	33/102
⚖ Civil Justice	—	0.56	3/18	8/31	39/102
🏛 Criminal Justice	▲	0.5	2/18	8/31	38/102

— South Africa — Sub-Saharan Africa — Upper middle income group   ▲ Trending up ▼ Trending down ▨ Low Medium ☐ High

🏛 Constraints on Government Powers

1.1 Limits by legislature	0.64
1.2 Limits by judiciary	0.63
1.3 Independent auditing	0.51
1.4 Sanctions for official misconduct	0.5
1.5 Non-governmental checks	0.73
1.6 Lawful transition of power	0.67

💰 Absence of Corruption

2.1 No corruption in the executive branch	0.46
2.2 No corruption in the judiciary	0.66
2.3 No corruption in the police/military	0.55
2.4 No corruption in the legislature	0.36

📱 Open Government

3.1 Publicized laws and government data	0.53
3.2 Right to information	0.6
3.3 Civic participation	0.7
3.4 Complaint mechanisms	0.63

👤 Fundamental Rights

4.1 Equal treatment / no discrimination	0.53
4.2 Right to life and security	0.63
4.3 Due process of law	0.5
4.4 Freedom of expression	0.73
4.5 Freedom of religion	0.75
4.6 Right to privacy	0.53
4.7 Freedom of association	0.77
4.8 Labor rights	0.61

👮 Order and Security

5.1 Absence of crime	0.51
5.2 Absence of civil conflict	1
5.3 Absence of violent redress	0.35

📋 Regulatory Enforcement

6.1 Effective regulatory enforcement	0.51
6.2 No improper influence	0.59
6.3 No unreasonable delay	0.41
6.4 Respect for due process	0.57
6.5 No expropriation w/out adequate compensation	0.69

⚖ Civil Justice

7.1 Accessibility and affordability	0.47
7.2 No discrimination	0.47
7.3 No corruption	0.63
7.4 No improper gov. influence	0.61
7.5 No unreasonable delay	0.47
7.6 Effective enforcement	0.57
7.7 Impartial and effective ADRs	0.72

🏛 Criminal Justice

8.1 Effective investigations	0.47
8.2 Timely and effective adjudication	0.47
8.3 Effective correctional system	0.35
8.4 No discrimination	0.52
8.5 No corruption	0.56
8.6 No improper gov. influence	0.65
8.7 Due process of law	0.5

Spain

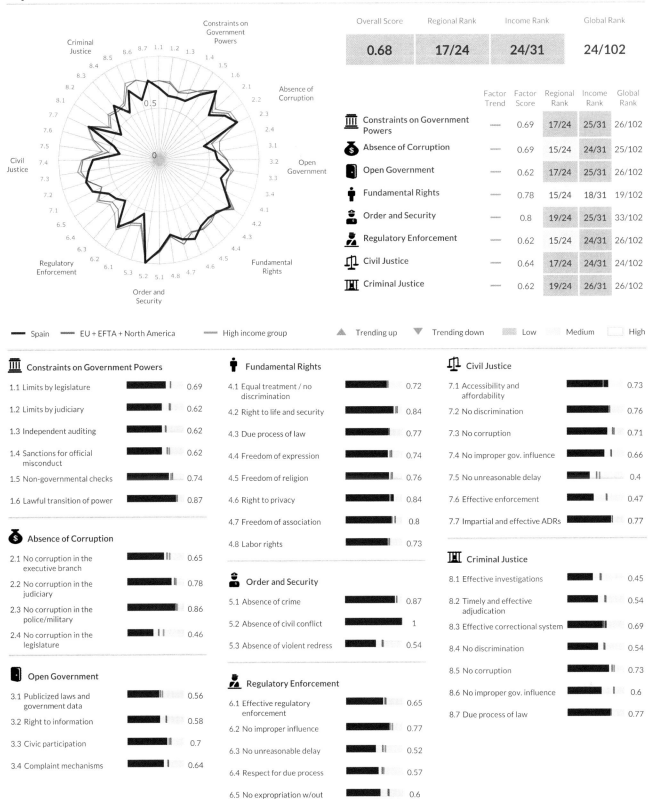

	Overall Score	Regional Rank	Income Rank	Global Rank
	0.68	17/24	24/31	24/102

	Factor Trend	Factor Score	Regional Rank	Income Rank	Global Rank
Constraints on Government Powers	—	0.69	17/24	25/31	26/102
Absence of Corruption	—	0.69	15/24	24/31	25/102
Open Government	—	0.62	17/24	25/31	26/102
Fundamental Rights	—	0.78	15/24	18/31	19/102
Order and Security	—	0.8	19/24	25/31	33/102
Regulatory Enforcement	—	0.62	15/24	24/31	26/102
Civil Justice	—	0.64	17/24	24/31	24/102
Criminal Justice	—	0.62	19/24	26/31	26/102

— Spain   — EU + EFTA + North America   — High income group   ▲ Trending up   ▼ Trending down   ▒ Low   Medium   □ High

Constraints on Government Powers

1.1 Limits by legislature		0.69
1.2 Limits by judiciary		0.62
1.3 Independent auditing		0.62
1.4 Sanctions for official misconduct		0.62
1.5 Non-governmental checks		0.74
1.6 Lawful transition of power		0.87

Absence of Corruption

2.1 No corruption in the executive branch		0.65
2.2 No corruption in the judiciary		0.78
2.3 No corruption in the police/military		0.86
2.4 No corruption in the legislature		0.46

Open Government

3.1 Publicized laws and government data		0.56
3.2 Right to information		0.58
3.3 Civic participation		0.7
3.4 Complaint mechanisms		0.64

Fundamental Rights

4.1 Equal treatment / no discrimination		0.72
4.2 Right to life and security		0.84
4.3 Due process of law		0.77
4.4 Freedom of expression		0.74
4.5 Freedom of religion		0.76
4.6 Right to privacy		0.84
4.7 Freedom of association		0.8
4.8 Labor rights		0.73

Order and Security

5.1 Absence of crime		0.87
5.2 Absence of civil conflict		1
5.3 Absence of violent redress		0.54

Regulatory Enforcement

6.1 Effective regulatory enforcement		0.65
6.2 No improper influence		0.77
6.3 No unreasonable delay		0.52
6.4 Respect for due process		0.57
6.5 No expropriation w/out adequate compensation		0.6

Civil Justice

7.1 Accessibility and affordability		0.73
7.2 No discrimination		0.76
7.3 No corruption		0.71
7.4 No improper gov. influence		0.66
7.5 No unreasonable delay		0.4
7.6 Effective enforcement		0.47
7.7 Impartial and effective ADRs		0.77

Criminal Justice

8.1 Effective investigations		0.45
8.2 Timely and effective adjudication		0.54
8.3 Effective correctional system		0.69
8.4 No discrimination		0.54
8.5 No corruption		0.73
8.6 No improper gov. influence		0.6
8.7 Due process of law		0.77

    Complete country profiles available at: data.worldjusticeproject.org

Sri Lanka

Colombo, Negombo, Kandy
Region: **South Asia** | Income group: **Lower middle income**

	Overall Score	Regional Rank	Income Rank	Global Rank
	0.51	2/6	9/25	58/102

		Factor Trend	Factor Score	Regional Rank	Income Rank	Global Rank
🏛	Constraints on Government Powers	▼	0.47	4/6	16/25	75/102
💰	Absence of Corruption	—	0.46	1/6	6/25	54/102
📱	Open Government	—	0.53	3/6	8/25	52/102
👤	Fundamental Rights	▼	0.49	3/6	16/25	77/102
👮	Order and Security	—	0.69	2/6	13/25	65/102
👷	Regulatory Enforcement	—	0.49	2/6	7/25	58/102
⚖	Civil Justice	—	0.47	1/6	11/25	69/102
🏛	Criminal Justice	—	0.45	2/6	5/25	46/102

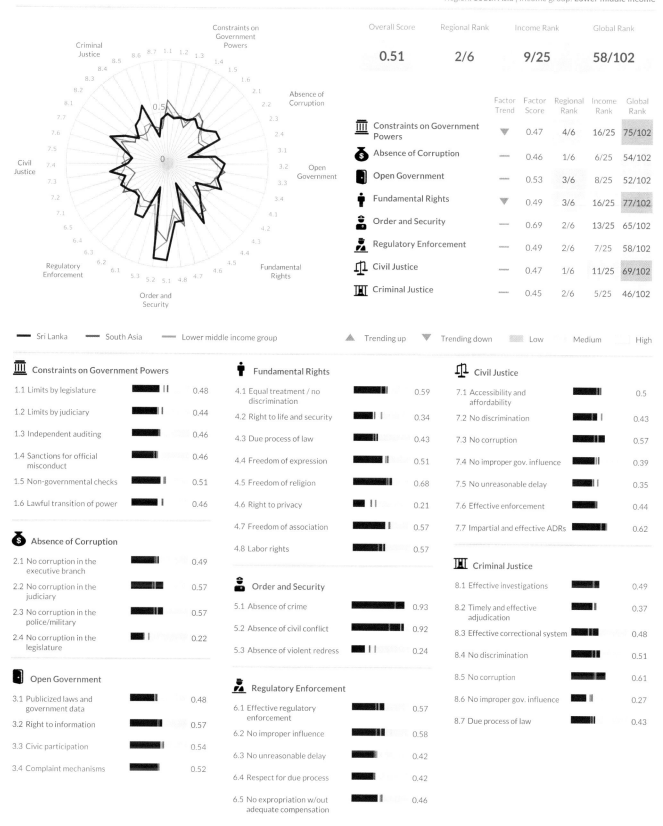

— Sri Lanka   — South Asia   — Lower middle income group   ▲ Trending up   ▼ Trending down   ▨ Low   Medium   High

🏛 Constraints on Government Powers

1.1 Limits by legislature	0.48
1.2 Limits by judiciary	0.44
1.3 Independent auditing	0.46
1.4 Sanctions for official misconduct	0.46
1.5 Non-governmental checks	0.51
1.6 Lawful transition of power	0.46

💰 Absence of Corruption

2.1 No corruption in the executive branch	0.49
2.2 No corruption in the judiciary	0.57
2.3 No corruption in the police/military	0.57
2.4 No corruption in the legislature	0.22

📱 Open Government

3.1 Publicized laws and government data	0.48
3.2 Right to information	0.57
3.3 Civic participation	0.54
3.4 Complaint mechanisms	0.52

👤 Fundamental Rights

4.1 Equal treatment / no discrimination	0.59
4.2 Right to life and security	0.34
4.3 Due process of law	0.43
4.4 Freedom of expression	0.51
4.5 Freedom of religion	0.68
4.6 Right to privacy	0.21
4.7 Freedom of association	0.57
4.8 Labor rights	0.57

👮 Order and Security

5.1 Absence of crime	0.93
5.2 Absence of civil conflict	0.92
5.3 Absence of violent redress	0.24

👷 Regulatory Enforcement

6.1 Effective regulatory enforcement	0.57
6.2 No improper influence	0.58
6.3 No unreasonable delay	0.42
6.4 Respect for due process	0.42
6.5 No expropriation w/out adequate compensation	0.46

⚖ Civil Justice

7.1 Accessibility and affordability	0.5
7.2 No discrimination	0.43
7.3 No corruption	0.57
7.4 No improper gov. influence	0.39
7.5 No unreasonable delay	0.35
7.6 Effective enforcement	0.44
7.7 Impartial and effective ADRs	0.62

🏛 Criminal Justice

8.1 Effective investigations	0.49
8.2 Timely and effective adjudication	0.37
8.3 Effective correctional system	0.48
8.4 No discrimination	0.51
8.5 No corruption	0.61
8.6 No improper gov. influence	0.27
8.7 Due process of law	0.43

Sweden

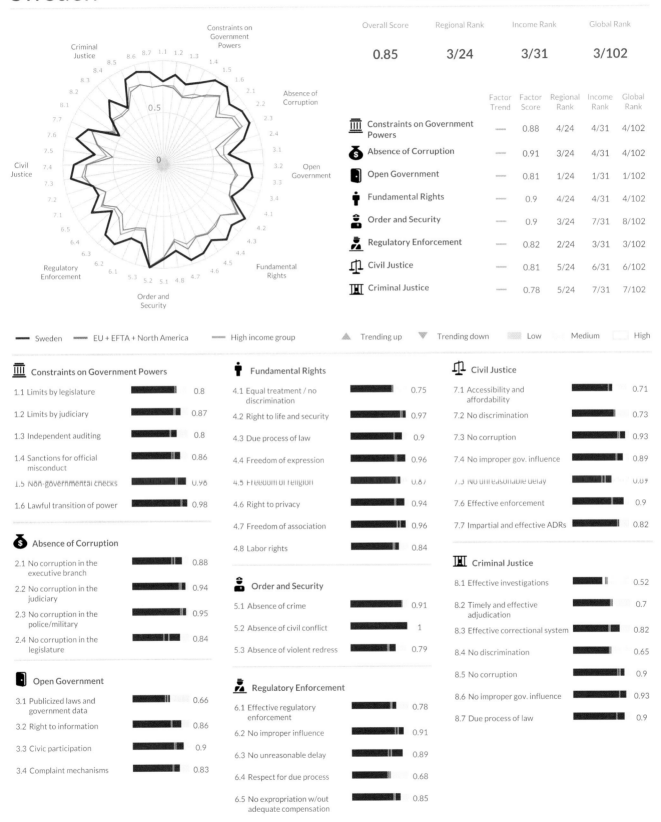

	Overall Score	Regional Rank	Income Rank	Global Rank
	0.85	3/24	3/31	3/102

	Factor Trend	Factor Score	Regional Rank	Income Rank	Global Rank
Constraints on Government Powers	—	0.88	4/24	4/31	4/102
Absence of Corruption	—	0.91	3/24	4/31	4/102
Open Government	—	0.81	1/24	1/31	1/102
Fundamental Rights	—	0.9	4/24	4/31	4/102
Order and Security	—	0.9	3/24	7/31	8/102
Regulatory Enforcement	—	0.82	2/24	3/31	3/102
Civil Justice	—	0.81	5/24	6/31	6/102
Criminal Justice	—	0.78	5/24	7/31	7/102

— Sweden   — EU + EFTA + North America   — High income group   ▲ Trending up   ▼ Trending down   Low   Medium   High

Constraints on Government Powers

1.1 Limits by legislature	0.8
1.2 Limits by judiciary	0.87
1.3 Independent auditing	0.8
1.4 Sanctions for official misconduct	0.86
1.5 Non-governmental checks	0.98
1.6 Lawful transition of power	0.98

Absence of Corruption

2.1 No corruption in the executive branch	0.88
2.2 No corruption in the judiciary	0.94
2.3 No corruption in the police/military	0.95
2.4 No corruption in the legislature	0.84

Open Government

3.1 Publicized laws and government data	0.66
3.2 Right to information	0.86
3.3 Civic participation	0.9
3.4 Complaint mechanisms	0.83

Fundamental Rights

4.1 Equal treatment / no discrimination	0.75
4.2 Right to life and security	0.97
4.3 Due process of law	0.9
4.4 Freedom of expression	0.96
4.5 Freedom of religion	0.87
4.6 Right to privacy	0.94
4.7 Freedom of association	0.96
4.8 Labor rights	0.84

Order and Security

5.1 Absence of crime	0.91
5.2 Absence of civil conflict	1
5.3 Absence of violent redress	0.79

Regulatory Enforcement

6.1 Effective regulatory enforcement	0.78
6.2 No improper influence	0.91
6.3 No unreasonable delay	0.89
6.4 Respect for due process	0.68
6.5 No expropriation w/out adequate compensation	0.85

Civil Justice

7.1 Accessibility and affordability	0.71
7.2 No discrimination	0.73
7.3 No corruption	0.93
7.4 No improper gov. influence	0.89
7.5 No unreasonable delay	0.89
7.6 Effective enforcement	0.9
7.7 Impartial and effective ADRs	0.82

Criminal Justice

8.1 Effective investigations	0.52
8.2 Timely and effective adjudication	0.7
8.3 Effective correctional system	0.82
8.4 No discrimination	0.65
8.5 No corruption	0.9
8.6 No improper gov. influence	0.93
8.7 Due process of law	0.9

Tanzania

Dar es Salaam, Mwanza, Shinyanga
Region: **Sub-Saharan Africa** | Income group: **Low income**

	Overall Score	Regional Rank	Income Rank	Global Rank
	0.47	6/18	3/15	72/102

	Factor Trend	Factor Score	Regional Rank	Income Rank	Global Rank
Constraints on Government Powers	—	0.53	8/18	5/15	55/102
Absence of Corruption	—	0.37	9/18	5/15	77/102
Open Government	—	0.51	5/18	2/15	62/102
Fundamental Rights	—	0.51	9/18	6/15	71/102
Order and Security	—	0.58	14/18	12/15	91/102
Regulatory Enforcement	—	0.43	11/18	5/15	77/102
Civil Justice	—	0.51	7/18	2/15	57/102
Criminal Justice	—	0.37	9/18	4/15	67/102

--- Tanzania --- Sub-Saharan Africa --- Low income group ▲ Trending up ▼ Trending down Low Medium High

Constraints on Government Powers

1.1 Limits by legislature	0.69
1.2 Limits by judiciary	0.54
1.3 Independent auditing	0.36
1.4 Sanctions for official misconduct	0.45
1.5 Non-governmental checks	0.58
1.6 Lawful transition of power	0.57

Absence of Corruption

2.1 No corruption in the executive branch	0.4
2.2 No corruption in the judiciary	0.33
2.3 No corruption in the police/military	0.35
2.4 No corruption in the legislature	0.39

Open Government

3.1 Publicized laws and government data	0.41
3.2 Right to information	0.44
3.3 Civic participation	0.58
3.4 Complaint mechanisms	0.59

Fundamental Rights

4.1 Equal treatment / no discrimination	0.49
4.2 Right to life and security	0.52
4.3 Due process of law	0.29
4.4 Freedom of expression	0.59
4.5 Freedom of religion	0.68
4.6 Right to privacy	0.55
4.7 Freedom of association	0.6
4.8 Labor rights	0.31

Order and Security

5.1 Absence of crime	0.53
5.2 Absence of civil conflict	1
5.3 Absence of violent redress	0.21

Regulatory Enforcement

6.1 Effective regulatory enforcement	0.41
6.2 No improper influence	0.39
6.3 No unreasonable delay	0.3
6.4 Respect for due process	0.44
6.5 No expropriation w/out adequate compensation	0.58

Civil Justice

7.1 Accessibility and affordability	0.47
7.2 No discrimination	0.62
7.3 No corruption	0.36
7.4 No improper gov. influence	0.42
7.5 No unreasonable delay	0.42
7.6 Effective enforcement	0.56
7.7 Impartial and effective ADRs	0.71

Criminal Justice

8.1 Effective investigations	0.4
8.2 Timely and effective adjudication	0.51
8.3 Effective correctional system	0.16
8.4 No discrimination	0.28
8.5 No corruption	0.39
8.6 No improper gov. influence	0.6
8.7 Due process of law	0.29

Thailand

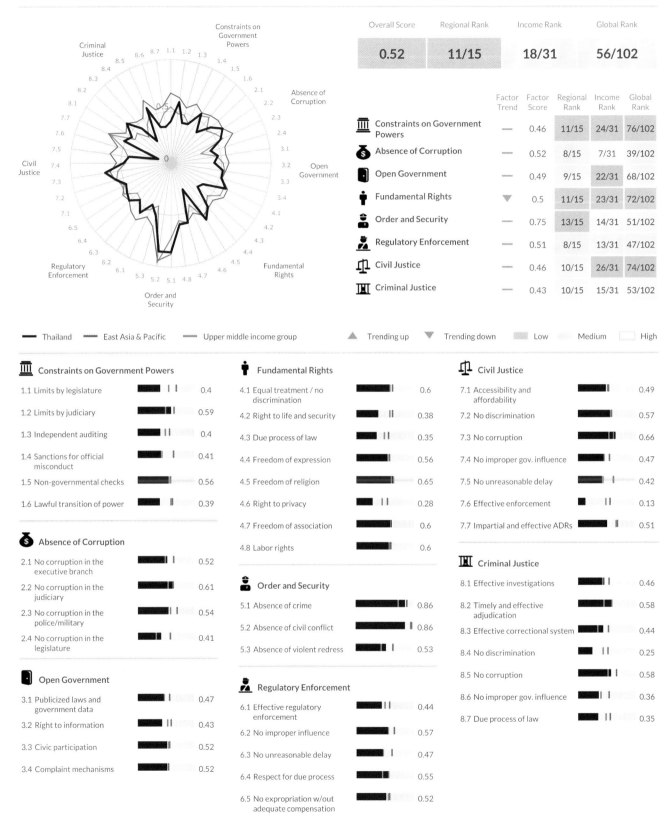

	Overall Score	Regional Rank	Income Rank	Global Rank
	0.52	11/15	18/31	56/102

		Factor Trend	Factor Score	Regional Rank	Income Rank	Global Rank
🏛	Constraints on Government Powers	—	0.46	11/15	24/31	76/102
💰	Absence of Corruption	—	0.52	8/15	7/31	39/102
📖	Open Government	—	0.49	9/15	22/31	68/102
👤	Fundamental Rights	▼	0.5	11/15	23/31	72/102
👮	Order and Security	—	0.75	13/15	14/31	51/102
🧑‍🌾	Regulatory Enforcement	—	0.51	8/15	13/31	47/102
⚖	Civil Justice	—	0.46	10/15	26/31	74/102
🏛	Criminal Justice	—	0.43	10/15	15/31	53/102

— Thailand   **—** East Asia & Pacific   **—** Upper middle income group   ▲ Trending up   ▼ Trending down   ░ Low   Medium   ☐ High

🏛 Constraints on Government Powers

1.1 Limits by legislature	0.4
1.2 Limits by judiciary	0.59
1.3 Independent auditing	0.4
1.4 Sanctions for official misconduct	0.41
1.5 Non-governmental checks	0.56
1.6 Lawful transition of power	0.39

💰 Absence of Corruption

2.1 No corruption in the executive branch	0.52
2.2 No corruption in the judiciary	0.61
2.3 No corruption in the police/military	0.54
2.4 No corruption in the legislature	0.41

📖 Open Government

3.1 Publicized laws and government data	0.47
3.2 Right to information	0.43
3.3 Civic participation	0.52
3.4 Complaint mechanisms	0.52

👤 Fundamental Rights

4.1 Equal treatment / no discrimination	0.6
4.2 Right to life and security	0.38
4.3 Due process of law	0.35
4.4 Freedom of expression	0.56
4.5 Freedom of religion	0.65
4.6 Right to privacy	0.28
4.7 Freedom of association	0.6
4.8 Labor rights	0.6

👮 Order and Security

5.1 Absence of crime	0.86
5.2 Absence of civil conflict	0.86
5.3 Absence of violent redress	0.53

🧑‍🌾 Regulatory Enforcement

6.1 Effective regulatory enforcement	0.44
6.2 No improper influence	0.57
6.3 No unreasonable delay	0.47
6.4 Respect for due process	0.55
6.5 No expropriation w/out adequate compensation	0.52

⚖ Civil Justice

7.1 Accessibility and affordability	0.49
7.2 No discrimination	0.57
7.3 No corruption	0.66
7.4 No improper gov. influence	0.47
7.5 No unreasonable delay	0.42
7.6 Effective enforcement	0.13
7.7 Impartial and effective ADRs	0.51

🏛 Criminal Justice

8.1 Effective investigations	0.46
8.2 Timely and effective adjudication	0.58
8.3 Effective correctional system	0.44
8.4 No discrimination	0.25
8.5 No corruption	0.58
8.6 No improper gov. influence	0.36
8.7 Due process of law	0.35

Complete country profiles available at: data.worldjusticeproject.org

Tunisia

	Overall Score	Regional Rank	Income Rank	Global Rank
	0.56	3/7	10/31	43/102

	Factor Trend	Factor Score	Regional Rank	Income Rank	Global Rank
Constraints on Government Powers	▲	0.62	1/7	4/31	34/102
Absence of Corruption	—	0.5	3/7	12/31	44/102
Open Government	—	0.51	1/7	19/31	59/102
Fundamental Rights	—	0.54	2/7	20/31	62/102
Order and Security	—	0.75	4/7	13/31	50/102
Regulatory Enforcement	—	0.52	4/7	10/31	43/102
Civil Justice	—	0.52	4/7	14/31	49/102
Criminal Justice	—	0.49	3/7	9/31	41/102

— Tunisia — Middle East & North Africa — Upper middle income group ▲ Trending up ▼ Trending down ▦ Low Medium High

Constraints on Government Powers

1.1 Limits by legislature	0.7
1.2 Limits by judiciary	0.59
1.3 Independent auditing	0.57
1.4 Sanctions for official misconduct	0.48
1.5 Non-governmental checks	0.69
1.6 Lawful transition of power	0.71

Absence of Corruption

2.1 No corruption in the executive branch	0.52
2.2 No corruption in the judiciary	0.46
2.3 No corruption in the police/military	0.63
2.4 No corruption in the legislature	0.4

Open Government

3.1 Publicized laws and government data	0.43
3.2 Right to information	0.5
3.3 Civic participation	0.65
3.4 Complaint mechanisms	0.46

Fundamental Rights

4.1 Equal treatment / no discrimination	0.54
4.2 Right to life and security	0.5
4.3 Due process of law	0.49
4.4 Freedom of expression	0.7
4.5 Freedom of religion	0.61
4.6 Right to privacy	0.23
4.7 Freedom of association	0.72
4.8 Labor rights	0.54

Order and Security

5.1 Absence of crime	0.82
5.2 Absence of civil conflict	1
5.3 Absence of violent redress	0.44

Regulatory Enforcement

6.1 Effective regulatory enforcement	0.53
6.2 No improper influence	0.59
6.3 No unreasonable delay	0.4
6.4 Respect for due process	0.42
6.5 No expropriation w/out adequate compensation	0.65

Civil Justice

7.1 Accessibility and affordability	0.48
7.2 No discrimination	0.62
7.3 No corruption	0.46
7.4 No improper gov. influence	0.52
7.5 No unreasonable delay	0.47
7.6 Effective enforcement	0.48
7.7 Impartial and effective ADRs	0.59

Criminal Justice

8.1 Effective investigations	0.44
8.2 Timely and effective adjudication	0.53
8.3 Effective correctional system	0.45
8.4 No discrimination	0.46
8.5 No corruption	0.57
8.6 No improper gov. influence	0.51
8.7 Due process of law	0.49

Turkey

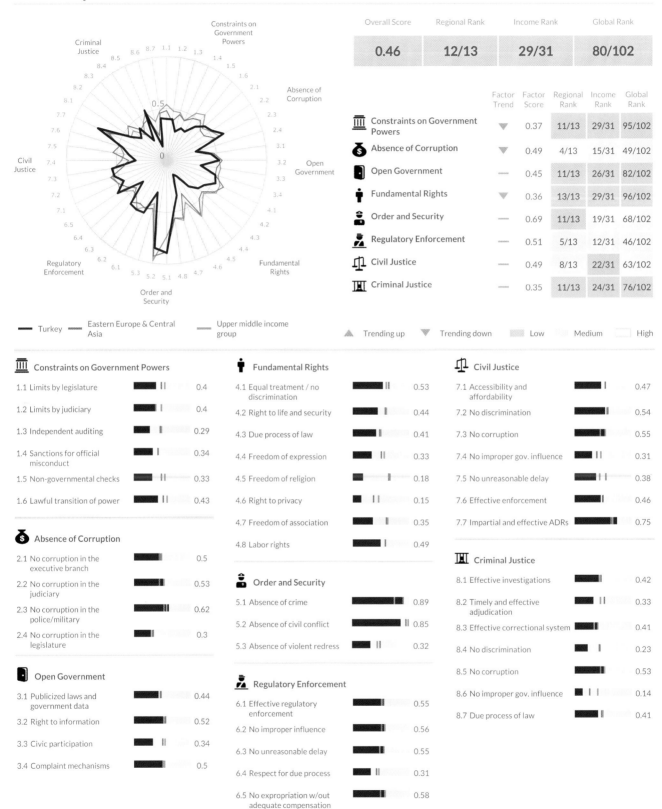

	Overall Score	Regional Rank	Income Rank	Global Rank
	0.46	12/13	29/31	80/102

		Factor Trend	Factor Score	Regional Rank	Income Rank	Global Rank
🏛	Constraints on Government Powers	▼	0.37	11/13	29/31	95/102
💰	Absence of Corruption	▼	0.49	4/13	15/31	49/102
📱	Open Government	—	0.45	11/13	26/31	82/102
👤	Fundamental Rights	▼	0.36	13/13	29/31	96/102
👮	Order and Security	—	0.69	11/13	19/31	68/102
📋	Regulatory Enforcement	—	0.51	5/13	12/31	46/102
⚖	Civil Justice	—	0.49	8/13	22/31	63/102
🏛	Criminal Justice	—	0.35	11/13	24/31	76/102

— Turkey   — Eastern Europe & Central Asia   — Upper middle income group

▲ Trending up   ▼ Trending down   ▓ Low   Medium   High

🏛 Constraints on Government Powers

1.1 Limits by legislature	0.4
1.2 Limits by judiciary	0.4
1.3 Independent auditing	0.29
1.4 Sanctions for official misconduct	0.34
1.5 Non-governmental checks	0.33
1.6 Lawful transition of power	0.43

💰 Absence of Corruption

2.1 No corruption in the executive branch	0.5
2.2 No corruption in the judiciary	0.53
2.3 No corruption in the police/military	0.62
2.4 No corruption in the legislature	0.3

📱 Open Government

3.1 Publicized laws and government data	0.44
3.2 Right to information	0.52
3.3 Civic participation	0.34
3.4 Complaint mechanisms	0.5

👤 Fundamental Rights

4.1 Equal treatment / no discrimination	0.53
4.2 Right to life and security	0.44
4.3 Due process of law	0.41
4.4 Freedom of expression	0.33
4.5 Freedom of religion	0.18
4.6 Right to privacy	0.15
4.7 Freedom of association	0.35
4.8 Labor rights	0.49

👮 Order and Security

5.1 Absence of crime	0.89
5.2 Absence of civil conflict	0.85
5.3 Absence of violent redress	0.32

📋 Regulatory Enforcement

6.1 Effective regulatory enforcement	0.55
6.2 No improper influence	0.56
6.3 No unreasonable delay	0.55
6.4 Respect for due process	0.31
6.5 No expropriation w/out adequate compensation	0.58

⚖ Civil Justice

7.1 Accessibility and affordability	0.47
7.2 No discrimination	0.54
7.3 No corruption	0.55
7.4 No improper gov. influence	0.31
7.5 No unreasonable delay	0.38
7.6 Effective enforcement	0.46
7.7 Impartial and effective ADRs	0.75

🏛 Criminal Justice

8.1 Effective investigations	0.42
8.2 Timely and effective adjudication	0.33
8.3 Effective correctional system	0.41
8.4 No discrimination	0.23
8.5 No corruption	0.53
8.6 No improper gov. influence	0.14
8.7 Due process of law	0.41

Uganda

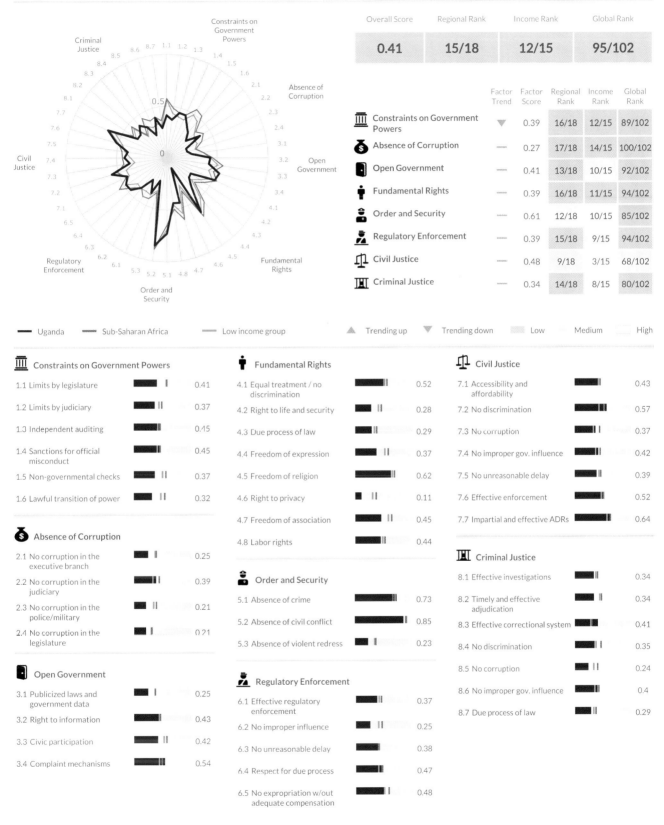

	Overall Score	Regional Rank	Income Rank	Global Rank
	0.41	**15/18**	**12/15**	**95/102**

	Factor Trend	Factor Score	Regional Rank	Income Rank	Global Rank
Constraints on Government Powers	▼	0.39	16/18	12/15	89/102
Absence of Corruption	—	0.27	17/18	14/15	100/102
Open Government	—	0.41	13/18	10/15	92/102
Fundamental Rights	—	0.39	16/18	11/15	94/102
Order and Security	—	0.61	12/18	10/15	85/102
Regulatory Enforcement	—	0.39	15/18	9/15	94/102
Civil Justice	—	0.48	9/18	3/15	68/102
Criminal Justice	—	0.34	14/18	8/15	80/102

—— Uganda ━━ Sub-Saharan Africa —— Low income group ▲ Trending up ▼ Trending down Low Medium High

Constraints on Government Powers

1.1 Limits by legislature	0.41
1.2 Limits by judiciary	0.37
1.3 Independent auditing	0.45
1.4 Sanctions for official misconduct	0.45
1.5 Non-governmental checks	0.37
1.6 Lawful transition of power	0.32

Absence of Corruption

2.1 No corruption in the executive branch	0.25
2.2 No corruption in the judiciary	0.39
2.3 No corruption in the police/military	0.21
2.4 No corruption in the legislature	0.21

Open Government

3.1 Publicized laws and government data	0.25
3.2 Right to information	0.43
3.3 Civic participation	0.42
3.4 Complaint mechanisms	0.54

Fundamental Rights

4.1 Equal treatment / no discrimination	0.52
4.2 Right to life and security	0.28
4.3 Due process of law	0.29
4.4 Freedom of expression	0.37
4.5 Freedom of religion	0.62
4.6 Right to privacy	0.11
4.7 Freedom of association	0.45
4.8 Labor rights	0.44

Order and Security

5.1 Absence of crime	0.73
5.2 Absence of civil conflict	0.85
5.3 Absence of violent redress	0.23

Regulatory Enforcement

6.1 Effective regulatory enforcement	0.37
6.2 No improper influence	0.25
6.3 No unreasonable delay	0.38
6.4 Respect for due process	0.47
6.5 No expropriation w/out adequate compensation	0.48

Civil Justice

7.1 Accessibility and affordability	0.43
7.2 No discrimination	0.57
7.3 No corruption	0.37
7.4 No improper gov. influence	0.42
7.5 No unreasonable delay	0.39
7.6 Effective enforcement	0.52
7.7 Impartial and effective ADRs	0.64

Criminal Justice

8.1 Effective investigations	0.34
8.2 Timely and effective adjudication	0.34
8.3 Effective correctional system	0.41
8.4 No discrimination	0.35
8.5 No corruption	0.24
8.6 No improper gov. influence	0.4
8.7 Due process of law	0.29

Ukraine

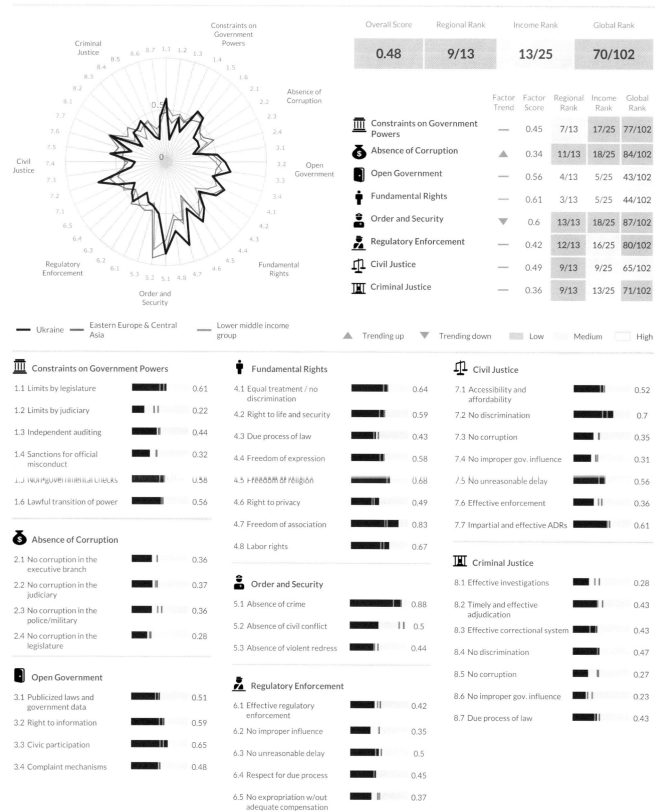

	Overall Score	Regional Rank	Income Rank	Global Rank
	0.48	9/13	13/25	70/102

	Factor Trend	Factor Score	Regional Rank	Income Rank	Global Rank
Constraints on Government Powers	—	0.45	7/13	17/25	77/102
Absence of Corruption	▲	0.34	11/13	18/25	84/102
Open Government	—	0.56	4/13	5/25	43/102
Fundamental Rights	—	0.61	3/13	5/25	44/102
Order and Security	▼	0.6	13/13	18/25	87/102
Regulatory Enforcement	—	0.42	12/13	16/25	80/102
Civil Justice	—	0.49	9/13	9/25	65/102
Criminal Justice	—	0.36	9/13	13/25	71/102

— Ukraine — Eastern Europe & Central Asia — Lower middle income group

▲ Trending up ▼ Trending down ▓ Low Medium High

Constraints on Government Powers

1.1 Limits by legislature	0.61
1.2 Limits by judiciary	0.22
1.3 Independent auditing	0.44
1.4 Sanctions for official misconduct	0.32
1.5 Non-governmental checks	0.58
1.6 Lawful transition of power	0.56

Absence of Corruption

2.1 No corruption in the executive branch	0.36
2.2 No corruption in the judiciary	0.37
2.3 No corruption in the police/military	0.36
2.4 No corruption in the legislature	0.28

Open Government

3.1 Publicized laws and government data	0.51
3.2 Right to information	0.59
3.3 Civic participation	0.65
3.4 Complaint mechanisms	0.48

Fundamental Rights

4.1 Equal treatment / no discrimination	0.64
4.2 Right to life and security	0.59
4.3 Due process of law	0.43
4.4 Freedom of expression	0.58
4.5 Freedom of religion	0.68
4.6 Right to privacy	0.49
4.7 Freedom of association	0.83
4.8 Labor rights	0.67

Order and Security

5.1 Absence of crime	0.88
5.2 Absence of civil conflict	0.5
5.3 Absence of violent redress	0.44

Regulatory Enforcement

6.1 Effective regulatory enforcement	0.42
6.2 No improper influence	0.35
6.3 No unreasonable delay	0.5
6.4 Respect for due process	0.45
6.5 No expropriation w/out adequate compensation	0.37

Civil Justice

7.1 Accessibility and affordability	0.52
7.2 No discrimination	0.7
7.3 No corruption	0.35
7.4 No improper gov. influence	0.31
7.5 No unreasonable delay	0.56
7.6 Effective enforcement	0.36
7.7 Impartial and effective ADRs	0.61

Criminal Justice

8.1 Effective investigations	0.28
8.2 Timely and effective adjudication	0.43
8.3 Effective correctional system	0.43
8.4 No discrimination	0.47
8.5 No corruption	0.27
8.6 No improper gov. influence	0.23
8.7 Due process of law	0.43

Complete country profiles available at: data.worldjusticeproject.org

United Arab Emirates

Dubai, Sharjah, Abu Dhabi
Region: **Middle East & North Africa** | Income group: **High income**

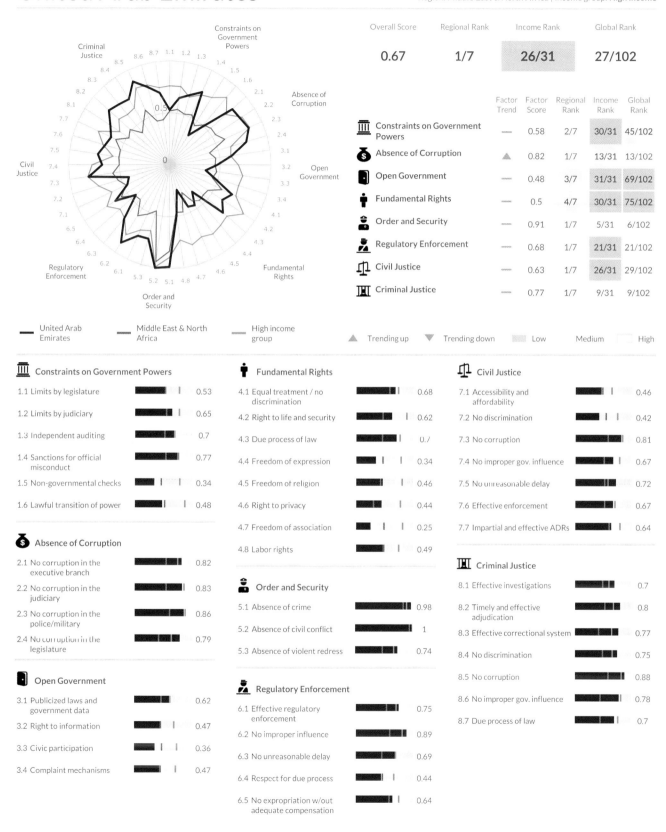

	Overall Score	Regional Rank	Income Rank	Global Rank
	0.67	1/7	26/31	27/102

		Factor Trend	Factor Score	Regional Rank	Income Rank	Global Rank
🏛	Constraints on Government Powers	—	0.58	2/7	30/31	45/102
💰	Absence of Corruption	▲	0.82	1/7	13/31	13/102
📖	Open Government	—	0.48	3/7	31/31	69/102
👤	Fundamental Rights	—	0.5	4/7	30/31	75/102
👮	Order and Security	—	0.91	1/7	5/31	6/102
📊	Regulatory Enforcement	—	0.68	1/7	21/31	21/102
⚖	Civil Justice	—	0.63	1/7	26/31	29/102
🏛	Criminal Justice	—	0.77	1/7	9/31	9/102

— United Arab Emirates   — Middle East & North Africa   — High income group   ▲ Trending up   ▼ Trending down   Low   Medium   High

🏛 Constraints on Government Powers

1.1 Limits by legislature	0.53
1.2 Limits by judiciary	0.65
1.3 Independent auditing	0.7
1.4 Sanctions for official misconduct	0.77
1.5 Non-governmental checks	0.34
1.6 Lawful transition of power	0.48

💰 Absence of Corruption

2.1 No corruption in the executive branch	0.82
2.2 No corruption in the judiciary	0.83
2.3 No corruption in the police/military	0.86
2.4 No corruption in the legislature	0.79

📖 Open Government

3.1 Publicized laws and government data	0.62
3.2 Right to information	0.47
3.3 Civic participation	0.36
3.4 Complaint mechanisms	0.47

👤 Fundamental Rights

4.1 Equal treatment / no discrimination	0.68
4.2 Right to life and security	0.62
4.3 Due process of law	0.7
4.4 Freedom of expression	0.34
4.5 Freedom of religion	0.46
4.6 Right to privacy	0.44
4.7 Freedom of association	0.25
4.8 Labor rights	0.49

👮 Order and Security

5.1 Absence of crime	0.98
5.2 Absence of civil conflict	1
5.3 Absence of violent redress	0.74

📊 Regulatory Enforcement

6.1 Effective regulatory enforcement	0.75
6.2 No improper influence	0.89
6.3 No unreasonable delay	0.69
6.4 Respect for due process	0.44
6.5 No expropriation w/out adequate compensation	0.64

⚖ Civil Justice

7.1 Accessibility and affordability	0.46
7.2 No discrimination	0.42
7.3 No corruption	0.81
7.4 No improper gov. influence	0.67
7.5 No unreasonable delay	0.72
7.6 Effective enforcement	0.67
7.7 Impartial and effective ADRs	0.64

🏛 Criminal Justice

8.1 Effective investigations	0.7
8.2 Timely and effective adjudication	0.8
8.3 Effective correctional system	0.77
8.4 No discrimination	0.75
8.5 No corruption	0.88
8.6 No improper gov. influence	0.78
8.7 Due process of law	0.7

United Kingdom

London, Birmingham, Glasgow
Region: **EU + EFTA + North America** | Income group: **High income**

	Overall Score	Regional Rank	Income Rank	Global Rank
	0.78	**8/24**	**12/31**	**12/102**

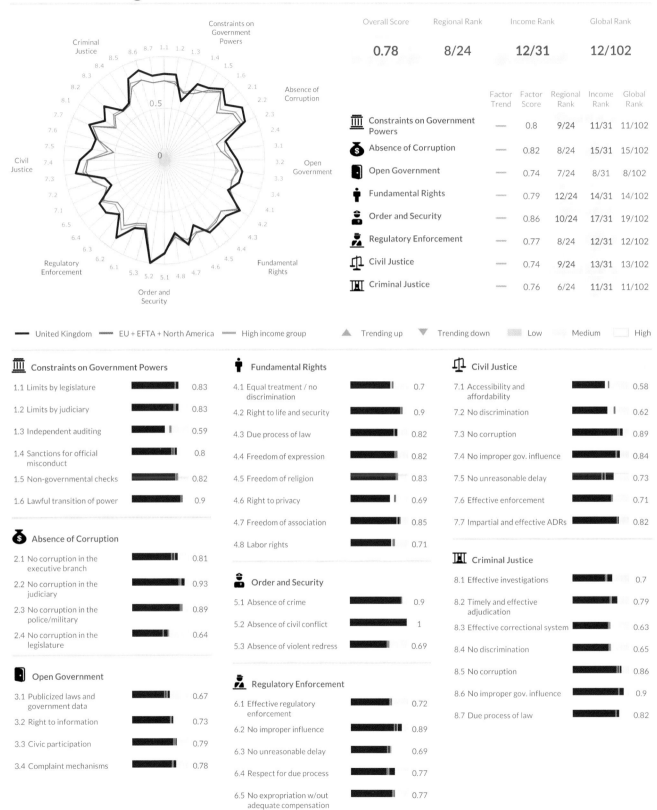

	Factor Trend	Factor Score	Regional Rank	Income Rank	Global Rank
Constraints on Government Powers	—	0.8	9/24	11/31	11/102
Absence of Corruption	—	0.82	8/24	15/31	15/102
Open Government	—	0.74	7/24	8/31	8/102
Fundamental Rights	—	0.79	12/24	14/31	14/102
Order and Security	—	0.86	10/24	17/31	19/102
Regulatory Enforcement	—	0.77	8/24	12/31	12/102
Civil Justice	—	0.74	9/24	13/31	13/102
Criminal Justice	—	0.76	6/24	11/31	11/102

Legend: ▬ United Kingdom · ▬ EU + EFTA + North America · ▬ High income group · ▲ Trending up · ▼ Trending down · Low · Medium · High

Constraints on Government Powers

1.1 Limits by legislature	0.83
1.2 Limits by judiciary	0.83
1.3 Independent auditing	0.59
1.4 Sanctions for official misconduct	0.8
1.5 Non-governmental checks	0.82
1.6 Lawful transition of power	0.9

Absence of Corruption

2.1 No corruption in the executive branch	0.81
2.2 No corruption in the judiciary	0.93
2.3 No corruption in the police/military	0.89
2.4 No corruption in the legislature	0.64

Open Government

3.1 Publicized laws and government data	0.67
3.2 Right to information	0.73
3.3 Civic participation	0.79
3.4 Complaint mechanisms	0.78

Fundamental Rights

4.1 Equal treatment / no discrimination	0.7
4.2 Right to life and security	0.9
4.3 Due process of law	0.82
4.4 Freedom of expression	0.82
4.5 Freedom of religion	0.83
4.6 Right to privacy	0.69
4.7 Freedom of association	0.85
4.8 Labor rights	0.71

Order and Security

5.1 Absence of crime	0.9
5.2 Absence of civil conflict	1
5.3 Absence of violent redress	0.69

Regulatory Enforcement

6.1 Effective regulatory enforcement	0.72
6.2 No improper influence	0.89
6.3 No unreasonable delay	0.69
6.4 Respect for due process	0.77
6.5 No expropriation w/out adequate compensation	0.77

Civil Justice

7.1 Accessibility and affordability	0.58
7.2 No discrimination	0.62
7.3 No corruption	0.89
7.4 No improper gov. influence	0.84
7.5 No unreasonable delay	0.73
7.6 Effective enforcement	0.71
7.7 Impartial and effective ADRs	0.82

Criminal Justice

8.1 Effective investigations	0.7
8.2 Timely and effective adjudication	0.79
8.3 Effective correctional system	0.63
8.4 No discrimination	0.65
8.5 No corruption	0.86
8.6 No improper gov. influence	0.9
8.7 Due process of law	0.82

Complete country profiles available at: data.worldjusticeproject.org

United States

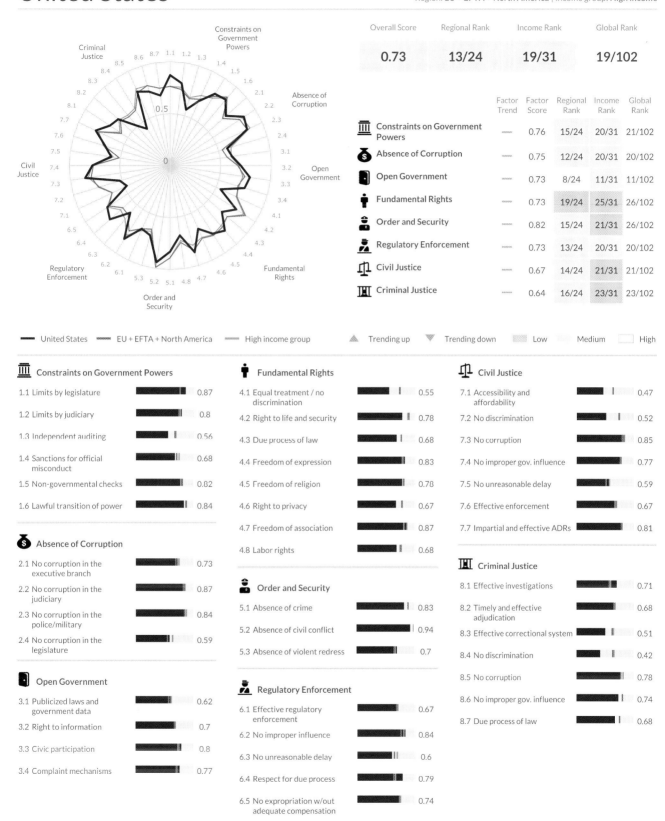

	Overall Score	Regional Rank	Income Rank	Global Rank
	0.73	**13/24**	**19/31**	**19/102**

		Factor Trend	Factor Score	Regional Rank	Income Rank	Global Rank
🏛	Constraints on Government Powers	—	0.76	15/24	20/31	21/102
💰	Absence of Corruption	—	0.75	12/24	20/31	20/102
📱	Open Government	—	0.73	8/24	11/31	11/102
👤	Fundamental Rights	—	0.73	19/24	25/31	26/102
👮	Order and Security	—	0.82	15/24	21/31	26/102
👷	Regulatory Enforcement	—	0.73	13/24	20/31	20/102
⚖	Civil Justice	—	0.67	14/24	21/31	21/102
⚖	Criminal Justice	—	0.64	16/24	23/31	23/102

— United States ▬ EU + EFTA + North America — High income group   ▲ Trending up   ▼ Trending down   ▨ Low   ▨ Medium   ☐ High

🏛 Constraints on Government Powers

1.1 Limits by legislature	0.87
1.2 Limits by judiciary	0.8
1.3 Independent auditing	0.56
1.4 Sanctions for official misconduct	0.68
1.5 Non-governmental checks	0.82
1.6 Lawful transition of power	0.84

💰 Absence of Corruption

2.1 No corruption in the executive branch	0.73
2.2 No corruption in the judiciary	0.87
2.3 No corruption in the police/military	0.84
2.4 No corruption in the legislature	0.59

📱 Open Government

3.1 Publicized laws and government data	0.62
3.2 Right to information	0.7
3.3 Civic participation	0.8
3.4 Complaint mechanisms	0.77

👤 Fundamental Rights

4.1 Equal treatment / no discrimination	0.55
4.2 Right to life and security	0.78
4.3 Due process of law	0.68
4.4 Freedom of expression	0.83
4.5 Freedom of religion	0.78
4.6 Right to privacy	0.67
4.7 Freedom of association	0.87
4.8 Labor rights	0.68

👮 Order and Security

5.1 Absence of crime	0.83
5.2 Absence of civil conflict	0.94
5.3 Absence of violent redress	0.7

👷 Regulatory Enforcement

6.1 Effective regulatory enforcement	0.67
6.2 No improper influence	0.84
6.3 No unreasonable delay	0.6
6.4 Respect for due process	0.79
6.5 No expropriation w/out adequate compensation	0.74

⚖ Civil Justice

7.1 Accessibility and affordability	0.47
7.2 No discrimination	0.52
7.3 No corruption	0.85
7.4 No improper gov. influence	0.77
7.5 No unreasonable delay	0.59
7.6 Effective enforcement	0.67
7.7 Impartial and effective ADRs	0.81

⚖ Criminal Justice

8.1 Effective investigations	0.71
8.2 Timely and effective adjudication	0.68
8.3 Effective correctional system	0.51
8.4 No discrimination	0.42
8.5 No corruption	0.78
8.6 No improper gov. influence	0.74
8.7 Due process of law	0.68

Uruguay

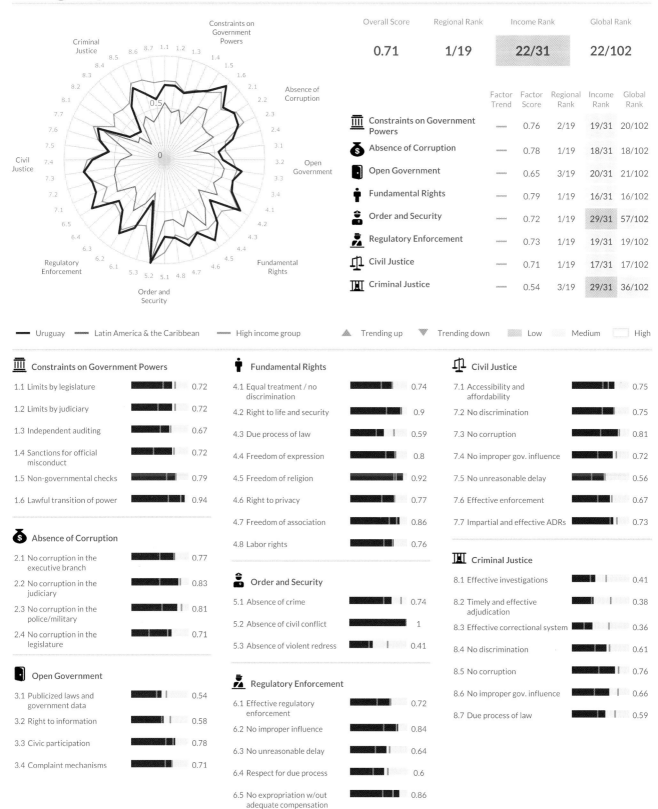

	Overall Score	Regional Rank	Income Rank	Global Rank
	0.71	1/19	22/31	22/102

		Factor Trend	Factor Score	Regional Rank	Income Rank	Global Rank
🏛	Constraints on Government Powers	—	0.76	2/19	19/31	20/102
💰	Absence of Corruption	—	0.78	1/19	18/31	18/102
📗	Open Government	—	0.65	3/19	20/31	21/102
👤	Fundamental Rights	—	0.79	1/19	16/31	16/102
👮	Order and Security	—	0.72	1/19	29/31	57/102
📋	Regulatory Enforcement	—	0.73	1/19	19/31	19/102
⚖	Civil Justice	—	0.71	1/19	17/31	17/102
🏛	Criminal Justice	—	0.54	3/19	29/31	36/102

Legend: ── Uruguay ── Latin America & the Caribbean ── High income group ▲ Trending up ▼ Trending down ▨ Low ▨ Medium ☐ High

🏛 Constraints on Government Powers

1.1 Limits by legislature	0.72
1.2 Limits by judiciary	0.72
1.3 Independent auditing	0.67
1.4 Sanctions for official misconduct	0.72
1.5 Non-governmental checks	0.79
1.6 Lawful transition of power	0.94

💰 Absence of Corruption

2.1 No corruption in the executive branch	0.77
2.2 No corruption in the judiciary	0.83
2.3 No corruption in the police/military	0.81
2.4 No corruption in the legislature	0.71

📗 Open Government

3.1 Publicized laws and government data	0.54
3.2 Right to information	0.58
3.3 Civic participation	0.78
3.4 Complaint mechanisms	0.71

👤 Fundamental Rights

4.1 Equal treatment / no discrimination	0.74
4.2 Right to life and security	0.9
4.3 Due process of law	0.59
4.4 Freedom of expression	0.8
4.5 Freedom of religion	0.92
4.6 Right to privacy	0.77
4.7 Freedom of association	0.86
4.8 Labor rights	0.76

👮 Order and Security

5.1 Absence of crime	0.74
5.2 Absence of civil conflict	1
5.3 Absence of violent redress	0.41

📋 Regulatory Enforcement

6.1 Effective regulatory enforcement	0.72
6.2 No improper influence	0.84
6.3 No unreasonable delay	0.64
6.4 Respect for due process	0.6
6.5 No expropriation w/out adequate compensation	0.86

⚖ Civil Justice

7.1 Accessibility and affordability	0.75
7.2 No discrimination	0.75
7.3 No corruption	0.81
7.4 No improper gov. influence	0.72
7.5 No unreasonable delay	0.56
7.6 Effective enforcement	0.67
7.7 Impartial and effective ADRs	0.73

🏛 Criminal Justice

8.1 Effective investigations	0.41
8.2 Timely and effective adjudication	0.38
8.3 Effective correctional system	0.36
8.4 No discrimination	0.61
8.5 No corruption	0.76
8.6 No improper gov. influence	0.66
8.7 Due process of law	0.59

Uzbekistan

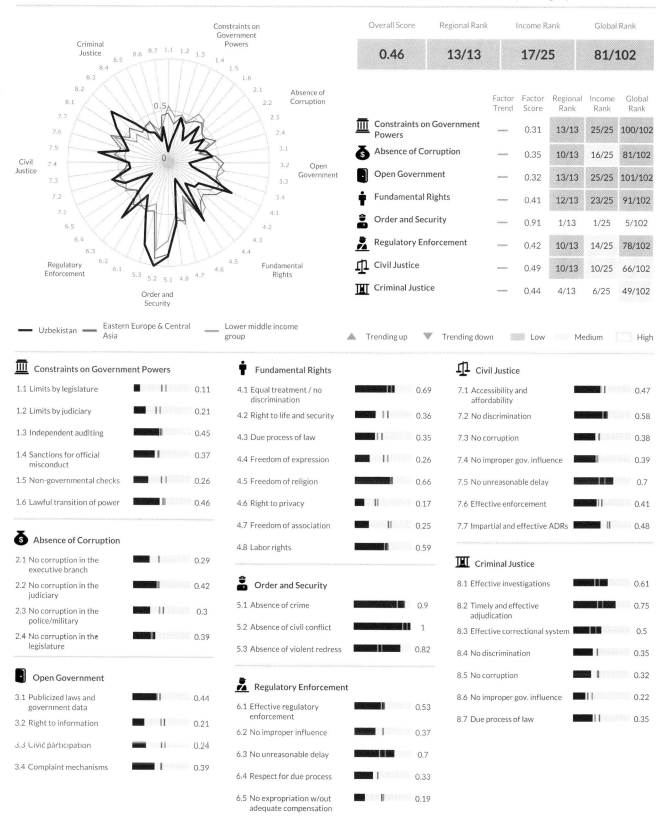

	Overall Score	Regional Rank	Income Rank	Global Rank
	0.46	13/13	17/25	81/102

	Factor Trend	Factor Score	Regional Rank	Income Rank	Global Rank
Constraints on Government Powers	—	0.31	13/13	25/25	100/102
Absence of Corruption	—	0.35	10/13	16/25	81/102
Open Government	—	0.32	13/13	25/25	101/102
Fundamental Rights	—	0.41	12/13	23/25	91/102
Order and Security	—	0.91	1/13	1/25	5/102
Regulatory Enforcement	—	0.42	10/13	14/25	78/102
Civil Justice	—	0.49	10/13	10/25	66/102
Criminal Justice	—	0.44	4/13	6/25	49/102

— Uzbekistan — Eastern Europe & Central Asia — Lower middle income group

▲ Trending up   ▼ Trending down   ▨ Low   ▨ Medium   ▢ High

Constraints on Government Powers

1.1 Limits by legislature		0.11
1.2 Limits by judiciary		0.21
1.3 Independent auditing		0.45
1.4 Sanctions for official misconduct		0.37
1.5 Non-governmental checks		0.26
1.6 Lawful transition of power		0.46

Absence of Corruption

2.1 No corruption in the executive branch		0.29
2.2 No corruption in the judiciary		0.42
2.3 No corruption in the police/military		0.3
2.4 No corruption in the legislature		0.39

Open Government

3.1 Publicized laws and government data		0.44
3.2 Right to information		0.21
3.3 Civic participation		0.24
3.4 Complaint mechanisms		0.39

Fundamental Rights

4.1 Equal treatment / no discrimination		0.69
4.2 Right to life and security		0.36
4.3 Due process of law		0.35
4.4 Freedom of expression		0.26
4.5 Freedom of religion		0.66
4.6 Right to privacy		0.17
4.7 Freedom of association		0.25
4.8 Labor rights		0.59

Order and Security

5.1 Absence of crime		0.9
5.2 Absence of civil conflict		1
5.3 Absence of violent redress		0.82

Regulatory Enforcement

6.1 Effective regulatory enforcement		0.53
6.2 No improper influence		0.37
6.3 No unreasonable delay		0.7
6.4 Respect for due process		0.33
6.5 No expropriation w/out adequate compensation		0.19

Civil Justice

7.1 Accessibility and affordability		0.47
7.2 No discrimination		0.58
7.3 No corruption		0.38
7.4 No improper gov. influence		0.39
7.5 No unreasonable delay		0.7
7.6 Effective enforcement		0.41
7.7 Impartial and effective ADRs		0.48

Criminal Justice

8.1 Effective investigations		0.61
8.2 Timely and effective adjudication		0.75
8.3 Effective correctional system		0.5
8.4 No discrimination		0.35
8.5 No corruption		0.32
8.6 No improper gov. influence		0.22
8.7 Due process of law		0.35

Venezuela

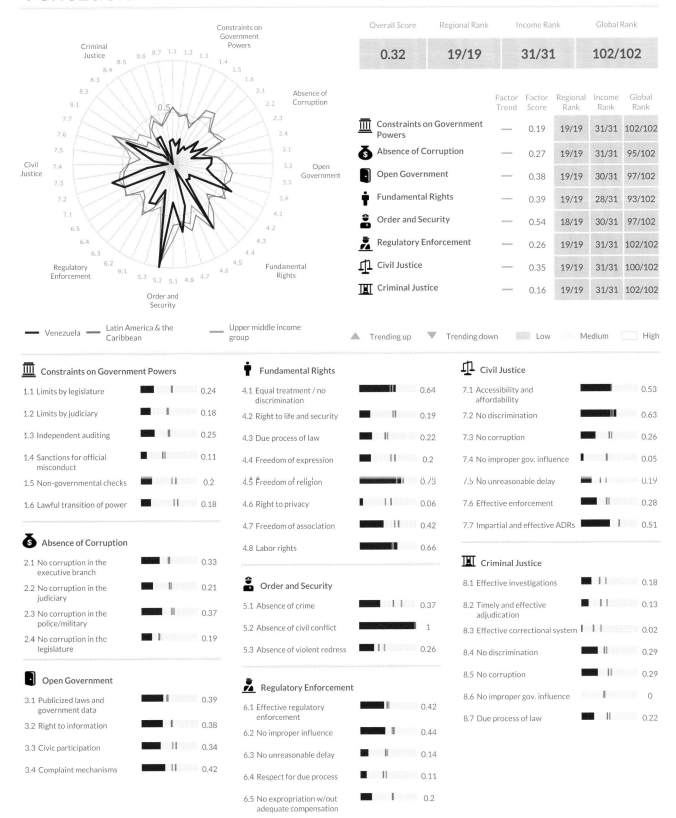

	Overall Score	Regional Rank	Income Rank	Global Rank
	0.32	19/19	31/31	102/102

	Factor Trend	Factor Score	Regional Rank	Income Rank	Global Rank
🏛 Constraints on Government Powers	—	0.19	19/19	31/31	102/102
💰 Absence of Corruption	—	0.27	19/19	31/31	95/102
📱 Open Government	—	0.38	19/19	30/31	97/102
👤 Fundamental Rights	—	0.39	19/19	28/31	93/102
👮 Order and Security	—	0.54	18/19	30/31	97/102
👷 Regulatory Enforcement	—	0.26	19/19	31/31	102/102
⚖ Civil Justice	—	0.35	19/19	31/31	100/102
🏛 Criminal Justice	—	0.16	19/19	31/31	102/102

Legend: — Venezuela　— Latin America & the Caribbean　— Upper middle income group　▲ Trending up　▼ Trending down　　Low　Medium　High

🏛 Constraints on Government Powers

1.1 Limits by legislature	0.24
1.2 Limits by judiciary	0.18
1.3 Independent auditing	0.25
1.4 Sanctions for official misconduct	0.11
1.5 Non-governmental checks	0.2
1.6 Lawful transition of power	0.18

💰 Absence of Corruption

2.1 No corruption in the executive branch	0.33
2.2 No corruption in the judiciary	0.21
2.3 No corruption in the police/military	0.37
2.4 No corruption in the legislature	0.19

📱 Open Government

3.1 Publicized laws and government data	0.39
3.2 Right to information	0.38
3.3 Civic participation	0.34
3.4 Complaint mechanisms	0.42

👤 Fundamental Rights

4.1 Equal treatment / no discrimination	0.64
4.2 Right to life and security	0.19
4.3 Due process of law	0.22
4.4 Freedom of expression	0.2
4.5 Freedom of religion	0.73
4.6 Right to privacy	0.06
4.7 Freedom of association	0.42
4.8 Labor rights	0.66

👮 Order and Security

5.1 Absence of crime	0.37
5.2 Absence of civil conflict	1
5.3 Absence of violent redress	0.26

👷 Regulatory Enforcement

6.1 Effective regulatory enforcement	0.42
6.2 No improper influence	0.44
6.3 No unreasonable delay	0.14
6.4 Respect for due process	0.11
6.5 No expropriation w/out adequate compensation	0.2

⚖ Civil Justice

7.1 Accessibility and affordability	0.53
7.2 No discrimination	0.63
7.3 No corruption	0.26
7.4 No improper gov. influence	0.05
7.5 No unreasonable delay	0.19
7.6 Effective enforcement	0.28
7.7 Impartial and effective ADRs	0.51

🏛 Criminal Justice

8.1 Effective investigations	0.18
8.2 Timely and effective adjudication	0.13
8.3 Effective correctional system	0.02
8.4 No discrimination	0.29
8.5 No corruption	0.29
8.6 No improper gov. influence	0
8.7 Due process of law	0.22

Vietnam

Hanoi, Haiphong, Ho Chi Minh City
Region: **East Asia & Pacific** | Income group: **Lower middle income**

	Overall Score	Regional Rank	Income Rank	Global Rank
	0.5	12/15	11/25	64/102

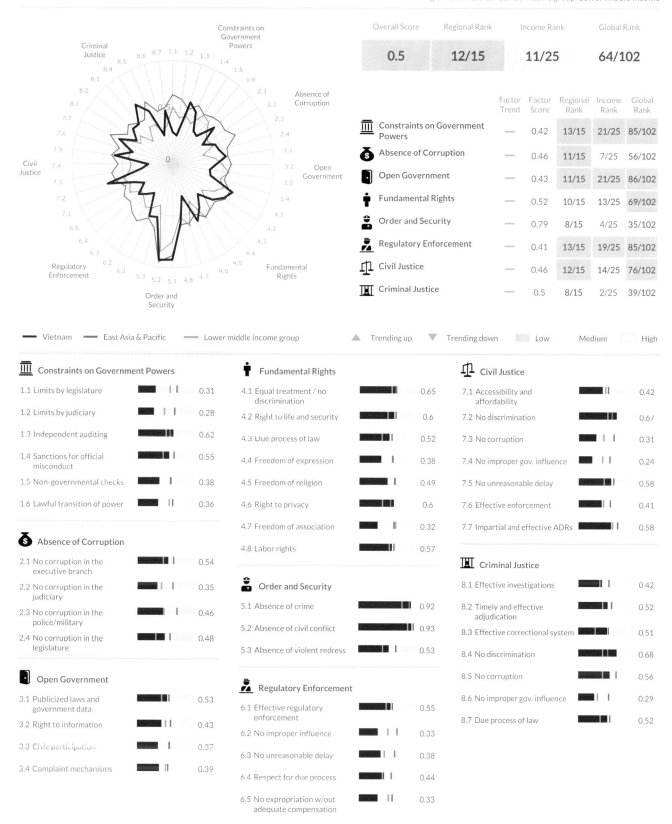

	Factor Trend	Factor Score	Regional Rank	Income Rank	Global Rank
🏛 Constraints on Government Powers	—	0.42	13/15	21/25	85/102
💰 Absence of Corruption	—	0.46	11/15	7/25	56/102
📖 Open Government	—	0.43	11/15	21/25	86/102
👤 Fundamental Rights	—	0.52	10/15	13/25	69/102
👮 Order and Security	—	0.79	8/15	4/25	35/102
👔 Regulatory Enforcement	—	0.41	13/15	19/25	85/102
⚖ Civil Justice	—	0.46	12/15	14/25	76/102
🏛 Criminal Justice	—	0.5	8/15	2/25	39/102

— Vietnam   — East Asia & Pacific   — Lower middle income group   ▲ Trending up   ▼ Trending down   ▒ Low   Medium   High

🏛 Constraints on Government Powers

1.1 Limits by legislature	0.31
1.2 Limits by judiciary	0.28
1.3 Independent auditing	0.62
1.4 Sanctions for official misconduct	0.55
1.5 Non-governmental checks	0.38
1.6 Lawful transition of power	0.36

💰 Absence of Corruption

2.1 No corruption in the executive branch	0.54
2.2 No corruption in the judiciary	0.35
2.3 No corruption in the police/military	0.46
2.4 No corruption in the legislature	0.48

📖 Open Government

3.1 Publicized laws and government data	0.53
3.2 Right to information	0.43
3.3 Civic participation	0.07
3.4 Complaint mechanisms	0.39

👤 Fundamental Rights

4.1 Equal treatment / no discrimination	0.65
4.2 Right to life and security	0.6
4.3 Due process of law	0.52
4.4 Freedom of expression	0.38
4.5 Freedom of religion	0.49
4.6 Right to privacy	0.6
4.7 Freedom of association	0.32
4.8 Labor rights	0.57

👮 Order and Security

5.1 Absence of crime	0.92
5.2 Absence of civil conflict	0.93
5.3 Absence of violent redress	0.53

👔 Regulatory Enforcement

6.1 Effective regulatory enforcement	0.55
6.2 No improper influence	0.33
6.3 No unreasonable delay	0.38
6.4 Respect for due process	0.44
6.5 No expropriation w/out adequate compensation	0.33

⚖ Civil Justice

7.1 Accessibility and affordability	0.42
7.2 No discrimination	0.67
7.3 No corruption	0.31
7.4 No improper gov. influence	0.24
7.5 No unreasonable delay	0.58
7.6 Effective enforcement	0.41
7.7 Impartial and effective ADRs	0.58

🏛 Criminal Justice

8.1 Effective investigations	0.42
8.2 Timely and effective adjudication	0.52
8.3 Effective correctional system	0.51
8.4 No discrimination	0.68
8.5 No corruption	0.56
8.6 No improper gov. influence	0.29
8.7 Due process of law	0.52

Zambia

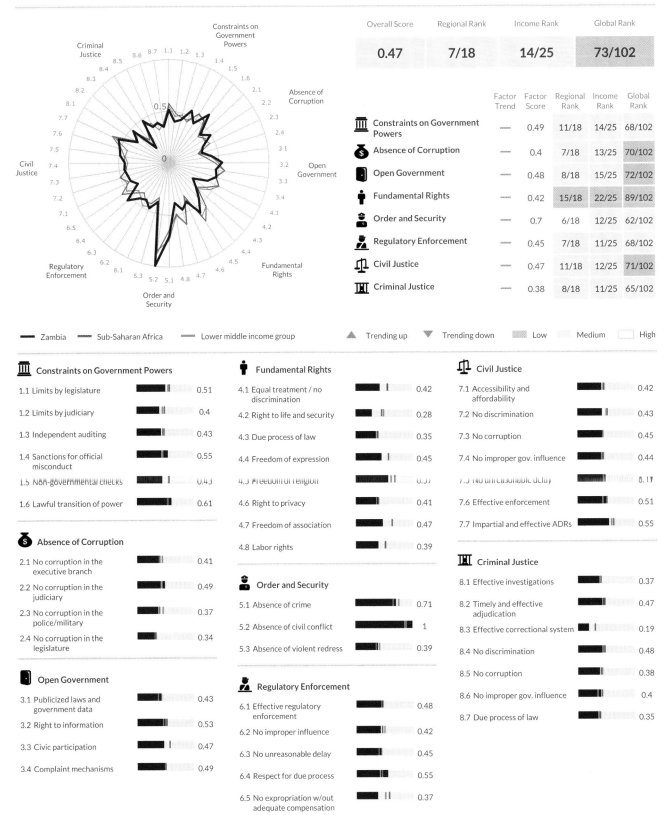

		Overall Score	Regional Rank	Income Rank	Global Rank
		0.47	7/18	14/25	73/102

		Factor Trend	Factor Score	Regional Rank	Income Rank	Global Rank
🏛	Constraints on Government Powers	—	0.49	11/18	14/25	68/102
💰	Absence of Corruption	—	0.4	7/18	13/25	70/102
▯	Open Government	—	0.48	8/18	15/25	72/102
🧍	Fundamental Rights	—	0.42	15/18	22/25	89/102
👮	Order and Security	—	0.7	6/18	12/25	62/102
🧑‍⚖	Regulatory Enforcement	—	0.45	7/18	11/25	68/102
⚖	Civil Justice	—	0.47	11/18	12/25	71/102
🏛	Criminal Justice	—	0.38	8/18	11/25	65/102

Legend: — Zambia · ···· Sub-Saharan Africa · — Lower middle income group · ▲ Trending up · ▼ Trending down · Low · Medium · High

🏛 Constraints on Government Powers

1.1 Limits by legislature	0.51
1.2 Limits by judiciary	0.4
1.3 Independent auditing	0.43
1.4 Sanctions for official misconduct	0.55
1.5 Non-governmental checks	0.43
1.6 Lawful transition of power	0.61

💰 Absence of Corruption

2.1 No corruption in the executive branch	0.41
2.2 No corruption in the judiciary	0.49
2.3 No corruption in the police/military	0.37
2.4 No corruption in the legislature	0.34

▯ Open Government

3.1 Publicized laws and government data	0.43
3.2 Right to information	0.53
3.3 Civic participation	0.47
3.4 Complaint mechanisms	0.49

🧍 Fundamental Rights

4.1 Equal treatment / no discrimination	0.42
4.2 Right to life and security	0.28
4.3 Due process of law	0.35
4.4 Freedom of expression	0.45
4.5 Freedom of religion	0.57
4.6 Right to privacy	0.41
4.7 Freedom of association	0.47
4.8 Labor rights	0.39

👮 Order and Security

5.1 Absence of crime	0.71
5.2 Absence of civil conflict	1
5.3 Absence of violent redress	0.39

🧑‍⚖ Regulatory Enforcement

6.1 Effective regulatory enforcement	0.48
6.2 No improper influence	0.42
6.3 No unreasonable delay	0.45
6.4 Respect for due process	0.55
6.5 No expropriation w/out adequate compensation	0.37

⚖ Civil Justice

7.1 Accessibility and affordability	0.42
7.2 No discrimination	0.43
7.3 No corruption	0.45
7.4 No improper gov. influence	0.44
7.5 No unreasonable delay	0.17
7.6 Effective enforcement	0.51
7.7 Impartial and effective ADRs	0.55

🏛 Criminal Justice

8.1 Effective investigations	0.37
8.2 Timely and effective adjudication	0.47
8.3 Effective correctional system	0.19
8.4 No discrimination	0.48
8.5 No corruption	0.38
8.6 No improper gov. influence	0.4
8.7 Due process of law	0.35

Complete country profiles available at: data.worldjusticeproject.org

Zimbabwe

		Overall Score	Regional Rank	Income Rank	Global Rank
		0.37	18/18	14/15	100/102

		Factor Trend	Factor Score	Regional Rank	Income Rank	Global Rank
🏛	Constraints on Government Powers	—	0.26	18/18	15/15	101/102
💰	Absence of Corruption	—	0.28	13/18	9/15	92/102
📱	Open Government	—	0.32	18/18	15/15	102/102
🧍	Fundamental Rights	—	0.29	18/18	15/15	101/102
👮	Order and Security	—	0.63	9/18	8/15	78/102
🛠	Regulatory Enforcement	—	0.35	18/18	14/15	100/102
⚖	Civil Justice	—	0.45	13/18	6/15	79/102
🏛	Criminal Justice	—	0.36	11/18	6/15	72/102

Legend: — Zimbabwe — Sub-Saharan Africa — Low income group ▲ Trending up ▼ Trending down ▒ Low ░ Medium ▢ High

🏛 Constraints on Government Powers

1.1 Limits by legislature	0.36
1.2 Limits by judiciary	0.26
1.3 Independent auditing	0.31
1.4 Sanctions for official misconduct	0.36
1.5 Non-governmental checks	0.19
1.6 Lawful transition of power	0.1

💰 Absence of Corruption

2.1 No corruption in the executive branch	0.25
2.2 No corruption in the judiciary	0.41
2.3 No corruption in the police/military	0.27
2.4 No corruption in the legislature	0.19

📱 Open Government

3.1 Publicized laws and government data	0.23
3.2 Right to information	0.4
3.3 Civic participation	0.23
3.4 Complaint mechanisms	0.41

🧍 Fundamental Rights

4.1 Equal treatment / no discrimination	0.36
4.2 Right to life and security	0.28
4.3 Due process of law	0.27
4.4 Freedom of expression	0.19
4.5 Freedom of religion	0.55
4.6 Right to privacy	0.04
4.7 Freedom of association	0.21
4.8 Labor rights	0.43

👮 Order and Security

5.1 Absence of crime	0.51
5.2 Absence of civil conflict	1
5.3 Absence of violent redress	0.37

🛠 Regulatory Enforcement

6.1 Effective regulatory enforcement	0.34
6.2 No improper influence	0.32
6.3 No unreasonable delay	0.37
6.4 Respect for due process	0.42
6.5 No expropriation w/out adequate compensation	0.3

⚖ Civil Justice

7.1 Accessibility and affordability	0.53
7.2 No discrimination	0.54
7.3 No corruption	0.44
7.4 No improper gov. influence	0.17
7.5 No unreasonable delay	0.47
7.6 Effective enforcement	0.55
7.7 Impartial and effective ADRs	0.47

🏛 Criminal Justice

8.1 Effective investigations	0.5
8.2 Timely and effective adjudication	0.52
8.3 Effective correctional system	0.34
8.4 No discrimination	0.48
8.5 No corruption	0.3
8.6 No improper gov. influence	0.12
8.7 Due process of law	0.27

Methodology

Methodology

The WJP Rule of Law Index is the first attempt to systematically and comprehensively quantify the rule of law around the world, and remains unique in its operationalization of rule of law dimensions into concrete questions.

The *WJP Rule of Law Index 2015* report presents information on eight composite factors that are further disaggregated into 44 specific sub-factors (see Table 2). Factor 9, informal justice, is included in the framework, but has been excluded from the aggregated scores and rankings in order to provide meaningful cross-country comparisons. In attempting to present an image that accurately portrays the rule of law as experienced by ordinary people, each score of the Index is calculated using a large number of questions drawn from two original data sources collected by the World Justice Project in each country: a General Population Poll (GPP) and a series of Qualified Respondents' Questionnaires (QRQs).

These two data sources collect up-to-date firsthand information that is not available at the global level, and constitute the world's most comprehensive dataset of its kind. They capture the experiences and perceptions of ordinary citizens and in-country professionals concerning the performance of the state and its agents and the actual operation of the legal framework in their country. The country scores and rankings presented in this report are built from more than five hundred variables drawn from the assessments of more than 100,000 citizens and legal experts in 102 countries and jurisdictions, making it the most accurate portrayal of the factors that contribute to shaping the rule of law in a nation.

Table 2: The Indicators of the World Justice Project's Rule of Law Index®

The World Justice Project's Rule of Law Index comprises 44 sub-factors organized around eight factors. The following table presents a summary of the concepts underlying each of these sub-factors. A full map of the variables used to calculate the Index scores is available in the methodology section of the WJP Rule of Law Index website.

Factor 1: Constraints on Government Powers

1.1 Government powers are effectively limited by the legislature
Measures whether legislative bodies have the ability in practice to exercise effective checks and oversight of the government.

1.2 Government powers are effectively limited by the judiciary
Measures whether the judiciary has the independence and the ability in practice to exercise effective checks on the government.

1.3 Government powers are effectively limited by independent auditing and review
Measures whether comptrollers or auditors, as well as national human rights ombudsman agencies, have sufficient independence and the ability to exercise effective checks and oversight of the government.

1.4 Government officials are sanctioned for misconduct
Measures whether government officials in the executive, legislature, judiciary, and the police are investigated, prosecuted, and punished for official misconduct and other violations.

1.5 Government powers are subject to non-governmental checks
Measures whether an independent media, civil society organizations, political parties, and individuals are free to report and comment on government policies without fear of retaliation.

1.6 Transition of power is subject to the law
Measures whether government officials are elected or appointed in accordance with the rules and procedures set forth in the constitution. Where elections take place, it also measures the integrity of the electoral process, including access to the ballot, the absence of intimidation, and public scrutiny of election results.

Factor 2: Absence of Corruption

2.1 Government officials in the executive branch do not use public office for private gain
Measures the prevalence of bribery, informal payments, and other inducements in the delivery of public services and the enforcement of regulations. It also measures whether government procurement and public works contracts are awarded through an open and competitive bidding process, and whether government officials at various levels of the executive branch refrain from embezzling public funds.

2.2 Government officials in the judicial branch do not use public office for private gain
Measures whether judges and judicial officials refrain from soliciting and accepting bribes to perform duties or expedite processes, and whether the judiciary and judicial rulings are free of improper influence by the government, private interests, and criminal organizations.

2.3 Government officials in the police and the military do not use public office for private gain
Measures whether police officers and criminal investigators refrain from soliciting and accepting bribes to perform basic police services or to investigate crimes, and whether government officials in the police and the military are free of improper influence by private interests or criminal organizations.

2.4 Government officials in the legislative branch do not use public office for private gain
Measures whether members of the legislature refrain from soliciting or accepting bribes or other inducements in exchange for political favors or favorable votes on legislation.

Factor 3: Open Government

3.1 Publicized laws and government data

Measures whether basic laws and information on legal rights are publicly available, presented in plain language, and are made accessible in all languages. It also measures the quality and accessibility of information published by the government in print or online, and whether administrative regulations, drafts of legislation, and high court decisions are made accessible to the public in a timely manner.

3.2 Right to information

Measures whether requests for information held by a government agency are granted, whether these requests are granted within a reasonable time period, if the information provided is pertinent and complete, and if requests for information are granted at a reasonable cost and without having to pay a bribe. It also measures whether people are aware of their right to information, and whether relevant records are accessible to the public upon request.

3.3 Civic participation

Measures the effectiveness of civic participation mechanisms, including the protection of the freedoms of opinion and expression, assembly and association, and the right to petition the government. It also measures whether people can voice concerns to various government officers, and whether government officials provide sufficient information and notice about decisions affecting the community.

3.4 Complaint mechanisms

Measures whether people are able to bring specific complaints to the government about the provision of public services or the performance of government officers in carrying out their legal duties in practice, and how government officials respond to such complaints.

Factor 4: Fundamental Rights

4.1 Equal treatment and absence of discrimination

Measures whether individuals are free from discrimination - based on socio-economic status, gender, ethnicity, religion, national origin, or sexual orientation, or gender identity - including with respect to public services, employment, court proceedings, and the justice system.

4.2 The right to life and security of the person is effectively guaranteed

Measures whether the police inflict physical harm upon criminal suspects during arrest and interrogation, and whether political dissidents or members of the media are subjected to unreasonable searches or to arrest, dentention, imprisonment, threats, abusive treatment or violence.

4.3 Due process of law and rights of the accused

Measures whether the basic rights of criminal suspects are respected, including the presumption of innocence and the freedom from arbitrary arrest and unreasonable pre-trial detention. It also measures whether criminal suspects are able to access and challenge evidence used against them, whether they are subject to abusive treatment, and whether they are provided with adequate legal assistance. In addition, it also measures whether the basic rights of prisoners are respected once they have been convicted of a crime.

4.4 Freedom of opinion & expression is effectively guaranteed

Measures whether an independent media, civil society organizations, political parties, and individuals are free to report and comment on government policies without fear of retaliation.

4.5 Freedom of belief and religion is effectively guaranteed

Measures whether members of religious minorities can worship and conduct religious practices freely and publicly, and whether non-adherents are protected from having to submit to religious laws.

4.6 Freedom from arbitrary interference with privacy is effectively guaranteed

Measures whether the police or other government officials conduct physical searches without warrants, or intercept electronic communications of private individuals without judicial authorization.

4.7 Freedom of assembly and association is effectively guaranteed

Measures whether people can freely attend community meetings, join political organizations, hold peaceful public demonstrations, sign petitions, and express opinions against government policies and actions without fear of retaliation.

4.8 Fundamental labor rights are effectively guaranteed

Measures the effective enforcement of fundamental labor rights, including freedom of association and the right to collective bargaining, the absence of discrimination with respect to employment, and freedom from forced labor and child labor.

Factor 5: Order & Security

5.1 Crime is effectively controlled
Measures the prevalence of common crimes, including homicide, kidnapping, burglary and theft, armed robbery, and extortion, as well as people's general perceptions of safety in their communities.

5.2 Civil conflict is effectively limited
Measures whether people are effectively protected from armed conflict and terrorism.

5.3 People do not resort to violence to redress personal grievances
Measures whether people resort to intimidation or violence to resolve civil disputes amongst themselves, or to seek redress from the government, and whether people are free from mob violence.

 Factor 6: Regulatory Enforcement

6.1 Government regulations are effectively enforced
Measures whether government regulations, such as labor, environmental, public health, commercial, and consumer protection regulations, are effectively enforced.

6.2 Government regulations are applied and enforced without improper influence
Measures whether the enforcement of regulations is subject to bribery or improper influence by private interests, and whether public services, such as the issuance of permits and licenses and the administration of public health services, are provided without bribery or other inducements.

6.3 Administrative proceedings are conducted without unreasonable delay
Measures whether administrative proceedings at the national and local levels are conducted without unreasonable delay.

6.4 Due process is respected in administrative proceedings
Measures whether the due process of law is respected in administrative proceedings conducted by national and local authorities, including in such areas as the environment, taxes, and labor.

6.5 The government does not expropriate without lawful process and adequate compensation
Measures whether the government respects the property rights of people and corporations, refrains from the illegal seizure of private property, and provides adequate compensation when property is legally expropriated.

Factor 7: Civil Justice

7.1 People can access and afford civil justice
Measures the accessibility and affordability of civil courts, including whether people are aware of available remedies, can access and afford legal advice and representation, and can access the court system without incurring unreasonable fees, encountering unreasonable procedural hurdles, or experiencing physical or linguistic barriers.

7.2 Civil justice is free of discrimination
Measures whether the civil justice system discriminates in practice based on socio-economic status, gender, ethnicity, religion, national origin, sexual orientation, or gender identity.

7.3 Civil justice is free of corruption
Measures whether the civil justice system is free of bribery and improper influence by private interests.

7.4 Civil justice is free of improper government influence
Measures whether the civil justice system is free of improper government or political influence.

7.5 Civil justice is not subject to unreasonable delay
Measures whether civil justice proceedings are conducted and judgments are produced in a timely manner without unreasonable delay.

7.6 Civil justice is effectively enforced
Measures the effectiveness and timeliness of the enforcement of civil justice decisions and judgments in practice.

7.7 Alternative dispute resolution mechanisms are accessible impartial, and effective
Measures whether alternative dispute resolution mechanisms (ADRs) are affordable, efficient, enforceable, and free from corruption.

Factor 8: Criminal Justice

8.1 Criminal investigation system is effective
Measures whether perpetrators of crimes are effectively apprehended and charged. It also measures whether police, investigators, and prosecutors have adequate resources, are free of corruption, and perform their duties competently.

8.2 Criminal adjudication system is timely and effective
Measures whether perpetrators of crimes are effectively prosecuted and punished. It also measures whether criminal judges and other judicial officers are competent and produce speedy decisions.

8.3 Correctional system is effective in reducing criminal behavior
Measures whether correctional institutions are secure, respect prisoners' rights, and are effective in preventing recidivism.

8.4 Criminal system is impartial
Measures whether the police and criminal judges are impartial and whether they discriminate in practice based on socio-economic status, gender, ethnicity, religion, national origin, sexual orientation, or gender identity.

8.5 Criminal system is free of corruption
Measures whether the police, prosecutors, and judges are free from bribery and improper influence from criminal organizations.

8.6 Criminal system is free of improper government influence
Measures whether the criminal justice system is independent from government or political influence.

8.7 Due process of law and rights of the accused
Measures whether the basic rights of criminal suspects are respected, including the presumption of innocence and the freedom from arbitrary arrest and unreasonable pre-trial detention. It also measures whether criminal suspects are able to access and challenge evidence used against them, whether they are subject to abusive treatment, and whether they are provided with adequate legal assistance. In addition, it measures whether the basic rights of prisoners are respected once they have been convicted of a crime.

DATA SOURCES

Every year the WJP collects data from representative samples of the general public (the General Population Polls or GPPs) and legal professionals (the Qualified Respondents' Questionnaires or QRQs) to compute the Index scores and rankings. The GPP surveys provide firsthand information on the experiences and the perceptions of ordinary people regarding a range of pertinent rule of law information, including their dealings with the government, the ease of interacting with state bureaucracy, the extent of bribery and corruption, the availability of dispute resolution systems, and the prevalence of common crimes to which they are exposed. The GPP questionnaire includes 87 perception-based questions and 56 experience-based questions, along with socio-demographic information on all respondents. The questionnaire is translated into local languages, adapted to common expressions, and administered by leading local polling companies using a probability sample of 1,000 respondents in the three largest cities of each country. Depending on the particular situation of each country, three different polling methodologies are used: face-to-face, telephone, or online. The GPPs are carried out in each country every other year. The polling data used in this year's report was collected during the fall of 2012 (for 5 countries), the fall of 2013 (for 43 countries), and the fall of 2014 (for 54 countries). Detailed information regarding the cities covered, the polling companies contracted to administer the questionnaire, and the polling methodology employed in each of the 102 countries is presented in Table 3.

The Qualified Respondents' Questionnaires (QRQs) complement the polling data with assessments from in-country professionals with expertise in civil and commercial law, criminal justice, labor law, and public health. These questionnaires gather timely input from practitioners who frequently interact with state institutions, including information on the efficacy of courts, the strength of regulatory enforcement, and the reliability of accountability mechanisms. The questionnaires contain closed-ended perception questions and several hypothetical scenarios with highly detailed factual assumptions aimed at ensuring comparability across countries. The QRQ surveys are conducted annually, and the questionnaires are completed by respondents selected from directories of law firms, universities and colleges, research organizations, and non-governmental organizations (NGOs), as well as through referrals from the WJP global network of practitioners, and vetted by WJP staff based on their expertise. The expert surveys are administered in three languages: English, French, and Spanish. The QRQ data for this report includes over 2,500 surveys, which represents an average of 25 respondents per country. These data were collected from October 2014 through January 2015.

DATA CLEANING AND SCORE COMPUTATION

Once collected, the data are carefully processed to arrive at country-level scores. As a first step, the respondent-level data are edited to exclude partially-completed surveys, suspicious data, and outliers (which are detected using the Z-score method). Individual answers are then mapped onto the 44 sub-factors of the Index (or onto the intermediate categories that make up each sub-factor), codified so that all values fall between 0 (least rule of law) and 1 (most rule of law), and aggregated at the country level using the simple (or un-weighted) average of all respondents. To allow for aggregation, the resulting scores are normalized using the Min-Max method. These normalized scores are then successively aggregated from the variable level all the way up to the factor level to produce the final country scores and rankings. In most cases, the GPP and QRQ questions are equally weighted in the calculation of the scores of the intermediate categories (sub-factors and sub-sub-factors). A full picture of how questions are mapped onto indicators and how they are weighted is presented in Botero and Ponce (2011).

DATA VALIDATION

As a final step, data are validated and cross-checked against qualitative and quantitative third-party sources to provide an additional layer of analysis and to identify possible mistakes or inconsistencies within the data. The third-party data sources used to cross-check the Index scores are described in Botero and Ponce (2011).

Table 3: City Coverage and Polling Methodology in the 102 Indexed Countries & Territories

Country/Territory	Cities Covered	Polling Company	Methodology	Sample	Year
Afghanistan	Kabul, Kandahar, Herat	ACSOR Surveys, a subsidiary of D3 Systems, Inc.	Face-to-face	1000	2014
Albania	Tirana, Durres, Shkodra	Market Research & Polls - EURASIA (MRP-EUR-ASIA)	Face-to-face	1000	2013
Argentina	Buenos Aires, Cordoba, Rosario	Statmark Group	Face-to-face	1000	2013
Australia	Sydney, Melbourne, Brisbane	Survey Sampling International	Online	1000	2013
Austria	Vienna, Graz, Linz	Survey Sampling International	Online	1008	2014
Bangladesh	Dhaka, Chittagong, Khulna	Org-Quest Research	Face-to-face	1000	2013
Belarus	Minsk, Gomel, Mogilev	Market Research & Polls - EURASIA (MRP-EUR-ASIA)	Face-to-face	1000	2014
Belgium	Antwerp, Ghent, Charleroi	Survey Sampling International	Online	1000	2013
Belize	Belize City, San Ignacio, Belmopan	CID-Gallup Latin America	Face-to-face	1020	2014
Bolivia	La Paz, Santa Cruz, Cochabamba	Prime Consulting	Face-to-face	1201	2013
Bosnia and Herzegovina	Sarajevo, Tuzla, Banja Luka	Market Research & Polls - EURASIA (MRP-EUR-ASIA)	Face-to-face	1000	2014
Botswana	Gaborone, Francistown, Molepolole	SIS International Research	Face-to-face	1045	2012
Brazil	Rio de Janeiro, Salvador, Sao Paolo	IBOPE Market Research	Face-to-face	1000	2014
Bulgaria	Sofia, Plovdiv, Varna	Alpha Research	Face-to-face	1027	2013
Burkina Faso	Ouagadougou, Bobo Dioulasso, Dédougou	TNS-RMS	Face-to-face	1000	2014
Cambodia	Phnom Penh, Battambang, Kampong Cham	Indochina Research	Face-to-face	1000	2014
Cameroon	Douala, Yaounde, Bamenda	Liaison Marketing	Face-to-face	997	2013
Canada	Toronto, Montreal, Vancouver	Survey Sampling International	Online	920	2014
Chile	Santiago, Valparaiso, Concepcion	D3 Systems, Inc.	Face-to-face	1000	2014
China	Shanghai, Beijing, Guangzhou	IBI Partners	Face-to-face	1002	2013
Colombia	Bogota, Medellin, Baranquilla	Statmark Group	Face-to-face	1017	2013
Costa Rica	San Jose, Alajuela, Cartago	CID-Gallup Latin America	Face-to-face	1020	2014
Cote d'Ivoire	Abidjan, San Pedro, Bouake	TNS-RMS	Face-to-face	1000	2014
Croatia	Zagreb, Split, Rijeka	Market Research & Polls - EURASIA (MRP-EURASIA)	Face-to-face	1000	2013
Czech Republic	Prague, Brno, Ostrava	Survey Sampling International	Online	997	2014
Denmark	Copenhagen, Arhus, Odense	SIS International Research	Online	1050	2014
Dominican Republic	Santo Domingo, Distrito Nacional, Santiago	CID-Gallup Latin America	Face-to-face	1000	2013
Ecuador	Quito, Guayaquil, Cuenca	Statmark Group	Face-to-face	1000	2014
Egypt	Cairo, Alexandria, Giza	D3 Systems, Inc./WJP in collaboration with local partner	Phone/Face-to-face	300/1000	2014/2012
El Salvador	San Salvador, San Miguel, Santa Ana	CID-Gallup Latin America	Face-to-face	1009	2013
Estonia	Tallinn, Tartu, Narva	Norstat	Online	800	2014
Ethiopia	Addis Ababa	Infinite Insight	Face-to-face	570	2014
Finland	Helsinki, Espoo, Tampere	SIS International Research	Online	1050	2014
France	Paris, Lyon, Marseille	Survey Sampling International	Online	1001	2013
Georgia	Tbilisi, Kutaisi, Batumi	ACT	Face-to-face	1000	2014
Germany	Berlin, Hamburg, Munich	Survey Sampling International	Online	1000	2013
Ghana	Accra, Kumasi, Sekondi-Takoradi	FACTS International Ghana Limited	Face-to-face	1005	2013
Greece	Athens, Thessaloniki, Patras	Survey Sampling International	Online	1000	2014
Guatemala	Guatemala City, Quetzaltenango, Escuintla	CID-Gallup Latin America	Face-to-face	1026	2013
Honduras	Tegucigalpa, San Pedro Sula, La Ceiba	CID-Gallup Latin America	Face-to-face	1020	2014
Hong Kong SAR, China	Hong Kong	IBI Partners	Face-to-face	1010	2014
Hungary	Budapest, Debrecen, Szeged	Market Research & Polls - EURASIA (MRP-EUR-ASIA)	Face-to-face	1000	2014
India	Mumbai, Delhi, Bangalore	Ipsos Public Affairs	Face-to-face	1047	2013
Indonesia	Jakarta, Surabaya, Bandung	MRI-Marketing Research Indonesia	Face-to-face	1011	2014
Iran	Teheran, Mashad, Isfahan	WJP in collaboration with local partner	Face-to-face	1045	2013
Italy	Rome, Milan, Naples	Survey Sampling International	Online	1000	2014
Jamaica	Kingston & St. Andrew, St. Catherine, St. James	Statmark Group	Face-to-face	1000	2014
Japan	Tokyo, Yokohama, Osaka	IBI Partners	Face-to-face	1002	2013

Country/Territory	Cities Covered	Polling Company	Methodology	Sample	Year
Jordan	Amman, Irbid, Zarqa	WJP in collaboration with local partner	Face-to-face	1004	2013
Kazakhstan	Almaty, Astana, Shymkent	VCIOM	Face-to-face	1002	2013
Kenya	Nairobi, Mombasa, Nakuru	TNS-RMS	Face-to-face	1003	2013
Kyrgyzstan	Bishkek, Osh, Jalalabad	VCIOM	Face-to-face	1000	2013
Lebanon	Beirut, Tripoli, Sidon	IIACSS	Face-to-face	1003	2014
Liberia	Monrovia, Kakata, Gbarnga	FACTS International Ghana Limited	Face-to-face	1000	2013
Macedonia, FYR	Skopje, Kumanovo, Bitola	Market Research & Polls - EURASIA (MRP-EUR-ASIA)	Face-to-face	1000	2014
Madagascar	Antananarivo, Antsirabe, Toamasina	DCDM Research	Face-to-face	1000	2014
Malawi	Blantyre, Lilongwe, Mzuzu	Consumer Options Ltd.	Face-to-face	997	2014
Malaysia	Kuala Lumpur, Johor Bahru, Ipoh	IBI Partners	Face-to-face	1011	2014
Mexico	Mexico City, Guadalajara, Monterrey	Data Opinion Publica y Mercados	Face-to-face	1005	2014
Moldova	Chisinau, Balti, Cahul	Market Research & Polls - EURASIA (MRP-EUR-ASIA)	Face-to-face	1000	2014
Mongolia	Ulaanbaatar, Darkhan, Erdenet	Sant Maral	Face-to-face	1000	2014
Morocco	Casablanca, Rabat, Marrakesh	Ipsos Public Affairs	Face-to-face	1000	2013
Myanmar	Mandalay, Naypyidaw, Yangon	IBI Partners	Face-to-face	1004	2013
Nepal	Kathmandu, Pokhara, Biratnagar	Solutions Consultant	Face-to-face	1000	2014
Netherlands	Amsterdam, Rotterdam, The Hague	Survey Sampling International	Online	1000	2013
New Zealand	Auckland, Wellington, Christchurch	IBI Partners	Telephone	1003	2014
Nicaragua	Managua, Masaya, Leon	CID-Gallup Latin America	Face-to-face	1020	2014
Nigeria	Lagos, Oyo, Kano	Marketing Support Consultancy	Face-to-face	1048	2013
Norway	Oslo, Bergen, Trondheim	SIS International Research	Online	1050	2014
Pakistan	Karachi, Lahore, Faisalabad	Gallup Pakistan	Face-to-face	2007	2014
Panama	Panama City, San Miguelito, David	CID-Gallup Latin America	Face-to-face	1020	2014
Peru	Lima, Trujillo, Arequipa	Prime Consulting	Face-to-face	1231	2013
Philippines	Manila, Davao, Cebu	IBI Partners	Face-to-face	1000	2013
Poland	Warzaw, Lodz, Cracow	Market Research & Polls - EURASIA (MRP-EUR-ASIA)	Face-to-face	1000	2013
Portugal	Lisbon, Villa Nova de Gaia, Sintra	Survey Sampling International	Online	1001	2014
Republic of Korea	Seoul, Busan, Incheon	IBI Partners	Face-to-face	1004	2013
Romania	Bucharest, Cluj-Napoco, Timisoara	Market Research & Polls - EURASIA (MRP-EUR-ASIA)	Face-to-face	1000	2013
Russia	Moscow, Saint Petersburg, Novosibirsk	VCIOM	Face-to-face	1000	2013
Senegal	Dakar, Thies, Saint-Louis	Liaison Marketing	Face-to-face	1001	2014
Serbia	Belgrade, Novi Sad, Nis	Market Research & Polls - EURASIA (MRP-EUR-ASIA)	Face-to-face	1000	2014
Sierra Leone	Freetown, Kenema, Makeni	TNS-RMS Cameroun Ltd.	Face-to-face	1005	2012
Singapore	Singapore	Survey Sampling International	Online	1000	2014
Slovenia	Ljubljana, Maribor, Oelje	Market Research & Polls - EURASIA (MRP-EUR-ASIA)	Face-to-face	1000	2014
South Africa	Johannesburg, Cape Town, Durban	Quest Research Services	Face-to-face	1000	2013
Spain	Madrid, Barcelona, Valencia	Survey Sampling International	Online	1000	2013
Sri Lanka	Colombo, Negombo, Kandy	PepperCube Consultants	Face-to-face	1030	2014
Sweden	Stockholm, Gothenburg, Malmo	Survey Sampling International	Online	1000	2013
Tanzania	Dar es Salaam, Mwanza, Shinyanga	Consumer Options Ltd.	Face-to-face	1000	2012
Thailand	Bangkok, Nonthaburi, Pak Kret	IBI Partners	Face-to-face	1008	2013
Tunisia	Tunis, Sfax, Sousse	BJKA Consulting (BJ Group)	Face-to-face	1000	2014
Turkey	Istanbul, Ankara, Izmir	TNS Turkey	Face-to-face	1003	2013
Uganda	Kampala, Mbale, Mbarara	TNS-RMS	Face-to-face	1002	2013
Ukraine	Kiev, Kharkiv, Odesa	Market Research & Polls - EURASIA (MRP-EUR-ASIA)	Face-to-face	1000	2014
United Arab Emirates	Dubai, Sharjah, Abu Dhabi	Dolfin Market Research & Consultancy (DolfinX)	Face-to-face	1610	2014
United Kingdom	London, Birmingham, Glasgow	Survey Sampling International	Online	1000	2013
United States	New York, Los Angeles, Chicago	Survey Sampling International	Online	1002	2014
Uruguay	Montevideo, Salto, Paysandu	Statmark Group	Telephone	1000	2012
Uzbekistan	Tashkent, Samarkand, Fergana	Market Research & Polls - EURASIA (MRP-EUR-ASIA)	Face-to-face	1000	2014
Venezuela	Caracas, Maracaibo, Barquisimeto	WJP in collaboration with local partner	Face-to-face	1000	2013
Vietnam	Hanoi, Haiphong, Ho Chi Minh City	Indochina Research	Face-to-face	1000	2014
Zambia	Lusaka, Ndola, Kitwe	Quest Research Services	Face-to-face	1000	2014
Zimbabwe	Harare, Bulawayo, Chitungwiza	SIS International Research	Face-to-face	1005	2012

METHODOLOGICAL CHANGES TO THIS YEAR'S REPORT

Every year, the WJP reviews the methods of data collection to ensure that the information produced is valid, useful, and continues to capture the status of the rule of law in the world. To maintain consistency with previous editions and to facilitate tracking changes over time, this year's questionnaires and data maps are closely aligned with those administered in the past.

In order to improve the accuracy of the QRQ results and reduce respondent burden, pro-active dependent interviewing techniques were used to remind respondents who participated in last year's survey of their responses in the previous year.

The most notable change to this year's Rule of Law Index was the broadening of the open government definition and the addition of new survey questions for better measurement for each of the four subfactors. 1) The "Publicized Laws and Government Data" category is an expansion of the category previously named "The laws are publicized and stable". The concept's definition has been broadened to include new information on the quality and accessibility of information published by the government in print and online. 2) The "Right to Information" category, which was previously named "Official information is available on request", has been expanded and now includes new survey questions on whether requests for government information are granted within a reasonable time period, whether the information provided is pertinent and complete, and whether requests for information are granted at a reasonable cost and without having to pay a bribe. 3) The "Civic Participation" category, previously named "Right to petition the government and public participation", has been broadened, and now includes survey questions on the freedom of opinion and expression, and the freedom of assembly and association. 4) The category "Complaint Mechanisms" is introduced and measures whether people are able to bring specific complaints to the government about the provision of public services or the performance of government officials. The category "The laws are stable", which was included as part of the open government factor in the Rule of Law Index, has been removed.

For these reasons, the scores and rankings provided in this report are not comparable to the previous "Factor 3: Open Government" scores and rankings presented in the Rule of Law Index.

TRACKING CHANGES OVER TIME

This year's report includes a measure to illustrate whether the rule of law in a country, as measured through the factors of the WJP Rule of Law Index, changed over the course of the past year. This measure is presented in the form of arrows and represents a summary of rigorous statistical testing based on the use of bootstrapping procedures (see below). For each factor, this measure takes the value of zero (no arrow) if there was no statistically significant change in the score since last year, a positive value (upward arrow) if there was a change leading to a statistically significant improvement in the score, and a negative value (downward arrow) if there was a change leading to a statistically significant deterioration in the score. This measure complements the numerical scores and rankings presented in this report, which benchmark each country's current performance on the factors and sub-factors of the Index against that of other countries.

The measure of change over time is constructed in four steps:

1. First, to allow for comparisons across last year's data and this year's data, the country-level raw values of each variable are mapped onto the 44 sub-factors (using this year's data map) and then normalized on a scale of 0-1 using the Min-Max method, so the maximum and minimum values of each variable over the two years equal one and zero, respectively.

2. The normalized variables are aggregated to yield country scores for each of the factors and sub-factors of the Index for each year. Last year's scores are then subtracted from this year's to obtain, for each country and each factor, the annual difference in scores.

3. To test whether the annual changes are statistically significant, a bootstrapping procedure is used to estimate standard errors, to calculate these errors, 100 samples of respondent-level observations (of equal size to the original sample) are randomly selected with replacement for each country from

the pooled set of respondents for last year and this year. These samples are used to produce a set of 100 country-level scores for each factor and each country, which are utilized to calculate the final standard errors. These errors – which measure the uncertainty associated with picking a particular sample of respondents – are then employed to conduct pair-wise t-tests for each country and each factor.

4. Finally, to illustrate the annual change, a measure of change over time is produced based on the value of the annual difference and its statistical significant (at the 95 percent level).

STRENGTHS AND LIMITATIONS

The Index methodology displays both strengths and limitations. Among its strengths is the inclusion of both expert and household surveys to ensure that the findings reflect the conditions experienced by the population. Another strength is that it approaches the measurement of rule of law from various angles by triangulating information across data sources and types of questions. This approach not only enables accounting for different perspectives on the rule of law, but it also helps to reduce possible bias that might be introduced by any other particular data collection method. Finally, it relies on statistical testing to determine the significance of the changes in the factor scores over the last year.

With the aforementioned methodological strengths come a number of limitations. First, the data shed light on rule of law dimensions that appear comparatively strong or weak, but are not specific enough to establish causation. Thus, it will be necessary to use the Index in combination with other analytical tools to provide a full picture of causes and possible solutions. Second, the methodology has been applied only in three major urban areas in each of the indexed countries. The WJP is therefore piloting the application of the methodology to rural areas. Third, given the rapid changes occurring in two countries, scores for some countries may be sensitive to the specific points in time when the data were collected. To address this, the WJP is piloting test methods of moving averages to account for short-term fluctuations. Fourth, the QRQ data may be subject to problems of measurement error due to the limited number of experts in some countries, resulting in less

precise estimates. To address this, the WJP works constantly to expand its network of in-country academic and practitioner experts who contribute their time and expertise to this endeavor. Finally, due to the limited number of experts in some countries (which implies higher standard errors) and the fact that the GPPs are carried out in each country every other year (which implies that for some countries, some variables do not change from one year to another). It is possible that the test described above fails to detect small changes in a country's situation over time.

OTHER METHODOLOGICAL CONSIDERATIONS

A detailed presentation of the methodology, including a table and description of the more than 500 variables used to construct the Index scores is available at www.worldjusticeproject.org and in Botero, J. and Ponce, A. (2011) "Measuring the Rule of Law": WJP Working Paper No. 1, available at www.worldjusticeproject.org/publications .

Contributing Experts

The *WJP Rule of Law Index® 2015* was made possible by the generous pro-bono contributions of academics and practitioners who contributed their time and expertise. The names of those experts wishing to be acknowledged individually are listed in the following pages.

This report was also made possible by the work of the polling companies who conducted fieldwork, and the thousands of individuals who have responded to the General Population Poll around the world.

Afghanistan

Amanullah Nuristani
Afghan Anti Corruption Network

Aschiana Organization

Augustine Kaheeru Bahemuka
M/s Kahuma, Khalayi & Kaheeru Advocates

Baryalai Hakimi
Kabul University

Hashmat Khalil Nadirpor
Legal Education Support Program-Afghanistan

Hosai Rahim Wardak

Idrees Zaman
Cooperation for Peace and Unity

Jürgen Baumann
GIZ German Development Corporation

Kakail Nuristani
Basic Needs Support Organization Afghanistan

Khalid Massoudi
Massoudi Legal Consultancy

Khalid Sekander

Mohammad Naeem Salimee
Coordination of Afghan Relief

Mohammad Tareq Eqtedary
Assistance to Legislative Bodies of Afghanistan

Nabil Shariq
Shajjan & Associates

Niamatullah Barakzai
Lex Ferghana

R. Michael Smith
Bowie & Jensen, LLC

Sammar Serat
NIL

Sanzar Kakar
Afghanistan Holding Group

Selay Ghaffar
HAWCA

Shoaib Timory
American University of Afghanistan

Suraya Sadeed
Help the Afghan Children, Inc.

Wahidullah Amiri
Nangarhar University

Zabihullah
Coordination of Afghan Relief

Anonymous Contributors

Albania

Artan Bozo
BOZO & Associates

Dorant Ekmekçiu
Hoxha, Memi & Hoxha

Drini Hakorja

Enver Roshi
Faculty of PublicHealth Medical University of Tirana

Gentiana Tirana
Tirana Law Firm

Gjergji Gjika
Gjika & Associates

Jonida Braja Melani
Wolf Theiss shpk

Mitat Dautaj
Catholic University

Oltjan Hoxholli
LPA Law Firm Albania

Shirli Gorenca
Kalo & Associates

Anonymous Contributors

Argentina

Adrián Goldin
International Society for Labour and Social Security Law

Adrián Tellas

Agustín Allende

Alberto Gonzalez Torres
Baker & McKenzie. Sociedad Civil

Alejandro Carrió
Asociación por los Derechos Civiles

Alvaro Herrero
Laboratorio de Políticas Públicas

Alvaro José Galli
Estudio Beccar Varela

Analía Duran
Allende & Brea

Carlos Marin
Estudio Bullo

Claudio Jesús Santagati
Pontificia Universidad Católica de Argentina

Daniel Sabsay
Universidad de Buenos Aires y Fundación Ambiente y Recursos Naturales

Dante Omar Grana
Fundación Red de Vida

Diego Silva Ortiz
Silva Ortiz, Alfonso, Pavic & Louge

Enrique Mariano Stile
Marval, O'Farrell & Mairal

Federico A. Borzi Cirilli

Humberto Federico Rios
Estudio Rios Abogados

J. Sebastian Elias
Universidad de San Andrés

Joaquín E. Zappa
J.P. O'Farrell Abogados

Joaquín Odriozola
Curutchet - Odriozola

María Morena del Rio

Maria Paola Trigiani
Alfaro Abogados

Mario Glanc
Universidad Isalud

Maximo Julio Fonrouge
Colegio de Abogados

Mercedes Lorenzo
Hewlett-Packard Argentina SRL

Nicolas Francisco Niewolski Cesca
Estudio Ferrer Deheza

P. Eugenio Aramburu
PAGBAM

Sandra Guillan
De Dios & Goyena Abogados Consultores

Santiago Legarre
Pontificia Universidad Catolica Argentina

Anonymous Contributors

Australia

Andrew Frazer
University of Wollongong

Andrew Goldsmith
Flinders University Centre for Crime Policy & Research

Breen Creighton
RMIT University

Dan Williams
Minter Ellison

Esther Stern
Flinders University of South Australia

Fiona McDonald
Queensland University of Technology

George Williams
University of New South Wales

Greg Patmore
University of Sydney

Iain Stewart
Macquarie University

James Hunt
University of Newcastle

Justice Chris Maxwell
Supreme Court of Victoria

Kate Burns
Rule of Law Institute of Australia

Kate Eastman

Mary E Crock
University of Sydney

Neil James
Australia Defence Association

Nicholas Cowdery
University of Sydney; University of New South Wales

Peter Cashman
University of Sydney

Sarah Joseph
Castan Centre for Human Rights Law

Simon Rice
Australian National University

Sonia Allan
Macquarie University

Thomas Faunce
Australian National University

Veronica Siow
Allens

Anonymous Contributors

Austria

Christoph Konrath
Parliamentary Administration

Claudia Habl
GÖG - Health Austria

Doris Wydra
Salzburg Centre of European Union Studies

Gerhard Jarosch
Austrian Association of Prosecutors

Isabell Kirisits-Ilek
Hewlett-Packard

Isabelle Pellech

Ivo Greiter
Greiter Pegger Kofler & Partners

Jernej Sekolec

Karin Bruckmüller
Johannes Kepler University Linz

Karl Stöger
University of Graz

Magdalena Ziembicka
Barnert Egermann Illigasch Rechtsanwälte GmbH

Manfred Ketzer
Hausmaninger Kletter Rechtsanwälte GmbH

Martin Reinisch
BKP Brauneis Klauser Prändl Rechtsanwälte GmbH

Martin Risak
University of Vienna

Rupert Manhart
Austrian Bar Association

Thomas Frad
KWR Karasek Wietrzyk Rechtsanwälte GmbH

Thomas Hofmann
PALLAS Rechtsanwälte Partnerschaft

Anonymous Contributors

Bangladesh

Abdul Awal
NRDS

Abdullahel Baki
Law Portal

Abu Sayeed M M Rahman
United Hospital Limited

AKM Nasim
Solidarity Center

Al Amin Rahman
Fox Mandal Associates

Ali Asif Khan
Hossain & Khan Associates

ASM Alamgir
IEDCR

Debra Efroymson
HealthBridge

Imteaz Ibne Mannan
Save the Children

K.A.R. Sayeed
United Hospital Limited

M. R. I. Chowdhury
M. R. I. Chowdhury & Associates

Mahua Zahur
BRAC University

Masud Khan
The Legal Circle

Mirza Farzana Iqbal Chowdhury
Daffodil International University

Mohammad Nafiu Alam
FM Associates

Mohammed Mutahar Hossain
Hossain & Khan Associates

Nasirud Doulah
Doulah & Doulah

Rokib Bin Hossain
The Legal Circle

S M Shaikat
SERAC-Bangladesh

Saira Rahman Khan
Odhikar

Sarjean Rahman Lian
FM Associates

Sayed Rubayet
Save the Children

Sheikh Abdur Rahim
Daffodil International University

Shusmita Khan
Eminence

Syed Mizanur Rahman
Daffodil International University

Tanim Hussain Shawon

Anonymous Contributors

Belarus

Alexander Botian
Borovtsov & Salei law firm

Alexey Darvin
Revera Consulting Group

Anastasia Byckowskaya
Stepanovski, Papakul and Partners

Denis Aleinikov
Aleinikov & Partners Law Firm

Dmitry Kovalchik
Stepanovski, Papakul and Partners

Dmitry Semashko
Stepanovski, Papakul and Partners

Elena Selivanova
Sysouev, Bondar, Khrapoutski SBH

Eugenia Chenverikova
Revera Consulting Group

Helen Mourashko
Revera Consulting Group

Helen Mourashko, Olga Korobeiko,
Yulia Oshmyan
Revera Consulting Group

Olga Zdobnova
Vlasova Mikhel & Partners

Vadzim Samaryn
Belarusian State University

Valentina Ogarkova
Stepanovski, Papakul and Partners

Anonymous Contributors

Belgium

Abayo J-P
CHRVS

Andrée Puttemans
Université Libre de Bruxelles

Anne-Lise Sibony
University of Liège

Cindy Stalmans
Hewlett-Packard

Damien Gerard
Université Catholique de Louvain

Fontaine
Chu Liege Belgique

Henry
Avocats.Be

Nicolas Cariat

Olivier De Witte
Hospital Erasme ULB

Patrick Goffaux
Université Libre de Bruxelles

Patrick Wautelet
University of Liège

Pierre-Olivier Mahieu
Allen & Overy LLP

Yves Lejeune
Université Catholique de Louvain

Anonymous Contributors

Belize

Andrew Bennett
Glenn D. Godfrey & Co. LLP

Estevan Perera
Glenn D. Godfrey & Co. LLP

Fred Lumor
Fred Lumor & Co.

Marvin Manzanero
Ministry of Health of Belize

Melissa Balderamos Mahler
Marin Balderamos Arthurs LLP

Rondine Twist
Government of Belize

Said W. Musa S.C.
Musa Balderamos LLP

Victor Lizarraga
Universal Health Services Ltd.

Anonymous Contributors

Bolivia

Adrian Barrenechea
BM&O Abogados

Arletta Añez
OPS/OMS

Astruval Columba Joffre
AC Consultores Legales

Carlos Gerke Siles
Estudio Jurídico Gerke. Soc. Civ.

Cesar Burgoa Rodríguez
Bufete Burgoa

Efraín Freddy Suárez Chávez

Ivan Lima Magne

Javier Mir Peña
Mir & Abogados

Lucy Mejia Montoya
Sociedad Boliviana de Salud Pública

María Eugenia Antezana Virreira
Criales, Urcullo & Antezana - Abogados

Mirko Antezana
Soliplast SRL

Pablo Carrasco
Pablo Carrasco Firma de Abogados

Raul Baldivia
Baldivia Unzaga & Asociados

Rosario Baptista Canedo

Salomón Eid
Ferrere Abogados

Sandra Salinas

Sergio Reynolds Ruiz
Bufete Reynolds Legal Advice

Victor Vargas Montaño
Herrera & Abogados Soc. Civ.

William Herrera Añez
Herrera & Abogados Soc. Civ.

Anonymous Contributors

Bosnia and Herzegovina

Adis Arapovic
Centres for Civic Initiatives

Adisa Omerbegovic Arapovic
University of Sarajevo

Adnan Durakovic
University of Zenica

Aida Pojskić
Kantonalna Bolnica Zenica

Aleksandar Sajic
SAJIC Banja Luka

Andrea Zubovic-Devedzic
CMS Reich-Rohrwig Hainz

Arijana Hadžiahmetović
Marić & Co. Law Firm

Boris Stojanović
Boris Stojanović Law Office

Danijela Saller Osenk

Davorin Marinkovic

Edin Halapic

Esad Oruc
International Burch University

Hajrija Sijerčić-Čolić
University of Sarajevo

Hana Korać
University of Travnik

Kasim Trnka

Lana Bubalo
University of "Džemal Bijedić"Mostar

Mehmed Spaho
Law Office Spaho

Mersida Suceska
University of Sarajevo

Milorad Sladojevic
Municipal Court Bugojno

Miodrag Simović
Constitutional Court of Bosnia and Herzegovina

Mirjana Šarkinović

Nedžad Smailagić
University of Poitiers

Randzana Hadzibegovic Haracic
Municipal Court Bugojno

Sakib Softić
University of Sarajevo

Samil Ramić
Municipal Court Bugojno

Slaven Dizdar
Marić & Co. Law Firm

Tarik Prolaz
PETOSEVIC

Zlatan Balta
CMS Reich-Rohrwig Hainz

Zoran Dakic
Health Center Bijeljina

Anonymous Contributors

Botswana

Buhlebenkosi Ncube
Y S Moncho Attorneys

Dick Bayford
Bayford & Associates

Jaloni Pansiri
University of Botswana

John McAllister
University of Botswana

Kagiso Jani
Tshekiso Ditiro & Jani Legal Practice

Kwadwo Osei-Ofei
Osei-Ofei Swabi & Co.

Munyaka Wadaira Makuyana
Makuyana Legal Practice

Patrick Athiany
Pakmed Group

Piyush Sharma
Piyush Sharma Attorneys & Co.

Rekha A. Kumar
University of Botswana

Setho Mokobi
Bookbinder Business Law

Anonymous Contributors

Brazil

Alexandre Fragoso Silvestre
Miguel Neto Advogados

Andre de Melo Ribeiro
Dias Carneiro Advogados

Anna Thereza Monteiro de Barros
Pinheiro Neto Advogados

Carlos Ayres
Trench, Rossi e Watanabe Advogados

Cesar Augusto Infante Basso
Hewlett-Packard

Daniel Arbix
Google

Daniel Bushatsky
Advocacia Bushatsky

Daniela Muradas
Universidade Federal de Minas Gerais

Denise Provasi Vaz
Moraes Pitombo Advogados

Edson Mazieiro
Murray Law Firm

Elival da Silva Ramos
São Paulo University

Fabio Martins Di Jorge
Peixoto & Cury Advogados

Fábio Peixinho Gomes Corrêa
Lilla, Huck, Otranto e Camargo Advogados

Felipe Asensi
Rio de Janeiro State University

Fernanda Vargas Terrazas
National Council of Municipal Health Secretaries

Fernando Aith
University of São Paulo

Gabriel Costa
Shell Brasil Petroleo Ltda.

Heloísa Estellita
Fundação Getúlio Vargas

Igor Parente
Shell Brasil

João Otávio Pinheiro Olivério
Campos Mello Advogados

Joaquim Falcao
Fundação Getúlio Vargas

Joel Ferreira Vaz Filho
Garcia & Keener Advogados

José Ricardo dos Santos Luz Júnior
Duarte Garcia, Caselli Guimarães e Terra Advogados

Luciano Feldens
Pontifícia Universidade Católica do Rio Grande do Sul

Luiz Guilherme Marinoni

Luiz Guilherme Primos
Primos e Primos Advocacia

Maria Celina Bodin de Moraes
Bodin de Moraes Vilela & Fernandes

Maria Valeria Junho Penna
Universidade Federal do Rio de Janeiro

Mario de Barros Duarte Garcia
Duarte Garcia, Caselli Guimarães e Terra Advogados

Mauricio Faragone
Faragone Advogados

Michael Freitas Mohallem
Fundação Getúlio Vargas

Oscar Vilhena Vieira
Fundação Getúlio Vargas

Paulo Fernando Giugliodori Grippa
Hewlett-Packard

Pedro Augusto Gravatá Nicoli
Universidade Federal de Minas Gerais

Rafael Villac Vicente de Carvalho
Peixoto & Cury Advogados

Rosa Lima
Rosa Lima, PC

Sergio Cruz Arenhart
Ministério Público Federal and Universidade Federal do Paraná

Soraia Saleh
Leite, Tosto e Barros Advogados Associados

Thiago Bottino
FGV Direito Rio

Victor Hugo Criscuolo Boson
Universidade Federal de Minas Gerais

Anonymous Contributors

Bulgaria

Assen Vassilev
Center for Economic Strategy

Atanas Politov
PILnet

Atanas Slavov
Sofia University

Boyko Guerginov
CHSH

Delchev & Partners Law Firm

Denitsa Sacheva
International Healthcare and Health Insurance Institute

Georgi P. Dobrev
Georgi P. Dobrev Law Office

Gergana Ilieva
KSK and Partners

Iana Roueva Madey

Irina Stoeva
Stoeva, Kuyumdjieva & Vitliemov

Ivo Baev
Ivo Baev & Partners

Jean Crombois
American University in Bulgaria

Lachezar Raichev
Penkov, Markov & Partners

Lidia M. Georgieva
Medical University - Sofia

Momiana Guneva
Burgas Free University

Nikolai Hristov
Medical University - Sofia

Petko Salchev
Institute of Economic Research-Bulgarian Academy of Science

Stanislav Hristov

Stanley B. Gyoshev
Xfi Centre for Finance & Investment, University of Exeter

Todor Dotchev
Institute for Political and Legal Studies

Veselka Petrova

Anonymous Contributors

Burkina Faso

Adrien Sosthène Zongo
Cabinet d'Avocats Sosthène A. M. Zongo

Apollinaire Joachimson Kyélem de Tambèla
Avocat au Barreau du Burkina Faso

Fako Bruno Ouattara
Etude Fako Bruno Ouattara et Cinesda

Julien Lalogo

K. Frederic Hermann Minoungou
SCPA LEGALIS

K. Timothée Zongo
Avocat au Barreau du Burkina Faso

Maliki Derra
Avocat au Barreau du Burkina Faso

Martine Tologho
Cabinet d'Avocats

Neya Ali
Cabinet d'Avocats Ali Neya

Paré Biencomma
Société Civilie Professionnelle d'Avocats Yaguibou et Yanogo

Paulin Marcellin Salambere
Barreau du Burkina Faso

Roland Patrick Bouda
SCPA Consilium

Anonymous Contributors

Cambodia

Alex Larkin
DFDL

Chak Sopheap
Cambodian Center for Human Rights

Chandy NY
Legal Town Lawyer Group

Kem Ley

Narin Chum
Community Legal Education Center

Run Saray
Legal Aid of Cambodia

Sek Sophorn
Rights & Business Law Office

Sia Phearum
Housing Rights Task Force

Sophea IM

Thida Khus
Silaka

Tola Moeun
Community Legal Education Center

Vichuta Ly
Legal Support for Children and Women

Anonymous Contributors

Cameroon

Abane Stanley
Abeng Law Firm

Alain Bruno Woumcou Nzetchie
Cabinet d'Avocats Josette KADJI

Atsishi Fon-Ndikum
Fon-Ndikum & Partners

Barthélemy Tchepnang
CAJAD

Cabinet d'Avocat Henri Job

Christian Dudieu Djomga
Isis Attorneys

Etakong Tabyang
The Global Citizens Initiative

Hyacinthe Fansi
SCP Ngassam Njikè & Associes

Innocent Takougang
Foundation for Health Research & Development

Jean Joseph Claude Siewe
Siewe & Partners Law Firm

John Esandua Morfaw
Strategic Development Initiatives

Marie-José Essi
Faculté de Médecine et des Sciences Biomédicales

Martin Kamako
Cabinet Kamako

Nelson Enyih

Nkenglefac Yochembeng
Cabinet Marie-Andree Ngwe

Nkongme Dorcas Mirette
Nkongme Law Firm

Nyamboli Joyce Ngwe
Destiny Chambers

Patrick Menyeng Manga
Fiduciaire Associes en Afrique

Paul Watsop
Cabinet d'Avocats

Samuel Nko'o-Amvene
Faculte de Médecine et des Sciences Biomédicales

Tarh Bocong Frambo
American University

Tchuisseu Miranda Chanda
Universal Law Chambers

Tougoua Djokouale Guy Alaïn
Tougoua and Partners Law Firm

Zakariaou Njoumemi
Université de Yaoundé I

Anonymous Contributors

Canada

[name]
Cassels Brock & Blackwell LLP

Brian Langille
University of Toronto

Brian Pukier
Stikeman Elliott

Bruce Grist
Fasken Martineau DuMoulin LLP

C.G. Harrison
Fasken Martineau DuMoulin LLP

Colin L. Soskolne

Constance MacIntosh
Dalhousie Health Law Institute

Daniel M. Campbell
Cox & Palmer

Fabien Gélinas
McGill University

Finn Makela
Université de Sherbrooke

Frédéric Bachand
McGill University

Gaynor Roger
Shibley Righton LLP

Glen Luther
University of Saskatchewan

Jabeur Fathally
University Of Ottawa

Jula Hughes
University of New Brunswick

Karen Busby
University of Manitoba

Louis Letellier de St-Just
Institut Phillippe Pinel de Montréal

Marc Laporta
Montreal WHO Collaborating Centre

Orie Niedzviecki
Ellyn Law LLP

Richard Perras
Richard Perras

Rick Molz
Concordia University

Sonny Goldstein
Goldstein Financial Consultants

William Goodridge
Supreme Court of Newfoundland and Labrador

Anonymous Contributors

Chile

Alfonso Canales Undurraga
UH&C Abogados

Andrea Abascal Marín
Jara del Favero Abogados

Carlos Maturana Toledo
Universidad de Concepción

Carlos Ossandon Salas
Eluchans y Compañía

Caterina Guidi Moggia
Universidad Adolfo Ibáñez

Cristian Fabres
Guerrero Olivos

Cristián Muga Aitken
Puga Ortiz Abogados

Cristián Vásquez Goerit
BAZ Abogados

Daniela Horvitz Lennon
Horvitz & Horvitz Abogados

Diego Miranda Reyes
Phillipi Yrarrázaval Pulido & Brunner

Fernando Lolas
Universidad de Chile

Fernando Maturana Crino
Eyzaguirre y Cía., Abogados

Gabriel del Río
Aninat Schwencke & Cía.

Gonzalo Cisternas Sobarzo
Cisternas & Cortes

Gonzalo Hoyl Moreno
Hoyl, Alliende & Cía. Abogados

Irene Rojas Miño
Universidad de Talca

Jorge Canales G.
Estudio Jurídico PGYA

Jorge Sandrock Carrasco
Fundación Hanns Seidel

Jorge Wahl S.
Larraín & Asociados

Juan Enrique Vargas
Universidad Diego Portales

Lorena Pavic
Carey Abogados

Luis Eugenio García-Huidobro
Philippi, Prietoçarrizosa & Uría

Luis Felipe Hubner
UH&C Abogados

Luis Parada
Bahamondez, Alvarez & Zegers

Manuel Jiménez Pfingsthorn
Jara del Favero Abogados

Maria Elena Santibánez Torres
Pontificia Universidad Católica de Chile

María Isabel Cornejo Plaza
Universidad de Chile

Maria Norma Oliva Lagos
Defensoria laboral, Corporacion Asistencia Judicial del Bio Bio.

Martin Besio Hernández
Rivadeneira Colombara Zegers

Matías Donoso Lamas
Urenda & Cía.

Omar Morales C.
Montt y Cía. Abogados

Orlando Palominos
Morales & Besa

Patricio Morales Aguirre

Paula Sánchez Birke
Bofill Mir & Álvarez Jana Abogados

Roberto Guerrero del Rio
Guerrero Olivos

Sergio Gamonal Contreras
Universidad Adolfo Ibáñez

Anonymous Contributors

China

JIA Ping
Health Governance Initiative

Jiaona Chen
Hewlett-Packard

Kaiming Liu
Institute of Contemporary Observation

Liu Xin
China University of Political Science and Law

Matthew Murphy
MMLC Group

Qiong Yan
Hewlett-Packard

Xia Yu
MMLC Group

Zhigang Yu
China University of Political Science and Law

Anonymous Contributors

Colombia

Ana Liliana Rios García
Universidad del Norte

Angela Maria Ruiz Sternberg
Universidad del Rosario

Camilo Torres Serna
Universidad Libre de Cali

Carlos Andrés Gómez González
Universidad Jorge Tadeo Lozano

Carlos Arturo Toro Lopez

Carolina Posada Isaacs
Posse Herrera Ruiz

Diego Felipe Valdivieso Rueda
VS+M Abogados

Diego Muñoz Tamayo
Muñoz Tamayo & Asociados

Eduardo Cárdenas
Cárdenas & Cárdenas Abogados

Enrique Alvarez Posada
Lloreda Camacho & Co.

Fernando Pabon
Pabon Abogados

Gonzalo Anibal Parrado Ochoa
Parrado Ochoa Holguín Abogados

Guillermo Hernando Bayona Combariza

Gustavo Quintero Navas

Gustavo Tamayo
Lloreda Camacho & Co.

Ignacio Santamaria
Lloreda Camacho & Co.

Joe Bonilla Gálvez
Muñoz Tamayo & Asociados

Jorge Acosta-Reyes
Universidad del Norte

Jorge Diaz Cardenas
Diaz Cardenas Abogados

Lucas Fajardo Gutiérrez
Brigard & Urrutia Abogados

Luis Alberto Tafur Calderón
Universidad del Valle

Luis Fernando Ramire Contreras
Tribunal Superior de Bogotá

[name]
Hewlett-Packard

Marcela Castro-Ruiz
Universidad de los Andes

Mario Pérez
Prieto Carrizosa Abogados

Martín Acero
Prietocarrizosa

Mauricio A. Bello Galindo
Baker & McKenzie

Olga Santamaría Aguilera
Prietocarrizosa

Rafael Tuesca Molina
Universidad del Norte

Raúl Alberto Suárez Arcila
Suárez Arcila & Abogados Asociados

Ricardo Posada Maya
Universidad de los Andes

Sandra Catalina Charris Rebellón

Santiago Martínez
Godoy Córdoba Abogados

Tomás Calderón-Mejía
Lloreda Camacho & Co.

Anonymous Contributors

Costa Rica

Alejandro Batalla Bonilla
Batalla Abogados

Alfonso Carro
Central Law Quirós Abogados

Armando A. Guardia
Guardia & Cubero

César Hines Céspedes

J. Federico Campos Calderón
LEXPENAL - Abogados Penalistas

José Luis Campos Vargas
Batalla Abogados

Jose Luis Pacheco Murillo
AB&P Consultores Jurídicos

Luis Ángel Sánchez Montero
Bufete Facio & Cañas

Marlen León Guzmán
Universidad de Costa Rica

Miguel Ruíz Herrera
Lex Counsel

Sergio Amador
Batalla Abogados

Anonymous Contributors

Cote d'Ivoire

Dable
SCPA Dogue Abbe Yao

Dugbemin Kone G.
SCPA Nambeya-Dogbemin & Associes

Mᵉ Lynda Dadié-Sangaret
Dadié-Sangaret & Associés

Raphael Abauleth

Sylvia Soro
l'Université de Bordeaux

Yabasse Lucien Abouya
Atchan For All

Youan Gotre Jules
ONG AMEPOUH

Anonymous Contributors

Croatia

Alan Soric
Attorneys Soric & Tomekovic Dunda

Ana Padjen
Macesic & Partners Law Offices LLC

Ana Stavljenic-Rukavina
DIU Libertas International University

Anita Krizmanic
Macesic & Partners Law Offices LLC

Arsen Bacic
University of Split

Boris Kozjak
Lawyers Office

Boris Šavorić
Šavoric & Partners

Božidar Feldman
Matić & Feldman

Darko Jurišić
General Hospital "Dr.Josip Benčević"

Emir Bahtijarević
DTB

I Irvoje Banfic
University of Zagreb

Ivan Kos
PETOŠEVIĆ

Ivana Manovelo
Macesic & Partners Law Offices LLC

Ivo Grga

Luka Kovačić
Andrija Stampar School of Public Health

Marin Labar
Poliklinika Labar D.O.O.

Marko Lovric

Matko Pajčić
University of Split

Rudolf Gregurek
University of Zagreb

Sunčana Roksandić Vidlička
University of Zagreb

Visnja Drenski Lasan
Law Firm Drenski Lasan

Zlatko Vlajcic
University Hospital Dubrova

Zoran Vujasin
Law Firm Vujasin & Duk J.T.D.

Zvonko Sosic
University of Zagreb

Anonymous Contributors

Czech Republic

Denisa Bellinger
Hewlett-Packard

Lukáš Prudil
AK Prudil a Spol., S.R.O.

Marek Antos
Charles University in Prague

Maria Janková

Martin Strnad
Havel, Holášek & Partners

Matej Smolar
FELIX A SPOL Advokatni Kancelar

Michal Hanko
Bubník, Mysli & Partners

Pavel Černý
Frank Bold

Pavel Holec
Holec, Zuska & Partners

Radek Matouš
Balcar Polanský Eversheds

Tomas Cihula
Kinstellar

Tomas Matejovsky
CMS Cameron McKenna

Anonymous Contributors

Denmark

Amin Alavi
Aarhus University

Anne Brandt Christensen
HopeNow

Anne Skjold Qvortrup
Gorrissen Federspiel

Bitten Elizabeth Hansen
Gorrissen Federspiel

Chalida Svastisalee
Metropolitan University College

Hans Henrik Edlund
University of Aarhus

Jacob Sand
Gorrissen Federspiel

Jakob S. Johnsen
HjulmandKaptain

Jens Rye-Andersen
Advokatfirmaet Jens Rye-Andersen

Jørn Vestergaard
University of Copenhagen

Lars Lindencrone Petersen
Bech-Bruun Law Firm

Marianne Granhol and Soren Moller Rasmussen
Kormann Reumert

Michael Hansen Jensen
Aarhus University

Morten Broberg
University of Copenhagen

Paul Krüger Andersen
Aarhus University

Per Andersen
Aarhus University

Poul Hvilsted
Horten Law Firm

Thomas Neumann
University of Aarhus

Anonymous Contributors

Dominican Republic

Ana Isabel Caceres
Troncoso y Cáceres

Carlos Hernandez
Hernandez Contreras & Herrero. Abogados

Edwin Grandel Capellán

Elisabetta Pedersini
Aaron Suero & Pedersini

Enrique De Marchena Kaluche and Nelson MI. Jaquez Suarez
DMK Lawyers - Central Law

Fernando Roedán Hernández
Ortiz & Hernández Abogados Asociados

Jesus Maria Troncoso
Troncoso y Cáceres

Juan Manuel Suero
Aaron Suero & Pedersini

Leandro Corral
Estrella & Tupete

Mary Fernandez Rodriguez
Headrick Rizik. Alvarez & Fernandez

Miguel Valerio Jiminián
Valerio Jiminián Roa Abogados

Plinio C. Pina Mendez
Pina Mendez & Asoc.

Richard A. Benoit Dominguez
Benoit Dominguez & Asociados

Ulises Morlas Pérez
Cabral & Díaz Abogados

Virgilio A. Mendez Amaro
Mendez & Asociados

Virgilio Bello González
Bello Rosa & Bello González, Abogados

Anonymous Contributors

Ecuador

Andrea Izquierdo
Sempertegui Ontaneda Abogados

Carlos I Ierdoiza
Arizaga y Co. Abogados

James Pilco Luzuriaga
Universidad del Azuay

Juan Carlos Riofrio Martínez-Villalba
Universidad de Los Hemisferios

Santiago Solines Moreno
Solines & Asociados

Ximena Moreno de Solines
Solines & Asociados

Anonymous Contributors

Egypt

Ahmed El-Gammal
El-Shalakany Law Firm

Bassem S Wadie
Urology and Nephrology Center

Habiba Hassan-Wassef
National Research Center

Ibrahim Kharboush
Alexandria University

Khaled El Shalakany
Shalakany Law Office

Laila El Baradei
American University in Cairo

Mohamed Abdelaal
Alexandria University

Mohamed Hanafi Mahmoud Mohamed
Egyptian Ministry of Justice

Nada El Ezaby
Zaki Hashem & Partners

Nagwa Mohamed El Sadek Mahdy
Administrative Prosecution Authority

Somaya Hosny
Suez Canal University

Walid Hegazy
Hegazy Law Firm

Anonymous Contributors

El Salvador

Ana Yesenia Granillo de Tobar
Escuela Superior de Economia y Negocios

Antonio R. Méndez Llort
Romero Pineda & Asociados

Benjamin Valdez Iraheta
Consortium Centro América Abogados

Celina de Parada

David Claros
García & Bodán - Attorneys and Counselors at Law

Délmer Edmundo Rodríguez Cruz
Escuela Superior de Economia y Negocios

Diego Martin Menjivar
Consortium Centro America Abogados

Eduardo Suárez
Ministerio de Salud

Jaime Salinas Olivares
Garcia & Bodan El Salvador

Jose Eduardo Barrientos Aguirre
SBA, Firma Legal y Consultora

José Freddy Zometa Segovia
Romero Pineda & Asociados

Julio Vides
Consortium El Salvador

Oscar Samour
Consortium Centro América Abogados

Oscar Torres Cañas
Garcia & Bodan El Salvador

Piero Antonio Rusconi Gutiérrez
Central Law

Rebeca Atanacio de Basagoitia
Escalon & Atancio

Ricardo A. Cevallos
BLP

Roberto Romero Pineda
Romero Pineda & Asociados

Rommell Ismael Sandoval Rosales
I&D Consulting; SBA Legal Firm

Yudy Aracely Jimenez Rivera
Gold Service S.A. de C.V.

Anonymous Contributors

Estonia

Andres Parmas
Tallinn Circuit Court

Andres Vutt
University of Tartu

Anneli Soo
University of Tartu

Gaabriel Tavits
University of Tartu

Irene Kull
University of Tartu

Jüri Saar
University of Tartu

Kaja Põlluste
University of Tartu

Karl Käsper
Estonian Human Rights Centre

Madis Kiisa
Law Office Laus & Parners

Maksim Greinoman
Advokaadibüroo Greinoman & Co

Margit Vutt
Supreme Court of the Republic of Estonia

Martin Käerdi
University of Tartu

Merle Erikson
University of Tartu

Pirkko-Liis Harkmaa
LAWIN Attorneys at Law

Tanel Kerikmäe
Tallinn University of Technology

Triinu Hiob
LAWIN Attorneys at Law

Anonymous Contributors

Ethiopia

Aberra Degefa Nagawo
Addis Ababa University

Afework Kassu
Addis Ababa University

Endalkachew Geremew Negash
University of Gondar

Fikadu Asfaw
Fikadu Asfaw and Associates Law Office

Guadie Sharew
Bahir Dar University

Hiruy Wubie Gebreegziabher
University of Gondar

Kumsa Girma Kassa
Adama Science and Technology University

Lubo Teferi Kerorsa
Adama Science and Technology University

Mehari Redae
Addis Ababa University

Mulu Abraha

Tameru Wondm Agegnehu
Tameru Wondm Agegnehu Law Offices

Wondimu S. Yirga
Haramaya University College of Health Sciences

Yordanos Seifu Estifanos

Anonymous Contributors

Finland

Ari Miettinen
Fimlab Laboratories Ltd.

Iikka Sainio
Attorneys-at-Law Juridia Bützow Ltd

Johanna Niemi
University of Turku

Jukka Peltonen
Peltonen LMR Attorneys Ltd

Jussi Tapani
University of Turku

Liisa von Plato
Hewlett-Packard

Markku Fredman
Fredman & Mansson

Matti Ilmari Niemi
University of Eastern Finland

Matti Reinikainen
Attorney's Office Kolari & Co.Oy

Matti Tolvanen
University of Eastern Finland

Mika J Lehtimaki
Attorneys-at-Law TRUST

Mika Launiala
University of Eastern Finland

Patrick Lindgren
Advocare Law Office

Pekka Viljanen
University of Turku

Raimo Isoaho
University of Turku

Sanna Leisti
Rule of Law Finland - ROLFI

Anonymous Contributors

France

Anicee Van Engeland
SOAS

Carlos M. Herrera
Université de Cergy-Pontoise -CP.IP

Catherine Cathiard
Jeantet et Associés

David Levy

Delga

Francis Tartour

Gauthier Chassang
INSERM

Marie-Christine Cimadevilla
Cimadevilla Avocats

Nataline Fleury
Ashurst

Nicolas Mathieu
Skadden, Arps, Slate, Meagher & Flom LLP

Nicole Stolowy
HEC Paris

Olivier de Boutiny
BBG Associés

Pascale Lagesse
Bredin Prat

Patrice Le Maigat
Université de Rennes

Philippe Marin
IM Avocats

Philippe Portier
Jeantet Avocats

Samira Denfer

Thierry Berland
SCP Avocats Berland & Sevin Dijon

Virginie Hailey des Fontaines
Université Pierre et Marie Curie

Yanick Alvarez-de Selding

Anonymous Contributors

Georgia

Ana Chelidze
Basisbank

Davit Atabegashvili
Basisbank

Ekaterina Aleksidze
BGI Advisory Services Georgia

George Gotsadze
Curatio International Foundation

George Nanobashvili
UNDP Georgia

Giorgi Chkheidze

Gocha Svanidze
Law Firm Svanidze & The Partners

Grigol Gagnidze
NNLE, Georgian Barristers & Lawyers International Observatory

Imeda Dvalidze

Kakha Sharabidze
Business Legal Bureau

Ketevani Krialashvili
Economic Policy Experts Center

Lasha Gogiberidze
BGI Legal

Nata Kazakhashvili
Iv. Javakhishvili Tbilisi State University

Otar Gzirishvili
JSC "Basisbank"

Otar Vasadze
University of Georgia

Revaz Beridze
Eristavi & Partners

Tamara Tevdoradze
BGI Legal

Tinatin Gugunava
IDECO

Tsotne Murghulia
City Council of Zugdidi

Vera Doborjginidze
Lexpert Group Law Firm

Zurab Mukhuradze
Legal and Business Consulting

Anonymous Contributors

Germany

Alexander Baron von Engelhardt

Alexander Putz
Putz und Partner Steuerberater & Rechtsanwälte

Anna Lindenberg

Antje Schwarz
Daimler AG

Astrid Stadler
Universtiy of Konstanz

Axel Nagler
Rechtsanwälte Nagler & Partner

Barbara Baur

Bernd Weller
Heuking Kühn Lüer Wojtek

Brigitte Kolb

Burkhard Klüver
Ahlers & Vogel Rechtsanwälte

C E Naundorf
Schirp Neusel & Partner Rechtsanwälte mbB

Carsten Momsen
Leibniz University

Catherine Hess

Christian Schultze
AB&D Attorneys Berlin

Christian Wolff
Schock Rechtsanwalte GbR

Christina Reifelsberger

Christof Kerwer
University of Würzburg

Christoph Lindner

Dirk Vielhuber
Berufsgenossenschaft der Bauwirtschaft

Dominik Steiger
Freie Universität

Friederike Lemme
Lemme + Al Abed Rechtsanwälte

Gernot A. Warmuth
Scheiber & Partner

Gregor Dornbusch

Hauke Achim Hagena
Lüders Warneboldt & Partner

Henning Rosenau
University of Augsburg

Hermann Bietz

Hubertus Becker
Becker Sennheinn Schuster Rechtsanwälte

Ingo Klaus Wamser
Rechtsanwalt Wamser

Jan Ricken
Kliemt & Vollstädt

Jessica Jacobi
Kliemt & Vollstädt

Juergen Nazarek

Lars Nitzsche
Kanzlei Joachim Ledele, Kehl, Germany

Lars Rieck
IPCL Rieck & Partner Rechtsanwälte

M. Nodorf

Manfred Weiss
Goethe University, Frankfurt

Martin Sträßer
RAe Sträßer Rehm Barfield

Mathias Bröring

Matthias Kaiser
Wittch & Kaiser Notar Rechtsanwälte

Michael Zoebisch
rwzh Rechtsanwälte

Nelles Reinhold

Nicola Kreutzer
Law Firm Kreutzer & Kreuzau

Oliver Schellbach

Oliver Thamerus

Othmar K. Traber
Ahlers & Vogel Rechtsanwälte PartG mbB

Piet Klemeyer
Goliub Klemeyer Fachanwälte - Partnerschaft mbB

R. Kunz-Hallstein

RA Oliver Bolthausen
BridgehouseLaw

Rainer W. Hofmann
Kanzlei im Hofhaus

Robert H. Leitermann
Thelen & Reiners

Roland Gross
Gross::Rechtsanwaelte

Sabine Barth
Dostal & Sozien Rechtsanwälte

Stefan Sasse
GÖHMANN Rechtsanwälte

Stephan Sander
Terhedebrügge Heyn Sander

Storch Katharina

Thomas B. Belitz
Advopartner Rechtsanwälte Belitz & Partner

Thomas Feltes
Ruhr-Universität Bochum

Thomas Jürgens
Jürgens Rechtsanwaltsgesellschaft mbH

Torsten Koller
Hewlett-Packard

Ulrich Keil
University of Muenster

Wolf Stahl
Kanzlei fuer Wirtschaftsrecht

Wolfgang Grüttner

Wolfgang Hau
University of Passau

Anonymous Contributors

Ghana

Araba Sefa-Dedeh
University of Ghana Medical School

Azanne Kofi Akainyah
A & A Law Consult

Dinah Baah-Odoom
Ghana Health Service

Kwame Owusu Agyeman
University of Cape Coast

Nana Tawiah Okyir
Ghana Institute of Management and Public Administration

Nii Nortey Hanson-Nortey
Ghana Health Service

Richmond Aryeetey
University of Ghana School of Public Health

Sam Okudzeto
Sam Okudzeto & Associates

Sam Poku
The Business Council for Africa

Anonymous Contributors

Greece

Alex Afouxenidis
National Centre for Social Research

Anastasia Tsakatoura
KTLEGAL Law Offices

Anna Damaskou
Transparency International Greece

Anthony Mavrides
Ballas, Pelecanos & Associates L.P.C.

Athanasios Kikis
Athanasios Kikis & Partners Law Office

Christina Papadopoulou
IRCT

Dionysios Pantazis
Pantazis & Associates Law Firm

Dionyssis Balourdos
National Centre for Social Research

Fotini N. Skopouli
Harokopio University

George Ballas
Ballas, Pelecanos & Associates L.P.C.

George Konstantinopoulos
ECOCITY NGO

Grace Ch. Katsoulis
Ballas, Pelecanos & Associates L.P.C.

Ilias Anagnostopoulos
Anagnostopoulos Law Firm

Ionna Chryssiis Argyraki
I.K. Rokas & Partners Law Firm

Konstantinos Apostolopoulos
Patras Law Firm

Konstantinos Kanellakis
K. Kanellakis & Partners Law Office

Kostoula Mazaraki
Nomos Law Firm

Nigel Bowen-Morris
Stephenson Harwood LLP

Nikolaos Kondylis
N. Kondylis & Partners Law Office

Olga Theodorikakou
Klimaka NGO

Panagiotis Gioulakos

Stavros Karageorgiou
Karageorgiou & Associates

Stelios Gregoriou
Gregoriou Law Offices & Associates

Themis Tosounidis
KPAG Kosmidis & Partners Law Firm

Theodoropoulou Virginia
Pandeion University

Yota Kremmida
Hewlett-Packard Hellas EPE

Anonymous Contributors

Guatemala

Alexander Aizenstatd
Universidad Rafael Landivar

Alvaro R. Cordon
Cordon, Ovalle & Asociados

Ana Gisela Castillo
Saravia y Muñoz

Andrés Hernández L.
Carrillo y Asociados

Carlos Roberto Cordón Krumme
Cordón, Ovalle & Asociados

David Erales Jop
Consortium-Guatemala

David Ernesto Chacón estrada
Universidad de San Carlos de Guatemala

Edson López
Integrum

Emanuel Callejas A.

Gabriel Muadi
Muadi, Murga y Jimenez

Juan Jose Porras Castillo
Palomo y Porras

Luis Pablo Cobar Benard
Integrum

Marcos Palma
Integrum

Maricarmen Rosal
Integrum

Mario Augusto Alcántara Velásquez
Carrillo y Asociados

Mario René Archila Cruz
Arias & Muñoz

Mario Roberto Guadron Rouanet
Palomo y Porras

Pedro Mendoza Montano
Universidad Francisco Marroquín

Pedro Trujillo
Universidad Francisco Marroquín

Rodolfo Alegría
Carrillo & Asociados

Rodrigo Callejas
Carrillo & Asociados

Anonymous Contributors

Honduras

Aldo F. Cosenza Bungener
Bufete Honduraslaw

Carlos Danzilo
Bufete Honduraslaw

Claudia Midence
Bufete Arias & Muñoz

Daniela Puerto Irias
Consultorio Jurídico Puerto

Gerardo Emilio Martínez Aguilar
Bufete Martínez y Asociados

Heidi Dayana Luna Duarte
Garcia & Bodán, Abogados y Notarios

Juan José Alcerro Milla
Aguilar Castillo Love

Miguel Joaquín Melgar Guevara
Garcia & Bodán, Abogados y Notarios

Milton Carcamo

Roberto M. Zacarias

Ruben A. Rodezno
Bufete Danzilo & Asociados

Yadira Alejandra Maradiaga Rivera
Arias & Muñoz

Anonymous Contributors

Hong Kong SAR, China

Avnita Lakhani
City University of Hong Kong

Danny Chan
Century Chambers

David Donald
The Chinese University of Hong Kong

Farzana Aslam
University of Hong Kong

James A. Rice
Lingnan University

James Wong
Century Chambers

Liza Jane Cruden
Des Voeux Chambers Hong Kong

Lok Sang Ho
Lingnan University

Michael Chai
Bernacchi Chambers

Raymond Leung
Hong Kong Bar Association

Rick Glofcheski
University of Hong Kong

Robert Gregory Chan

Shahla Ali
University of Hong Kong

Tsui Fung Ling Sara
City University of Hong Kong

Victor Yang
Boughton Peterson Yang Anderson

Xiangdong Wei
Lingnan University

Yun Zhao
University of Hong Kong

Anonymous Contributors

Hungary

Akos Sule
Sule Law Firm

András Jakab
Hungarian Academy of Sciences

Gabor Baruch
Baruch Law Office

Katalin Parti
National Institute of Criminology

Petra Bard
National Institute of Criminology

Zsolt Zengödi

Anonymous Contributors

India

A. Nagarathna
National Law School of India University

Abhimanyu Shandilya
Hewlett-Packard India Sales Pvt. Ltd.

Anil Paleri
Institute of Palliative Medicine

Ashok Ramgir
Harsh Impex

Bontha V. Babu
ICMR

E.N. Thambi Durai

I C Dwivedi
National Election Watch

Jayant Kumar Thakur
Dimension Data India Ltd

Jhelum Chowdhury

KS Subramanian

Nirmal Kanti Chakrabarti
KIIT University

Priyesh Poovanna
Hewlett-Packard

Puneet Misra
AIIMS

Rajas Kasbekar
Partner, Little & Co., Advocates & Solicitors

Rebbapragada Ravi
Samata

Ruchi Sinha
Centre For Criminology and Justice

Sankaran Ramakrishnan

Satish Murthi
Murti & Murti International Law Practice

Saurabh Misra
Saurabh Misra & Associates

Shaffi Mather
Mather and Krishna

Shankar Das
TISS

Shomona Khanna

Subhadra Menon
Public Health Foundation of India

Subhash Chandra Bhatnagar

Subhrarag Mukherjee
HEWLETT-PACKARD

T. Ramakrishna
NLSIU, Bangalore

Vidya Bhushan Rawat

Vipender Mann
KNM & Partners, Law Offices

Yadlapalli S. Kusuma
All India Institute of Medical Sciences

Yashomati Ghosh
National Law School of India University

Anonymous Contributors

Indonesia

Alamo D. Laiman
Legisperitus Lawyers

Daniel Alfredo
Legisperitus Lawyers

Erline Herrmann
Berwin Leighton Paisner LLP

Lia Alizia
Makarim & Taira S.

Mardjono Reksodiputro
University of Indonesia; The National Law Commssion of the Republic of Indonesia

Marini Suiaeman
Legisperitus Lawyers

Ricardo Simanjuntak
Ricardo Simanjuntak & Partners

Sandi Adila

Sunardjo Sumargono
Law Office of Semar Suryakencana Cipta Justiceindo

Tauvik M. Cakradipura
Paramdina Graduate School of Diplomacy and Strategic International Policies

Tristam Moeliono
Fakultas Hukum Universitas Katolik Parahyangan

Anonymous Contributors

Iran

Abdolkarim Hamedi
Imam Reza Hospital

Ahmad Daryani
Mozandaran University of Medical Sciences

Arash Izadi
Izadi Law Firm

Mohammad H. Zarei
Zarei Legal Services Institution

Mohammad Rasekh
Shahid-Beheshti University

Parviz Azadfallah
Tarbiat Modares University

Samaneh Hassanli
UNHCR

Yahya Rayegani
Farjam Law Office

Anonymous Contributors

Italy

Alberto Fantini
Tonucci & Partners

Alberto Lama
Bureau Plattner

Alberto Zucconi
Istituto dell'Approccio Centrato sulöla Persona

Anna Simonati
University of Trento

Annita Larissa Sciacovelli
University of Bari

Antonella Antonucci
University of Bari

Antonio Viscomi
Università "Magna Graecia" di Catanzaro

Astolfo di Amato
Astolfo di Amato e Associati

Carlo Casonato
University of Trento

Daniela Rampani
Hewlett-Packard

Davide Cacchioli

Emanuele Corlesi
Caffi Maroncelli & Associati

Emanuele Scafato
Società Italiana di Alcologia

Enrico Maria Mancuso
Università Cattolica del Sacro Cuore

Francesca Valerii
Direzione Centrale Salute

Francesco Maria Avato
University of Ferrara

Gianantonio Barelli
Studio Caffi Maroncelli e Associati

Giovanni Pasqua
ISISC

Giuseppe Lorenzo Rosa
Giuseppe L.Rosa & Associated Counsels

Lorenzo Zoppoli
Università di Napoli Federico II

Luigi Mori
Biolato Longo Ridola & Mori

Marco Esposito
Università di Napoli Parthenope

Mariano Cingolani
University of Macerata

Mario Perini
Università Degli Studi di Siena

Mario Rusciano
Università di Napoli Federico II

Mitja Gialuz
University of Trieste

Pierpaolo Martucci
University of Trieste

Pietrantonio Ricci
Magna Graecia University

Pietro Faraguna
New York University School of Law

Riccardo Del Punta
University of Florence

Roberto Bin
University of Ferrara

Roberto Caranta
Turin University

Roberto Ceccon
Ceccon & Associati - Avvocati

Roberto Rosapepe
University of Salerno

Roberto Toniatti
University of Trento

Silvia Borelli
University of Ferrara

Stefania Scarponi
University of Trento

Anonymous Contributors

Jamaica

Aisha Mulendwe

Alan Barnett
University of the West Indies

Allan S Wood

Althea Bailey
University of the West Indies

Anthony Clayton
University of the West Indies

Audrey Brown

Christopher Bovell
DunnCox

Eris D. Schoburgh
University of the West Indies

Harvey L. Reid
University of the West Indies

Jason M. Wilks
Florida State University

Jimmy Tindigarukayo
University of the West Indies

Joanne Wood Rattray
DunnCox

Marie Freckleton
University of the West Indies

Narda Graham
DunnCox

Norma Anderson

Orville W. Taylor
University of the West Indies

Orville Wayne Beckford
University of the West Indies

Pauline E. Dawkins
University of the West Indies

Rachael Irving
University of the West Indies

Shirley-Ann Eaton
University of the West Indies

Suzanne Soares-Wynter
University of the West Indies

Sylvia Mitchell
University of the West Indies

Verona Henry Ferguson
University of the West Indies

William Aiken
University of the West Indies

Anonymous Contributors

Japan

Eduardo Campos
Nagasaki University

Hiroshi Nishihara
Waseda University

Kaoru Haraguchi
Haraguchi International Law Office

Mark Nakamura
International Education, Information Center

Masanori Tanabe
Sakai Law Office

Nobuo Koinuma
Tohoku Pharmaceutical University

Shigeji Ishiguro
Oguri & Ishiguro Law Offices

Toshiaki Higashi
University of Occupational and Environmental Health

Yasuhiro Fujii
Law Office of Yasuhiro Fujii

Yasushi Higashizawa
Kasumigaseki Sogo Law Offices

Anonymous Contributors

Jordan

Al-nawasyieh Abedulellah
Mutah University

Anwar Mahmoud Batieha
Jordan University of science and Technology

Atallah Rabi
Jordan University of Science and Technology

Azzam Zalloum
Zalloum & Laswi Law Firm

Firas T. Malhas
IBLAW

George Hazboun
International Consolidated for Legal Consultations

Mahasen Mohammad Aljaghoub
University of Jordan

Mahmoud Ali Quteishat

Mohamed Y Olwan
Petra University

Mohammed Abdullah Al Shawabken
American University in the Emirates-Dubai

Nisreen Mahasneh

Rasha Laswi
Zalloum & Laswi Law Firm

Tamara Al Rawwad
University of Houston

Thaer Najdawi
A&T Najdawi Law Firm

Yousef Saleh Khader
Jordan University of Science and Technology

Anonymous Contributors

Kazakhstan

Arlan Yerzhanov
BMF Group LLP

Asset Kussaiyn & Larissa Orlova
Michael Wilson & Partners, Ltd.

Nurzhan Albanov
Dentons Kazakhstan LLP

Yerjanov Timur
al-Farabi Kazakh National University

Zhanat Alimanov
Kimep University

Anonymous Contributors

Kenya

Angela Ochumba
New York University

Connie Martina Tanga Gumo

Dennis Mungata
Gichimu Mungata & Co Advocates

Francis Kairu
Transparency International Kenya

James Mang'erere
Mang'erere J and Co. Advocates

John Mudegu Vulule
Kenya Medical Research Institute

Kamau Karori
Iseme, Kamau & Maema Advocates

Kiingati Indirangu
Kairu Mbuthia & Kiingati Advocates

Laila Abdul Latif
Rachier & Amollo Advocates

Leonard Samson Opundo
Opundo & Associates Advocates

Noelle Kyanya

Peter Gachuhi
Kaplan & Stratton Advocates

Remigeo P. Mugambi
Muthoga Gaturu & Co Advocates

Thomas Nyakambi Maosa
Maosa and Company Advocates

Yvonne Wangui Machira
Tatiti Research Group Ltd.

Anonymous Contributors

Kyrgyzstan

Aikanysh Jeenbaeva

Aizhan Albanova

Akbar Suvanbekov
Republican Medical Scientific Library

Azamat Kerimbaev
ABA Rule of Law Initiative

Dinara Asanbaeva
AUCA

Elida K. Nogoibaeva
American University of Central Asia

Ermek Mamaev

Esenkulova Begaiym
American University of Central Asia

Idaiat Toktash
Lex Law Firm

Jyldyz Tagaeva

Nurlan Alymbaev
Law Firm Alymbaev LLC

Saltanat Moldoisaeva
Ministry of Health

Valentin Chernyshev

Anonymous Contributors

Lebanon

Antoine G. Ghafari

Carlos Abou Jaoude
Abou Jaoude & Associates Law Firm

Elias Mattar
Abou Jaoude & Associates Law Firm

Jean Akl
Akl Law Practice

Jihad Irani

Khatoun Haidar
Synergy-Takamol

Roger El Khoury
HiiL

Roula Zayat
The Arab Center for the Development of the Rule of Law and Integrity

Salah Mattar
Salah Mattar Law Firm

Souraya Machnouk
Abou Jaoude & Associates Law Firm

Wissam Kabbara
Lebanese American University

Anonymous Contributors

Liberia

Alfred Hill
The Carter Center

Cecil Griffiths
Liberia National Law Enforcement Association

F. Augustus Caesar
Caesar Architects Inc.

Frederick A.B. Jayweh
Liberian Law Consultants, Ltd

James C.R. Flomo
Public Defense System of Liberia

Lury T. Nkouessom
Carter Center

Meredith Guardino

Peter Hne Wilson
United States African Development Foundation

Robert Nyanhbui Gharbot
The Carter Center

Sayma Syrenius Cephus
Justice & Public Interest Consortium Africa

Anonymous Contributors

Macedonia

Aleksandar Godjo
Godzo, Kiceec & Novakovski

Aleksandar Ickovski

Aleksandra Baleva Grozdanova
Godzo, Kiceec & Novakovski

Aleksandra Bojadjieva

Andon Majhovey
University "Goce Delchev" Stip

Besa Arifi
South East European University

Dance Gudeva Nikovska
Ss. Cyril and Methodius University

Deljo Kadiev

Doncho M. Donev
Ss. Cyril and Methodius University

Dori Kimova
Kimova Law Office

Ilija Nedelkoski
Cakmakova Advocates

Jadranka Denkova
University "Goce Delchev" Stip

Katerina Lazareska
Savic Law Office

Leonid Trpenoski
Trpenoski Law Firm

Ljupka Noveska
Karanovic and Nikolic Law Firm

Maja Jakimovska
Cukmukovu Advocates

Maja Risteska
A.D. Insurance Policy

Marija Blazevska A
Law Office Pepeljugoski

Neda Milevska
CRPRC Studiorum

Pamela Veljanoska
Law Office Pepeljugoski

Sami Mehmeti
Southeast European University

Sinisha Dimitrovski
THEMIS SB Law Firm

Suzana Stojkoska
Law Firm Cakmakova advocates

Svetlana Necheva
Law Office Pepeljugoski

Svetlana Veljanovska
Faculty of Law-Kichevo Macedonia

Anonymous Contributors

Madagascar

Alexandra Rajerison
Cabinet Rojerison

Bakoly Razaiarisolo

Francesco Andrianjanahary
Barreau de Madagascar

Jacques Rakotomalala
Cabinet d'Avocats Rakotomalala

Jean Pierre Rakotovao
Faculte de Medecine Antananarivo

Jonarisona Julien Abdon
Cabinet d'Avocat JAJ

Ketakandriana Rahtoson
Liberty 32

Léonard Velozandry
Avocat au Barreau de Madagascar

Mamison Rakotondramanana
JurisConsult Madagascar

Michèle Vonintsoa Razafimbelo
Cabinet d'Avocats Rakotomalala

Njara Andrianasoavina
Cabinet d'Avocats

Olivia Rajerison
Cabinet Rajerison

Rija Rakotomalaia
Cabinet d'Avocats Rakotomalala

Rindra Hasimbelo Rabarinirinarison
Magistrature Malgache

Tianasoa Jeannine Nathalie Rakotomalala
MIARO ZO

Anonymous Contributors

Malawi

Adamson S. Muula
University of Malawi

Allan Hans Muhome
Malawi Law Society

Annabel Mtalimanja
Republic of Malawi Judiciary

Charles Mangani
University of Malawi

Elton Jangale
PFI Partnerships, Law Consultants

Eric Umar
University of Malawi

Fiona Mwale
High Court of Malawi

Gabriel Kamhale
GK Associates

Gloria Alinafe Kalebe
Office of the Ombudsman

Jack N riva
Industrial Relations Court of Malawi

Jacques Carstens
Democratic Governance Programme

Justin G.K Dzonzi
Justice Link-NGO

Martha Kaukonde
Competition and Fair Trading Commission

Mwiza Jo Nkhata
University of Malawi

Patrice Nkhono
Mbendera & Nkhono Associates

Redson Edward Kapindu
High Court of Malawi

Anonymous Contributors

Malaysia

Ashgar Ali Ali Mohamed
International Islamic University Malaysia

Dato' Vignesh Kumar Krishnasamy
M/s Balendran Chong

Nurhafilah Musa
National University Malaysia

Ravindra Kumar Rengasamy

S. B. Cheah
S. B. Cheah & Associates

Sharon Jeyaraman
Hewlett-Packard

Anonymous Contributors

Mexico

Alejandra Moreno Altamirano
Universidad Nacional Autónoma de Mexico

Alfonso Rodriguez-Arana
LEGALMEX S.C.

Alfredo Kupfer-Dominguez
Sanchez Devanny Eseverri, S.C.

Alonso Gonzalez Villalobos

Aurea Esther Grijalva Eternod
Catedras Conacyt/Universidad de Guadalajara-CUCEA

Carlos de Buen Unna
Bufete de Buen

Daniel Carranca de la Mora
Instituto Mexicano para la Justicia A.C.

Elias Huerta Psihas
Asociación Nacional de Doctores en Derecho

Enrique Camarena Dominguez
Maqueo Abogados, S.C.

Esteban Maqueo Barnetche
Maqueo Abogados, S.C.

Esteban Puentes-Rosas

Franz Erwin Oberarzbacher
Instituto Tecnológico Autónomo de México

Gilberto M Valle Zulbaran
Basham Ringe y Correa, S.C.

Guillermo A. Gatt Corona
ITESO

Guillermo Piecarchic
PMC Law S.C.

Hugo Hernández-Ojeda Alvirez
Hogan Lovells BSTL, S.C.

Iván Garcia Gárate
Universidad del Claustro de Sor Juana

Jorge Luis Silva Méndez
Banco Mundial

Jose Alberto Campos Vargas
Sanchez de Vanny

Juan Carlos Tornel
Hewlett-Packard

Juan Francisco Torres Landa R.
Hogan Lovells BSTL, S.C.

Juan Manuel Juarez Meza
Nino Gallegos & Asociados

L. Alberto Balderas Fernández
Jauregui y Del Valle, S.C.

Luciano Mendoza Cruz
UNAM

Maribel Trigo Aja
Goodrich, Riquelme y Asociados

Mario Alberto Rocha
PricewaterhouseCoopers

Monica Schiaffino
Littler Mendelson

Oliva López Arellano
Universidad Autónoma Metropolitana - Xochimilco

Sergio López Moreno
Universidad Autónoma Metropolitana - Xochimilco

Teresa Carmona Arcos
Consultores Jurídicos

Anonymous Contributors

Moldova

Adrian Belii
Université d'Etat de Médecine et Pharmacie

Alexander Turcan
Turcan Cazac Law Office

Alexey Croitor
Law Offices of Alexey Croitor

Ana Galus
Turcan Cazac Law Firm

Andrei Borsevski
Institute for Democracy

Chesov Ion
Universite d'Etat de Médecine et Pharmacie

Eugeniu Graur
NGO "CERTITUDE"

Iulia Furtuna
Turcan Cazac Law Firm

Marica Dumitrasco
Academy of Sciences of Moldova

Serghei Ostaf
Resource Center for Human Rights

Zama Vitalie

Anonymous Contributors

Mongolia

B. Enkhbat
MDS & KhanLex

Badamragchaa Purevdorj
Open Society Forum

Batragchaa Ragchaa
A&A Partners Law Firm

Bayar Budragchaa
ELC LLP Advocates

Byambaa Saranchimeg
National Statistical Office of Mongolia

Erdenebalsuren Damdin
Supreme Court of Mongolia

G.Batjargal
MDS & KhanLex LLP

Ganbat Byambaa
City Health Services

Khishigsaikhan
Open Society Forum

Maizorig Janchivdorj
MDS and KhanLex LLP

Munkhjargal Munkhbat
MJL Attorneys

Oyunchimeg Dovdoi
Public Participation for Sustainable Development NGO

Sarangerel Batbayar
The National Legal Institute of Mongolia

Zanaa Jurmed
Center for Citizen's Alliance

Anonymous Contributors

Morocco

Abdellah Bakkali
Bakkali Law Firm

Ali Lachgar Essahili
Ali Lachgar Essahili Law Firm

Anis Mouafik
Anis Mouafik Law Firm

Briou Mustapha Said
BriouLaw

Lhassan M'barki

Mimoun Charqi
Charqi Lex Consulting

Mohamed Akinou

Mohamed Baske Manar

Mokhtar Benabdallaoui
MADA Center

Moulay El Amine El Hammoumi Idrissi
Hajji & Associés

Nassri Ilham
L'Institut National d'Hygiène

Nesrine Roudane
NERO Boutique Law Firm

Omar M. Bendjelloun
Cabinet Bendjelloun

Richard D. Cantin
Juristructures LLP

Rita Kettani
Kettani Law Firm

Saad Moummi
Cour de cassation du Maroc

Soulaimane Fenjiro

Tarik Mossadek
Université Hassan I. Settat

Zineb Idrissia Hamzi

Anonymous Contributors

Myanmar

Cho Cho Myint
Interactive Co., Ltd.

Joseph Lovell
BNG Legal Myanmar

Nang Htawn Hla
Myanmar Nurse and Midwife Association

Thu Ya Zaw

Tin Sein
Polastri Wint & Partners Legal Services Ltd.

U Mya Thein
U Mya Thein & Legal Group

Wint Thandar Oo
Polastri Wint & Partners Legal Services Ltd.

Anonymous Contributors

Nepal

Bijaya Mishra
Kalyan Law Firm

Bishnu Luitel
BG Law Foundation

Budhi Karki

Gourish Krishna Kharel
Kto Inc.

Madhab Raj Ghimire
PSM Global Consultants P. Ltd

Rabin Subedi
PILAL

Ram Chandra Subedi
Apex Law Chamber

Rudra Prasad Pokhrel
R P Pokhrel & Associates

Rup Narayan Shrestha
Avenue Law Firm

Sajjan Bar Singh Thapa
Legal Research Associates

Shankar Limbu
United Law Associates

Shirshak Ghimire
Pradhan & Associates

Shiva Rijal
Pioneer Law Associates

Sudeep Gautam
CeLRRd, Nepal

Sudheer Shrestha
Kusum Law Firm

Anonymous Contributors

Netherlands

Aldo Verbruggen & Anamarija Kristic
Houthoff Buruma

Annieke Bloemberg
Mesland & Vroegh Advocaten

Arjen Tillea
Transparency International Nederland

Arnold Versteeg
Macro & Versteeg Advocaten

Catelijne C.J. Muller
Trade Union Confederation for Professionals

Else Frishman-Jansen

Eugenie Nunes
Boekel De Neree N.V

Gerben den Hertog
Galavazi Den Hertog

H. Broeksteeg
Radboud University of Nijmegen

Hans J. Hoegen Dijkhof
Hoegen Dijkhof Advocaten

Henk J. Snijders
University of Leiden

JAC Meeuwissen
Trimbos Institute

Jacqueline van den Bosch
Ivy Advocaten

Jeroen Bijnen
Hewlett-Packard

Joost Italianer
NautaDutilh

Lars van Vilet
Maastricht University

M.J. de Heer
Vakbond De Unie

N.B. (Bernard) Spoor
De Brauw Blackstone Westbroek

R.H.G. Klatten
Qurrent Nederland B.V.

S.F.H. Jellinghaus
Tilburg University

Anonymous Contributors

New Zealand

Ålan Knowsley
Rainey Collins

Alastair Hercus
Buddle Findlay

Alberto Costi
Victoria University of Wellington

Andrew Geddis
University of Otago

Andrew Schulte
Cavell Leitch

Asha Stewart
Quigg Partners

Austin Forbes

Brian Keene

C. S. Henry
Refugee Council of New Zealand

Caroline McLorinan
Auld Brewer Mazengarb and McEwen

Chris Noonan
University of Auckland

D J Lyon
Lyon O'Neale Arnold Lawyers

David V Williams
University of Auckland

Dean Kilpatrick
Anthony Harper

Denise Arnold
Lyon O'Neale Arnold Lawyers

Erich Bachmann
Hesketh Henry

Evgeny Orlov
Equity Law

Feona Sayles
Massey University

Gay Morgan
University of Waikato

Gordon Anderson
Victoria University of Wellington

Graham McCready
New Zealand Private Prosecution Service Limited

Helen Kelly
New Zealand Council of Trade Unions

Jennifer Wademan
Thomas Dewar Sziranyi Letts

Jessica Palmer
University of Otago

Jim Roberts
Hesketh Henry

Jyostana Haria
Justitia Chambers

Kathryn Guise
Brown Partners

Kevin Riordan
Office of the Judge Advocate General

Kim Workman
Robson Hanan Trust

Kris Gledhill
University of Auckland

Malcolm Rabson

Marcelo Rodriguez Ferrere
University of Otago

Marie Bismark
University of Melbourne

Marie Grills
RPB Law

Mark Bennett
Victoria University of Wellington

Mark Winger
Holmden Horrocks

Mary-Rose Russell
Auckland University of Technology

Matthew Berkahn
Massey University

Michael Bott

Michael Appleby

N R Wheen
University of Otago

Nick Crang
Duncan Cotterill Law Firm

Nigel Hampton

Pam Nuttall
AUT University Law School

Paul Gooby

Paul Michalik

Paul Roth
University of Otago

Penny Bright

Peter Watts
University of Auckland

Peter Thirkell

Petra Butler
Victoria University of Wellington

Rob Ord

Sarah Bierre
University of Otago

Scott Wilson
Duncan Cotterill Law Firm

Sonja M Cooper
Cooper Legal

Stephen Eliot Smith
University of Otago

Stephen Franks
Franks Ogilvie

Steven Zindel
Zindels

Sylvia Bell
New Zealand Human Rights Commission

Tony Ellis

Trevor Daya-Winterbottom
University of Waikato

W. John Hopkins
University of Canterbury

W. Murray Thomson
University of Otago

Warren Brookbanks
University of Auckland

William Akel
Simpson Grierson

Anonymous Contributors

Nicaragua

Angelica Maria Toruño Garcia
Universidad Evangelica Nicaraguense Martin Luther King Jr.

Aubree Gordon
University of Michigan

Carlos Eduardo Téliez Páramo
García & Bodan

Edgard Leonel Torres Mendieta
Arias & Muñoz Nicaragua

John Lordsal Minnella-Romano
Minnella Romano y Asociados

Luis Manuel Perezalonso Lanzas
Bufete Juridico

Roger Pérez Grillo
Arias & Muñoz

Victor Mendez Dussan
Asociacion Nicaraguense de Salud Publica

Anonymous Contributors

Nigeria

Abdulhamid Abdullahi Bagara
Community Health and Research Initiative

Abraham Oladipupo
Ountoye & Oguntoye

Adamu M. Usman
F.O. Akinrele & Co.

Adewale Akande
Stachys & Apelles Solicitors

Aluko & Oyebode

Anse Agu Ezetah
Chief Law Agu Ezetah & co.

Ayodele Atsenuwa
Legal Research and Resource Development Centre, Lagos

Ayotunde Ologe
Synergy Legal Practitioners

B.O. Jibogun
Legal Aid Council of Nigeria

Bolaji Owasanoye
Human Development Initiatives

Chinedum Umeche
Banwo & Ighodalo

Chioma Kanu Agomo
University of Lagos

Chudi Nelson Ojukwu
Infrastructure Consulting Partnership

Chukwuemeka Castro Nwabuzor
Nigerian Institute of Advanced Legal Studies

Cosmas Emeziem
Uzoma 'Onyiaka & Acceciatac LR

Deji Adekunle
Nigerian Institute of Advanced Legal Studies

E. L Okiche
University of Nigeria

E.M. Azariah
Legal Aid Council of Nigeria

Eno Ebong
Hewlett-Packard

Femi David Ikotun
Ziongates Chambers

Festus Okechukwu Ukwueze
University of Nigeria

Gbenga Odusola
Gbenga Odusola & Co

Gbite Adeniji
Advisory, Legal Consultants

Godwin Etim
Aelex

Godwin Obla San
Obla and Co

Idowu Durosinmi-Etti
Adepetun, Caxton-Martins, Agbor & Segun

Innocent Abidoye
Nnenna Ejekam Associates

Joe Okei-Odumakin
Women Arise for Change Initiative

Joseph E. O. Abugu
Abugu & Co., Solicitors

L. Omolola Ikwuagwu
George Ikoli & Okagbue

Michael Abayomi Bisade Alliyu
Chief Yomi Alliyu & Co.

Michael C Asuzu
University of Ibadan College of Medicine

Nelson C.S Ogbuanya
Nocs Consults

Obiajulu Nnamuchi
University of Nigeria

Oghogho Makinde
Aluko & Oyebode

Okechukwu Nwizu
George Ikoli & Okagbue

Oladimeji Oladepo
University of Ibadan College of Medicine

Olasupo Olaibi
Supo Olaibi & Company

Olumide Ekisola
Adejumo & Ekisola

Olusoji Elias
Olusoji Elias + Company

Oluwadamilare Yomi-Alliyu
Chief Yomi Alliyu & Co.

Oluwole Agbo
Oluwole Agbo & Co.

Onjefu Adoga
Brooke Chambers Law Firm

Patrick Okonjo
Okonjo, Odiawa & Ebie

Pontian N. Okoli
University of Dundee Law School

Precious O. Aderemi
Babalakin & Co.

Teingo Inko-Tariah
Accord Legal Practice

Terrumun Z. Swende
Benue State University

Titilola Ayotunde-Rotifa
Valuespeak Solicitors

Vitalis Chukwunalu Ihedigbo
Punuka Attorneys & Solicitors

Yomi Dare
Yomi Dare & Company

Yusuf Ali San
Yusuf O Ali & Co

Anonymous Contributors

Norway

Arild Vaktskjold
Høgskulen i Hedmark

Eivind Smith
University of Oslo

Erling Lind
Advokatfirmaet Wiersholm

Ivar Alvik
University of Oslo

Jan Fridthjof Bernt
University of Bergen

Karl Harald Søvig
University of Bergen

Katrina Hames
University of Bergen

Liss Sunde
Advokatfirma Ræder DA

Magne Strandberg
University of Bergen

Niels R. Kiær
Rime Advokatfirma DA

Ola Mestad
University of Oslo

Stella Tuft
Microsoft

Terje Einarsen
University of Bergen

Tina Søreide
University of Bergen

Tor Vale

Ulf Stridbeck
University of Oslo

Anonymous Contributors

Pakistan

Abdul Ghaffar Khan
Supreme Court

Faiza Muzaffar
Legis Inn Attorneys & Corporate Consultants

Hina Jilani
AGHS Legal Aid Cell

Khalid A Rehman
Surridge & Beecheno

Mansoor Hassan Khan
Khan & Associates

Muhammad Akram Sheikh
Akram Sheikh Law Associates

Muhammad Farhad Tirmazi
Farhad & Associates

Muhammad Nouman Shams
Qazi Law Associates

Muhammad Tahir Mansoori
International Islamic University Islamabad

Muzaffar Islam
Legis Inn Attorneys & Corporate Consultants

Naheed Humayun Sheikh
Akhtar Saeed Medical & Dental College

Nuzhat Huma
Gandhara University Peshawar

Rai Muhammad Saleh Azam
Azam & Rai

Salman Safdar
Chmaber of Barrister Salman Safdar

Sarah Saleem
Aga Khan University

Shams ul Haque Joiya
Right Law Company

Umer Farooq
Ayub Medical College

Waheed Ahmad
Waheed Law Firm

Anonymous Contributors

Panama

Alcides Gabriel Castillo Rivera
Aparicio, Castillo Cedeño & Real

Carlos Ernesto González Ramírez
Fundación Libertad

Ibis Sanchez-Serrano
Core Model Corporation, S.A.

Mario Rognoni
Arosemena, Noriega & Contreras

Mercedes Arauz de Grimaldo
Morgan & Morgan

Milagros Caballero
Morgan & Morgan

Victor Delgado
Universidad Catolica Santa Maria La Antigua

Anonymous Contributors

Peru

Alberto Varillas
Garcia Sayan Abogados

Arturo Gárate Salazar
Universidad Nacional "Federico Villareal"

Carlos J. Torres Berrio
Muñiz, Ramirez, Pérez-Taiman & Olaya Abogados

Cecilia Ma
Ministerio de Salud

César Puntriano Rosas
PwC Perú

Danilo Sanchez Coronel
Instituto nacional de Ciencias Neurologicas

Dennis Vilchez Ramírez
Estudio Ghersi Abogados

Elena Timoteo

Fernando M. Ramos Guevara
Barrios & Fuentes, Abogados

Gonzalo Garcia Calderon Moreyra

Gonzalo Mendoza del Solar
Hospital Goyeneche - MINSA

Gustavo de los Rios Woolls
Rey & de los Rios - Abogados

Ismael Cornejo-Rosello Dianderas
Universidad San Agustin Arequipa Perú

Jaime Durand

Jean Paul Borit
Hewlett-Packard

Jorge Martin Gavidia
Clinica Anglo Americana

Ludmin Gustavo Jiménez Coronado
Revista Actualidad Empresarial

Luis Villar
Seguro Social del Perú - EsSalud y Universidad San Martin

Marcos Ricardo Revatta Salas
Universidad Nacional San Luis Gonzaga de Ica

María del Pilar Pozo Garcia
Hospital Central Fuerza Aérea del Perú

Mario Pasco
Universidad del Pacifico

Mercedes Neves Murillo
Universidad Nacional de San Agustin de Arequipa

Nelson Ramirez Jiménez
Estudio Muñiz

Paula Devescovi
Barrios & Fuentes, Abogados

Ricardo Antonio Pauli Montenegro

Rossana Maccera de Alayza
Grupo Decide

Teodoro German Jiménez Borra
Muñiz, Ramirez, Pérez-Taiman & Olaya Abogados

Anonymous Contributors

Philippines

Afdal Kunting
Zamboanga City Medical Center

Alfredo Z. Pio de Roda, III
Quasha Ancheta Peña & Nolasco Law Office

Carmelita Gopez Nuqui
Development Action for Women Network

Emerico O. De Guzman
Accra Law Offices

Ferdinand M. Lavin
National Bureau of Invetigation

Fidel T. Valeros, Jr.
Puyat Jacinto & Santos Law

Jesusito G. Morallos
Follosco Morallos & Herce Law Firm

Joanne B. Babon
Follosco Morallos & Herce Law Firm

Jonathan P. Sale
University of the Philippines School of Labor and Industrial Relations

Karen S. Gomez Dumpit
Commission on Human Rights

Louisa M. Viloria-Yap
The Law Firm of Garcia Inigo & Partners

Miguel B. Liceralde
Alga Law

Nancy Joan M. Javier
Javier Law

Ordelio Azevedo Sette

Reginald A. Tongol
Regie Tongol Law and Communications Firm

Reynald Trillana
Philippine Center for Civic Education and Democracy

Rhea Quimson
Hewlett-Packard

Sherwin Dwight O. Ebalo
Follosco Morallos & Herce Law Firm

Anonymous Contributors

Poland

Agnieszka Helsztynska
Kancelaria Adwokacka

Andrzej Brodziak
Institute of Occupational Medicine and Environmental Healh

Jacek Wierciński
University of Warsaw

Janusz Bojarski
Nicolaus Copernicus University

Joanna Kobza
School of Public Health

Joanna Kosińska-Wiercińska
Kancelaria Adwokacka Adwokat dr Joanna Kosińska Wiercińska

Julian Bielicki
Drzewiecki, Tomaszek & Partners

Krzysztof Rastawicki
RMS Rastawicki Mianowski Sowicki sp.k.

Maciej Pakuła
Medical University of Gdansk

Marcin Olechowski
Soltysinski Kawecki & Szlezak

Michal Raczkowski
Uniwersytet Warszawski

Monika Hartung
Wardyński & Partners

Piotr Jakub Rastawicki
Polish Academy of Sciences

Piotr Sadownik
Gide, Tokarczuk, Grześkowiak - Spółka Komandytowa

Radosław Skowron
KKPW Law Office

Tomasz Trojanowski
St. Wojciech Hospital

Anonymous Contributors

Portugal

Ana Carla Carvalho
RSA

Ana Paula Cabral
ISCET

António Casa Nova
Escola Superior de Saúde de Portalegre

Carlos Lopes Ribeiro
CR Advogados

Catarina Gouveia Carneiro
ACE - Sociedade de Advogados

Duarte Vera Jardim
Jardim, Sampaio, Magalhães e Silva e Associados - Sociedade de Advogados, RL

Eduardo Azevedo
CRMA & Associados, Soc. de Advogados

Eduardo Buisson Loureiro

Fernando Alves Correia
University of Coimbra

Fernando Antas da Cunha
Miranda Law Firm

Joana Barrilaro Ruas
Ferreira da Conceição, Menezes & Associados, Sociedade de Advogados, R.L.

José Alves Do Carmo
AVM Advogados

Libertário Teixeira
LTCF - Sociedade de Advogados RL

Luis Miguel Amaral
Luis Miguel Amaral Advogados

Margarida Lucas Rodrigues
ACE - Sociedade de Advogados

Miguel Andrade
Miguel Andrade Law Office

Octávio Castelo Paulo
Advogado

Pedro Pinto
PBBR & Associados

Rui Tavares Correia
Abreu & Marques e Associados

Sandrine Bisson Marvão

Teresa Anselmo Vaz
AVA - Anselmo Vaz, Afra & Associados, Sociedade de Advogados, R.L.

Anonymous Contributors

Republic of Korea

Haksoo Ko
Seoul National

Hwang Lee
Korea University

Hye Jeong Lee
Ahnse Law Offices

Jaeseop Song
Shin&Kim

Jinsu Yune
Seoul National University

Junsok Yang
The Catholic University of Korea

Lee Chang Woo
Donghwa Labor Counsultng Company

Sang Won Lee
Seoul National University

Sangbong Lee
Hwang Mok Park PC.

Sang-Il Kim
Ewha W. University

Sean C. Hayes
IPG Legal

Soyoon Jang
Hewlett-Packard

Youngjoon Kwon
Seoul National University

Anonymous Contributors

Romania

Ana Maria Placintescu
Musat & Asociatii

Anca Grigorescu
BPV Grigorescu Stefanica

Andrei Danciu
Cataniciu & Asociatii

AuxMundus - Las and Mediation company

Bogdan C. Stoica
Popovici Nitu & Asociatii SCA

Corpodean Alexandru

Cosmin Flavius Costaş
Costaş, Negru & Associates - Attorneys at law

Cristina Alexe
Cristina Alexe Law Office

Daniel Nitu
Babes-Bolyai University; SCA Iordachescu & Associates

Dariescu Cosmin
Alexandru Ioan Cuza University

Diana Lavinia Botau
Babes-Bolyai University

Dragos Daghie
Universitatea Dunarea de Jos Galati

Elena Simina Tanasescu
Bucharest University

Flaviu Nanu
Flaviu Nanu Law Office

Florin Streteanu
University of Cluj-Napoca

Florina Firaru
Petosevic

Gavrila Simona Petrina
University Dunarea de Jos Galati

George Nedelcu
George NEDELCU - Law office

Gherdan Sergiu Valentin
Gherdan Law Office

Ioan Lazăr

Larion Alina-Paula
Universitatea Stefan cel Mare Suceava, Romania

Laura Lazar
Babes-Bolyai University from Cluj-Napoca

Mariana Berbec Rostas
Open Society Human Rights Initiative

Mariana Sturza
Tuca Zbârcea & Asociaţii

Marius Balan
Alexandru Ioan Cuza University

Mihai Dunea
Alexandru Ioan Cuza University

Mihail Romeo Nicolescu
Romeo Nicolescu Law Office

Miloiu Ciprian
AuxMundus - International Law and Mediation Company

Moldoveanu Alexandru
Tuca Zbârcea & Asociaţii

Nicolae-Bogdan Bulai
University of Bucharest

Oana Lucia Cornescu
Tuca Zbârcea & Asociaţii

Ovidiu Podaru
Babes-Bolyai University

Radu Chirita
Chirita si Asociatii Law Firm

Radu Rizoiu
Rizoiu & Asociatii SCA

Roxana Iordachescu
SCA Iordachescu si Asociatii

Septimiue Panainte
Alexandru Ioan Cuza University

Serban Păslaru
Tuca Zbârcea & Asociaţii

Stoia Iulian Alexander
Bucharest Bar Association

Valerian Cioclei
University of Bucharest

Valerius M. Ciuca
Alexandru Ioan Cuza University

Anonymous Contributors

Russia

A. Romanov
RANEPA

Andrei Neznamov

Demin Alexey Afanasievich
Universidad Estatal de Moscu Lomonosov

Dmitry V. Kravchenko
Asnis & Partners

Eduard Margulyan
Margulyan & Kovalev

Elena Sapegina
Beiten Burkhardt

Galina Osokina
Tomsk State University

Gennady Kipor
ARCDM "Zaschita"

Konstantin Konstantinov
Chadbourne & Parke LLP

Maria Safarova
Hewlett-Packard

Maxim Likholetov
Magnusson

Nikolai Kostenko
Moscow Helsinki Group

Sergey Budylin
Roche & Duffay

Sergey Stepanov
Institute of Private Law

Viacheslav Vhasnyk
Saint-Petersburg State Pediatric Medical University

Vladimir Yarkov
The Urals State Law University

Anonymous Contributors

Senegal

Diéne Ousseynou Diouf
Université de Ziguinchor

Diop Ibrahima Thione
Université Cheikh Anta Diop

El Hadji Mame Gning

Ibrahima Baïdy Niane
Avocats Sans Frontières

Khaled Abou El Houda

Mamadou BA
USADF

Mbaye Seck
SCP GENI & KEBE

Moustapha Ndoye
Cabinet d'Avocats

Ndiaye Semou
Université Cheikh Anta Diop

Samba Cor Sarr
Ministere de la Santé et de l'Action Sociale

Anonymous Contributors

Serbia

Danijela Korać-Mandić
Novi Sad Humanitarian Centre

Danilo Curcic
YUCOM - Lawyers' Committee for Human Rights

Dijana Malbasa
Novi Sad Humanitarian Centre

Dragan Psodorov
Joksovic, Stojanovic & Partners

Dusan S. Dimitrijevic
Law Office Dimitrijevic

Dušan Stojković
Stojković & Prekajski

Jane Paunkovic
Faculty of Management

Jelena Zeleskov Djoric
Institute of Criminological and Sociological Research

Nebojsa Stankovic
Stankovic & Partners Law Office

Nikola Janković
JPM Janković, Popović, Mitic

Petar Stojanovic
Joskovic, Stojanovic & Partners

Simonida Sladojevic - Stanimirovic

Valentina Krković
Law Office of Valentina Krkovic

Vladimir Marinkov
Guberina - Marinkov Law Office

Anonymous Contributors

Sierra Leone

Augustine Sorie-Sengbe Marrah
Yada Williams and Associates

Editayo Pabs -Garnon
Lambert & Partners

Emmanuel Saffa Abdulai
Society for Democratic Initiatives

Kortor Kamara
Saddleback Re

Lornard Taylor
Taylor & Associates

Moses Manskanu

Anonymous Contributors

Singapore

Boon Teck Chia
Chia Wong LLP

Elizabeth Siew-Kuan Ng
National University of Singapore

Eric Tin
Donaldson & Burkinshaw LLP

Eugene K.B. Tan
Singapore Management University School of Law

Foo Cheow Ming
Templars Law LLC, Advocates & Solicitors

Gary Chan
Singapore Management University

Simon Chesterman
National University of Singapore

Stefanie Yuen Thio
TSMP Law Corporation

Anonymous Contributors

Slovenia

Andrej Bukovnik
Petosevic Law Offices

Anton Gradišek
Dagra D.O.O.

Grega Strban
University of Ljubljana

Josip Sever

Matija Repolusk
Repolusk Attorneys at Law

Matjaž Jan
ODI Law Firm

Primoz Rozman
Blood Transfusion Centre of Slovenia

Suzana Kraljić
University of Maribor

Tjaša Ivanc
University of Maribor

Anonymous Contributors

South Africa

Altair Richards
Edward Nathan Sonnenbergs, Inc.

Anne Pope
University of Cape Town

Avinash Govindjee
Nelson Mandela Metropolitan University

Budeli Mpfariseni
University of South Africa

Charnelle van der Bijl
University of South Africa

Christa Rautenbach
North-West University

Clarence Tshoose
University of South Africa

Coenraad Visser
University of South Africa

Daphney Nozizwe Conco
DENOSA Professional Institute

Darcy du Toit
Social Law Project, University of the Western Cape

Dejo Olowu
North-West University

Derek Hellenberg
University of Cape Town

Fawzia Cassim
University of South Africa

Francois Venter
North-West University

FT Abioye
University of South Africa

Gabriel Meyer
Norton Rose Fulbright South Africa

Graham Damant
Bowman Gilfillan Inc

Gusha X. Ngantweni
University of South Africa

Henri Fouche
University of South Africa

Hugh Corder
University of Cape Town

J.S. Horne
University of South Africa

Johan Burger
Institute for Security Studies

Johan Kruger
Centre for Constitutional Rights

Johan Olivier
Webber Wentzel

Johann Kriegler
Freedom Under Law

John Faris
Institute for Dispute Resolution in Africa, University of South Africa

M A du Plessis
University of the Witwatersrand

Marcel van der Watt
University of South Africa

Marinda Surridge
Hewlett-Packard

Marlize Ingrid van Jaarsveld
Fairleigh Dickinson University

Milton Seligson

Moses Phooko
University of South Africa

Neil Cameron
Stellenbeosch University

Ntombifikile Mtshali
University of KwaZulu-Natal

Paul Hoffman
Accountability Now

Pierre de Vos
University of Cape Town

Pieter Bakker
University of South Africa

Pieter du Toit
North-West University

PJ Schwikkard
University of Cape Town

Professor Basdeo
University of South Africa

Rudolph Zinn
University of South Africa

SS Terblanche
University of South Africa

Stephen M Monye
University of South Africa

Stuart Harrison
ENSafrica

Susan Goldstein
Soul City Institute for Health and Development Communication

Tamara Cohen
University of Kwazulu-Natal

Victoria Bronstein
University of the Witwatersrand

Yousuf Vawda
University of Kwazulu-Natal

Anonymous Contributors

Spain

Ana de la Puebla Pinilla
Universidad Autónoma de Madrid

Antonio Fernández
Garrigues Abogados

Antonio Pedrajas Quiles
Abdón Pedrajas Abogados

Bernardo E. Macías G.
Servicio Canario de la Salud

Carlos Alvarez-Dardet
Universidad de Alicante

Carlos Campillo-Artero

Carlos Gómez de la Escalera
Universidad Carlos III de Madrid

César Aguado Renedo
Universidad Autónoma de Madrid

Daniel Marín Moreno
Gómez-Acebo & Pombo Abogados, S.L.P.

Eduardo Trigo Sierra

Esther Algarra Prats
Universidad de Alicante

Esther Fernández Molina
Universidad de Castilla-La Mancha

Federico Durán López
Universidad de Córdoba

Federico Rodríguez Morata
Universidad de Castilla-La Mancha

Félix Fernández Hinojal
Hewlett-Packard

Francisco Javier Dávila González
Universidad de Cantabria

Gustavo Larraz
ECBA, NACDL SPAIN

Gustavo Raúl de las Heras Sánchez
Universidad de Castilla-La Mancha

Iñigo Sagardoy
Sagardoy Abogados

Jacobo Dopico Gómez-Aller
Universidad Carlos III de Madrid

Javier Ramírez
Hewlett-Packard

Jesús Padilla Gálvez
Universidad de Castilla-La Mancha

Joan R. Villalbí
Agència de Salut Pública de Barcelona

Jorge Sirvent García
Universidad Carlos III de Madrid

Jose Fernandez-Rañada
J&A Garrigues S.L.P.

Jose Luis Cembrano Reder
Abogadocivil.Es

Jose Luis de Peray

José M. Labeaga
Universidad Nacional de Educación a Distancia

Jose Mª Ordóñez Iriarte
Sociedad Española de Sanidad Ambiental

José Manuel Mateo
J&A Garrigues S.L.P.

José Muñoz Lorente
Universidad Carlos III de Madrid

José V. Martí Bosca
Universitat de València

Juan Antonio Lascurain
Universidad Autónoma de Madrid

Juan Francisco Aguiar Rodríguez
Servicio Canario de la Salud

Juan María Terradillos
Universidad de Cadiz

Juan Oliva-Moreno
Universidad de Castilla-La Mancha

Juana María Serrano García
Universidad de Castilla-La Mancha

Luis Gaite Pindado
Hospital Valdecilla

Magdalena Ureña Martinez
Universidad de Castilla-La Mancha

Manuel Alvarez Feijoo
Uría Menéndez Abogados

Manuel Ángel de las Heras García
Universidad de Alicante

Maria Acale Sánchez
Universidad de Cádiz

María José Aguilar Idañez
Universidad de Castilla-La Mancha

Marina Lorente
Garrigues Abogados

Montserrat Casamitjana
Societat de Salut Publica de Catalunya i Balears

Orlanda Díaz-García
Universidad de Castilla-La Mancha

Oscar Morales

Pablo de la Vega Cavero
Garrigues Abogados

Paz M. De la Cuesta Aguado
Universidad de Cantabria

Rafael Ortiz Cervelló
Garrigues Abogados

Rebeca Benarroch Benarroch
Consejeria de Sanidad y Consumo de Ceuta

Remedios Menéndez Calvo
Universidad de Alcalá

Roberto Gutierrez Gavilan
Universidad de Cantabria

Roberto Mazorriaga Las Hayas
Rambla Abogados y Asesores SL

Rosario Vicente Martínez
Universidad de Castilla-La Mancha

Santiago Fernandez Redondo
Hospital Universitario La Princesa

Teresa Martin Zuriaga
Gobierno de Aragon

Teresa Rodriguez Montañés
Universidad de Alcala

Xavier Castells
Universidad Autónoma de Barcelona

Anonymous Contributors

Sri Lanka

Anusha Wickramasinghe

Camena Guneratne
Open University of Sri Lanka

Chrishantha Abeysena
University of Kelaniya

Gamini Perera
Law Chambers Sri Lanka

Kandiah Neelakandan
Neelakandan & Neelakandan, Attorneys-at-Law & Notaries Public

N. Sivarajah
University of Jaffna

P.A.D. Coonghe
University of Jaffna

Theshika Mahaneewarajah
Kotelawala Defence University

R. Surenthirakumaran
University of Jaffna

Sunil Madhawa Lokusooriya

Anonymous Contributors

Sweden

Anne Ramberg
Swedish Bar Association

Åsa Esbjörnson Carlberg
Hewlett-Packard Sverige AB

Birgitta Nystrom
Lund University

Bjorn Ohde
Advokataktiebolaget Roslagen

Boel Flodgren
Lund University

Catherine Lions
Umea University

Christer Thordson
Legal Edge AB

Claes Sandgren
Stockholm University

Daniel Drott
Advokatfirman Delphi

Fredrik Gustafsson
DLA Nordic KB

Gabriel Donner
Donner & Partners AB

Göran Millqvist
Stockholm University

Gunilla Lindmark
University of Uppsala

Gustaf Sjöberg
Stockholm University

Jack Ägren
Stockholm University

Johan Sangborn
Swedish Bar Association

Karl Arne Olsson
Gärde Wesslau Advokatbyrå

Karol Nowak
Lund University

Lars Hartzell
Elmzell Advokatbyrå AB

Laura Carlson
Stockholm University

Lennart Köhler
Nordic School of Public Health NHV

Madeleine Leijonhufvud
Stockholm University

Malin Sjöstrand
University of Lund

Malin Winbom
Hewlett-Packard

Märten Lundmark
Danowsky & Partners

Mats Hellström
Hellström Law

Mauro Zamboni
Stockholm University

Mikael Johansson
Raoul Wallenberg Institute of Human Rights and Humanitarian Law

Olle Marsater
University of Uppsala

Reinhold Fahlbeck
Lund university

Sverker Jönsson
Lund University

Anonymous Contributors

Tanzania

Blandina Selle Gogadi

Eliud Wandwalo
Mukikute

Elizabeth Samuel Karua
Mkono & Co. Advocates

Eustard Peter Athanace Ngatale
PMO-RALG Dodoma Tanzania

M.T. Leshabari
Muhimvbili University of Health and Allied Sciences

Octavian William Temu
Octavian & Company Advocates

Thomas Nyakambi Maosa
Maosa and Co. Advocates

Anonymous Contributors

Thailand

Anant Akanisthaphichat
Thai Law Firm

Chanvit Tharathep
Ministry of Public Health

Chulapong Yukate
ZICOlaw

Jeeranun Klaewkla
Mahidol university

Pawinee Chumsri
Cross Cultural Foundation

Peter Shuler
Siam Prmeier International Law Office

Phil Robertson
Human Rights Watch

Piyatida Pavasutti
Asia Inter Law Co., Ltd.

Anonymous Contributors

Tunisia

Abdelwahab Hechiche
University of South Florida

Amine Hamdi
Zaanouni Law Firm & Associates

Amira Yahyaoui
Al Bawsala

Ben Nasr Mohamed Mehdi
Cabinet d'Avocats Ben Nasr

Ben Nasr Taoufik
Cabinet d'Avocats Ben Nasr

Elies Ben Letaifa
Juris International

Eya Essif
Alliance Culture & Nature

Hassine Fekih Ahmed

Hechmi Louzir
Institut Pasteur de Tunis

Hedia Kedadi
Cabinet Kedadi

Imed Oussaifi
Avocat Prés La Cour D'appel, Sousse TUNISIE

Imen Nasri

Kais Ben Brahim
Tunisie Legal

Khedija Anane

Lassâad Dhaouadi
Expert fiscal

Mohamed Mokdad
Ministry of Health Tunisia

Nadhir Ben Ammou

Nizar Sdiri
Nizar Sdiri Law Firm

Radia Hennessey
Vineeta Foundation

Ridha Mezghani
R. Mezghani Law Office

Wajdi Hamza
Hamza Wajdi Avocats

Zied Gallala
Gallala Law Firm

Anonymous Contributors

Turkey

Altan Liman
Aydas Liman Kurman

Banu Uckan Hekimler
Anadolu Universitesi

Berrin Gökçek
Anadolu Universitesi

Bertil Oder
Koç University

Burcay Erus
Bogazici University

Cagatay Yilmaz
Yilmaz Law Offices

Ece Göztepe
Bilkent University

Esenyel Barak Bal
Cailliau & Çolakel Law Firm

Fatih Selim Yurdakul
Yurdakul Law Office

Filiz Tepecik
Anadolu Universitesi

Gulum Ozcelik
Bilkent University

Halil I. Kardicali
Hewlett-Packard

Mahmut Bayazit
Sabanci University

Mahmut Kacan
MK Law Office

Nuray Gokcek Karaca
Anadolu Universitesi

Onur Demirci
DEMIRCI Law Office

Osman Hayran
Istanbul Medipol University

R. Murat Önok
Koç University & Press Council

Rukiye Seyran Çam
Cailliau & Çolakel Law Firm

Sinan Aslan

Ufuk Aydin
Anadolu Universitesi

Anonymous Contributors

Uganda

Adrian Jjuuko
Human Rights Awareness and Promotion Forum

Andrew Bwengye Ankunda
MMAKS Advocates

Andrew Kasirye
Kasirye, Byaruhanga & Co Advocates

Birungyi Cephas Kagyenda
Birungyi, Barata & Associates

Brian Kalule
AF Mpanga Advocates

Busingye Kabumba
Development Law Associates & Makerere University

Damalie E. Naggita-Musoke
Makerere University

Daniel Ronald Ruhweza
Makerere University

Edith Kibalama
Kituo Cha Katiba

Edward Ssebbombo
Bobo Eco Farm Limited

Emmanuel Luyirika
African Palliative Care Association

Francis Opedun
EvaMoR International Limited

George Omunyokol
GP Advocates and Solicitors

J.B. Rwakimari
Abt Associates, Inc.

John Magezi
Magezi Ibale & Co. Advocates

Jude Byamukama
BNB Advocates

Justus Orishaba Bagamuhunda
National Foundation for Democracy and Human Rights in Uganda

Kallu C. Kalumiya
Kampala Associated Advocates

Kobel Allan
Magezi Ibale & Co. Advocates

Kwikiriza Benson A
Uganda Law Society

Laura Nyirinkindi
Pro Initiatives Agency

Lilian Keene-Mugerwa
Platform for Labour Action

Namusobya Salima
Initiative for Social and Economic Rights

Nicholas Opiyo
Chapter Four Uganda

Timothy Kyepa
Development Law Associates

Violet Gwokyalya
Mothers Against Malnutrition and Hunger

Anonymous Contributors

Ukraine

Alena Zolotarevskaya
Hewlett-Packard

Andrii Gorbatenko
Legal Alliance

Chernenko Zoryana
National University Kyiv Mohyla Academy

Eugene Pismensky
Lugansk State University of Internal Affairs

Igor Svechkar
Asters

Ivan Horodyskyy
Rule of Law Center of Ukrainian Catholic University

Ivan Lishchyna
AstapovLawyers

Karchevskiy Nickolay
Lugansk State University of Internal Affairs

Kostin Ilya
Legal Alliance

Lyubomyr Drozdovskyy
Khasin and Drozdovskyy Barristers Association

Maksym Litvinov
Cybercrime Division MIA of Ukraine

Markian Malskyy
Arzinger

Misiats Andrii
Attorney Co. Misiats and Partners

Oksana Holovko-Havrysheva
Ukrainian Catholic University

Oksana Kneychuk
AstapovLawyers International Law Group

Oleksandr Liemienov
Center for Political Studies and Analysis

Oleksandr Skliarenko
Skliarenko and Partners

Pavlo Lukomskyi
Salkom Law Firm

Sergei Nezhurbida
Chernivtsi National University

Sergiy Oberkovych
Gvozdiy & Oberkovych Law Firm

Tarasov Andrey
LC Tarasov & Partners

Anonymous Contributors

United Arab Emirates

Abhimanyu Jalan
Clyde & Co

Chris Williams
Bracewell & Giuliani LLP

Fahmy I. El Khatib
AlSuwaidi & Company

Ibrahim Elsadig
Dentons

Karim Fawaz
Clyde & Co

Kavitha S. Panicker
Panicker Partners

Mirza R. Baig
Dubai Pharmacy College

Mohammad Kawasmi
Al Tamimi and Company

Salah Eldin Al Nahas
Hadef & Partners

Shakeel A. Mian
Prudential Middle East Legal Consultants, UAE

Stuart Paterson
Herbert Smith Freehills LLP

Tarek Nakkach
Hewlett-Packard

Anonymous Contributors

United Kingdom

Alan J. Masson W.S.
Anderson Strathern LLP

Amy Holcroft
Hewlett-Packard

Anne Bradshaw
Imperial College Healthcare NHS Trust

Cassam Tengnah
Swansea University

Christopher May
Lancaster University

Gareth Davies
Hewlett-Packard

Jacqueline Laing
London Metropolitan University

James Bell
Slater and Gordon LLP UK

Jeffrey Golden
The P.R.I.M.E. Finance Foundation

Jill Stavert
Edinburgh Napier University

John Gardner
University of Oxford

JS Nguyen-Van-Tam
University of Nottingham

Katja Samuel
University of Reading

Kiron Reid
University of Liverpool & ZNU Ukraine

Maryellen Reynolds
Reynolds Fitgerald Levine Walker Wong Wu Johnson

Pat Walsh
Dickson Poon School of Law, King's College London

Peter Hungerford-Welch
City University London

Peter McTigue
Nottingham Trent University

Rajkumar Bidla
Sathi All For Partnerhsips

Richard Ashcroft
Queen Mary University of London

Richard W Whitecross
Edinburgh Napier University

Sara Fovargue
Lancaster University

Simon Honeyball
University of Exeter

Tonia Novitz
University of Bristol

Tony Ward
University of Hull

Anonymous Contributors

United States

A Renee Pobjecky
Pobjecky & Pobjecky LLP

Andrew Kaizer
Calhoun & Lawrence, LLP

Anjali B. Dooley
Law Office of Anjali B. Dooley, LLC

Anthony A Dean
Gibbons P.C.

Arthur L. Hunter, Jr
Orleans Parish Criminal District Court

Barbara J. Fick
University of Notre Dame Law School

Blair Glencorse
Accountability Lab

Bruce R. Frumich
Ohio Northern University College of Law

Bryan A. Liang
Global Health Policy Institute, UC San Diego

Catherine C. Carr
Community Legal Services of Philadelphia

Christopher R. Kelley
University of Arkansas

Claudia Rast
Butzel Long

Daniel Cody
Reed Smith LLP

David E Birenbaum

Earl Johnson, Jr.
USC Law School/Western Center on Law and Poverty

Earl V. Brown, Jr.
Solidarity Center

Eleanor D. Kinney
Indiana University

Foeng Tham
University of Nevada, Las Vegas

H. David Kelly, Jr
Beins Axelrod, PC

Jack Saul
International Trauma Studies Program

James F. Cleary
University of Wisconsin School of Medicine and Public Health

James H. Pietsch
University of Hawaii

Jane H. Aiken
Georgetown University Law Center

Jeffrey Aresty
Internet Bar Organization

John Hummel
Deschutes County, Oregon, USA

John Pollock
Public Justice Center

John R. LaBar
Henry, McCord, Bean, Miller, Gabriel & LaBar, P.L.L.C.

Jonathan Hiatt
American Federation of Labor-Congress of Industrial Organizations

Kepler B. Funk
Funk, Szachacz & Diamond, LLC

Laurel G. Bellows
The Bellows Law Group, P.C.

Leonard A. Sandler
University of Iowa Clinical Law Programs

Mary Joyce Carlson
National Fast Food Organizing Committee

Michele Forzley
O'Neill Institute for National and Global Health Law

Myrna M. Weissman
Columbia University College of Physicians and Surgeons

Patrick Del Duca
Zuber Lawler & Del Duca LLP

Paul Bender
Arizona State University

Peter Edelman
Georgetown University Law Center

Renaldy J. Gutierrez
Gutierrez & Associates

Renée M. Landers
Suffolk University Law School

Reynolds, Levine, Walker, Wong, Wu, Johnson
Attorneys Judicial Consulting Team

Ricks P. Frazier
Massachusetts Executive Office of Housing and Economic Development

Robert Burt
Yale Law School

Robert J. Collins
University of Pennsylvania

Sara Elizabeth Dill
Law Offices of Sara Elizabeth Dill

Sherman L. Cohn
Georgetown University

Stephen C. Veltri
Northern University

Thomas Y. Mandler
Hinshaw & Culbertson

Tim K. Mackey
UC San Diego - School of Medicine

Timothy E. Dolan
Texas A&M International University

Vernellia Randall
University of Dayton

Anonymous Contributors

Uruguay

Beatriz Murguía
Murguía - Aguirre Abogados

Escandor El Ters

Gabriel Gari
Queen Mary University of London

Gonzalo Gari Irureta Goyena
Posadas, Posadas, & Vecino

Haroldo Espalter
Hughes & Hughes

Juan Andrés Fuentes Larghero
Arcia Storace Fuentes Medina Abogados

Martin Fridman
Ferrere Abogados

Martin Risso Ferrand
Universidad Católica del Uruguay

Ricardo Mezzera
Mezzera Abogados

Santiago Pereira Campos
Rueda Abadi Pereira

Anonymous Contributors

Uzbekistan

Scott Radnitz
University of Washington

Shukhrat Khudayshukurov
Advokat-Himoya Law office

Anonymous Contributors

Venezuela

Alberto Garcia Lares
Colegio de Abogados del Estado Zulia

Alberto Jurado
Asesoria Legal Corporativa, A.C.

Andrea Cruz Suárez
Torres, Plaz & Araujo

Andres Halvorssen
RDHOO Abogados

Andrés Milano Garcia

Catherina Gallardo
Zambrano Gallardo y Asociados

Dorelys Coraspe
Hewlett-Packard

Gabriel Ruan Santos
Academia de Ciencias Políticas y Sociales

Gonzalo Himiob Santomé
Foro Penal Venezolano

Gregory Odreman Ordozgoitty
Odreman & Asociados

J.C. Garantón-Blanco
Universidad Católica Andrés Bello

Jaime Martinez Estévez
Rodner, Martinez & Asociados

Jesus Escudero
Torres, Plaz & Araujo

José Manuel Ortega Pérez
Palacios, Ortega y Asociados

Juan M. Raffalli A.
RDHOO Abogados

Mariana Villasmil Blanchard
Borges & Lawton

Mark A. Melilli Silva
Hoet Pelaez Castillo & Duque

Rafael Prado Moncada

Ramón José Medina
Instituto de Estudios Parlamentarios Fermin Toro

Saúl Crespo Lossada
Borges & Lawton

Simon Jurado Blanco Sandoval

Xiomara Magdaleno
HPCD Consultor

Anonymous Contributors

Vietnam

Cao Thi Huyen Thuong
Van phong Luat su Le Nguyen

Huyen Dinh
Hewlett-Packard

Kent A. Wong
VCI Legal

Le Thi Thuy Huong
Russin & Vecchi L.L.P

Linh D. Nguyen
VILAF

Ngo Huu Nhi
Thien An Law Office

Nguyen Huu Phuoc
Phuoc & Partners

Nguyen Khac Hai
Vietnam National University

Pham Van Phat
An Phat Pham Law Firm

Juan A. Phung
VCI Legal

Tung Tran
Phuoc & Partners

Võ Đức Duy
Santa Lawyers Company

Vu Dzung

Anonymous Contributors

Zambia

Anne Namakando - Phiri
University of Zambia

Chifumu K Banda

Fares Florence Phiri
FFP

Kakoma K Ernest
Ministry of Health

Melvin L M Mbao
North West University, South Africa

Naomy Kanyemba Lintini
RayBeam Enterprises

Pamela Mumbi
Street Law Zambia Project

Sydney Chisenga
Corpus Legal Practitioners

Anonymous Contributors

Zimbabwe

Andrew Makoni
Mbidzo Muchadehama & Makoni Legal Practitioners

Casper Pound
Family Aids Support Organisation

Christopher Mhike
Atherstone & Cook Legal Practitioners

Clever Bere
Organising for Zimbabwe

John T. Burombo
International Bridges to Justice

Mercia Monica Tshuma
Zambezi Law Trust/ Masawi &Partners Legal Practitioners

Mordecai Pilate Mahlangu
Gill Godlonton & Gerrans

Norma Lole
Women and Children Support Group

Nyasha Pamella Timba
Kantor & Immerman Legal Practitioners

Obey Shava
Mbidzo Muchadehama and Makoni Legal Practitioners

Otto Saki
Governance Resources Group

Sharon Bwanya
Mawere & Sibanda Legal Practitioners

Simplicio Bhebhe
Kantor & Immerman Legal Practitioners

Anonymous Contributors

Acknowledgments

Acknowledgements

The World Justice Project's Honorary Chairs, Directors, Officers, Staff, Financial Supporters, and Sponsoring Organizations listed in the last section of this report.

The polling companies and research organizations listed in the Methodology section of this report, and the contributing experts.

Academic advisors: Mark David Agrast, American Society of International Law; Jose M. Alonso, World Wide Web Foundation; Rolf Alter, OECD; Eduardo Barajas, Universidad del Rosario; Maurits Barendrecht, Tilburg University; Christina Biebesheimer, The World Bank; Tim Besley, London School of Economics; Paul Brest, Stanford University; Jose Caballero, IMD Business School; David Caron, Kings College, London; Thomas Carothers, Carnegie Endowment; Marcela Castro, Universidad de los Andes; Eduardo Cifuentes, Universidad de los Andes; Sherman Cohn, Georgetown University; Christine M. Cole, Crime & Justice Institute; Mariano-Florentino Cuellar, Stanford University; Larry Diamond, Stanford University; Claudia J. Dumas, Transparency International USA; Sandra Elena, Center for the Implementation of Public Policies; Brad Epperly, University of South Carolina; Julio Faundez, Warwick University; Hazel Feigenblatt, Global Integrity; Todd Foglesong, Munk School of Global Affairs at the University of Toronto; Tom Ginsburg, University of Chicago; Joseph Foti, Open Government Partnership; James Goldston, Open Society Justice Initiative (OSJI); Jorge Gonzalez, Universidad Javeriana; Alejandro Gonzalez-Arriola, Open Government Partnership; Jon Gould, American University; Martin Gramatikov, HiiL; Brendan Halloran, Transparency and Accountability Initiative; Linn Hammergren; Tim Hanstad, Landesa; Wassim Harb, Arab Center for the Development of Rule of Law and Integrity; Nathaniel Heller, Open Government Partnership; Vanessa Herringshaw, Transparency and Accountability Initiative; Susan Hirsch, George Mason University; Ronald Janse, University of Amsterdam Law School; Erik G. Jensen, Stanford University; Rachel Kleinfeld, Carnegie Endowment; Jack Knight, Duke University; Harold H. Koh, Yale University; Margaret Levi, University of Washington; Iris Litt, Stanford University; Clare Lockhart, The Institute for State Effectiveness; Zsuzsanna Lonti, OECD; Diego Lopez, Universidad de los Andes; William T. Loris, Loyola University; Paul Maassen, Open Government Partnership; Beatriz Magaloni, Stanford University; Jenny S. Martinez, Stanford University; Toby McIntosh, FreedomInfo.org; Toby Mendel, Centre for Law and Democracy; Ghada Moussa, Cairo University; Sam Muller, HiiL; Robert L. Nelson, American Bar Foundation and Northwestern University; Alfonsina Peñaloza, Hewlett Foundation; Harris Pastides, University of South Carolina; Randal Peerenboom, La Trobe University and Oxford University; Angela Pinzon, Universidad del Rosario; Shannon Portillo, George Mason University; Michael H. Posner, New York University; Roy L. Prosterman, University of Washington; Anita Ramasastry, University of Washington; Mor Rubinstein, Open Knowledge Foundation; Angela Ruiz, Universidad del Rosario; Audrey Sacks, The World Bank; Lutforahman Saeed, Kabul University; Michaela Saisana, EU-JRC; Andrea Saltelli, EU-JRC; Moises Sanchez, Alianza Regional por la Libertad de Expresion; Andrei Shleifer, Harvard University; Jorge Luis Silva, The World Bank; Gordon Smith, University of South Carolina; Christopher Stone, Open Society Foundations; Rene Uruena, Universidad de los Andes; Stefan Voigt, University of Hamburg; Barry Weingast, Stanford University; Michael Woolcock, The World Bank.

Roland Abeng; Lukman Abdul-Rahim; Priya Agarwal-Harding; Lina Alameddine; Sarah Alexander; Rose Karikari Anang; Evelyn Ankumah; Jassim Alshamsi; Ekaterina Baksanova; Hamud M. Balfas; Laila El Baradei; Sophie Barral; April Baskin; Ivan Batishchev; Rachael Beitler; Laurel Bellows; Ayzada Bengel; Dounia Bennani; Clever Bere; Rindala Beydoun; Karan K. Bhatia; Eric C. Black; Cherie Blair; Rob Boone; Juan Manuel Botero; Oussama Bouchebti; Raúl Izurieta Mora Bowen; Ariel Braunstein; Kathleen A. Bresnahan; Michael Brown; Susanna Brown; William R. Brownfield; David Bruscino; Josiah Byers; Carolina Cabrera; Ted Carrol; Javier Castro De León; Fahima Charaffeddine; David Cheyette; Jose Cochingyan, III; Kate Coffey; Sonkita Conteh; Barbara Cooperman; Hans Corell; Adriana Cosgriff; Alexander E. Davis; James P. DeHart; Brackett B. Denniston, III; Russell C. Deyo; Surya Dhungel; Adama Dieng; Sandra Elena; Roger El Khoury; Adele Ewan; Fatima Fettar; Eric Florenz; Abderrahim Foukara; Kristina Fridman; Morly Frishman; Viorel Furdui; Minoru Furuyama; William H. Gates, Sr.; Anna Gardner; Dorothy Garcia; Sophie Gebreselassie; Dwight Gee; Sujith George; Adam Gerstenmier; Jacqueline Gichinga; Brian Gitau; Arturo Gomez; Nengak Daniel Gondyi; Lindsey Graham; Deweh Gray; Michael S. Greco; Elise Groulx; Paula F. Guevara; Arkady Gutnikov; Karen Hall; Kunio Hamada; Leila Hanafi; Sana Hawamdeh; Alvaro Herrero; Sheila Hollis; Michael Holston; R. William Ide, III; Murtaza Jaffer; Chelsea Jaeztold; Hassan Bubacar Jallow; Sunil Kumar Joshi; Marie-Therese Julita; Anne Kelley; Howard Kenison; Junaid Khalid; Elsa Khwaja; Se Hwan Kim; Laurie Kontopidis; Simeon Koroma; Steven H. Kraft; Larry D. Kramer; Jack Krumholtz; Lianne Labossiere; Joanna Lim; Deborah Lindholm; Hongxia Liu; Annie Livingston; Jeanne L. Long; Stephen Lurie; Ahna B. Machan; Maha Mahmoud; Biawakant Mainali; Andrew Makoni; Dijana Malbaša; Frank Mantero; Madison Marks; Roger Martella; Vivek Maru; John Mason; Elisa Massimino; Hiroshi Matsuo; Michael Maya; Matthew Mead; Sindi Medar-Gould; Nathan Menon; Ellen Mignoni; Aisha Minhas; Claros Morean; Liliana Moreno; Junichi Morioka; Carrie Moore; Katrina Moore; Marion Muller; Xavier Muller; Jenny Murphy; Rose Murray; Norhayati Mustapha; Reinford Mwangonde; Doreen Ndishabandi; Ilija Nedelkoski; Patricia van Nispen; Daniel Nitu; Elida Nogoibaeva; Victoria Norelid; Justin Nyekan;

Sean O'Brien; Peggy Ochanderena; Bolaji Olaniran; Joy Olson; Mohamed Olwan; Gustavo Alanis Ortega; Bolaji Owasanoye; Kedar Patel; Angeles Melano Paz; Karina Pena; John Pollock; Cynthia Powell; Nathalie Rakotomalia; Javier Ramirez; Eduardo Ramos-Gómez; Daniela Rampani; Richard Randerson; Claudia Rast; Yahya Rayegani; Adrian F. Revilla; Ludmila Mendonça; Lopes Ribeiro; Nigel H. Roberts; Liz Ross; Steve Ross; Patricia Ruiz de Vergara; Irma Russell; Bruce Sewell; Humberto Prado Sifontes; Uli Parmlian Sihombing; Hajrija Sijerčić-Čolić; William Sinnott; Lumba Siyanga; Brad Smith; Lourdes Stein; Thomas M. Susman; Elizabeth Thomas-Hope; Laurence Tribe; Robert Varenik; Jessica Villegas; Raymond Webster; Robin Weiss; Dorothee Wildt; Jennifer Wilmore; Jason Wilks; Malin Winbom; Russom Woldezghi; Stephen Zack; Jorge Zapp-Glauser; Roula Zayat; Fanny Zhao.

Altus Global Alliance; APCO Worldwide; Fleishman-Hillard; The Center for Advanced Study in the Behavioral Sciences, Stanford University; The Center on Democracy, Development, and the Rule of Law, Stanford University; The German Bar Association in Brussels; The Hague Institute for the Internationalisation of Law (HiiL); The Legal Department of Hewlett-Packard Limited; The Legal Department of Microsoft Corporation; The Whitney and Betty MacMillan Center for International and Area Studies, Yale University; Rule of Law Collaborative, University of South Carolina; Vera Institute of Justice.

About the World Justice Project

About the World Justice Project

The World Justice Project® (WJP) is an independent, multidisciplinary organization working to advance the rule of law around the world.

Effective rule of law reduces corruption, combats poverty and disease, and protects people from injustices large and small. It is the foundation for communities of peace, opportunity, and equity—underpinning development, accountable government, and respect for fundamental rights.

Traditionally, the rule of law has been viewed as the domain of lawyers and judges. But everyday issues of safety, rights, justice, and governance affect us all; everyone is a stakeholder in the rule of law.

The World Justice Project (WJP) engages citizens and leaders from across the globe and from multiple work disciplines to advance the rule of law. Through our mutually-reinforcing lines of business — Research and Scholarship, the WJP Rule of Law Index, and Engagement — WJP seeks to increase public awareness about the foundational importance of the rule of law, stimulate policy reforms, and develop practical, on-the-ground programs at the community level.

Founded by William H. Neukom in 2006 as a presidential initiative of the American Bar Association (ABA), and with the initial support of 21 other strategic partners, the World Justice Project transitioned into an independent 501(c)(3) non-profit organization in 2009. Its offices are located in Washington, DC, and Seattle, WA, USA.

OUR APPROACH

The work of the World Justice Project is founded on two premises: 1) the rule of law is the foundation of communities of peace, opportunity, and equity, and 2) multidisciplinary collaboration is the most effective way to advance the rule of law. Based on this, WJP's mutually-reinforcing lines of business employ a multi-disciplinary, multi-layered approach through original research and data, an active and global network, and practical, on-the-ground programs to advance the rule of law worldwide.

RESEARCH AND SCHOLARSHIP

The WJP's Research & Scholarship work supports research about the meaning and measurement of the rule of law, and how it matters for economic, socio-political, and human development. The Rule of Law Research Consortium (RLRC) is a community of leading scholars from a variety of fields harnessing diverse methods and approaches to produce research on the rule of law and its effects on society.

WJP RULE OF LAW INDEX®

The WJP Rule of Law Index is a quantitative assessment tool that measures how the rule of law is experienced by ordinary people in 102 countries around the globe. It offers a detailed view of the extent to which countries adhere to the rule of law in practice. Index scores are derived from perceptions and experiences as reported in household surveys (180,000 have been collected to date) as well as questionnaire responses from in-country experts.

ENGAGEMENT

Engagement efforts include connecting and developing a global network, organizing strategic convenings, and fostering practical, on-the-ground programs. At our biennial World Justice Forum, regional conferences, and single-country sorties, citizens and leaders come together to learn about the rule of law, build their networks, and design pragmatic solutions to local rule of law challenges. In addition, the World Justice Challenge provides seed grants to support practical, on-the-ground programs addressing discrimination, corruption, violence, and more.

HONORARY CHAIRS

The World Justice Project has the support of outstanding leaders representing a range of disciplines around the world. The Honorary Chairs of the World Justice Project are:

Madeleine Albright, Giuliano Amato, Robert Badinter, James A. Baker III, Cherie Blair, Stephen G. Breyer, Sharan Burrow, David Byrne, Jimmy Carter, Maria Livanos Cattaui, Hans Corell, Hilario G. Davide, Jr., Hernando de Soto, Adama Dieng, William H. Gates, Sr., Ruth Bader Ginsburg, Richard J. Goldstone, Kunio Hamada, Lee H. Hamilton, Mohamed Ibrahim, Hassan Bubacar Jallow, Tassaduq Hussain Jillani, Anthony M. Kennedy, Beverley McLachlin, George J. Mitchell, John Edwin Mroz, Indra Nooyi, Sandra Day O'Connor, Ana Palacio, Colin L. Powell, Roy L. Prosterman, Richard W. Riley, Mary Robinson, Petar Stoyanov, Richard Trumka, Desmond Tutu, Antonio Vitorino, Paul A. Volcker, Harold Woolf, Andrew Young

BOARD OF DIRECTORS

Sheikha Abdulla Al-Misnad, Emil Constantinescu, William C. Hubbard, Suet-Fern Lee, Mondli Makhanya, William H. Neukom, Ellen Grace Northfleet, James R. Silkenat.

DIRECTORS EMERITUS

President Dr. Ashraf Ghani Ahmadzai

OFFICERS AND STAFF

William C. Hubbard, *Chairman of the Board*; William H. Neukom, *Founder and CEO*; Deborah Enix-Ross, *Vice President*; Suzanne E. Gilbert, *Vice President*; James R. Silkenat, *Director and Vice President*; Lawrence B. Bailey, *Treasurer*; Gerold W. Libby, *General Counsel and Secretary*.

Staff: Juan Carlos Botero, *Executive Director*; Alejandro Ponce, *Chief Researcher*; Rebecca Billings; Sophie Barral; Josiah Byers; Bryce de Flamand; Alyssa Dougherty; Radha Friedman; Amy Gryskiewicz; Margaret Halpin; Matthew Harman; Sarah Long; Debby Manley; Joel Martinez; Nikki Ngbichi-Moore; Christine Pratt; Kelly Roberts; Nancy Ward.

FINANCIAL SUPPORTERS

Foundations. Allen & Overy Foundation; Bill & Melinda Gates Foundation; Carnegie Corporation of New York; Chase Family Philanthropic Fund; The Edward John and Patricia Rosenwald Foundation; Ewing Marion Kauffman Foundation; Ford Foundation; GE Foundation; Gordon and Betty Moore Foundation; Judson Family Fund at The Seattle Foundation; Neukom Family Foundation; North Ridge Foundation; Oak Foundation; Pinnacle Gardens Foundation; Salesforce Foundation; The William and Flora Hewlett Foundation.

Corporations: AmazonSmile; Anonymous; Apple, Inc.; The Boeing Company; E.I. DuPont de Nemours & Company; Google, Inc.; General Electric Company; Hewlett-Packard Company; Intel Corporation; Invest In Law Ltd; Johnson & Johnson; LexisNexis; McKinsey & Company, Inc.; Merck & Co., Inc.; Microsoft Corporation; Nike, Inc.; PepsiCo; Texas Instruments, Inc.; Viacom International, Inc.; WalMart Stores, Inc.

Law Firms: Allen & Overy LLP; Boies, Schiller & Flexner, LLP; Cochingyan & Peralta Law Offices; Drinker Biddle & Reath LLP; Fulbright & Jaworski; Garrigues LLP; Gómez-Acebo & Pombo; Haynes and Boone, LLP; Holland & Knight LLP; Hunton & Williams; K&L Gates; Mason, Hayes+Curran; Nelson Mullins Riley & Scarborough LLP; Roca Junyent; Sullivan & Cromwell LLP; SyCip Salazar Hernandez & Gatmaitan; Troutman Sanders LLP; Turner Freeman Lawyers; Uría Menéndez; White & Case LLP; Winston & Strawn LLP

Governments: Irish Aid; National Endowment for Democracy; U.S. Department of State

Professional Firms and Trade Associations: American Bar Association (ABA); ABA Section of Administrative Law and Regulatory Practice; ABA Section of Antitrust Law; ABA Business Law Section; ABA Criminal Justice Section; ABA Section of Dispute Resolution; ABA Section of Environment, Energy, and Resources; ABA Health Law Section; ABA Section of Individual Rights & Responsibilities; ABA Section of Intellectual Property Law; ABA Section of International Law; ABA Judicial Division; ABA Section of Labor and Employment Law; ABA Section of Litigation; ABA Section of Real Property, Trust and Estate Law; ABA Section of State and Local Government Law; ABA Section of Taxation; Major, Lindsey & Africa; Union of Turkish Bar Associations; United States Chamber of Commerce & Related Entities; Welsh, Carson, Andersen & Stowe.

Institutions: Eastminister Presbyterian Church; Society of the Cincinnati.

Individual Donors: Mark Agrast; Randy J. Aliment; H. William Allen; William and Kay Allen; David and Helen Andrews; Anonymous; Keith A. Ashmus; Kirk Baert; Robert Badinter; Lawrence B. Bailey; Martha Barnett; Richard R. Barnett, Sr.; April Baskin; David Billings;

Juan Carlos Botero; Pamela A. Bresnahan; Toby Bright;
Jack Brooms; Richard D. Catenacci; Valerie Colb; Lee and
Joy Cooper; Russell C. Deyo; Sandra Disner; Mark S. Ellis;
Deborah Enix-Ross; Matthew and Valerie Evans; William
and Janet Falsgraf; Jonathan Fine; Malcolm Fleming;
William Forney; Suzanne Gilbert; Jamie S. Gorelick;
Lynn T. Gunnoe; Margaret Halpin; Harry Hardin; Joshua
Harkins-Finn; Norman E. Harned; Albert C. Harvey;
Judith Hatcher; Thomas Z. Hayward, Jr.; Benjamin H.
Hill, III; Claire Suzanne Holland; Kathleen Hopkins; Avery
Horne; R. Thomas Howell, Jr.; William C. and Kappy
Hubbard; R. William Ide; Marina Jacks; Patricia Jarman;
George E. Kapke; Peter E. Halle and Carolyn Lamm;
Suet-Fern Lee; Myron and Renee Leskiw; Margaret Levi;
Gerold Libby; Paul M. Liebenson; Iris Litt; Hongxia Liu;
Karla Mathews; Lucile and Gerald McCarthy; Sandy
McDade; M. Margaret McKeown; James Michel; Leslie
Miller; Liliana Moreno; Nelson Murphy; Justin Nelson;
Robert Nelson; William H. Neukom; Jitesh Parikh; Scott
Partridge; J. Anthony Patterson Jr.; Lucian T. Pera;
Maury and Lorraine Poscover; David Price; Llewelyn G.
Pritchard; Michael Reed; Joan and Wm. T Robinson III;
Daniel Rockmore; Rachel Rose; Robert Sampson; Erik
A. Schilbred; Judy Schulze; James R. Silkenat; Rhonda
Singer; Thomas Smegal; Ann and Ted Swett; Joan Phillips
Timbers; Nancy Ward; H. Thomas Wells; Dwight Gee and
Barbara Wright

STRATEGIC PARTNERS

American Bar Association; American Public Health
Association; American Society of Civil Engineers;
Arab Center for the Development of the Rule of Law
and Integrity; Avocats Sans Frontières; Canadian
Bar Association; Club of Madrid; Hague Institute for
the Internationalisation of Law; Human Rights First;
Human Rights Watch; Inter-American Bar Association;
International Bar Association; International Chamber of
Commerce; International Institute for Applied Systems
Analysis; International Organization of Employers;
International Trade Union Confederation; Inter-Pacific
Bar Association; Karamah: Muslim Women Lawyers
for Human Rights; Landesa; NAFSA: Association of
International Educators; Norwegian Bar Association;
People to People International; Transparency
International USA; Union Internationale des Avocats;
Union of Turkish Bar Associations; U.S. Chamber of
Commerce; The World Council of Religious Leaders;
World Federation of Engineering Organisations; World
Federation of Public Health Associations

"Laws of justice which Hammurabi, the wise king, established… That the strong might not injure the weak, in order to protect the widows and orphans…, in order to declare justice in the land, to settle all disputes, and heal all injuries."

-CODEX HAMMURABI

"I could adjudicate lawsuits as well as anyone. But I would prefer to make lawsuits unnecessary."

-ANALECTS OF CONFUCIUS

"It is more proper that law should govern than any one of the citizens."

- ARISTOTLE, POLITICS (350 BCE)

"If someone disobeys the law, even if he is (otherwise) worthy, he must be punished. If someone meets the standard, even if he is (otherwise) unworthy, he must be found innocent. Thus the Way of the public good will be opened up, and that of private interest will be blocked."

- THE HUAINANZI 139 BCE (HAN DYNASTY, CHINA)

"We are all servants of the laws in order that we may be free."

- CICERO(106 BCE - 43 BCE)

"The Law of Nations, however, is common to the entire human race, for all nations have established for themselves certain regulations exacted by custom and human necessity."

-CORPUS JURIS CIVILIS

"Treat the people equally in your court and give them equal attention, so that the noble shall not aspire to your partiality, nor the humble despair of your justice."

-JUDICIAL GUIDELINES FROM 'UMAR BIN AL-KHATTAB, THE SECOND KHALIFA OF ISLAM

"No freeman is to be taken or imprisoned or disseised of his free tenement or of his liberties or free customs, or outlawed or exiled or in any way ruined, nor will we go against such a man or send against him save by lawful judgement of his peers or by the law of the land. To no-one will we sell or deny or delay right or justice."

-MAGNA CARTA

"Where-ever law ends, tyranny begins."

- JOHN LOCKE, TWO TREATISES OF GOVERNMENT (1689)

"Good civil laws are the greatest good that men can give and receive. They are the source of morals, the palladium of property, and the guarantee of all public and private peace. If they are not the foundation of government, they are its supports; they moderate power and help ensure respect for it, as though power were justice itself."

-JEAN-ÉTIENNE-MARIE PORTALIS. DISCOURS PRÉLIMINAIRE DU PREMIER PROJET DE CODE CIVIL

"All human beings are born free and equal in dignity and rights… Everyone is entitled to all the rights and freedoms set forth in this Declaration, without distinction of any kind, such as race, colour, sex, language, religion, political or other opinion, national or social origin, property, birth or other status."

-UNIVERSAL DECLARATION OF HUMAN RIGHTS